Whitestein Series in Software Agent Technologies and Autonomic Computing

Series Editors:
Monique Calisti (Editor-in-Chief)
Marius Walliser
Stefan Brantschen
Marc Herbstritt

The Whitestein Series in Software Agent Technologies and Autonomic Computing reports new developments in agent-based software technologies and agent-oriented software engineering methodologies, with particular emphasis on applications in the area of autonomic computing & communications.

The spectrum of the series includes research monographs, high quality notes resulting from research and industrial projects, outstanding Ph.D. theses, and the proceedings of carefully selected conferences. The series is targeted at promoting advanced research and facilitating know-how transfer to industrial use.

About Whitestein Technologies

Whitestein Technologies is a leading innovator in the area of software agent technologies and autonomic computing & communications. Whitestein Technologies' offering includes advanced products, solutions, and services for various applications and industries, as well as a comprehensive middleware for the development and operation of autonomous, self-managing, and self-organizing systems and networks.
Whitestein Technologies' customers and partners include innovative global enterprises, service providers, and system integrators, as well as universities, technology labs, and other research institutions.

www.whitestein.com

CASCOM:
Intelligent Service
Coordination in the
Semantic Web

Michael Schumacher
Heikki Helin
Heiko Schuldt
Editors

Birkhäuser
Basel · Boston · Berlin

Editors:

Michael Schumacher
Institute of Business Information Systems
University of Applied Sciences Western Switzerland
TechnoArk 3
3960 Sierre
Switzerland
e-mail: michael.schumacher@hevs.ch

Heikki Helin
TeliaSonera
P. O. Box 970
00051 Sonera
Finland
e-mail: heikki.j.helin@teliasonera.com

Heiko Schuldt
Database and Information Systems Group
Universität Basel
Bernoullistrasse 16
4056 Basel
Switzerland
e-mail: heiko.schuldt@unibas.ch

2000 Mathematical Subject Classification: 68-02, 68T35, 68U35
1998 ACM Computing Classification: I.2.11 [Artificial Intelligence]: Distributed Artificial
Intelligence: Intelligent Agents, Multiagent Systems, Coherence and coordination; H.3.5
[Information Storage and Retrieval]: Online Information Systems: Web-based services;
H.3.4 [Information Storage and Retrieval]: Systems and Software: Distributed Systems.

Library of Congress Control Number: 2008932709

Bibliographic information published by Die Deutsche Bibliothek
Die Deutsche Bibliothek lists this publication in the Deutsche Nationalbibliografie;
detailed bibliographic data is available in the Internet at <http://dnb.ddb.de>.

ISBN 978-3-7643-8574-3 Birkhäuser Verlag AG, Basel – Boston – Berlin

© 2008 Birkhäuser Verlag, P.O. Box 133, CH-4010 Basel, Switzerland
Part of Springer Science+Business Media
Printed on acid-free paper produced from chlorine-free pulp. TCF ∞
Printed in Germany

ISBN 978-3-7643-8574-3

e-ISBN 978-3-7643-8575-0

9 8 7 6 5 4 3 2 1

www.birkhauser.ch

Contents

III Trials and Results   329

List of Figures

List of Tables

Abbreviations

3GPP 3rd Generation Partnership Project
ABox Assertional Object Knowledge Base
ACC Agent Communication Channel
ACL Agent Communication Language
ADL Action Description Language
AI Artificial Intelligence
AIC Agent Interaction Component
ALL Abstract Logic Language
AMS Agent Management System
API Application Programming Interface
BAN Body Area Network
BPEL Business Process Execution Language
CAD Computer Aided Dispatching
CBD Criteria Based Dispatching
CDC Connected Device Configuration
CLDC Connected Limited Device Configuration
CMU Carnegie-Mellon University
CoBrA Context Broker Architecture
CORBA Common Object Request Broker Architecture
CORBA-ORB CORBA Object Request Broker
CQA Conjunctive Query Answering
CSCW Computer Supported Cooperative Worw
CWA Closed World Assumption
DAML DARPA Agent Mark-Up Language
DAML-S DAML for Services
DF Directory Facilitator
DHT Distributed Hash Table
DL Description Logic
DLP Description Logic Programming
DMZ demilitarized network zone
DS Directory Service
DSD DIANE Service Description of Project DIANE
EC European Community

ECG   Electrocardiogram
e-Health   Electronic Health
ESSI   European Semantic Systems Initiative
ETSI   European Telecommunications Standards Institute
FIPA   Foundation for Intelligent Physical Agents
FIPA ACL   FIPA Agent Communication Language
FIPA SL   FIAPA Semantic Language
FIPA-SL0   FIPA Semantic Language Profile 0
FLC   Functional-Level Composition
FOL   First-Order Logic
FP/FN   False-Positives/False-Negatives
FP5   Framewok Programme 5
FP6   Framewok Programme 6
GCMAS   Generic Context Management and Acquisition System
GPRS   General Packet Radio Service
GPS   global positioning system
GSM   global system for mobile communications
GUI   graphical user interface
HH   home hospital
HIP   Host Identity Protocol
HSDPA   High-Speed Downlink Packet Access
HTN   Hierarchical Task Network
HTTP   HyperText Transfer Protocol
HTTPS   Hypertext Transfer Protocol over Secure Socket Layer
I D E   Itegrated Development Environment
I/O   Input / Output
ICP3   International Planning Competition
ICT   Information and Communication Technology
IDL   Interface Description Language
IEEE   Institute of Electrical and Electronics Engineers
IETF   Internet Engineering Task Force
IIOP   Internet Inter-Orb Protocol
IMTP   Internal Message Transport Protocol
IOPE   Input-Output-Precondition-Effect
IP   Internet Protocol
IP2P   Intelligent Peer-to-Peer
IR   Information Retrieval
IRP   Invocation and Reasonable Persistence
J2ME   Java 2 Platform, Micro Edition
J2SE   Java 2 Platform, Standard Edition
JADE   Java Agent Development Framework
JDK   Java SE Development Kit
JENA   Semantic Web framework for Java
JESS   Java Expert System Shell

JICP   JADE Intercontainer Protocol
KIF   Knowledge Interchange Format
LAN   local area network
LARKS   Language for Advertisement and Request for Knowledge Sharing
LCWA   Local Closed World Assumption
LEAP   Lightweight Extensible Agent Platform
LH   local hospital
LL   Linear Logic
LP   Logic Programming
MaMaS   MatchMaker-Service
MBU   Mobile Base Unit
MDP   Markov-Decision Process
m-Health   Mobile Health
MIDP   Mobile Information Device Profiles
MTP   Message Transport Protocol
MTS   Message Transport Service
NAT   Network Address Translation
NFC   Near Field Communication
NGG   Next Generation Grid
OIL   Onotlogy Interchange Language
OMA   Open Mobile Alliance
OMS   Online Medicine Selling Domain
OS   operating system
OSIRIS   Open Service Infrastructure for Reliable and Integrated process Support
OWA   Open World Assumption
OWL   Web Ontology Language
OWL-DL   OWL Description Logic
OWL?S   Web Ontology Language for Services
P2P   Peer-to-Peer
PA   Personal Agent
PAN   Personal Area Network
PCEM   Precondition-Effect Matchmaker
PDA   Personal Digital Assistant
PDDL   Planning Domain Definition Language
PDDLXML   XML Surface Syntax of PDDL Language
PDF   Probability Density Function
PLC   Process-Level Composition
POMDP   Partially Observable Markov Decision Process
QoS   Quality of Service
RACER   Renamed ABox and Concept Expression Reasoner
RAM   Random Access Memory
RDF   Resource Description Framework
RDFS   RDF Schema
RDFS   RDF Schema

REST   REpresentational State Transfer
RFID   Radio Frequency IDentification
RICA   Role/Interaction/Communicative Action
RMI   Remote Method Invocation
ROWLS   Role-based Service Matchmaker
RP   Relaxed Plan
RPG   Relaxed Planning Graph
RS2D   Risk Based Semantic Service Discovery
SAWSDL   Semantically Annotated WSDL
SAX   Simple API for XML
sCAP   Smart Context-Aware Packets.
SCPA   Service Composition and Planning Agent
SDA   Service Discovery Agent
SEA   Service Execution Agent
SEDA   Staged Event-Driven Architecture
SL   Semantic Language
SMA   Service Matchmaking Agent
SOAP   Simple Object Access Protocol
SPARQL   Standard Semantic Web Ontology Query Language
STS   State-Transition System
SWRL   Semantic Web Rule Language
SWS   Semantic Web Service
SWSL   Semantic Web Service Language
TBox   Terminological Knowledge Base
TMS   Truth Maintenance System
TTL   Time-To-Live
UDDI   Universal Description, Discovery and Integration
UMA   Unlicensed Mobile Access
UMBC   University of Maryland at Baltimore County
UML   Unified Modeling Language
UMTS   Universal Mobile Telecommunications System
URI   Uniform Resource Identifier
URL   Uniform Resource Locator
VAT   Value Added Tax
W3C   World Wide Web Consortium
WAP   Wireless Application Protocol
WASP   Web Architectures for Service Platforms
WLAN   wireless local area network
WS-CDL   Web Service Choreography Description Langauge
WSDir   Web Services Directories
WSDL   Web Service Description Language
WSDL-S   Web Service Semantics
WSMF   WSMO Web Service Modelling Framework
WSML   Web Service Modeling Language

WSMO   Web Service Modeling Ontology
WSMO4J   WSMO for Java
WSMX   WSMO Web Service Execution Environment
WSPDS   Web Services Peer-to-peer Discovery Service
WWAN   Wireless Wide Area Network
XML   eXtensible Markup Language
XML Schema   eXtensible Markup Language Schema
XSP   eXtended Service Platform
YAWL   Yet Another Workflow Language

Preface

CASCOM started with a vision of what could be achieved in the future for mobile service environments. The challenge was to address how ubiquitous application services could be flexibly coordinated and pervasively provided to mobile users operating in highly dynamic environments. The CASCOM approach was sound and involved combining and significantly extending existing complementary technologies (agent capability, Peer-to-Peer systems, mobile computing, and semantic web services coordination) in order to develop an architecture capable of reaching its vision.

From its outset the work had ambitious objectives. In order for these to be fulfilled, many technical and scientific barriers would have to be met and overcome. Many questions had to be answered, not least: If there is an assumption of no fixed architecture what changes would be needed to deal with agent communication? How can service coordination be provided with agents and P2P environments in nomadic situations? What were the implications for service discovery architectures taking into account the dynamic topology of IP2P networks, the fluctuating QoS of wireless network connections, and the limited capacity of devices? What solutions could be found for service discovery, service composition planning, service execution monitoring, and failure recovery for open, secure IP2P environments taking into account resource-poor devices? Finally, how could the notions of context and situation awareness be made more precise for IP2P environments.

The overall CASCOM system has involved many innovative solutions for individual problems such as service discovery, matching algorithms and service composition planning, etc. Furthermore, the integration of these components, together with aspects dealing with privacy and context, etc. have resulted in a coherent and impressive system.

In order to demonstrate the power of the architecture and to see how it could truly support mobile users the group chose the challenging and fundamental service of health care. Providing emergency medical assistance to travellers epitomises the difficulties of integrating, coordinating and exchanging information between physically distributed and nomadic actors operating over a variety of networks. The team put a strong emphasis on user group input. This input has been essential throughout the work, not only for testing but also for influencing the development. It would have been easy to trial the system in simple and straightforward conditions. However, the team chose a more difficult and realistic route trialling the system in some extreme conditions and demanding environments. This was coupled with quantitative performance testing of the system in the laboratory. The results are impressive and the system is simplistically easy to use masking the technological achievements of the work.

Technologically the CASCOM solution can be considered as being ahead of its time. The principles of the approach have been demonstrated and the benefits to the different actors involved in this arena (end users, network operators and service providers) are clear. The potential use of both the individual CASCOM components and of the complete architecture itself is large. The components dealing with service provision, discovery, composition and monitoring, etc. can be taken and used individually. The open-source nature of much of the software will greatly facilitate its adoption and use within the community. For the whole system a critical factor in its potential uptake is the adaptability of the system to other applications. Being domain independent the framework would require little modification if applied to another scenario.

CASCOM met and exceeded its objectives pushing ahead and producing advances in many domains. The CASCOM approach has demonstrated how it is possible to have ubiquitous application services for mobile users using constrained devices in dynamically changing open environments without any assumption of a fixed architecture. At a purely theoretical level the results would be impressive. However, the work is not merely blue-skies research but the demonstration of the system in action has shown the potential of the approach, thus forging the way for next-generation global, large-scale intelligent service environments.

Julie Dugdale, July 2008

Acknowledgements

This book is the result of a three years specific targeted research project (STREP) supported by the European Commission under the project CASCOM (grant FP6-IST-511632-CASCOM). The project Web site can be found under *http://www.ist-cascom.org*, with all deliverables, publications and software.

All CASCOM partners:

- Deutsches Forschungszentrum für Künstliche Intelligenz (DFKI), Germany,

- TeliaSonera AB, Finland,

- Associação para o Desenvolvimento das Telecomunicaões e Técnicas de Informática (ADETTI), Portugal,

- Universidad Rey Juan Carlos (URJC), Spain,

- Ecole Polytechnique Fédérale de Lausanne (EPFL), Switzerland,

- University of Basel, Switzerland,

- FRAMeTech S.R.L., Italy,

- Emergency Medical Assistance Group Ltd., Finland,

- University for Medical Informatics and Technology (UMIT), Austria

thank the European Commission, the reviewers, and the additional partners from the healthcare domain – especially from the Tyrolean Hospital Consortium TILAK – for their support and enthusiasm for the CASCOM project.

The project was not only a pure research project in computer science. It was a real human experience, which was very stimulating for every single participant. We thank all members of the 'CASCOM family' warmly for their work and contributions to the success of the project.

Chapter 1

Introduction

Heikki Helin, Michael Schumacher and Heiko Schuldt

1.1 Introduction

The ever-growing number of services on the Web provides enormous business opportunities. In particular, there is a huge potential for creating added value through service coordination. For this to happen, technology must be developed to be capable of pervasively providing and flexibly coordinating ubiquitous business application services to mobile users and workers in the dynamically changing contexts of open, large-scale and pervasive application domains.

One possible step toward the realization of this vision is the development of an intelligent agent-based peer-to-peer (IP2P) environment. IP2P environments are extensions to conventional P2P architectures with components for mobile and ad-hoc computing, wireless communications, and a broad range of mobile devices. Basic IP2P facilities come as Web Services, while their reliable, task-oriented, resource-bounded, and adaptive coordination-on-the-fly characteristics call for agent-based software technology. A major challenge in IP2P environments is to guarantee a secure spread of (personal) service requests across multiple transmission infrastructures and ensure the trustworthiness of services that may involve a broad variety of providers.

This book presents a general architecture for service delivery and coordination in IP2P environments that has been developed within the CASCOM research project. This architecture aims at providing support for business services for mobile workers and users across mobile and fixed networks. For end users, the CASCOM architecture provides easy and seamless access to Semantic Web Services anytime, anywhere, and using any device. This gives more freedom to mobile workers to do their job whenever and wherever needed. For network operators, it aims towards a vision of seamless service experience providing better customer satisfaction, which in turn helps to retain current customer relations as well as attract new customers. To service providers the CASCOM architecture offers an innovative platform for various mobile business application services.

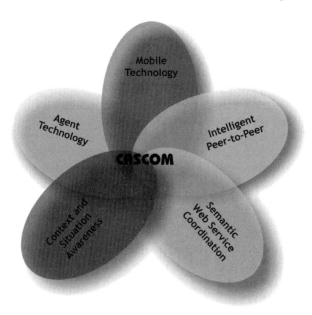

Figure 1.1: CASCOM technologies

1.2   Background

The CASCOM approach is an innovative combination of agent technology, Semantic Web Service coordination, peer-to-peer, context-awareness, and mobile computing for intelligent peer-to-peer mobile service environments (see Figure 1.1).

Software agents are a key technology to address the challenges of the CASCOM architecture as they offer an adequate abstraction for dealing with services from pervasive devices in IP2P environments. On the other hand, IP2P networks provide a suitable environment for agents to collaborate as peers sharing information, tasks, and responsibilities with each other. Agents can help to manage the complexity of P2P networks. The inherently autonomous nature of intelligent agents helps achieving peer node autonomy, which is a requirement to operate efficiently in very dynamic environments. Innovations done in this domain concerns the development of context-aware agent-based semantic Web services and flexible resource-efficient co-ordination of such services in the nomadic computing field. Using agents in nomadic computing has been studied extensively. We built on the previous work by using existing agent platforms as a basis of the CASCOM architecture. However, the P2P aspects were insufficiently taken into account in these platforms and therefore CASCOM research represented advancements in this direction. For example, the architecture provides solutions for agent communication between agents without assumption of any fixed infrastructure.

Service co-ordination mechanisms of P2P systems can be applied to multi-agent systems to improve their efficiency. Although this may be accepted on a conceptual level, the combination of agents and P2P environments certainly deserved more innovative research, especially regarding nomadic environments. The dynamic topology of IP2P networks, characteristics of wireless network connections, and the limited capacity or mobile devices pose several challenges that have been addressed inadequately in conventional service discovery architectures. The CASCOM architecture provides mechanisms for service discovery algorithms for dynamic IP2P environments.

The problem of service co-ordination can be split into several sub problems: discovery, composition planning, execution monitoring, and failure recovery. CASCOM carried out innovative research on how these problems can be solved in IP2P environments. Especially, the architecture provides flexible and efficient matching algorithms to be performed in large scale and resource-limited IP2P environments.

Agent-based IP2P applications may be largely pervasive thus inherit the main characteristic of minimally intrusive pervasive applications: context-awareness. These concepts have been intensively investigated in many contexts. In CASCOM, we investigated these issues in the context of IP2P environment and develop context-aware agents which provide various business application services.

1.3 Motivation: CASCOM in Emergency Assistance

Consider the following use case (depicted in Figure 1.2) which exemplifies how the CASCOM system supports mobile users in accessing information, relevant for their current context, via Semantic Web Services.

Juha, a business man from Finland, is attending on a trade fair in Austria when he suddenly feels severe pain in his chest. Before starting his trip, he installed the CASCOM mobile agent suite on his mobile phone. Thus, he can use the CASCOM personal agent on this device for an emergency call even though he does not speak German. The agent asks a few questions on the nature and intensity of his pain and transfers the information, together with Juha's identity and his current location, in parallel to a local emergency dispatch center and the Finnish Emergency Medical Assistance service center (EMA).

The dispatch center immediately sends an ambulance to Juha's place. Usually, a major challenge in emergency healthcare is to make the best decision on the treatment of a patient, without having seen him or her before, i.e., without having any background knowledge of the patient's medical history, allergies, etc. In the case of Juha, the emergency physicians in the ambulance car are also equipped with mobile devices which run the CASCOM system. After Juha's case has been transferred to them, the CASCOM system automatically selects the Semantic Web Services which provide access to parts of Juha's medical history. Healthcare organizations more and more open up their information systems via Semantic Web Services, in order to allow other physicians to access patient data,

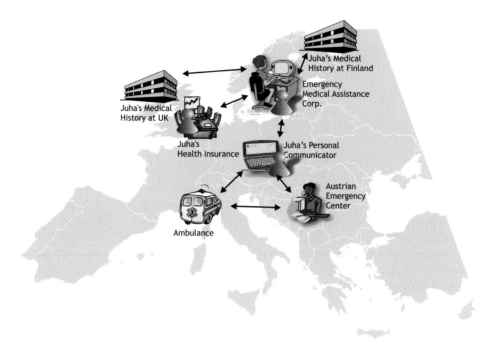

Figure 1.2: Application of CASCOM in emergency assistance

especially in emergency situations. Juha has recently moved within Finland and
has also worked in the past several years in the UK. This means that his medical record is fragmented and also physically distributed. The CASCOM service
discovery agent identifies all the services and their providers relevant for the information need of the emergency physicians, by using directory services hosted
by EMA. Afterwards, the CASCOM planner agent creates an ad-hoc application
which composes the calls to the individual Semantic Web Services identified in the
previous step. In the case of Juha, this includes access to all healthcare information
systems where parts of his medical record are stored (i.e., Semantic Web Services
which are interfaces to the clinical information system of his home hospital, to the
database of his former family doctor and to the information system of his former
health insurance in the UK). The CASCOM execution agent finally invokes all
services as specified by the planner and applies failure handling mechanisms, if
needed. As a result of this dynamically composed ad-hoc application, information
on Juha's medical history is collected from the different sources and transferred
to the personal agent on the physician's device (together with the emergency call,
Juha also authorizes the local emergency physicians to access parts of his medical records). Thus, the physicians are able to get an in-depth overview on Juha's
health state already in the ambulance car on the way to Juha, without having
seen him before. In particular, they can take a look at the most recent ECG data

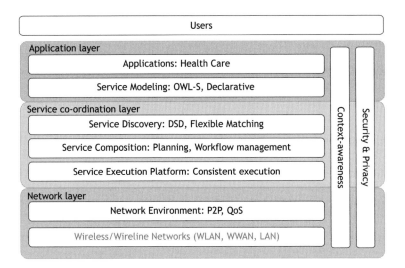

Figure 1.3: Layered model of the CASCOM architecture

and will be informed that Juha is allergic to certain drugs.

In order for the physician's personal agent to finally retrieve all relevant information, communication between the different agents of the CASCOM system is required. However, since some of the involved agents are mobile, a fixed network infrastructure cannot be guaranteed. Assume, for instance, that the application is started in the base station of the emergency center where a WLAN connection is available. As soon as the emergency car leaves the base station, it also leaves the connection range of the WLAN and the agent communication has to be seamlessly migrated to UMTS without affecting the CASCOM application.

Similarly, CASCOM technology can also be applied to organize Juha's repatriation, if needed, and/or to exchange information between healthcare organizations in the process of his after-treatment.

1.4   Overview of the Approach

As stated in Section 1.2, the architecture aims at the innovative combination of intelligent agent technology, Semantic Web Services, peer-to-peer, and mobile computing for intelligent peer-to-peer mobile service environments. For this purpose, conceptually, the architecture relies on a layered approach (see Figure 1.3). The four main components of this architecture link the application layer with the underlying networks and are described in more detail below.

The Networking Layer provides a generic, secure, and open Intelligent P2P network infrastructure taking into account varying Quality of Service (QoS) of wireless communication paths, limitations of resource-poor mobile devices, and contextual variability of nomadic environments. Especially, it provides the following functionality:

1. efficient, secure, and reliable agent message transport communication over wireless (and wireline) communication paths independently of the access technology.

2. provision the context subsystem with network-related context information,

3. low-level service discovery in IP2P environment, and

4. agent execution environment for resource-constrained mobile devices.

Setting out from the services of the networking layer, and based on the functionalities offered by both the context-awareness and the security and privacy subsystems, the Service Coordination Layer takes an agent-based approach towards flexible Semantic Web Service discovery and coordination. Its main functionality is twofold: Semantic service discovery (service discovery and semantic matchmaking) and service coordination (service composition and execution, and replanning).

The context subsystem, orthogonal to the above described layers, is in charge of acquiring, storing, and providing context information to both layers. Generally speaking, there will be contextual information for each of the system components. Each of them will be able to acquire it using the following set of functionalities: Discovery and acquisition of context information, subscription of context listeners and acquisition of context events/changes in the environment, and access to context information repository.

The Security and Privacy Subsystem, also orthogonal to the Networking and Service Coordination Layer, is responsible for ensuring security and privacy of information throughout the different components of the infrastructure. One of the main things we need to protect is the information (data) that every node of the network maintains. In detail, data confidentiality, integrity, and availability are topics of concern that any approach to security must address. The security and privacy functionality was considered at every level of the CASCOM architecture. This enables instant take-up of the CASCOM concepts for service-oriented business applications.

1.5   Overall View of the Book

This book is divided into three parts.

Part I (Chapters 2 to 6) covers the overall technical themes of CASCOM and describes the limitations of the current state of the art that CASCOM addressed.

Chapter 2 considers the state-of-the-art from the viewpoint of the network and network environment of the CASCOM architecture. An overview of enabling technologies is given including wireless network technologies, end-user devices, seamless mobility, agent communication in wireless environments, ontologies for the wireless world, and overlay networks.

Chapters 3 and 4 give an overview of Semantic Web Services. Those chapters survey different approaches to semantic service matchmaking and service composition planning.

Chapter 5 presents definitions of context-awareness and it presents a description of the solutions aimed at acquiring, modeling and processing context information. Further, it describes developed architectures of context-aware systems.

Chapter 6 concludes Part I focusing on CASCOM's main evaluation domain: healthcare. The chapter describes the evolution of the use of technology in this domain, from medical informatics, telehealth and telemedicine to the newly extended term e-health.

Part II (Chapters 7 – 13) introduces the CASCOM solution in detail. Chapter 7 describes the technical approach at high level and envisions the conceptual architecture able to provide the required functionality. The chapter concludes by describing in which ways the architecture can be instantiated.

Chapter 8 presents some essential enablers for agents in wireless environments. Firstly, the chapter introduces an agent platform that is usable in resource-constrained devices. Secondly, it describes how agent messaging over a wireless communication path is implemented in the CASCOM architecture including a performance analysis of implemented communication stack.

Chapter 9 introduces a federated directory system used in CASCOM called WSDir. Its main functionality is to let heterogeneous semantic web service descriptions be registered and searched by certain clients. As such, it realizes a lookup function with basic retrieval schemes.

Chapter 10 provides an overview of semantic service discovery in CASCOM, giving a detailed description of two agents intervening in this process, namely service discovery agents and semantic service matchmaker agents. The chapter gives details on the integrated service matchmaking algorithms.

Chapter 11 summarizes the CASCOM composition planning approach, followed by the detailed description of a pre-filtering module, and two composition planners for OWL-S services developed in the project.

Chapter 12 presents a framework to enable the execution of semantic web services in the CASCOM architecture. The chapter describes two approaches to reliable service execution: a centralized approach, where a single agent can execute an entire composite service; and a dynamically distributed approach, where different coordinated and co-operating agents contribute to the execution of parts of a composite service.

Chapters 13 and 14 present the orthogonal layers of the CASCOM architecture. Chapter 13 addresses the CASCOM approach regarding context acquisition and management. It presents context representation decisions (the content and structure of the ontologies used to model context) and an architecture for acquiring, monitoring, representation and storing context information. Chapter 14 deals with a stochastic model of trust that measurably captures trust in two-party interactions and a general-purpose framework that the CASCOM architecture provides to enable the realization of secure, privacy-aware and trust-aware multiagent systems.

Part III (chapters 15 and 16) present the qualitative and the quantitative evaluation of the CASCOM solution. The main objective of all realized tests was to verify that they can be effectively used in real world settings.

Chapter 15 discusses laboratory and field trials of the motivating application scenario to obtain qualitative feedback from end users. To make those trials realistic, they have been conducted under controlled conditions using real network services, resources, devices, and terminals.

Finally, Chapter 16 deals with tests of the Service Matchmaker Agent, the Service Discovery Agent, the Service Composition Planner Agent, the Service Execution Agent, and the Distributed Directories WSDir.

Part I

State of the Art

Chapter 2

Intelligent Agent-based Peer-to-Peer Systems (IP2P)

Heikki Helin and Ahti Syreeni

2.1 Introduction

One step toward the realization of the CASCOM vision is the development of an intelligent agent-based peer-to-peer (IP2P) environment. IP2P environments are extensions to conventional P2P architectures with components for mobile and ad hoc computing, wireless communications, and a broad range of pervasive devices. Software agents will be a key technology to address the challenges of CASCOM as they offer an adequate abstraction for dealing with services from pervasive devices in IP2P environments. However, agents in wireless environments need support from the underlying architecture. For example, communication over wireless connection needs to be designed carefully. Further, the underlying agent platform shall be tailored to resource-constrained mobile devices.

This chapter considers the state-of-the-art from the network environment viewpoint of the CASCOM architecture. The rest of this chapter is organized as follows. In Section 2.2, an overview of enabling technologies is given, including wireless network technologies, end-user devices, seamless mobility, agent communication in wireless environments, and existing ontologies for the wireless world. In Section 2.3, a short overview of overlay networks is introduced.

2.2 IP2P Enabling Technologies

2.2.1 Wireless Networks

Wireless network technologies can be divided into three categories: wireless wide-area networks (WWAN), wireless local area networks (WLAN), and personal area networks (PAN). Further, wireless wide-area network technologies can be divided into the following categories: (1) Analog cellular networks (e.g., Advanced Mobile Phone System (AMPS), Total Access Communication Systems (TACS), and Nordic Mobile Telephone (NMT) [28]), (2) digital cellular networks (e.g., GSM [23, 33]), and (3) mobile data networks (e.g., Mobitex [18] and CDPD [2, 5]). Wireless local area networks can be divided into cordless networks and Wireless LANs. At the transport layer, mobile data networks and WLANs are packet networks, and others are usually circuit switched networks. Circuit switched networks are mainly designed for voice transmittal, but can also be used to transfer data.

Perhaps the most well known example of digital cellular networks is GSM. In the first phase, it was possible to transfer data over GSM using relatively low speeds (9.6 Kb/s). The High Speed Circuit Switched Data (HSCSD) [11, 13] made it possible to transfer data in the GSM network using speeds up to 56 Kb/s. This was possible by allocating more time slots per user and by using a different channel coding. The General Packet Radio System (GPRS) [12] is a GSM Phase 2+ bearer service that provides a packet data access to mobile GSM users. The main feature of GPRS is that it allocates resources to users only when needed. Therefore it is especially suitable for bursty traffic such as web browsing. GPRS supports data rates up to 115 Kb/s. Further GSM evolution came with EDGE (Enhanced Data rates for Global Evolution) [10]. EDGE allows usage of GSM radio bands at speeds up to 384 Kb/s. Universal Mobile Telephone Service (UMTS) [43] will provide even higher data rates, but only in limited areas. UMTS is a 3rd generation (3G) mobile system being developed by ETSI within ITUs IMT-2000 framework. UMTS provides data rates up to 2 Mb/s in certain areas. Further, HSDPA (High-Speed Downlink Packet Access) is a technology which increases data transfer speed in UMTS-based networks up to 14.4 Mb/s.

Examples of local area wireless networks include Wireless LANs (802.11, 802.16, HiperLAN) [6, 21, 27]. Wireless LANs are typically employed in closed environments, for example, in offices, hotels, and so on. Emerging wireless LAN standards such as IEEE802.16 (WIMAX) will provide more bandwidth with significantly larger coverage area in the future. Technologies for implementing PANs include Bluetooth [3], and Infrared [40] connections. Bluetooth and Infrared connections are typically point-to-point connections, for example, between a PDA and a laptop computer. Nowadays almost all equipment targeted for mobile computing –smart phones, PDAs, laptops, and so on– are equipped with infrared communication capabilities.

The introduction of high-speed wireless capabilities, including GPRS and UMTS, enables new services, such as multimedia, that mobile users can use wherever needed and whenever needed. However, the gap between wireless and wireline networks will remain. No matter how fast wireless networks will be in the future, the wireline networks will be even faster. Furthermore, as the speed in the wireline networks increases, the application programmers tend to develop new applications that will take advantage of increased speeds. Soon after, the mobile users will also want to use these new applications.

Communication System	Typical bandwidth
Ethernet LAN	> 100 Mb/s
Wireless LAN (IEEE802.16; WiMax)	< 75 Mb/s
Wireless LAN (IEEE802.11g)	54 Mb/s
HSDPA	< 14.4 Mb/s
Wireless LAN (IEEE802.11b)	11 Mb/s
UMTS	$\ll$ 2 Mb/s
Infrared	19.2 Kb/s – 1 Mb/s
Bluetooth	720 Kb/s
EDGE	< 384 Kb/s
xDSL	< 24 Mb/s
GPRS	< 115 Kb/s
PSTN	< 56 Kb/s
HSCSD	< 43.2 Kb/s
CDPD	19.2 Kb/s
GSM	9.6 Kb/s

Table 2.1: Common communication systems

The environment of nomadic computing –wireless data communications and mobile devices– creates many challenges, which have been addressed insufficiently in today's distributed systems. First, in the wireless data communication environments the values of QoS parameters such as line-rate, delay, throughput, round-trip time, and error rate may change dramatically when a nomadic end-user moves from one location to another. While these new technologies will increase the performance of the wireless data communications, the basic problem will remain. Throughput, line rates, delays, and error rates may change, sometimes even more dramatically than in today's wireless networks. For example, when a nomadic-user roams from WLAN coverage to highly utilized GPRS coverage, the throughput may drop from (say) 10 Mb/s to 1 Kb/s. This has important consequences on application development. Table 2.1 summarizes the common communication systems.

2.2.2   End-user Devices

The variety of end-system technologies that end-users can use to gain access to Internet services are increasing rapidly. Nowadays there are several mobile computing devices ranging from powerful laptop computers to very small devices such as wristwatch computers. High-end laptop computers are typically almost as powerful as their desktop counterparts, but the display size, for example, is typically smaller.

These computing devices are able to run similar or almost all the same applications as the desktop computers if they operate in the same environment.

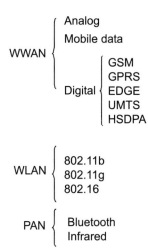

Figure 2.1: Wireless communication technologies

For example, they may have a similar connection to the network services, if such services are needed in order to run the application.

Personal Digital Assistants (PDAs) are more restricted in all areas; the processing power, amount of memory, and quality of display are significantly smaller. Applications similar to desktop versions must therefore be redesigned in order to catch the new restrictions. Furthermore, these computing devices typically have a variety of input devices, such as touch screen or voice command, which make the designing of the user interface somewhat different from designing the same interface for desktop or laptop computers [17].

PDAs, however, allow more flexibility in the user mobility. Typically, end-users are unwilling to carry their laptop computers everywhere. Small pocketsize PDA devices are easy to transport along all the time. In spite of the limited factors of PDAs, they still can be used for various tasks, such as reading email, word processing, and web browsing. Mobile phones have similar features as the PDAs, but are more restricted. Further, these devices typically have multiple wireless interfaces (e.g., IrDA/Bluetooth/GSM/GPRS/EDGE).

Today's devices are mainly used for standalone applications connecting if needed to existing services on a network. However, considering only the situation that the end-user has one device will be inadequate in the future. Instead, the future solutions for mobile/wireless environment should consider end-user devices as reconfigurable end-user systems [32]. In this view, the end-user has one core device that probes its surroundings looking for other devices and dynamically builds up the most appropriate auto-configurable end-user system. This obviously causes problems for applications, as they cannot anymore assume that end-user's device remains static even for a short time period.

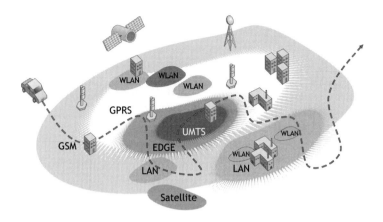

Figure 2.2: Seamless mobility

Obviously, in order to handle reconfigurable end-user systems, a lot of system support is needed. The best-known configuration descriptions today for wireless devices are W3C's CC/PP [45], OMA's UAProf [26], and FIPA's Device Ontology Specification [8]. These allow describing the terminal capabilities, but handling rapid and dynamic changes in the configuration is not considered in these standards. In addition to these standards, OMA has on-going work on Device Management [25] and W3C on Device Independence [44].

2.2.3   Seamless Mobility

Seamless mobility means that roaming from one location to another possibly switching the underlying access technology occurs without inconvenience to the user. Such a feature will be an important feature of the future nomadic applications. Figure 2.2 depicts a situation where the user drives through an urban area having several different access technologies.

A lot of research work is done in order to enable the seamless mobility at the IP layer. Relevant standardization organizations for IP mobility technologies at the moment are IETF [42], 3GPP [43] and IEEE [41]. The main emphasis is on the IETF standardization. However, it should be noted that seamless mobility cannot be solved completely at the IP layer. IP layer mobility is a particularly difficult problem in networking environment containing access networks with very different characteristics (e.g., 3G vs. WLAN) and across different administrative domains (e.g., handover between different operators). Seamless mobility will require tight integration to used networking environment and co-operation between different networking layers, and co-operation between different networking nodes. Further, it is envisioned that management issues (handovers between network technologies, IP address management, etc.) are going to be difficult to solve. This is mostly due to legacy systems and the differences in the access technologies that a mobile node (terminal, user equipment) can employ or access.

Currently the most relevant IP mobility technology is the Mobile IPv4 [29], which has reached required level of maturity from both a standardization and an implementation viewpoint. Mobile IPv4 is a standard track protocol, which adds mobility support for IPv4 based systems. The basic technology is mature and has been around since 1996. Both commercial and open source implementations are available.

In the future Mobile IPv6 [16] will most probably have an important role as an IP mobility enabling technology. Mobile IPv6 allows a mobile node to move from one network to another without changing the Mobile Node's home address. Packets may be routed to the Mobile Node using this address regardless of the Mobile Node's current point of attachment to the Internet. The mobile node may also continue to communicate with other nodes (stationary or mobile) after moving to a new network. The movement of a Mobile Node away from its home network is thus transparent to transport and higher-layer protocols and applications. The Mobile IPv6 protocol is just as suitable for mobility across homogeneous media as for mobility across heterogeneous media. For example, Mobile IPv6 facilitates node movement from one Ethernet segment to another as well as it facilitates node movement from an Ethernet segment to a WLAN, with the Mobile Node's IP address remaining unchanged in spite of such a movement. Mobile IPv6 does not attempt to solve all general problems related to the use of mobile computers or wireless networks.

Alternative IP mobility enabling protocols are also being actively developed. The Host Identity Protocol (HIP) [22] is one example of new alternative IP mobility enabling protocols being standardized in IETF. HIP is a new protocol that aims to separate the IP layer (routing) and transport layer from each other with a middle layer that defines a globally unique identity, the so-called Host Identity. This Host Identity is a cryptographic public key to the host. It adds two main features to Internet protocols. The first is a decoupling of the internetworking and transport layers. This will allow for independent evolution of the two layers and provide end-to-end services over multiple internetworking realms. The second feature is host authentication: because the Host Identifier is a public key, this key can be used to authenticate security protocols like IPsec.

2.2.4   Ontologies in the Wireless World

In this section, we give an overview of several ontologies developed for wireless environments.

Wireless Network Ontology

In [15], the authors introduce a wireless network ontology. The concepts defined in that ontology are intended to be used when describing wireless network instances. Three different use cases are identified. Firstly, a rather simple but useful use case could be that network operators provide information about their networks in the Web using the (wireless) network ontology. Many network operators provide already this information, but it is mainly meant for humans and therefore only usable for them. Developing an application that takes advantage of this information is hard if not impossible. The main reason for this is that the network operators have their own way of presenting their descriptions. Further, an operator may have different ways of presenting different kinds of networks. For example, if the operator provides both GSM and WLAN networks, the network information of these is presented in a different way, which further complicates the automatic usage of this information. Using the wireless network ontology, operators can use common terminology when defining instances of the networks they provide. This, obviously, presupposes that the ontology contains sufficient concepts for defining different kinds of networks.

Secondly, assuming that the majority of network providers publish the information about their networks using a common ontology, this allows third parties to develop value-added services based on this description. One such service could be searching networks based on location. For example, such service could answer questions like "Which networks are available at the Hotel Kmp Helsinki?" Some primitive services for answering this question are already available. For example, the GSM Association provides a database of GSM roaming agreements between operators as well as coverage maps[1]. Again, this information is mainly for humans. For example, coverage maps are not much of use for applications trying to reason whether some network is available at a given location. Another example of such a service is 'www.hotspot-locations.com', which provides information about WLAN access points available all over the world. Their interface is also meant for humans. Now, if both of these information sources could use the same terminology (i.e., ontology), it would be possible (to some extent) to automatically answer the aforementioned question about available networks at a given location. Obviously, a comprehensive answer is impossible if information about only GSM and WLAN networks is available.

The third use case comes from ISTAG[2] future scenarios [7]. In these scenarios, one of the requirements identified for the ambient intelligence is "a seamless mobile/fixed communications infrastructure". The (wireless) network ontology gives the basis to build such infrastructure. As for an example, let us take a look at the scenario 1: "Maria – The Road Warrior". In this scenario the user, Maria, is on a business trip and arrives at a foreign country. Maria is carrying a personalized communications device, P-Com, which automates various tasks during her way from the airport to the hotel: her visa is automatically checked at the immigration, her car rental is arranged beforehand, the P-Com recognizes and personalizes the car for Maria, real-time traffic instructions are provided during the drive, and finally, the hotel room facilities are customized for Maria by interactions between

---

[1]See http://www.gsmworld.com/roaming/gsminfo/index.shtml
[2]IST Advisory Group

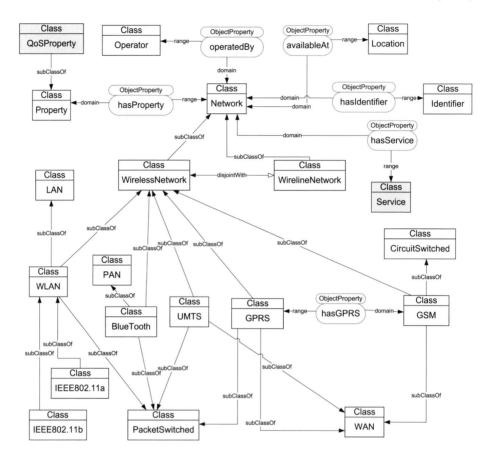

Figure 2.3: Core concepts of the wireless network ontology

the P-Com and the hotel room computing infrastructure. All of these tasks require
the knowledge of the networking infrastructure at the given time. At the airport
there might be WLAN hotspots available, and at the immigration there could be
local Bluetooth coverage. During the walk from the airport arrival hall to the car
garage a GPRS network is available, and once arrived at the car, there could be a
Bluetooth network specific to the car. During the drive to the hotel, the traffic information is delivered through a GPRS network, and at the hotel, the hotel room
provides a WLAN hotspot to control room facilities and to access the Internet. To
make all the different network infrastructures transparent to Maria, the P-Com
can make use of the (wireless) network ontology and location information, and
based on these, change seamlessly from one network to another.

The ontology defines a concept of GSM network, but it does not specify
instances of GSM networks. An instance could be, e.g., the GSM network that

Term	Explanation
LineRate	The bandwidth in one direction over a measured component.
Throughput	The number of user data bits successfully transferred in one direction across a measured component. Successful transfer means that no user data bits are lost, added or inverted in transfer.
RTT	Round-trip time, that is, the time required for a data segment to be transmitted to a peer entity and a corresponding acknowledgment sent back to the originating entity.
Delay	The (nominal) time required for a data segment to be transmitted to a peer entity.
MeanUpTime	The expected uptime of an established (logical) connection.
OmissionRate	The probability that a data segment is lost.
BER	The ratio of the number of bit errors to the total number of bits transmitted in a given time interval.
FrameError-Rate	The probability that a data segment is not transmitted correctly over a measured component.
ConnSetup-Delay	The delay to establish a connection between communicating entities.
ConnSetup-FailureProb	The ratio of total call attempts that result in call setup failure to the total call attempts in a population of interest.
Status	The connectivity status of a measured component.

Table 2.2: QoS terminology

TeliaSonera provides in Finland. Such instances are obviously necessary for effective usage of the ontology, but defining a complete set of these is impossible for individual organizations. However, we believe that if the ontology proves to be useful, innovative network operators will provide instances of their networks. This will lead towards achieving critical mass of users, and ultimately the ontology can be used in various applications. Therefore, it is essential that leading network operators provide initial sets of instances so that the critical mass of users is achieved rapidly. Figure 2.3 depicts the core concepts of the wireless network ontology. For details of this ontology, see [15].

QoS Ontology

Perhaps the most dominant characteristic of the wireless world is change of Quality of Service (QoS). This can happen both during the connection and between connections. During the connection, the values may vary because of a new user location or new radio conditions. Perhaps more significant changes occur between connections, especially when using different technologies. For example, the QoS changes significantly when roaming from a GSM network to a WLAN network, even if the user location remains static.

A network QoS ontology allows describing QoS properties of networks providing agents with means to communicate using QoS related terms. The original version of such an ontology was defined by FIPA (Foundation for Intelligent Physical Agents) [9]. It specifies several QoS attributes, and gives a natural language definition for each of them (see Table 2.2 and Figure 2.4). A more formal –although still quite informal– definition of this ontology is given in [14]. Both [9] and [14] discuss it only in abstract level and do not give any concrete encoding. However, in [15], a DAML encoding is presented (see Figure 2.4).

Device Ontology

In the environment of the CASCOM architecture, several different kinds of devices could be used. For managing and processing properly perceptions from a device –which may be a new one in the environment– a device ontology is needed. The capabilities of different devices are best expressed using an ontology, against which the profiles of those devices are validated.

There are several efforts to specify device ontologies. W3C has the Device Independence activity, which works with CC/PP (Composite Capability / Preference Profiles) [44] based on RDF [4]. A CC/PP profile contains CC/PP attribute names and associated values. The profile is structured allowing an entity to describe its capabilities by reference to a standard profile, accessible to a peer entity, and a smaller set of features that are in addition to or different than the standard profile. A CC/PP vocabulary consists of a set of CC/PP attribute names, permissible values and associated meanings. CC/PP is compatible with IETF media feature sets (CONNEG) [20] in the sense that all media feature tags and values can be expressed in CC/PP. However, not all CC/PP profiles can be expressed as media feature tags and values, and CC/PP does not attempt to express relationships between attributes.

FIPA has specified a device ontology that contains specifications for properties of devices [8]. Agents can use it when communicating about hardware and software properties of various devices. They pass profiles of devices to each other and validate them against the FIPA Device ontology. The profiles are useful, e.g., in a situation where memory- or processing-intensive actions take place; agent A1 can ask agent A2 whether device D has enough capabilities to handle some task A1 has in mind.

In [19], the authors introduce another approach to use ontologies in the context of devices. Ontology-based description of functional design knowledge of engineering devices is presented. In the proposed model generic concepts representing functionality of a device in the functional knowledge are provided by the functional concept ontology, which makes this knowledge consistent and applicable to other domains. In the case of CASCOM, the function concept ontology of wireless data communications equipment could be integrated with context ontologies.

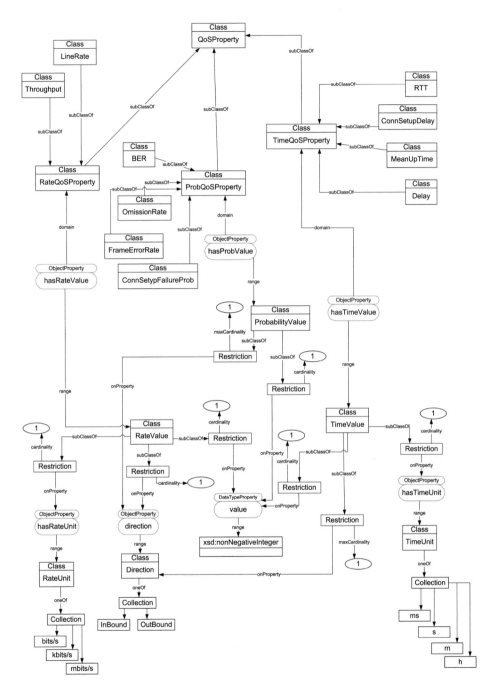

Figure 2.4: Concepts of QoS properties ontology

Standard Ontology for Pervasive Ontology

The goal of the Pervasive Computing Standard Ontology (PERCOM-SO)[3] is to define an ontology to support knowledge representation and communication interoperability in building pervasive computing applications. The PERCOM-SO ontology will be defined using OWL and published in RDF/XML representation. Even if it is a relatively new initiative, the following domains have been identified so far: (1) Spatial ontology that describes physical space and spatial relations, (2) temporal ontology that describes time and temporal relations, (3) person profile/user model ontology that describes profiles of persons, (4) event ontology that describes events that occur in a pervasive computing environment, (5) devices profile ontology that describes hardware and software attributes associated to a computing devices, (6) digital document ontology that describes attributes of associated digital documents, and (7) security and privacy policy ontology that describes policy rules for supporting access control and privacy protection in a pervasive computing environment.

Other Examples of Wireless World Ontologies

An interesting wireless world related ontology is presented in [1]. The authors introduce it for describing and discovering services in an ad-hoc networking environment like Bluetooth. This ontology enables far better service discovery than simple UUID-based descriptions used in the Bluetooth SDP system. It does not have a direct connection to our ontology, but gives an excellent example of using ontologies for supporting applications in the wireless world.

An example of a higher level ontology for mobile communications area can be found in [37]. This ontology defines concepts for services, networks, devices, as an example[4].

DAML-time[5] is an ontology for expressing temporal aspects of the contents of web resources and for expressing time-related properties of Web Services. Modeling time is very important in context-aware architectures and applications, and therefore ontologies, such as the DAML-time ontology, are an essential component of such a system.

2.3   Overlay Networks

An overlay network[6] consists of a collection of nodes implementing a network abstraction on top of the network infrastructure. The underlying network infrastructure may consist of several different network technologies (see Figure 2.5). In

---

[3]http://pervasive.semanticweb.org/percom-so-proposal.html

[4]The   specification   of   this   ontology   can   be   found   at http://www.ee.surrey.ac.uk/Personal/A.Zhdanova/ontologies/mobile_ontology/docs/

[5]http://www.cs.rochester.edu/ ferguson/daml/

[6]Sometimes overlay networks are called virtual networks (see. e.g., JXTA documentation)

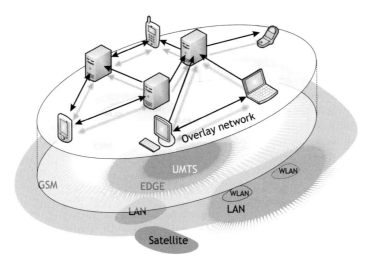

Figure 2.5: An overlay network

CASCOM, the functionality of the overlay network will be implemented using P2P technologies.

The P2P network, in general, can be defined as [36]:

A distributed network architecture may be called a Peer-to-Peer (P-to-P, P2P,...) network, if the participants share a part of their own hardware resources (processing power, storage capacity, network link capacity, printers,...). These shared resources are necessary to provide the Service and content offered by the network (e.g. file sharing or shared workspaces for collaboration). They are accessible by other peers directly, without passing intermediary entities. The participants of such a network are thus resource (Service and content) providers as well as resource (Service and content) requestors (Servent-concept).

Three basic architectures implementing overlay network can be identified: centralized, pure, and hybrid. These will be described briefly below.

2.3.1 Centralized P2P Architecture

The centralized overlay P2P architecture is essentially a client/server architecture [36]:

A Client/Server network is a distributed network which consists of one higher performance system, the Server, and several mostly lower performance systems, the Clients. The Server is the central registering unit as well as the only provider of content and service. A Client only re-

Figure 2.6: Centralized P2P architecture

quests content or the execution of services, without sharing any of its own resources.

In centralized (client/server) architecture, one node coordinates most of the operations in the network (see Figure 2.6). The advantage of centralized overlay network is fast resource lookup time ($O(1)$). However, the most significant disadvantage is that the centralized server is a single point of failure. Even though centralized architecture is not really a P2P architecture, it has been used in some P2P implementations (e.g., Napster [24]).

2.3.2   Pure P2P Architecture

A pure P2P network is defined as follows [36] (Figure 2.7):

> A distributed network architecture has to be classified as a "Pure" Peer-to-Peer network, if it is firstly a Peer-to-Peer network according to P2P network definition (see above) and secondly if any single, arbitrary chosen Terminal Entity can be removed from the network without having the network suffering any loss of network service.

The essential feature of a pure P2P architecture is that existence of any single node cannot be assumed. All the nodes are equal and can leave the network at any given time. Such very dynamic nature of pure P2P architecture gives tough requirements of any application relying on such architecture. For example, no single application can rely on the existence of directory services, but the nodes have to handle directory services in a highly distributed manner.

Example algorithms for pure P2P architectures include Pastry [35], Tapestry [46], CAN [34], and Chord [38, 39]. The Plaxton algorithm [30] was the first attempt towards massively scalable Distributed Hash Table (DHT) algorithms for pure P2P architectures. However, there are several limitations in that algorithm

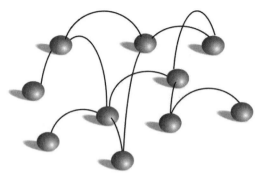

Figure 2.7: Pure P2P architecture

considering real-world applications. The most severe is that the algorithm lacks adaptability, that is, no nodes can join or leave the network at runtime. However, modern DHT algorithms do not have such limitations while preserving scalability of the Plaxton algorithm. For example, both Pastry and Tapestry are (directly) based on the Plaxton algorithm but overcome its limitations. The CAN (Content Addressable Network) is based on d-dimensional space. The Chord algorithm is perhaps the simplest algorithm of these four. However, same (or similar) computation complexity is achieved in Chord as in the other DHTs examples above. Given this, most of the new DHT algorithms are based on Chord.

2.3.3 Hybrid P2P Architecture

A hybrid P2P network is defined as follows [36] (Figure 2.8):

> A distributed network architecture has to be classified as a "Hybrid" Peer-to-Peer network, if it is firstly a Peer-to-Peer network according to P2P network definition (see above) and secondly a central entity is necessary to provide parts of the offered network services.

Compared to pure P2P architecture, the hybrid architecture is a bit simpler, because any given node can assume that there are some "super" nodes that can host different kind of services (e.g., directory services). An example of hybrid P2P architecture is JXTA [31]. However, since JXTA is basically only a collection of (P2P) protocols, it does not enforce hybrid P2P architectures.

2.4 Summary

This chapter considered the state-of-the-art from the network environment viewpoint of the CASCOM architecture. The foundation for wireless applications is

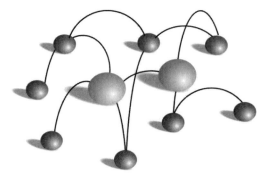

Figure 2.8: Hybrid P2P architecture

the availability of a wireless network. The development of different kind of wireless networks is rapid. Availability, reliability, and bandwidth are increasing at accelerating speed. Many mobile device has a WLAN radio, which enables fast communication but with limited mobility. There will always be different kind of wireless networks. Therefore, it is essential that mobile device can switch between network technologies without disturbing the user and applications. Technologies like WiMAX will enable fast communication with greater mobility in the future. At the same time, capabilities of mobile devices are increasing enabling more complex applications in very small devices. However, small display size and limited battery life still limits certain applications in mobile devices. But, new technologies, such as Near Field Communication (NFC), enable new kind of applications that are usable only in mobile devices.

Building intelligent applications for mobile devices requires ontologies not only related to application functionality but also to an environment in which the application is used. In the wireless world, this implies that ontologies related to wireless networks, network capabilities, and mobile devices are needed, as an example. Several such ontologies have been developed, although so far those are used only in small scale prototype applications.

References

[1] S. Avancha, A. Joshi, and T. Finin. Enhanced service discovery in bluetooth. *IEEE Computer*, 35(6):96–99, 2002.

[2] N. G. Badr. Cellular digital packet data CDPD. In *Proceedings of the IEEE 14th Annual International Phoenix Conference on Computers and Communications*, pages 659–665, Scottsdale, AZ, USA, March 1995.

[3] Bluetooth Special Interest Group. The Official Bluetooth SIG Website, 2007. Available from World Wide Web: <http://www.bluetooth.com>.

[4] D. Brickley and R. V. Guha, editors. *Resource Description Framework (RDF) Schema Specification 1.0*. World Wide Web Consortium, March 2000. W3C Candidate Recommendation.

[5] CDPD Consortium. *Cellular Digital Packet Data System Specification, Rel 1.0, Books I-V*. CDPD, 1993.

[6] B. P. Crow, I. Widjaja, J. G. Kim, and P. T. Sakai. IEEE 802.11 wireless local area networks. *IEEE Communications Magazine*, 35(9):116–126, September 1997.

[7] K. Ducatel, M. Bogdanowicz, F. Scapolo, J. Leijten, and J.C. Burgelman, editors. *Scenarios for Ambient Intelligence in 2010*. ISTAG, 2001.

[8] Foundation for Intelligent Physical Agents. *FIPA Device Ontology Specification*. Geneva, Switzerland, April 2001. Specification number SC00091.

[9] Foundation for Intelligent Physical Agents. *FIPA Quality of Service Ontology Specification*. Geneva, Switzerland, April 2001. Specification number SC00094.

[10] A. Furuskär, S. Mazur, F. Müller, and H. Olofsson. EDGE: Enhanced data rates for GSM and TDMA/136 evolution. *IEEE Personal Communications*, 6(3):56–66, June 1999.

[11] GSM Technical Specification, GSM 02.34. High speed circuit switched data (HSCSD), stage 1, July 1997. Version 5.2.0.

[12] GSM Technical Specification, GSM 02.60. GPRS service description, stage 1, 1998. Version 6.1.0.

[13] GSM Technical Specification, GSM 03.34. High speed circuit switched data (HSCSD), stage 2, May 1999. Version 5.2.0.

[14] H. Helin. *Supporting Nomadic Agent-based Applications in the FIPA Agent Architecture*. PhD thesis, University of Helsinki, Department of Computer Science, Helsinki, Finland, January 2003.

[15] H. Helin and M. Laukkanen. Wireless network ontology. In *Proceedings of the Wireless World Research Forum 9th Meeting*, Zürich, Switzerland, July 2003.

[16] D. Jonhson, C. Perkins, and J. Arkko. Mobility support in IPv6. Request for Comments 3755, IETF, June 2004.

[17] T. Kamba, S. A. Elson, T. Harpold, T. Stamper, and P. Sukaviriya. Using small screen space more efficiently. In *Proceedings of the Conference on Human Factors and Computing Systems (CHI'96)*, pages 383–390, Vancouver, Canada, April 1996. ACM Press.

[18] M. Khan and J. Kilpatrick. MOBITEX and mobile data standards. *IEEE Communications Magazine*, 33(3):96–101, March 1995.

[19] Y. Kitamura, T. Kasai, and R. Mizoguchi. Ontology-based description of functional design knowledge and its use in a functional way server. In *Proceedings of the Pacific Asian Conference on Intelligent Systems (PRIS'2001)*, pages 400–409, 2001.

[20] G. Klyne. A syntax for describing media feature sets. Request for Comments 2533, IETF, March 1999.

[21] R. O. LaMaire, A. Krishna, P. Bhagwat, and J. Panian. Wireless LANs and mobile networking: Standards and future directions. *IEEE Personal Communications*, 34(8):86–94, August 1996.

[22] R. Moskowitz and P. Nikander. Host identity protocol (HIP) architecture. Request for Comments 4423, IETF, May 2006.

[23] M. Mouly and M.-B. Pautet. *The GSM System for Mobile Communications*. Mouly and Pautet, 1992.

[24] Napster. The napster home page. www.napster.com.

[25] Open Mobile Alliance. OMA Device Management Version 1.1.2, January 2004.

[26] Open Mobile Alliance. OMA User Agent Profile Version 2.0, 2006.

[27] K. Pahlavan, A. Zahedi, and P. Krisnamurthy. Wideband local access: Wireless LAN and wireless ATM. *IEEE Communications Magazine*, 35(11):34–40, 1997.

[28] J. D. Parson, D. Jardine, and J. G. Gardiner. *Mobile Communication Systems*. Blackie, Glasgow, UK, 1989.

[29] C. Perkins. Ip mobility support for ipv4. Request for Comments 3344, IETF, August 2002.

[30] C. G. Plaxton, R. Rajamanen, and A.W. Richa. Accessing nearby copies of replicated objects in a distributed environment. Technical Report CS-TR-97-11, University of Texas at Austin, 1997.

[31] Project JXTA. JXTA home page, 2007. Available from World Wide Web: <http://www.jxta.org>.

[32] K. Raatikainen. A new look at mobile computing. In *Proceedings of ANWIRE Workshop*, Athens, May 2004.

[33] M. Rahnema. Overview of the GSM system and protocol architecture. *IEEE Communication Magazine*, 31(4):92–100, April 1993.

[34] S. Ratnasamy, P. Francis, M. Handley, R. Karp, and S. Shenker. A scalable content-addressable network. In *Proceedings of the ACM SIGCOMM 01*, San Diego, California, August 2001.

[35] A. Rowstron and P. Druschel. Pastry: Scalable, decentralized object location and routing for large-scale peer-to-peer systems. In *Proceedings of the ACM/IFIP Middleware*, 2001.

[36] R. Schollmeier. A definition of peer-to-peer networking for the classification of peer-to-peer architectures and applications. In *Proceedings of the First International Conference on Peer-to-Peer Computing (P2P'01)*, pages 101–102, Sweden, 2001.

[37] SPICE Consortium. Deliverable D3.1: Ontology Definition for the DCS and DCS Resource Description, User Rules, 2006.

[38] I. Stoica, R. Morris, D. R. Karger, M. F. Kaashoek, and H. Balakrishnan. Chord: A scalable peer-to-peer lookup service for internet applications. In *Proceedings of the ACM SIGCOMM 01*, San Diego, California, August 2001.

[39] I. Stoica, R. Morris, D. Liben-Nowell, D.R. Karger, M.F. Kaashoek, F. Dabek, and H. Balakrishnan. Chord: A scalable peer-to-peer lookup protocol for internet applications. *IEEE/ACM Transactions on Networking Software*, 11(1):17–32, 2003.

[40] The Infrared Data Association. IrDA homepage, 2007. Available from World Wide Web: <http://www.irda.org/>.

[41] The Institute of Electrical and Electronics Engineers. IEEE Home Page, 2007. Available from World Wide Web: <http://www.ieee.org>.

[42] The Internet Engineering Task Force. IETF Home Page, 2007. Available from World Wide Web: <http://www.ietf.org>.

[43] Third generation partnership project web site, 2007. Available from World Wide Web: <http://www.3gpp.org>.

[44] W3C. W3c device independence activity. Available from World Wide Web: <http://www.w3.org/2001/di/>.

[45] W3C. Composite capability/preference profiles (cc/pp): Structure and vocabularies, March 2003. W3C Working Draft.

[46] B. Y. Zhoa, J. D. Kubiatowicz, and A. D. Joseph. Tapestry: An infrastructure for fault-tolerant wide-area location and routing. Technical Report CSD-01-1141, University of California at Berkeley, 2001.

Chapter 3

Semantic Web Service Description

Matthias Klusch

3.1 Introduction

The convergence of Semantic Web with service-oriented computing is manifested by Semantic Web service (SWS) technology. It addresses the major challenge of automated, interoperable and meaningful coordination of Web services to be carried out by intelligent software agents. In this chapter, we briefly discuss prominent SWS description frameworks, that are the standard SAWSDL, OWL-S and WSML[1]. This is complemented by a critique, and selected references to further readings on the subject.

3.2 Issues of Semantic Service Description

Each semantic service description framework can be characterised with respect to (a) what kind of service semantics are described, (b) in what language or formalism, (c) allowing for what kind of reasoning upon the abstract service descriptions? Further, we distinguish between an abstract Web Service, that is the description of the computational entity of the service, and a concrete service as one of its instances or invocations that provide the actual value to the user [22]. In this sense, abstract service descriptions are considered complete but not necessarily correct: There might be concrete service instances that are models of the capability description of the abstract service but can actually not be delivered by the provider.

---

[1]Due to space limitations other semantic service description frameworks like SWSL (Semantic Web Service Language) and the DIANE service description language are excluded.

3.2.1   Functional and Non-Functional Service Semantics

In general, the functionality of a service can be described in terms of what it does, and how it actually works. Both aspects of its functional semantics (or capability) are captured by a service profile, respectively, service process model. The profile describes the signature of the service in terms of its input (I) and output (O) parameters, and its preconditions (P) and effects (E) that are supposed to hold before or after executing the service in a given world state, and some additional provenance information such as the service name, its business domain and provider. The process model of atomic or composite services describes how the service works in terms of the interplay between data and control flow based on a common set of workflow or control constructs like sequence, split+join, choice, and others.

This general distinction between profile and process model semantics is common to structured Web service description frameworks, while differences are in the naming and formal representation of what part of service semantics. We can further differentiate between stateless (IO), respectively, state-based (PE) abstract service descriptions representing the set of its instances, that are concrete services providing value to the user. The non-functional service semantics are usually described with respect to a quality of service (QoS) model including delivery constraints, cost model with rules for pricing, repudiation, availability, and privacy policy.

3.2.2   Structured Representation of Service Semantics

A domain-independent and structured representation of service semantics is offered by upper (top-level) service ontologies and languages such as OWL-S and WSML with formal logic groundings, or SAWSDL which comes, in essence, without any formal semantics. Neither OWL-S nor WSML provide any agreed formal but intuitive, standard workflow-based semantics of the service process model (orchestration and choreography). Alternatively, for abstract service descriptions grounded in WSDL, the process model can be intuitively mapped to BPEL orchestrations with certain formal semantics.

3.2.3   Monolithic Representation of Service Semantics

The formal specification of service semantics agnostic to any structured service description format can be achieved, for example, by means of a specific set of concept and role axioms in an appropriate logic (cf. Section 3.6). Since the service capability is described by means of one single service concept, this representation of service semantics is called monolithic and allows to determine the semantic relations between service descriptions fully within the underlying logical formalism based on concept satisfaction, subsumption and entailment. However, it does not provide any further information on how the service actually works in terms of the process model nor any description of non-functional semantics.

3.2.4 Data Semantics

The domain-dependent semantics of service profile parameters (also called data semantics) are described in terms of concepts, roles (and rules) taken from shared domain, task, or application ontologies. These ontologies are defined in a formal Semantic Web language like OWL, WSML or SWRL. If different ontologies are used, agents are supposed to automatically resolve the structural and semantic heterogeneities for interoperation to facilitate better Web Service discovery and composition. This process of ontology matching is usually restricted to ontologies specified in the same language, otherwise appropriate inter-ontology mappings have to be provided to the agents.

In subsequent sections, we briefly introduce prominent approaches to both types of service representation. For structured semantic service descriptions, we focus on OWL-S, WSML, and SAWSDL, and omit to discuss alternatives like DSD (DIANE service description format) and SWSL (Semantic Web service Language).

3.2.5 Reasoning about Semantic Service Descriptions

The basic idea of formally grounded descriptions of Web Services is to allow agents to better understand the functional and non-functional semantics through appropriate logic-based reasoning. For this purpose, it is commonly assumed that the applied type of logic reasoning complies with the underlying semantic service description framework. Further, the concept expressions used to specify the data semantics of service input and output parameters are assumed to build up from basic concepts and roles taken from formal application or domain ontologies which the requester and provider commonly refer to. We survey approaches to non-logic-based, logic-based, and hybrid reasoning means for Semantic Web Service discovery, and composition planning in the next chapter.

3.3 SAWSDL

The standard language WSDL for Web Services operates at the mere syntactic level as it lacks any declarative semantics needed to meaningfully represent and reason upon them by means of logical inferencing. In a first response to this problem, the W3C Working Group on Semantic Annotations for WSDL and XML Schema (SAWSDL) developed mechanisms with which semantic annotations can be added to WSDL components. The SAWSDL specification became a W3C candidate recommendation on January 26, 2007[2], and eventually a W3C recommendation on August 28, 2007.

---

[2]http://www.w3.org/2002/ws/sawsdl/

3.3.1   Annotating WSDL Components

Unlike OWL-S or WSML, SAWSDL does not specify a new language or top-level ontology for semantic service description but simply provides mechanisms by which ontological concepts that are defined outside WSDL service documents can be referenced to semantically annotate WSDL description elements. Based on its predecessor and W3C member submission WSDL-S[3] in 2005, the key design principles for SAWSDL are that (a) the specification enables semantic annotations of Web Services using and building on the existing extensibility framework of WSDL; (b) it is agnostic to semantic (ontology) representation languages; and (c) it enables semantic annotations for Web Services not only for discovering Web Services but also for invoking them.

Based on these design principles, SAWSDL defines the following three new extensibility attributes to WSDL 2.0 elements for their semantic annotation:

- An extension attribute, named `modelReference`, to specify the association between a WSDL component and a concept in some semantic (domain) model. This modelReference attribute is used to annotate XML Schema complex type definitions, simple type definitions, element declarations, and attribute declarations as well as WSDL interfaces, operations, and faults. Each modelReference identifies the concept in a semantic model that describes the element to which it is attached.

- Two extension attributes (`liftingSchemaMapping` and `loweringSchema-Mapping`) are added to the set of XML Schema element declarations, complex type definitions and simple type definitions. Both allow to specify mappings between semantic data in the domain referenced by modelReference and XML, which can be used during service invocation.

An example of a SAWSDL service, that is a semantically annotated WSDL service with references to external ontologies describing the semantics of WSDL elements, is given in Figure 3.1: The semantics of the service input parameter of type "OrderRequest" is defined by an equally named concept specified in an ontology "purchaseorder" which is referenced (URI) by the element tag "modelReference" attached to "OrderRequest". It is also annotated with a tag A tag "loweringSchemaMapping" which value (URI) points to a data type mapping, in this case an XML document, which shows how the elements of this type can be mapped from the referenced semantic data model (here RDFS) to XMLS used in WSDL.

3.3.2   Limitations

Major critic of SAWSDL is that it comes, as a mere syntactic extension of WSDL, without any formal semantics. In contrast to OWL-S and (in part) WSML, there is

---

[3]http://www.w3.org/Submission/WSDL-S/

```
<wsdl:types>
 <xs:schema targetNamespace="http://www.w3.org/2002/ws/sawsdl/spec/wsdl/order#" elementFormDefault="qualified">

   <xs:element name="OrderRequest"
        sawsdl:modelReference="http://www.w3.org/2002/ws/sawsdl/spec/ontology/purchaseorder#OrderRequest"
        sawsdl:loweringSchemaMapping="http://www.w3.org/2002/ws/sawsdl/spec/mapping/RDFOnt2Request.xml">
        <xs:complexType>
           <xs:sequence>
           <xs:element name="customerNo" type="xs:integer" />
           <xs:element name="orderItem" type="item" minOccurs="1" maxOccurs="unbounded" />
           </xs:sequence>
        </xs:complexType>
   </xs:element>

  <xs:complexType name="item">
     <xs:all> <xs:element name="UPC" type="xs:string" /> </xs:all>  <xs:attribute name="quantity" type="xs:integer" />
  </xs:complexType>

  <xs:element name="OrderResponse" type="confirmation" />
    <xs:simpleType name="confirmation"
        sawsdl:modelReference="http://www.w3.org/2002/ws/sawsdl/spec/ontology/purchaseorder#OrderConfirmation">
        <xs:restriction base="xs:string">
        <xs:enumeration value="Confirmed" />
        <xs:enumeration value="Pending" />
        <xs:enumeration value="Rejected" />
    </xs:restriction>
    </xs:simpleType>
 </xs:schema>
</wsdl:types>
```

Figure 3.1: Example of semantic annotation of WSDL elements in SAWSDL.

no defined formal grounding of neither the XML-based WSDL service components nor the referenced external metadata sources (via modelReference). Quoting from the SAWSDL specification: "Again, if the XML structures expected by the client and by the service differ, schema mappings can translate the XML structures into the semantic model where any mismatches can be understood and resolved." This makes any form of logic-based discovery and composition of SAWSDL service descriptions in the Semantic Web rather obsolete but calls for "magic" mediators outside the framework to resolve the semantic heterogeneities.

Another problem with SAWSDL today is its –apart from the METEOR-S framework by the developers of SAWSDL (WSDL-S) and related ongoing development efforts at IBM– still very limited software support compared to the considerable investments made in research and development of software for more advanced frameworks like OWL-S and WSMO world wide. However, the recent announcement of SAWSDL as a W3C recommendation does not only support a standardized evolution of the W3C Web service framework in principle (rather than a revolutionary technology switch to far more advanced technologies like OWL-S or WSML) but certainly will push software development in support of SAWSDL and reinforce research on refactoring these frameworks with respect to SAWSDL.

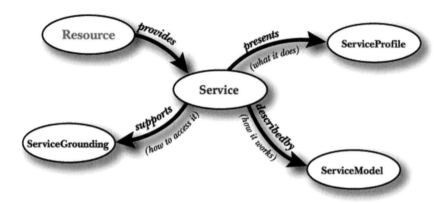

Figure 3.2: OWL-S service description elements.

3.4 OWL-S

OWL-S is an upper ontology used to describe the semantics of services based on the W3C standard ontology OWL and is grounded in WSDL. It has its roots in the DAML Service Ontology (DAML-S) released in 2001, and became a W3C candidate recommendation in 2005. OWL-S builds on top of OWL and consists of three main upper ontologies: the Profile, the Process Model, and the Grounding (cf. Figure 3.2).

In the following, we briefly summarize the underlying standard ontology language OWL and then present each of the main elements of OWL-S service descriptions.

3.4.1 Background: OWL

The standard ontology language for the Semantic Web is OWL [2, 4, 12] which is formally grounded in description logics (DL). OWL has its roots in the joint initiative DAML+OIL of researchers from the US and Europe in 2000 to develop a formal annotation or mark-up language for the Web. Only three years later, OWL became a W3C recommendation, and has been widely adopted by both industry and academics since then. The current version of OWL is OWL 1.1[4].

Variants

OWL comes in several variants, that are OWL-Full, OWL-DL, and OWL-Lite. Each variant corresponds to a DL of different expressivity and complexity. OWL-Lite and OWL-DL are an abstract syntactic form of the description logic SHIF(D), respectively, SHOIN(D).

---

[4]http://www.w3.org/Submission/2006/10/

OWL-Full. The most expressive but undecidable variant OWL-Full provides full compatibility with RDFS and covers the expressivity of the description logic SHOIQ(D)* which offers not only simple data types (D) but inverse roles (I), roles as subroles (a role hierarchy H), role transitivity (S) and qualified role cardinality restrictions (Q), as well as derived classes (classes used as individuals) together with non-primitive roles. Since OWL-Full allows in particular non-primitive roles (which can either be transitive or have transitive subroles) in role cardinality restrictions (S*), it is undecidable [14].

OWL-DL. Unlike OWL-Full, the less expressive variant OWL-DL (SHOIN(D)) allows only for unqualified number (role cardinality) restrictions, and does not permit to state that a role P is transitive or the inverse of another role $Q \neq P$. In particular, OWL-DL does not include relationships between (transitive) role chains which would cause its undecidability. That is, in role number restrictions, only simple roles which are neither transitive nor have transitive subroles are allowed; otherwise we gain undecidability even in SHN [14]. OWL-DL also does not allow classes to be used as individuals (derived classes), or to impose cardinality constraints on subclasses.

OWL-Lite. The variant OWL-Lite (SHIF(D)) is even less expressive than OWL-DL. It prohibits unions and complements of classes, does not allow the use of individuals in class descriptions (enumerated classes, nominals O), and limits role cardinalities to 0 or 1 (F). However, it is possible to capture all OWL-DL class descriptions except those containing either individuals or role cardinalities greater than 1 by properly exploiting the implicit negations introduced by disjointness axioms, and introducing new class names [13]. In role cardinality restrictions, only simple roles are allowed; however, it is unknown whether SHF or SHIF becomes undecidable without this restriction [14].

The syntactic transformation from OWL-Lite and OWL-DL ontologies to corresponding DL knowledge bases is of polynomial complexity. What makes OWL a Semantic Web language is not its semantics (which are quite standard for a DL) but the use of URI references for names, the use of XMLS datatypes for data values, and the ability to connect to documents in the Web.

Relation to RDFS

The abstract syntax of OWL can be mapped to the normative syntax of RDF [5]. In general, OWL adds constructors to RDFS for building class and property (role) descriptions (vocabulary) and new axioms (constraints) with model-theoretic semantics. In particular, the use of intersection (union) within (sub-)class descriptions, or universal/existential quantifications within super-/subclasses in OWL is not possible in RDFS[13]. However, the variants OWL-DL and OWL-Lite are extensions of a restricted use of RDFS whereas OWL-Full is fully upward compatible with RDFS. As mentioned above, OWL-DL and OWL-Lite do not allow classes to

---

[5]RDFS statements are equivalent to DL axioms of the form $C \sqsubseteq D$, $\top \sqsubseteq \forall P : C$, $\top \sqsubseteq \forall P^- . C$, $P \sqsubseteq Q$, $a : C$ and $(a, b) : P$.

be used as individuals, or to impose cardinality constraints on subclasses, and the language constructors cannot be applied to the language itself - which is possible in OWL-Full and RDFS.

It has been shown only recently in [21] that the formal semantics of a sublanguage of RDFS is compatible with that of the corresponding fragment of OWL-DL such that RDFS could indeed serve as a foundational language of the Semantic Web layer stack. Though checking whether a RDF graph is an OWL ontology and up-grading from RDFS to OWL remains hard in practice, and is topic of ongoing research. For a detailed treatment of this subject, we refer to [7]. The syntactic transformation from OWL-Lite and OWL-DL ontologies to corresponding DL knowledge bases is of polynomial complexity.

Complexity

As mentioned above, for OWL-Lite and OWL-DL, entailment reduced to concept satisfiability and ABox consistency is decidable in EXPTIME (complete), respectively, NEXPTIME (complete) [11, 26]. Though SHOIQ(D) is intractably co-NEXPTIME hard [26], its variant with non-primitive transitive roles in role cardinality restrictions (S*), hence OWL-Full, is undecidable [14]. Reasoning with data types and values (D) can be separated from reasoning with classes and individuals by allowing the DL reasoner to access a datatype oracle that can answer simple questions with respect to data types and values; this way, the language remains decidable if data type and value reasoning is decidable, i.e., if the oracle can guarantee to answer all questions of the relevant kind for supported datatypes.

Efficient query answering over DL knowledge bases with large ABoxes (instance stores) and static TBoxes is of particular interest in practice. Unfortunately, OWL can be considered insufficient for this purpose in general: Conjunctive query answering (CQA) for SHIQ and SHIF underlying OWL-Lite is decidable but only in time exponential in the size of the knowledge base (taxonomic complexity) and double exponential in the size of the query [7] (query and combined complexity); the CQA complexity for OWL-DL is unknown.

Another important inference on OWL ontologies is defined in terms of ontology entailment: Ontology O_1 entails another O_2, $O_1 \models O_2$, iff all interpretations that satisfy O_1 also satisfy O_2 in the DL sense. For both OWL-DL (SHOIN(D)) and OWL-Lite (SHIF(D)), ontology entailment checking can be polynomially reduced to the checking of the satisfiability of the corresponding DL knowledge bases O_1, O_2 (ontology consistency checking) which is decidable for both variants. The main criticism of the standard Semantic Web ontology language OWL is that it only allows for static declarative knowledge representation of limited expressivity and reasoning support.

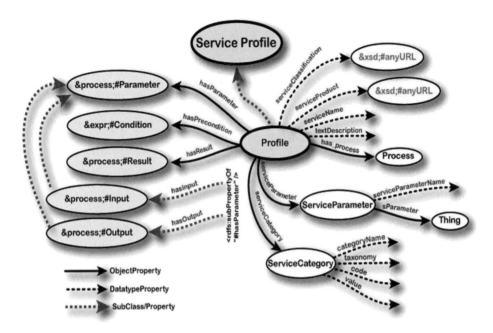

Figure 3.3: OWL-S service profile structure.

3.4.2 Service Profile

The OWL-S profile ontology is used to describe what the service does, and is meant to be mainly used for the purpose of service discovery. An OWL-S service profile or signature encompasses its functional parameters, i.e. hasInput, hasOutput, precondition and effect (IOPEs), as well as non-functional parameters such as serviceName, serviceCategory, qualityRating, textDescription, and meta-data (actor) about the service provider and other known requesters. Please note that, in contrast to OWL-S 1.0, in OWL-S 1.1 the service IOPE parameters are defined in the process model with unique references to these definitions from the profile (cf. Figure 3.3).

Inputs and outputs relate to data channels, where data flows between processes. Preconditions specify facts of the world (state) that must be asserted in order for an agent to execute a service. Effects characterize facts that become asserted given a successful execution of the service in the physical world (state). Whereas the semantics of each input and output parameter is defined as an OWL concept formally specified in a given ontology, typically in decidable OWL-DL or OWL-Lite, the preconditions and effects can be expressed in any appropriate logic (rule) language such as KIF, PDDL, and SWRL. Besides, the profile class can be subclassed and specialized, thus supporting the creation of profile taxonomies which subsequently describe different classes of services. An example of a Semantic

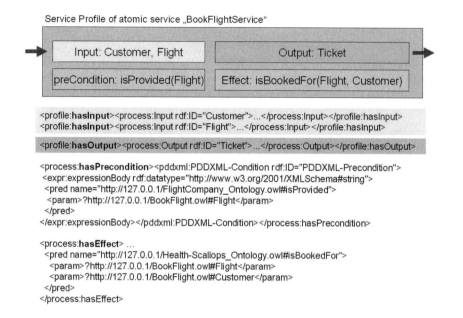

Figure 3.4: Example of OWL-S 1.1 service profile.

Web service profile in OWL-S 1.1 is given in figure 3.4.

3.4.3   Service Process Model

An OWL-S process model describes the composition (choreography and orchestration) of one or more services, that is the controlled enactment of constituent processes with respective communication pattern. In OWL-S this is captured by a common subset of workflow features like split+join, sequence, and choice (cf. Figure 3.5). Originally, the process model was not intended for service discovery but the profile by the OWL-S coalition.

More concrete, a process in OWL-S can be atomic, simple, or composite. An atomic process is a single, black-box process description with exposed IOPEs. Simple processes provide a means of describing service or process abstractions which have no specific binding to a physical service, thus have to be realized by an atomic process, e.g. through service discovery and dynamic binding at runtime, or expanded into a composite process. The process model of the example OWL-S service above is provided in Figure 3.6.

Composite processes are hierarchically defined workflows, consisting of atomic, simple and other composite processes. These process workflows are constructed using a number of different control flow operators including Sequence, Unordered (lists), Choice, If-then-else, Iterate, Repeat-until, Repeat-while, Split, and Split+Join. In OWL-S 1.1, the process model also specifies the inputs, outputs,

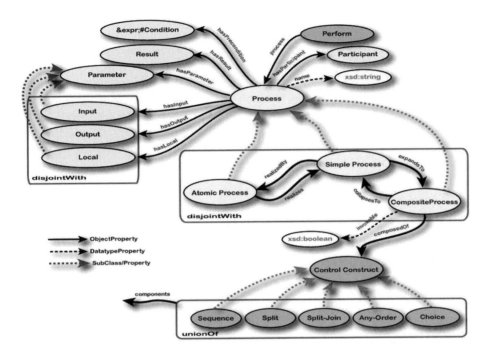

Figure 3.5: OWL-S service process model.

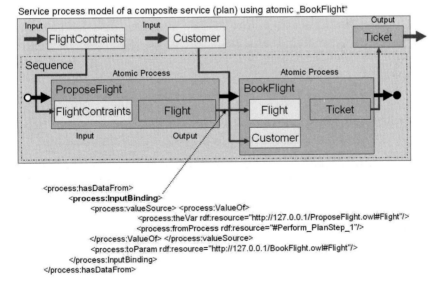

Figure 3.6: Example of OWL-S service process model.

preconditions, and effects of all processes that are part of a composed service, which are referenced in the profiles of the respective services[6]. An OWL-S process model of a composite service can also specify that its output is equal to some output of one of its subprocesses whenever the composite process gets instantiated. Moreover, for a composite process with a Sequence control construct, the output of one subprocess can be defined to be an input to another subprocess (binding).

Unfortunately, the semantics of the OWL-S process model are left undefined in the official OWL-S documents. Though there are proposals to specify these semantics in terms of, for example, the situation calculus [19], and the logic programming language GOLOG based on this calculus [20].

3.4.4 Service Grounding

The grounding of a given OWL-S service description provides a pragmatic binding between the logic-based and XMLS-based service definitions for the purpose of facilitating service execution. Such a grounding of OWL-S services can be, in principle, arbitrary but has been exemplified for a grounding in WSDL to pragmatically connect OWL-S to an existing Web service standard (cf. Figure 3.7).

In particular, the OWL-S process model of a service is mapped to a WSDL description through a thin (incomplete) grounding: Each atomic process is mapped to a WSDL operation, and the OWL-S properties used to represent inputs and outputs are grounded in terms of respectively named XML data types of corresponding input and output messages. Unlike OWL-S, WSDL cannot be used to express pre-conditions or effects of executing services. Any atomic or composite OWL-S service with a grounding in WSDL is executable either by direct invocation of the (service) program that is referenced in the WSDL file, or by a BPEL engine that processes the WSDL groundings of simple or orchestrated Semantic Web Services.

3.4.5 Software Support

One prominent software portal of the Semantic Web community is SemWebCentral[7] developed by InfoEther and BBN Technologies within the DAML program in 2004 with BBN continuing to maintain it today. As a consequence, it comes at no surprise that this portal offers a large variety of tools for OWL and OWL-S service coordination as well as OWL and rule processing. Examples of publicly available software support of developing, searching, and composing OWL-S services are as follows.

---

[6]This is in opposite to OWL-S 1.0, where the IOPES are defined in the profile and referenced in the process model.

[7]http://projects.semwebcentral.org/

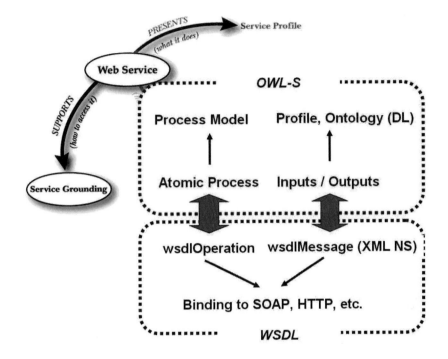

Figure 3.7: Grounding of OWL-S in WSDL.

- *Development.*
  OWL-S IDE integrated development environment[8], the OWL-S 1.1 API[9]
  with the OWL-DL reasoner Pellet[10] and OWL-S editors.

- *Discovery.*
  OWL-S service matchmakers OWLS-UDDI[11], OWLSM[12] and OWLS-MX[13]
  with test collection OWLS-TC2.

- *Composition.*
  OWL-S service composition planners OWLS-XPlan[14], GOAL[15].

---

[8]http://projects.semwebcentral.org/projects/owl-s-ide/
[9]http://projects.semwebcentral.org/projects/owl-s-api/
[10]http://projects.semwebcentral.org/projects/pellet/
[11]http://projects.semwebcentral.org/projects/mm-client/
[12]http://projects.semwebcentral.org/projects/owlsm/
[13]http://projects.semwebcentral.org/projects/owls-mx/
[14]http://projects.semwebcentral.org/projects/owls-xplan/
[15]http://www.smartweb-project.de

3.4.6   Limitations

Main critics of OWL-S concern its limited expressiveness of service descriptions in practice which, in fact, corresponds to that of its underlying description logic OWL-DL. Only static and deterministic aspects of the world can be described in OWL-DL, since it does not cover any notion of time and change, nor uncertainty. OWL-S allows specifying conditional effects, that are possible effects of the service each of which conditioned by its result (output) but not input. Besides, in contrast to WSDL, an OWL-S process model cannot contain any number of completely unrelated operations.

However, OWL-S bases on existing W3C Web standards, in particular the Web Services protocol stack: It extends OWL and has a grounding in WSDL. Furthermore, the large set of available tools and applications of OWL-S services, as well as ongoing research on Semantic Web rule languages on top of OWL such as SWRL and variants still support the adoption of OWL-S for Semantic Web Services, though this might be endangered by the choice of SAWSDL as a W3C standard just recently.

3.5   WSML

In this section, we informally introduce the reader to the basic elements of semantic service description in the Web service modeling language (WSML).

3.5.1   WSMO Framework

The WSMO (Web Service Modelling Ontology) framework[16] provides a conceptual model and a formal language WSML (Web Service Modeling Language) [17] for the semantic markup of Web services together with a reference implementation WSMX (Web Service Execution Environment). Historically, WSMO evolved from the Web Service Modeling Framework (WSMF) as a result of several European Commission funded research projects in the domain of Semantic Web Services like DIP, ASG, Super, TripCom, KnowledgeWeb and SEKT in the ESSI (European Semantic Systems Initiative) project cluster[18].

WSMO offers four key components to model different aspects of Semantic Web services in WSML (Web Service Modeling Language): Ontologies, goals, services, and mediators. Goals in goal repositories specify objectives that a client might have when searching for a relevant Web service. WSMO ontologies provide the formal logic-based grounding of information used by all other modeling components. Mediators bypass interoperability problems that appear between all these components at data (mediation of data structures), protocol (mediation of message exchange protocols), and process level (mediation of business logics) to "allow

---

[16] http://www.wsmo.org/TR/d2/v1.4/20061106
[17] http://www.wsmo.org/TR/d16/d16.1/v0.21/20051005/
[18] http://www.sdkcluster.org/

for loose coupling between Web services, goals (requests), and ontologies". Each of these components, called top-level elements of the WSMO conceptual model, can be assigned non-functional properties to be taken from the Dublin Core metadata standard by recommendation.

3.5.2 WSML Variants

The Web service modeling language WSML allows to describe a Semantic Web service in terms of its functionality (service capability), imported ontologies, and the interface through which it can be accessed for orchestration and choreography. The syntax of WSML is mainly derived from F-Logic extended with more verbose keywords (e.g., "hasValue" for $- >$, "p memberOf T" for p:T etc.), and has a normative human-readable syntax, as well as an XML and RDF syntax for exchange between machines. WSML comes in five variants with respect to the logical expressions allowed to describe the semantics of service and goal description elements. In the following, we informally introduce F-Logic and the WSML variants in very brief.

F-Logic. F-Logic is an object-oriented extension of first-order predicate logic with objects of complex internal structure, class hierarchies and inheritance, typing, and encapsulation in order to serve as a basis for object-oriented logic programming and knowledge representation. For modeling ontologies, it allows to define, for example, is-a object class (or type) hierarchies through subclass relationships like person::human denoting class "person" as a subclass of "human, a class of objects with structured properties (object type signature) like person[name $*\Rightarrow$ string, children $*\Rightarrow$ person], and instances of classes (typed objects) like john:person as well as rules like (R:region :- R1:region, R::R1.) and (L:location :- L:R, R:region.) denoting that every subclass "R" of an object class "R1" of type "region" is a region and that every member L of a region "R" is also a location. Rules may also be used to define virtual classes like the rule (X:redcar :- X:car, X[color $\rightarrow$ red].) defining the virtual class "redcar".

F-Logic comes in two flavors with respective variants: A first-order F-Logic variant (F-Logic(FO)) that includes an (OWL-DL/WSML-DL) description logic subset of classical predicate logic, and a full logic programming (LP) variant (F-Logic(LP)) that is LP extended with procedural built-ins (functions), and non-monotonic default inheritance and negation-as-(finite)-failure[19]. Non-monotonic (default) inheritance of F-Logic(LP) allows to override default property values of classes inherited by subclasses. For example, a class Elephant[color $*\rightarrow$ grey]

---

[19]In nonmonotonic LP, like semi-decidable PROLOG and F-Logic(LP), the default negation of fact p (**not** p) means "p is true if p cannot be proven in a given knowledge base KB in finite time" (under closed-world assumption). This is nonmonotonic, i.e., truth values of asserted and implied knowledge in KB do not grow monotonically: $(KB \models p)$ does *not* imply $(KB \cup \{q\} \models p)$, e.g., KB $= \{(p :\text{-} \textbf{not } q)\}$ implies p true $(KB \models p)$, but KB* $= \{q, (p :\text{-} \textbf{not } q)\}$ implies p false.

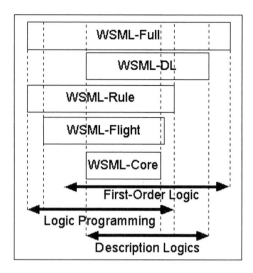

Figure 3.8: WSML language variants.

with default value "grey" of property "color" has a subclass royalElephant[color *→ white] for which objects this default value of inherited property "color" is overriden by (default) value "white". Hence, one can assert object fred[color → grey] as member of class "Elephant" (but not "royalElephant"), and clyde[color → white] as member of both classes. Semantics of F-Logic(LP) are derived from Van Gelder's well-founded (fix-point-based, minimal model) semantics of the non-monotonic part of logic programming [27]. F-Logic(LP) is more commonly used than F-Logic(FO) like in the LP-reasoners OntoBroker, Flora-2 and Florid. For more details on the syntax and semantics of F-Logic, we refer to [29, 28].

WSML variants. The formal semantics of WSML service description elements are specified as logical axioms and constraints in ontologies using one of five WSML variants: WSML-Core, WSML-DL, WSML-Flight, WSML-Rule and WSML-Full (cf. Figure 3.8).

Though WSML has a special focus on annotating Semantic Web services like OWL-S it tries to cover more representational aspects from knowledge representation and reasoning under both classical FOL and nonmononotic LP semantics. For example, WSML-DL is a decidable variant of F-Logic(FO) with expressivity close to the description logic SHOIN(D), that is the variant OWL-DL of the standard ontology Web language OWL. WSML-Flight is a decidable Datalog variant of F-Logic(LP) (function-free, non-recursive and DL-safe Datalog rules) with (nonmonotonic) default negation under perfect model semantics [23] of locally stratified F-Logic programs with ground entailment. WSML-Rule is a fully-fledged logic programming language with function symbols, arbitrary rules with inequality and nonmontonic negation, and meta-modeling elements such as treating concepts as instances, but does not feature existentials, strict (monotonic) negation, and equality reasoning. The semantics of WSML-Rule is defined through a mapping to undecidable (nonmonotonic, recursive) F-Logic(LP) variant with inequality and default negation under well-founded semantics [27]. WSML-Full shall unify the DL and LP paradigms as a superset of FOL with non-monotonic extensions to support nonmonotonic negation of WSML-Rule via Default Logic, Circumscription or Autoepistemic Logic. However, neither syntax nor semantics of WSML-Full have been completely defined yet.

3.5.3 Services in WSML

In general, the description of the semantics of a service and request (so-called goal) in WSML is structured into the parts of the service capability, the service interface used for orchestration and choreography, and the shared variables.

Goal. Like in OWL-S, a goal in WSMO represents the desired WSML service which is indicated with a special keyword "goal" instead of "webservice" in front of the service description. A goal refers to a desired state that can be described by help of a (world state) ontology. Such an ontology provides a basic vocabulary for specifying the formal semantics of service parameters and transition rules (TBox), and a set of concept and role instances (ABox) which may change their values from one world state to the other. It also specifies possible read-write access rights to instances and their grounding. A state is the dynamic set of instances of concepts, relations and functions of given state ontology at a certain point of time. The interpretation of a goal (and service) in WSML is not unique: The user may want to express that either all, or only some of the objects that are contained in the described set are requested [16].

Figure 3.9 gives an example of a goal in WSML to find a service, which as a result of its execution, offers to reserve a ticket for the desired trip. In this case, the only element of the capability the user is interested in, is the postcondition of the desired service.

Service Capability. A WSML service capability describes the state-based functionality of a service in terms of its precondition (conditions over the information space), postcondition (result of service execution delivered to the user), assumption (conditions over the world state to met before service execution), and effect (how does the execution change the world state). Roughly speaking, a WSML service capability consists of references to logical expressions in a WSML variant that are named by the scope (precondition, postcondition, assumption, effect, capability) they intend to describe. It also specifies non-functional properties and all-quantified shared variables (with the service capability as scope) for which the logical conjunction of precondition and assumption entails that of the postcondition and the effect.

```
namespace { _"http://example.org/goals#", dc _"http://purl.org/dc/elements/1.1#",
           tr _"http://example.org/tripReservationOntology",
           wsml _"http://www.wsmo.org/wsml/wsml-syntax#",
           loc _"http://www.wsmo.org/ontologies/locationOntology#"}

goal _"http://example.org/havingATicketReservationInnsbruckVenice"
    importsOntology { _"http://example.org/tripReservationOntology",
                      _"http://www.wsmo.org/ontologies/locationOntology"}
    capability
        postcondition definedBy
            ?reservation[ reservationHolder hasValue ?reservationHolder,
                          Item hasValue ?ticket ]
                memberOf tr#reservation and
            ?ticket[ trip hasValue ?trip ] memberOf tr#ticket and
            ?trip [ origin hasValue loc#innsbruck, destination hasValue loc#venice ]
                memberOf tr#trip.
```

Figure 3.9: Example of a service request (goal) in WSML.

```
capability BookTicketCapability

sharedVariables {?creditCard, ?initialBalance, ?trip, ?reservationHolder, ?ticket}

precondition
    definedBy
    ?reservationRequest[
        reservationItem hasValue ?trip,
        reservationHolder hasValue ?reservationHolder ]
        memberOf tr#reservationRequest
    and ?trip memberOf tr#tripFromAustria
    and ?creditCard[ balance hasValue ?initialBalance ] memberOf po#creditCard.
assumption
    definedBy po#validCreditCard(?creditCard)
            and ( ?creditCard[ type hasValue "PlasticBuy"] or
                  ?creditCard[ type hasValue "GoldenCard"] ).
postcondition
    definedBy
        ?reservation memberOf tr#reservation[ reservationItem hasValue ?ticket,
                                  reservationHolder hasValue ?reservationHolder ]
            and ?ticket[ trip hasValue ?trip ] memberOf tr#ticket.
effect
    definedBy
        ticketPrice(?ticket, "euro", ?ticketPrice)
        and ?finalBalance= (?initialBalance - ?ticketPrice)
        and ?creditCard[ po#balance hasValue ?finalBalance
```

in →

out →

Figure 3.10: Example of service capability in WSML.

```
interface BookTicketInterface
        importsOntology _http://www.example.org/BookTicketInterfaceOntology
        choreography BookTicketChoreography
        orchestration BookTicketOrchestration


choreography BookTicketChoreography
        state _"http://example.org/BookTicketInterfaceOntology"
        guardedTransitions BookTicketChoreographyTransitionRule

guardedTransitions BookTicketChoreographyTransitionRule
if ( reservationRequestInstance [ reservationItem hasValue ?trip,
                              reservationHolder hasValue ?reservationHolder ]
     memberOf bti#reservationRequest
     and ?trip memberOf tr#tripFromAustria
     and ticketInstance[ trip hasValue ?trip, recordLocatorNumber hasValue ?rln ]
         memberOf tr#ticket )
then temporaryReservationInstance[ reservationItem hasValue ticketInstance,
                              reservationHolder hasValue ?reservationHolder ]
     memberOf bti#temporaryReservation
```

Figure 3.11: Example of WSML service interface.

Figure 3.10 provides an example of a Web Service capability specified in WSML. This example service offers information about trips starting in Austria and requires the name of the person and credit card details for making the reservation. The assumption is that the credit card information provided by the requester must designate a valid credit card that should be of type either PlasticBuy or Golden-Card. The postcondition specifies that a reservation containing the details of a ticket for the desired trip and the reservation holder is the result of the successful execution of the Web Service. Finally, the effect in the world state is that the credit card is charged with the cost of the ticket.

Service Interface. A WSML service interface contains the description of how the overall functionality of the Web service is achieved by means of cooperation of different Web service providers (orchestration) and the description of the communication pattern that allows to one to consume the functionality of the Web service (choreography). A choreography description has two parts: the state and the guarded transitions. As mentioned above, a state is represented by an WSMO ontology, while guarded transitions are if-then rules that specify conditional transitions between states in the abstract state space.

Figure 3.11 provides an example of a service interface with choreography, and a guarded transition rule which requires the following to hold: If a reservation request instance exists (it has been already received, since the corresponding concept in the state ontology currently has the mode "in") with the request for a trip starting in Austria, and there exists a ticket instance for the desired trip in the Web service instance store, then create a temporary reservation for that ticket.

3.5.4   Software Support

The project web site www.wsmo.org provides, for example, a comprehensive set of links to software tools for developing WSMO oriented services (in WSML) most of which available under open source related licenses at sourceforge.net. Examples include the WSMO4J API[20], the WSMO studio[21] with WSML service editor, WSML-DL and WSML-Rule reasoner, WSML validator, and the WSMX service execution environment[22].

Remarkably, there are still neither implemented semantic WSML service composition planners nor full-fledged WSML service matchmakers available apart from a rather simple keyword-based and non-functional (QoS) parameter oriented WSML service discovery engine as part of the WSMX suite, and the hybrid match-maker WSMO-MX. This situation of weak software support of services in WSML, however, could drastically improve in near future for various reasons of both politics and science.

3.5.5   Limitations

The WSMO conceptual model and its language WSML is an important step forward in the SWS domain as it explicitly overcomes some but not all limits of OWL-S. Unfortunately, the development of WSMO and, in particular, WSML has been originally at the cost of its connection to the W3C Web service standard stack at that time. This raised serious concerns by the W3C summarized in its official response to the WSMO submission in 2005 from which we quote[23]: "The submission represents a development, but one which has been done in isolation of the W3C standards. It does not use the RDFS concepts of Class and Property for its ontology, and does not connect to the WSDL definitions of services, or other parts of the Web Services Architecture. These differences are not clearly explained or justified. The notion of choreography in WSMO is obviously very far from the definition and scope presented in WS-CDL. The document only gives little detail about mediators, which seem to be the essential contribution in the submission." To date, however, the connection of WSML with WSDL and SAWSDL (WSDL-S) has been established in part, and is under joint investigation by both WSMO and SAWSDL initiatives in relevant working and incubator groups of the standardisation bodies OASIS and W3C.

Another main critic on WSML concerns the lack of formal semantics of service capabilities in both the WSMO working draft as of 2006, and the WSML speci-

---

[20] http://wsmo4j.sourceforge.net/
[21] http://www.wsmostudio.org/download.html
[22] http://sourceforge.net/projects/wsmx/
[23] http://www.w3.org/Submission/2005/06/Comment

fication submitted to the Web consortium W3C in 2005. Recently, this problem has been partly solved by means of a semi-monolithic FOL-based representation of functional service semantics over abstract state spaces and (guarded) state space transitions by service execution traces [24]. Though, the formal semantics of the WSML service (orchestration and choreography) interface part is still missing — which is not worse than the missing process model semantics of OWL-S.

Further, principled guidelines for developing the proposed types of WSMO mediators for services and goals in concrete terms are missing. Besides, the software support for WSML services provided by the WSMO initiative appears reasonable with a fair number of downloads but is still not comparable to that of OWL-S in terms of both quantity and diversity.

Finally, as with OWL-S, it remains to be shown whether the revolutionary but rather academic WSMO framework will be adopted by major business stakeholders within their service application landscapes in practice. In general, this also relates to the key concern of insufficient scaling of logic-based reasoning to the Web scale as mentioned in the previous chapter.

3.6 Monolithic DL-Based Service Descriptions

As mentioned above, an alternative to formally specifying the functional semantics of a Web service agnostic to any structured service description formats like OWL-S, SAWSDL, or WSML, is the pure DL-based approach: The abstract service semantics is defined through an appropriate set of concept and role axioms in a given description logic. Any instantiation of this service concept corresponds to a concrete service with concrete service properties. That is, the extension S^I of a service concept S representing the abstract service to be described in an interpretation I of the concept over a given domain contains all service instances the provider of S is willing to accept for contracting with a potential requester of S. An example of a monolithic DL-based description of an abstract service and possible service instances is shown in Figure 3.12 ([8]).

In this example, the functional semantics or capability of the abstract Web service S is described by a set D_S of two DL concept axioms: The service concept S for the shipping of items with a weight less than or equal to 50kg from cities in the UK to cities in Germany; the concept *Shipping* (used to define S) which assures that instances of S specify exactly one location for origin and destination of the shipping. Semantic relations between such monolithically described service semantics can be determined fully within the underlying logical formalism, that is by DL-based inferencing. For a more detailed treatment of this topic, we refer to [8].

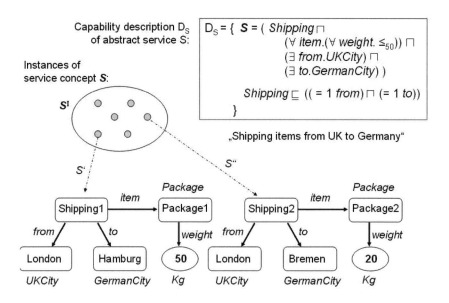

Figure 3.12: Example of a monolithic DL-based semantic service description.

3.7 Critique

Main critiques of Semantic Web services range from limitations of proposed frameworks via the lack of appropriate means of service coordination and software support to the legitimation of the research field as a whole. As one consequence, SWS technology still appears too immature for getting adopted by both common Web users and developers in practice, and industry for its commercial use on a large scale.

Do we really need formal service semantics? Some recent critics of SWS technology argue against the significance of its claimed benefits for practical Web service applications in general. Key justification of this argument, is related to the general critics on Semantic Web technologies. In fact, the need of having formal logic-based semantics specified for Web Services in practical human-centred applications is often questioned: It is completely unclear whether the complete lack of formal service semantics turns out to be rather negligible, or crucial for what kinds of service applications for the common Web user in practice, and on which scale.

Just recently, van Harmelen and Fensel [6] argued for a more tolerant and scalable Semantic Web reasoning based on approximated rather than strict logic-based reasoning. This is in perfect line with experimental results available for hybrid SWS matchmakers that combine both logic and approximated reasoning like the OWLS-MX [17], the WSMO-MX [15] and the syntactic OWLS-iMatcher [1].

Where are all the Semantic Web Services?   Another interesting question concerns the current reality of SWS technology in use. According to a recent survey of publicly available Semantic Web service descriptions in the surface Web [18], revealed that not more than around 1500 indexed semantic services in OWL-S, WSML, WSDL-S or SAWSDL are accessible in the Web of which only about one hundred are deployed outside special test collections like the OWLS-TC[24]. Though we expect the majority of Semantic Web Services being maintained in private project repositories and sites of the deep Web [10], it certainly does not reflect the strong research efforts carried out in the SWS domain world wide.

Of course, one might argue that this comes at no surprise in two ways. First, SWS technology is immature (with a standard announced just recently, that is SAWSDL) which still provides insufficient common ground supporting its exploitation by end users. Though this is certainly true, the other related side of this argument is that massive research and development of the field around the globe should have produced a considerable amount of even publicly visible Semantic Web service descriptions within the past half dozen of years.

Second, one might argue that it is not clear whether the surface Web and academic publications are the right place to look for Semantic Web service descriptions, as many of them would be intended for internal or inter-enterprise use but not visible for the public. Though this is one possible reason of the low numbers reported above, it indicates some lack of visibility to the common Web user to date.

Where are the easy to use SWS tools for the public?   As with Semantic Web application building in general, apart from the project prototypes and systems there is hardly any easy to use software support off the shelves available to the common user for developing, reusing and sharing her own Semantic Web Services — which might hamper the current confluence of the field with the Web 2.0 into the so called service Web 3.0 in practice.

How to efficiently coordinate Semantic Web Services?   Despite tremendous progress made in the field in European and national funded research projects like DIP, Super, CASCOM, Scallops and SmartWeb, there still is plenty of room for further investigating the characteristics, potential, and limits of SWS coordination in both theory and practice. The Semantic Web Services Challenge[25] attempts to qualitatively measure the minimal amount of programming required to adapt the semantics of given systems to new services. This acknowledges that the complete automation of composing previously unknown services is impossible, rather being a kind of Holy Grail of modern semantic technologies. Besides, the comparative

---

[24]projects.semwebcentral.org/projects/owls-tc/
[25]http://sws-challenge.org

evaluation of developed SWS discovery tools is currently hard, if not impossible, to perform since the required large scale service retrieval test collections are still missing even for the standard SAWSDL. Related to this, there are no large scale experimental results on the scalability of proposed service coordination means in practice available.

Apart from the problem of scalable and efficient SWS discovery and composition, another open problem of SWS coordination as a whole is privacy preservation. Though there are quite a few approaches to user data privacy preservation for each of the individual coordination processes (discovery, composition, and negotiation), there is no integrated approach that allows to coherently secure SWS coordination activities.

3.8 Summary

This chapter briefly introduced prominent frameworks of describing services in the Semantic Web together with some major critics of the domain. Overall, the interdisciplinary, vivid research and development of the Semantic Web did accomplish an impressive record in both theory and applications within just a few years since its advent in 2000. Though we identified several major gaps to bridge before the still immature Semantic Web services technology will make it to the common user of the Web, the ongoing convergence of the Semantic Web, Web 2.0, and services into a so called service Web 3.0 indicates its potential for future Web application services. In the next chapter, we survey prominent approaches to semantic discovery and composition planning of services in the Semantic Web.

Further readings. For more comprehensive information on Semantic Web Services in general, we refer to the accessible readings on the subject [25, 3, 5]. Examples of major funded research projects on Semantic Web Services are

- the European funded integrated projects DIP[26] and ASG (Adaptive semantic services grid technologies)[27]

- SmartWeb — Mobile multi-modal provision of Semantic Web Services[28],

- SCALLOPS[29] — Secure Semantic Web Service coordination,

- the European funded specific targeted research projects CASCOM[30], ARTEMIS[31] — Semantic Web Services for e-health applications (mobile, P2P)

---

[26] dip.semanticweb.org/
[27] asg-platform.org
[28] http://www.smartweb-project.de/
[29] http://www-ags.dfki.uni-sb.de/klusch/scallops/
[30] http://www.ist-cascom.org
[31] http://www.srdc.metu.edu.tr/webpage/projects/artemis/

For more information about Semantic Web service description frameworks, we refer to the respective documents submitted to the W3C:

- OWL-S[32]

- WSMO[33]

- SAWSDL[34]

- Semantic Web Services Framework SWSF[35] with SWSL-Rule[36] for monolithic FOL-based service representation by means of different variants of rule languages (DLP, HiLog, etc).

References

[1] A. Bernstein, C. Kiefer: Imprecise RDQL: Towards Generic Retrieval in Ontologies Using Similarity Joins. Proc. ACM Symposium on Applied Computing, Dijon, France, ACM Press, 2006.

[2] D. Calvanese, G. De Giacomo, I. Horrocks, C. Lutz, B. Motik, B. Parsia, P. Patel-Schneider: OWL 1.1 Web Ontology Language Tractable Fragments. W3C Member Submission, 19 December 2006. www.w3.org/Submission/2006/SUBM-owl11-tractable-20061219/. Updated version at www.webont.org/owl/1.1/tractable.html (6 April 2007)

[3] J. Cardoso, A. Sheth (Eds.): Semantic Web Services: Processes and Applications. Springer book series on Semantic Web & Beyond: Computing for human Experience, 2006.

[4] D. Connolly, F. van Harmelen, I. Horrocks, D. McGuinness, P. Patel-Schneider, L. Stein: DAML+OIL reference description. W3C Note, 18 December 2001. Available at www.w3.org/TR/2001/NOTE-daml+oil-reference-20011218.

[5] D. Fensel, H. Lausen, A. Polleres, J. de Bruijn, M. Stollberg, D. Roman, J. Domingue: Enabling Semantic Web Services — The Web Service Modeling Ontology. Springer, 2006.

[6] D. Fensel, F. van Harmelen: Unifying reasoning and search to Web scale. *IEEE Internet Computing*, March/April 2007.

[7] B. Glimm, I. Horrocks, C. Lutz, U. Sattler: Conjunctive Query Answering for the Description Logic SHIQ. Proceedings of International Joint Conference on AI (IJCAI), 2007.

---

[32] http://www.w3.org/Submission/OWL-S/
[33] www.w3.org/Submission/WSMO/
[34] www.w3.org/2002/ws/sawsdl/
[35] www.daml.org/services/swsf/
[36] www.w3.org/Submission/SWSF-SWSL/)

[8] S. Grimm: Discovery — Identifying relevant services. In [25], 2007.

[9] B. Grosof, I. Horrocks, R. Volz, S. Decker: Description Logic Programs: Combining Logic Programs with Description Logic. Proceedings of the 12th International World Wide Web Conference (WWW), 2003.

[10] B. He, M. Patel, Z. Zhang, K.Chang: Accessing the Deep Web. *Communications of the ACM*, 50(5), 2007.

[11] I. Horrocks, P. Patel-Schneider: Reducing OWL entailment to description logic satisfiability. Proceedings of International Semantic Web Conference (ISWC), 2003, Springer, LNCS, 2870, 2003.

[12] I. Horrocks, P. Patel-Schneider: A proposal for an OWL rules language. Proceedings of 13th International World Wide Web Conference (WWW), 2004.

[13] I. Horrocks, P. Patel-Schneider, F. van Harmelen: ¿From SHIQ and RDF to OWL: The Making of a Web Ontology Language. *Web Semantics*, 1, Elsevier, 2004.

[14] I. Horrocks, U. Sattler, S. Tobies: Practical Reasoning for Very Expressive Description Logics. Logic Journal of the IGPL, 8(3):239263, 2000.

[15] F. Kaufer and M. Klusch: Hybrid Semantic Web Service Matching with WSMO-MX. Proc. 4th IEEE European Conference on Web Services (ECOWS), Zurich, Switzerland, IEEE CS Press, 2006

[16] U. Keller, R. Lara, H. Lausen, A. Polleres, D. Fensel: Automatic Location of Services. Proceedings of the 2nd European Semantic Web Conference (ESWC), Heraklion, Crete, LNCS 3532, Springer, 2005.

[17] M. Klusch, B. Fries, K. Sycara: Automated Semantic Web Service Discovery with OWLS-MX. Proc. 5th Intl. Conference on Autonomous Agents and Multi-Agent Systems (AAMAS), Hakodate, Japan, ACM Press, 2006

[18] M. Klusch, Z. Xing: Semantic Web Service in the Web: A Preliminary Reality Check. Proc. First Intl. Joint ISWC Workshop SMR2 2007 on Service Matchmaking and Resource Retrieval in the Semantic Web, Busan, Korea, 2007.

[19] S. Narayanan, S. McIllraith: Simulation, verification and automated composition of Web Services. Proc. of 11th International COnference on the World Wide Web (WWW), Hawaii, 2002.

[20] S. McIllraith, T.C. Son: Adapting Golog for composition of Semantic Web Services. Proc. International Conference on Knowledge Representation and Reasoning KRR, Toulouse, France, 2002.

[21] J. Pan, I. Horrocks: RDFS(FA): Connecting RDF(S) and OWL DL. IEEE Transactions on Knowledge and Data Engineering, 19(2):192-206, 2007.

[22] C. Preist: Semantic Web Services — Goals and Vision. Chapter 6 in [25], 2007.

[23] T. C. Przymusinski: On the declarative and procedural semantics of logic programs. *Automated Reasoning*, 5(2):167-205, 1989.

[24] M. Stollberg, U. Keller, H. Lausen, S. Heymans: Two-phase Web Service discovery based on rich functional descriptions. Proceedings of European Semantic Web Conference, Buda, Montenegro, LNCS, Springer, 2007.

[25] R. Studer, S. Grimm, A. Abecker (eds.): Semantic Web Services. Concepts, Technologies, and Applications. Springer, 2007.

[26] S. Tobies: The Complexity of Reasoning with Cardinality Restrictions and Nominals in Expressive Description Logics. *Artificial Intelligence Research (JAIR)*, 12, 2000.

[27] A. van Gelder, K. Ross, J. S. Schlipf: The well-founded semantics for general logic programs. *ACM*, 38(3):620-650, 1991.

[28] G. Yang and M. Kifer: Well-Founded Optimism: Inheritance in Frame-Based Knowledge Bases. Proceedings of 1st International Conference on Ontologies, Databases and Applications of Semantics (ODBASE), Irvine, California, 2002.

[29] M. Kifer, G. Lausen, J. Wu: Logical Foundations of Object-Oriented and Frame-Based Languages. *Journal of the ACM*, 42(4), 1995.

Chapter 4

Semantic Web Service Coordination

Matthias Klusch

4.1 Introduction

Semantic service coordination aims at the coherent and efficient discovery, composition, negotiation, and execution of Semantic Web Services in a given environment and application context. What makes coordination of services in the Semantic Web different from its counterpart in the Web is its far more advanced degree of automation through means of logic-based reasoning on heterogeneous service and data semantics.

In this chapter, we only focus on approaches to semantic discovery and composition planning of Semantic Web services, and briefly comment on their interrelationships and selected open problems of both fields. For reasons of space limitations, the set of presented examples is representative but not exhaustive.

4.2 Semantic Service Discovery

Service discovery is the process of locating existing Web services based on the description of their functional and non-functional semantics. Discovery scenarios typically occur when one is trying to reuse an existing piece of functionality (represented as a Web service) in building new or enhanced business processes. A Semantic Web service, or in short semantic service, is a Web service which functionality is described by use of logic-based semantic annotation over a well-defined ontology (cf. Chapter 3). In the following, we focus on the discovery of semantic services. Both service-oriented computing and the Semantic Web envision intelligent agents to proactively pursue this task on behalf of their clients.

Semantic service discovery can be performed in different ways depending on the considered service description language, means of service selection and coordination through assisted mediation or performed in a peer-to-peer fashion. In general, any service discovery framework needs to have the following components ([37]).

- Service description language: A service description language (more precisely top-level ontologies, also called service description formats) is used to represent the functional and non-functional semantics of Web services. Examples of structured and logic-based semantic service description language are OWL-S and WSML. The standard Semantic Web service description language SAWSDL allows for a structured representation of service semantics in XML(S) with references to any kind of non-logic-based or logic-based ontology for semantic annotation.[1]. Alternatively, in so-called monolithic logic-based service descriptions the functionality of a service is represented by means of a single logical expression of an appropriate logic, usually a description logic like OWL-DL or WSML-DL.

- Service selection means: Service selection encompasses semantic matching and ranking of services to select a single most relevant service to be invoked, starting from a given set of available services. This set can be collected and maintained, for example, by front-end search engine, or given by providers advertising their services at registries or middle-agents like matchmakers and brokers. Semantic service matching, or in short: service matching, is the pairwise comparison of an advertised service with a desired service (query) to determine the degree of their semantic correspondence (semantic match). This process can be non-logic-based, logic-based or hybrid depending on the nature of reasoning means used.

    Non-logic-based matching can be perfomed by means of, for example, graph matching, data mining, linguistics, or content-based information retrieval to exploit semantics that are either commonly shared (in XML namespaces), or implicit in patterns or relative frequencies of terms in service descriptions. Logic-based semantic matching of services like those written in the prominent service description languages OWL-S (Ontology Web Language for Services), WSML (Web Service Modeling Language) and the standard SAWSDL (Semantically Annotated WSDL) exploit standard logic inferences. Hybrid matching refers to the combined use of both types of matching.

- Discovery architecture: The conceptual service discovery architecture concerns the environment in which the discovery is assumed to be performed. This includes assumptions about the (centralized or decentralized P2P) physical or semantic overlay of the network, the kind of service information storage (e.g., service distribution, registries, and ontologies) and location mechanisms such as query routing, as well as the agent society in the network (e.g., service consumers, providers, middle-agents).

---

[1]In this sense, SAWSDL services can be seen as a weaker form of semantic services while WSDL services are no semantic services.

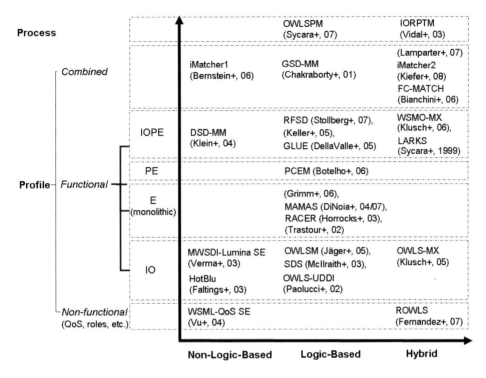

Figure 4.1: Categories of existing semantic Web service matchmakers.

In the following, we survey existing approaches to semantic service matching and discovery architectures. Examples of semantic service description languages were presented in the previous chapter.

4.2.1 Classification of Semantic Web Service Matchmakers

Semantic service matching determines whether the semantics of a desired service (or goal) conform to that of an advertised service. This is at the very core of any semantic service discovery framework. Current approaches to semantic service matching can be classified according to

- what kinds and parts of service semantics are considered for matching, and

- how matching is actually be performed in terms of non-logic-based or logic-based reasoning on given service semantics or a hybrid combination of both, within or partly outside the respective service description framework (cf. Figure 4.1).

Non-Logic, Logic, and Hybrid Semantic Service Matching.   The majority of Semantic Web service matchmakers performs deductive, that is logic-based semantic service matching. In this sense, they are keeping with the original idea of the Semantic Web to determine semantic relations (thus resolve semantic heterogeneities) between resources including services based on logical inferencing on their semantic annotations that are formally grounded in description logics (DL) and/or rules (cf. Chapter 3). As shown in figure 4.1, pure logic-based semantic matchmakers for services in OWL-S and WSML are currently prevalent. Non-logic-based semantic service matchmakers do not perform any logic-based reasoning to determine the degree of a semantic match between a given pair of service descriptions. Examples of non-logic-based semantic matching techniques are text similarity measurement, structured graph matching, and path-length-based similarity of concepts[2].

Service Profile and Process Model Matching.   Most Semantic Web service matchmakers perform service profile rather than service process model matching. Service profile matching (so-called "black-box" service matching) determines the semantic correspondence between services based on the description of their profiles. The profile of a service describes what it actually does in terms of its signature, that is its input and output (IO), as well as preconditions (P) and effects or postconditions (E), and non-functional aspects such as the relevant business category, name, quality, privacy and pricing rules of the service. We classify additional context information for service matching such as the organisational (social or domain) roles, or geographic location of service requesters and providers in their interaction as non-functional.

Service process-oriented matching (so-called "glass-box" service matching) determines the extent to which the desired operational behavior of a given service in terms of its process control and data flow matches with that of another service. Like with service profile matching, we can distinguish between non-logic based, logic based and hybrid semantic process matching approaches depending on whether automated reasoning on operational semantics specified in some certain logic or process algebraic language (e.g. CCS, π-calculus) is performed, or not. An overview of relevant approaches to process mining for process discovery is given in [110].

Supported Semantic Web Service Description Formats.   Each of the implemented Semantic Web service matchmakers shown in Figure 4.1 supports only one of the many existing Semantic Web service description formats (cf. Chapter 3) as follows. This list is representative but not exhaustive.

---

[2]Please note that any kind of semantic service matching that identifies concepts or rules (which are logically defined in a given ontology) by their names only does not classify as logic-based matching in the strict sense. Without any formal verification of the semantic relation between given (semantic service annotation) concepts based on their logical definitions, the matchmaker performs non-logic-based semantic service matching.

- **OWL-S** matchmakers: Logic-based semantic matchmakers for OWL-S services are the OWLSM [45] and OWLS-UDDI [81] focussing on service IO-matching, and the PCEM [18] that converts given OWL-S services to PDDL actions for PROLOG-based service PE-matching. Further OWL-S matchmakers are the hybrid service IO-matchmaker OWLS-MX [59], the hybrid non-functional profile matchmaker ROWLS [34], the hybrid (combined) profile matchmaker FC-MATCH [16], the non-logic-based (full) service matchmaker iMatcher1 [14] and its hybrid successor iMatcher2 [51]. An approach to logic-based OWL-S process model verification is in [109] while [11] presents an approach to the matching of OWL-S process dependency graphs based on syntactic similarity measurements, and [12] proposes a hybrid matchmaker that recursively compares the DAML-S process model dependency graphs.

- **WSML** matchmakers: Implemented approaches to WSML service discovery include the hybrid semantic matchmaker WSMO-MX [49], the logic-based matchmaker GLUE [27], and the syntactic search engine for QoS-enabled WSML service discovery in P2P networks [112]. Other approaches to logic-based WSML service IOPE matchmaking are presented in [48, 103], though it is unclear to what extent they have been implemented.

- **WSDL-S/SAWSDL** matchmakers: The METEOR-S WSDI discovery infrastructure [111] and the UDDI-based search component Lumina[3] are the only tool support of searching for SAWSDL services so far. While searching with Lumina is keyword-based, the MWSDI discovery of SAWSDL services relies on non-logic-based matching means.

- **Monolithic DL-based** matchmakers: Only very few matchmaker are agnostic to the above mentioned structured Semantic Web Service description formats without conversion by accepting monolithic descriptions of services in terms of a single service concept written in a given DL. In this case, semantic matching directly corresponds to DL inferencing, that is, semantic service matching is done exclusively within the logic theory such as performed by RACER [65], MaMaS[4] [29, 30], and in [38]. Recently, an implemented approach to matching of monolithic service descriptions in OWL-DL extended with (non-functional) pricing policies modeled in DL-safe SWRL rules according to given preferences using SPARQL queries to a service repository is presented in [62].

- **Others**: Non-logic-based service IOPE profile matchmakers for other structured service description formats are the DSD matchmaker [53] for DIANE services, the numeric service IO type matching based HotBlu matchmaker [25], and the hybrid service IOPE matchmaker LARKS for services in an equally named format [105].

---

[3]lsdis.cs.uga.edu/projects/meteor-s/downloads/Lumina/
[4]sisinflab.poliba.it/MAMAS-tng/

In the following, we discuss each category of Semantic Web service matching together with selected representative examples of the above mentioned Semantic Web service matchmakers in more detail. This is complemented by a classification of existing service discovery architectures for which these matchmakers have been designed for, or can be used in principle. As stand-alone implementation, each matchmaker classifies as centralized service discovery system, though a few matchmaker have been also tested for, or were originally developed for decentralized P2P service retrieval systems like the OWLS-MX and the OWLS-UDDI matchmaker, respectively, the WSMO-QoS search engine and the DReggie/GSD matchmaker[5].

4.2.2   Logic-Based Semantic Service Profile Matching

As mentioned above, logic-based semantic service matchmakers perform deductive reasoning on service semantics. The majority of such matchmakers pairwisely compare logic-based descriptions of service profile semantics. In order to define these semantics, logical concepts and rules are taken from respective ontologies as first-order or rule-based background theories with a shared minimal vocabulary. Different ontologies of service providers and service requester are matched or aligned either at design time, or at runtime as part of the logic-based service matching process.

Matching Degrees

The degree of logic-based matching of a given pair of semantic service profiles can be determined either (a) exclusively within the considered logic theory by means of logic reasoning, or (b) by a combination of logical inferences within the theory and algorithmic processing outside the theory. Prominent logic-based matching degrees are exact, plugin, subsumes, and disjoint which are defined differently depending on the parts of service semantics and the logic theory that is used to compute these degrees.

One prominent example for a software specification matching degree is the so-called plug-in match. A specification S plugs into (plug-in matches with) another specification R, if the effect of S is more specific than that of R, and vice versa for the preconditions of S and R [115]. If this definition is restricted to effects only, the matching degree is called a post plug-in match. Unfortunately, the original notion of plug-in match has been adopted quite differently by most logic-based Semantic Web service matchmakers for both monolithic and structured service descriptions.

---

[5]For reasons of readability, the implemented (stand-alone) Semantic Web service matchmakers shown in Figure 4.1 each representing a central discovery system by itself are not again listed in Figure 4.2, and vice versa, that is, those matchmaking approaches being inherent part of the functionality of each node of decentralized discovery systems (but not available as stand-alone matchmaker) are not listed in Figure 4.1.

Monolithic Logic-Based Service Matching

Matching of monolithic logic-based semantic service descriptions (cf. Chapter 3) is performed exclusively by means of logic inferences within the considered logic theory. That is, the functionality of a Web service is represented by a single (monolithic) expression in an appropriate logic, usually a description logic like OWL-DL or WSML-DL. As a consequence, monolithic logic-based semantic service matching reduces to standard first-order (description) logic reasoning such as checking the satisfiability of service and query concept conjunction, or the entailment of concept subsumption over a given knowledge base. Furthermore, it is agnostic to any form of structured stateless (I/O) or stateful (IOPE) representation of service semantics like in OWL-S and WSML. The prominent degrees of semantic matching used by the majority of monolithic logic-based semantic service matchmakers are logic equivalence, post-plug-in match, subsumes, and fail.

For example, the logical so-called post-plug-in match of an advertised service S with a service request R bases on the entailment of concept subsumption of S by R over a given knowledge base kb extended by the axioms of S and R: $kb \cup S \cup R \models S \sqsubseteq R$. That is, the matchmaker checks if in each first-order interpretation (possible world) I of kb, the set S^I of concrete provider services (service instances) is contained in the set R^I of service instances acceptable to the requester: $S^I \subseteq R^I$. This assures the requester that each provided service instance offers at least the requested functionality, maybe even more. In other words, service S is more specific than the request R, hence considered semantically relevant. In contrast, the so-called logical subsumes match assures the requester that her acceptable service instances are also acceptable to the provider: $kb \cup S \cup R \models R \sqsubseteq S$.

Some monolithic DL-based service matchmakers also check for a so-called intersection or potential match (Grimm, 2007)[37]. This matching degree indicates the principled compatibility of service S with request R with respect to the considered knowledge base kb by means of either concept intersection or non-disjointness. In the first case, the advertised service concept S potentially matches with the (desired service or) query concept R if their concept conjunction $S \sqcap R$ is satisfiable with respect to kb in some possible world I such that $S^I \cap R^I \neq \emptyset$ holds. In the second case, the monolithic logic-based semantic service matchmaker makes a stronger check by determining whether the intersection of both concept extensions is non-empty in each possible world.

In general, the complexity of matching monolithic DL-based service descriptions is equal to the combined DL complexity. For example, post-plug-in matching of service concepts in OWL-Full, that is SHOIQ$^+$ (including transitive non-primitive roles) has been shown to be undecidable [10] but decidable for OWL-DL, WSML-DL and DL-safe SWRL.

One problem of monolithic DL-based service matching is the risk to return false positives due to incomplete knowledge specified in service descriptions S, R or the domain ontology kb [38]. In other words, semantic matching of S with R with respect to kb based on monotonic DL reasoning under open-world assumption (OWA) can wrongly succeed due to the existence of possible but unwanted interpretations of concepts or roles used in S or R over kb. Such unwanted possible worlds of kb are intuitively ruled out by humans by default - which accounts for their usually non-monotonic reasoning under closed-world assumption[6].

One solution to this problem is to explicitly capture such default (common-sense) knowledge by adding, for example, appropriate concept disjointness axioms or object assertions to the knowledge base kb. This excludes possible worlds which are "obviously" wrong (but allowed due to open-world semantics) but is considered impracticable as it requires the modeler to somewhat "overspecify" the kb with "obvious" information.

An alternative solution is to perform semantic matching of services with local closed-world reasoning (cf. chapter 2) as proposed by [38]. Key idea is to exclude the unwanted possible worlds of knowledge base kb by means of an additional au-toepistemic logic operator $\mathbf{K}$[7] that allows to restrict the interpretation of certain concepts C and roles r used in advertised and desired service descriptions S and R to named individuals (nominals) in the ABox of kb which are definitely known or not known to belong to them (C, r)[8]. However, this local closure of concepts and roles in S, R for their interpretation in kb (i.e., locally closing off possible worlds of kb in S and R without any occurrence of $\mathbf{K}$ in kb) under the local closed world-assumption (LCWA)[9] by use of the $\mathbf{K}$-operator makes semantic matching dependent on the state of the world: It requires the existence of named individuals in the ABox of kb as representative (static) information on the locally closed con-

---

[6]The OWA states that the inability to deduce some fact from a knowledge base does not imply its contrary by default, that is, the fact may hold (not in all but) in some possible world (interpretations of kb). For example, the intersection match of $R = Flight \sqcap \forall from.UKCity$ with $S = Flight \sqcap \forall from.USCity$ with respect to the knowledge base $kb = \{UKCity \sqsubseteq EUCity, Flight \sqsubseteq \exists from.\top\}$ wrongly succeeds. The reason is that kb is underspecified in the sense that (due to the OWA) there can be possible worlds in which cities can be both in the UK and the US, which causes a false positive for the intersection match.

[7]The epistemic logic operator $\mathbf{K}$ allows to refer to definitely known facts by intersecting all possible worlds: $(\mathbf{K}C)^{I,E} = \bigcap_{I \in E} C^{I,E}$. The epistemic concept $\mathbf{K}C$ is interpreted as the intersection of extensions of concept C over all first-order interpretations of kb, that is the set of all individuals that are known to belong to C (in the epistemic model $E(kb)$ of kb, that is the maximal non-empty set of all first-order interpretations of kb).

[8]In the above example, the intersection match of the request $R = Flight \sqcap \forall from.\mathbf{K}UKCity$ with service $S = Flight \sqcap \forall from.\mathbf{K}USCity$ with respect to the matchmaker knowledge base $kb = \{UKCity \sqsubseteq EUCity, Flight \sqsubseteq \exists from.\top, UKCity(London)\}$ correctly fails, hence avoids to return a false positive. The satisfiability of the epistemic concept $S \sqcap R$ requires the existence of a named individual x in kb known to be both $UKCity$ and $USCity$ (that is kb entails $UKCity(x) \sqcap USCity(x)$, i.e. $kb \models UKCity(x)$ and $kb \models USCity(x)$, for every possible world I in the epistemic model $E(kb)$). While the named individual $London$ in the ABox of kb is definitely known to belong to the concept $UKCity$, and also known to belong to $EUCity$ due to the inclusion axiom in the TBox of kb, it is not definitely known to also belong to $USCity$ ($kb \nvDash USCity(London)$). There is also no other named individual in kb which is both known to be in $UKCity$ and $USCity$ such that $S \sqcap R$ is not satisfied. An intersection match of R with different service $S' = Flight \sqcap \forall from.\mathbf{K}EUCity$ correctly succeeds.

[9]The LCWA assumes that all individuals of some concept, or all pairs of individuals of some role are explicitly known in the local knowledge base (selected local concept or role closure).

cepts and roles[10]. Besides, using an autoepistemic extension of description logics like OWL-DL or WSML-DL for semantic service matching is still uncommon in practice, though (non-monotonic) reasoners such as for epistemic query answering in ALCK[11] can be easily integrated in a matchmaker.

Another application of non-monotonic reasoning to monolithic DL-based service matching is proposed in [24, 30]. The respective matchmaker MAMAS provides non-standard explanation services, that are non-monotonic logical abduction and contraction, for partial (also called approximated, intersection, or potential) matches. For example, concept contraction computes an explanation concept G to explain why a request concept R is not compatible with service concept S, that is, why $S \sqcap R$ is not satisfiable $(S \sqcap R) \sqsubseteq \bot$. For this purpose, it keeps the least specific concept expression K of concept R such that K is still compatible with S, i.e. $\neg(K \sqcap S) \sqsubseteq \bot$. The remaining set G of constraints of R represents the desired explanation of mismatch. Such kind of non-monotonic logical service matching is NP-hard already for the simple description logic ALN. However, research in this direction has just begun and is, in part, related to research on non-monotonic reasoning with Semantic Web rule languages.

Examples of implemented monolithic DL-based matchmakers for service concepts written in OWL(-DL) and DAML+OIL are MAMAS [29, 30], respectively, RACER. Remarkably, both matchmakers determine the degree of post-plug-in match inverse to its original definition in [115].

Service Specification Matching

The logic-based semantic matching of service specifications (so-called PE-matching) concerns the comparison of their preconditions (P) and effects (E) and originates from the software engineering domain. As mentioned above, the plug-in matching of two software components S, R requires that the logic-based definition of the effect, or postcondition of S logically implies that of R, while the precondition of S shall be more general than that of R [115]. In other words, a logic-based semantic plug-in match of service specifications S, R requires (in every model of given knowledge base kb) the effect of advertised service S to be more specific than requested, and its precondition to be more general than requested in R. Depending on the Semantic Web service description framework (cf. Chapter 3), the logic language for defining service preconditions and effects ranges from, for example, decidable def-Horn (DLP), WSML-DL and OWL-DL to undecidable SWRL, KIF and F-Logic(LP).

---

[10]In the above example, the intersection match $S' \sqcap R$ would (wrongly) fail, hence causes a false negative, if the named individual *London* would not have been explicitly stated in kb to belong to *UKCity* as its representative by default: There would be no named individual definitely known to belong to both *UKCity* and *EUCity* in all possible worlds. Though *UKCity*(*London*) has to be added to the kb of the matchmaker to avoid false positives and negatives of intersection matches by non-monotonic epistemic query answering kb with **K**, no (dynamic) information about concrete flights, i.e. individuals of concpet *Flight*, has to be additionally specified in kb.

[11]http://www.fzi.de/downloads/wim/KToy.zip

For example, the logic-based service-PE matchmaker PCEM (cf. Chapter 10) exploits the Java-based light-weight Prolog engine tuProlog[12] for logic-based exact matching of service preconditions and effects written in Prolog. In particular, the PCEM matchmaker checks whether there is a possibly empty variable substitution such that, when applied to one or both of the logical propositions (PE), this results into two equal expressions, and applies domain specific inference rules (for computing subPartOf relations).

The hybrid semantic WSML service matchmaker WSMO-MX [49] is checking an approximated query containment over a given finite service instance base for service effects (postconditions, constraints) written in undecidable F-Logic(LP) using OntoBroker. The approach to semantic service IOPE matchmaking described in [103] uses the VAMPIRE theorem prover for matching pairs of preconditions and effects written in FOL, while the hybrid service IOPE matchmaker LARKS [105] performs polynomial theta-subsumption checking of preconditions and postconditions written in Horn. There are no non-logic-based or hybrid semantic service PE matchmaker available yet.

Service Signature and IOPE Matching

Logic-based semantic matching of service signatures (input/output, IO), so called service profile IO-matching, is the stateless matching of declarative data semantics of service input and output parameters by logical reasoning within the theory and algorithmic processing outside the theory. For example, the logic-based plug-in matching of state-based service specifications (PE) can be adopted to the plug-in matching of stateless service signatures (IO): Service S is expected to return more specific output data whose logically defined semantics is equivalent or subsumed by those of the desired output in request R, and requires more generic input data than requested in R.

More concrete, the signature of S plugs into the signature of request R iff $\forall \text{IN}_S \; \exists \text{IN}_R: \text{IN}_S < \text{IN}_R \wedge \forall \text{OUT}_R \; \exists \text{OUT}_S: \text{OUT}_S \in \text{LSC}(\text{OUT}_R)$, with $LSC(C)$ the set of least specific concepts (direct children) C' of C, i.e. C' is a immediate sub-concept of C in the shared (matchmaker) ontology. The quantified constraint that S may require less input than specified in R guarantees at a minimum that S is, in principle, executable with the input provided by the user in R. This holds if and only if the logical service input concepts are appropriately mapped to the corresponding WSDL service input message data types in XMLS.

Examples of Semantic Web service matchmakers that perform logic-based semantic matching of service signatures only are the OWLSM [45] and the OWLS-UDDI [81]. Though the latter determines a signature plug-in matching degreee which is defined inverse to the original definition and restricted to the output. Approaches to logic-based semantic IOPE matching of Web services are proposed in [48, 103]. In general, logic-based matching of stateless service descriptions with I/O

---

[12]http://alice.unibo.it/xwiki/bin/view/Tuprolog/

concepts and conjunctive constraints on their relationship specified in OWL-DL, that is SHOIN has been proven decidable though intractable [42]. This indicates the respective decidability of service IOPE-matching for OWL-S (with OWL-DL) and WSML (with WSML-DL).

4.2.3 Non-logic-based Semantic Profile Matching

As mentioned above, non-logic-based Semantic Web service matchmaker do not perform any logical inferencing on service semantics. Instead, they compute the degree of semantic matching of given pairs of service descriptions based on, for example, syntactic similarity measurement, structured graph matching, or numeric concept distance computations over given ontologies. There is a wide range of means of text similarity metrics from information retrieval, approximated pattern discovery, and data clustering from data mining, or ranked keyword, and structured XML search with XQuery, XIRQL or TeXQuery [39, 6]. In this sense, non-logic-based semantic service matching means exploit semantics that are implicit in, for example, patterns, subgraphs, or relative frequencies of terms used in the service descriptions, rather than declarative IOPE semantics explicitly specified in the considered logic.

One example is the matchmaker iMatcher1 [14] which imprecisely queries a set of OWL-S service profiles that are stored as serialized RDF graphs in a RDF database with an extension of RDQL, called iRDQL, based on four (token and edit based) syntactic similarity metrics from information retrieval. The imprecise querying of RDF resources with similarity joins bases on TFIDF and the Levenshtein metric. The results are ranked according to the numerical scores of these syntactic similarity measurements, and a user-defined threshold.

The DSD matchmaker [53, 61] performs, in essence, graph matching over pairs of state-based service descriptions in the object oriented service description language DSD (with variables and declarative object sets) without any logic-based semantics. The matching process determines what assignment of IOPE variables is necessary such that the state-based service offer is included in the set (of service instances) defined by the request, and returns a numeric (fuzzy) degree of DSD service matching.

4.2.4 Hybrid Semantic Profile Matching

Syntactic matching techniques are first class candidates for the development of hybrid semantic service profile matching solutions that combine means of both crisp logic-based and non-logic-based semantic matching where each alone would fail. Indeed, first experimental evaluation of the performance of hybrid semantic service matchmakers OWLS-MX and iMatcher2 show that logic-based semantic service selection can be significantly outperformed by the former under certain conditions.

LARKS [105, 105] has been the first hybrid semantic service IOPE match-maker for services written in a frame-based language called LARKS. The match-maker OWLS-MX [59] bases in part on LARKS, and is the first hybrid semantic service signature (IO) matchmaker for OWL-S services. OWLS-MX complements deductive (DL) reasoning with approximated IR-based matching. For this pur-pose, each of its four hybrid variants OWLS-M1 to OWLS-M4 applies a selected token-based string similarity metric (cosine/TFIDF, extended Jaccard, Jensen-Shannon, LOI) to the given pair of service signature strings in order to determine their degree of text similarity-based matching. If the text similarity value exceeds a given threshold the failure of logic-based matching is tolerated, that means the service is eventually classified as semantically relevant to the given query. The ranking aggregates both types of matching degrees with respect to the total order of logic-based matching degrees. Experimental evaluation results over the test col-lection OWLS-TC together with a FP/FN-analysis of OWLS-MX showed that the performance of logic-based semantic matching can be improved by its combination with non-logic-based text similarity measurement [54, 55].

Similarly, the hybrid semantic service profile matchmaker iMatcher2 [51] uses multiple edit- or token-based text similarity metrics (Bi-Gram, Levenshtein, Monge-Elkan and Jaro similarity measures) to determine the degree of semantic matching between a given pair of OWL-S service profiles. Like OWLS-MX, the iMatcher2 transforms each structured service profile description into a weighted keyword vector that includes not only the names but terms derived by means of logic-based unfolding of its service input and output concepts. In this sense, iMatcher2 classifies as a hybrid matchmaker. The experimental evaluation of iMatcher2 over the test collection OWLS-TC2.1 confirmed, in principle, the pre-viously reported results of the evaluation of OWLS-MX.

In its adaptive mode, iMatcher2 can also be trained over a given retrieval training collection to predict the degree of semantic matching of unknown services to queries by means of selected regression models (support vector regression with a RBF kernel, linear and logistic regression). This regression-based induction is performed over the set of (a) the binary value of subjective semantic relevance as defined in the relevance sets, and (b) different text similarity values computed by means of the selected similarity metrics for each pair of query and service of the training collection. After training, the iMatcher2 first computes the text similar-ity values (using the selected similarity metrics) of a given query to all services of a given test collection, then uses the learned regression model to predict the combined similarity (or likelihood) of a match, and finally returns the answers in decreasing order of similarity. Experimental evaluation of the adaptive iMatcher2 showed that the combined logical deduction and regression-based learning of text similarities produces superior performance over logical inference only.

The hybrid semantic service matchmaker FC-MATCH [16] does a combined logic-based and text similarity-based matching of single service and query con-cepts written in OWL-DL. A service concept S is defined as logical conjunction of existential qualified role expressions where each role corresponds to a selected profile parameter: $S = \exists \mathrm{hasCategory}(C_1) \sqcap \exists \mathrm{hasOperation}(C_2) \sqcap \exists \mathrm{hasInput}(C_3) \sqcap \exists \mathrm{hasOutput}(C_4)$). Hybrid matching degrees are computed by means of (a) combined checking of logic-based subsumption of profile concepts (C_i) and (b) computing the so-called Dice (name affinity) similarity coefficient between terms occuring in these concepts according to the given terminological relationships of the thesaurus WordNet. FC-MATCH (FC stands for functional comparison) performs structured hybrid semantic matching of functional (I/O) and non-functional profile parameters (hasCategory, hasOperation). That is a combined matching of functional and non-functional parameters of OWL-S service profiles rewritten in special OWL-DL expressions. To the best of our knowledge, FC-MATCH has not been experimentally evaluated yet.

WSMO-MX [49] is the first hybrid semantic matchmaker for services written in a WSML-Rule variant, called WSML-MX. The hybrid service matching scheme of WSMO-MX is a combination of ideas of hybrid semantic matching as performed by OWLS-MX, the object-oriented graph matching of the matchmaker DSD-MM, and the concept of intentional matching of services in [48]. WSMO-MX applies different logic-based and text similarity matching filters to retrieve and rank services that are relevant to a query. The hybrid semantic matching degrees are recursively computed by aggregated valuations of (a) ontology-based type matching (logical concept subsumption), (b) logical (instance-based) constraint matching in F-logic(LP) through approximative query containment, (c) relation name matching, and (d) syntactic similarity measurement as well. The experimental evaluation of WSMO-MX over an initial WSML service retrieval test collection is ongoing work.

However, it is not yet known what kind of hybrid service matching will scale best to the size of the Web in practice. Research in this direction is in perfect line with the just recent call in [33] for a general shift in Semantic Web research towards scalable, approximative rather than strict logic-based reasoning.

4.2.5 Logic-based Semantic Process Matching

Semantic matching of service process models, in general, is very uncommon, and not intended by the designers of current Semantic Web Service description formats. Besides, the semantics of process models in OWL-S or WSML have not been formally defined yet, while neither SAWSDL nor monolithic service descriptions offer any process model. This problem can be partly solved by intuitively rewriting the process model descriptions in an appropriate logic with automated proof system and respective analysis tool support.

For example, in [109], OWL-S service process models are mapped into (intuitively) equivalent logical Promela statements that are then efficiently evaluated by the SPIN model checker[13]. This allows to verify the correctness of a given ser-

---

[13] A model checker verifies if a given system (service process) model satisfies a desirable prop-

vice process model in terms of consistency and liveness properties of an advertised service like the Delivery process always executes after the Buy process. The result of such service process model checking could be used for process-oriented OWL-S service selection (by identifying properties of service process models to be verified with queries to match); this is a topic of ongoing research.

Alternatively, the matching of process models of OWL-S services that are grounded in WSDL (cf. Chapter 3) can be, in principle, reduced to the matching of corresponding WSDL service orchestrations in BPEL. As mentioned before, the OWL-S process model captures a common subset of workflow features that can be intuitively mapped to BPEL (used to define WSDL service compositions) which offers an all-inclusive superset of such features (e.g. structured process activities in BPEL like Assignment, Fault Handler, Terminate are not available in OWL-S) [9]. Though BPEL has been given no formal semantics either yet, there are a few approaches to fill this gap based on Petri nets [69] and abstract state machines [32] that allow to verify liveness properties of WSDL service orchestrations in BPEL [72]. However, there are no approaches to exploit any of the proposed formal BPEL semantics for semantic matching of OWL-S process models that correspond to BPEL orchestrations of WSDL services.

4.2.6 Non-logic-based and Hybrid Semantic Process Model Matching

There are only a few approaches to non-logic-based Semantic Web service process model matching. One approach to the matching of (business) process dependency graphs based on syntactic similarity measurements is presented in [11]. [12] propose a hybrid matchmaker (IO-RPTM) that recursively compares the DAML-S process model dependency graphs based on given workflow operations and logical match between IO parameter concepts of connected (sub-)service nodes of the process graphs. On the other hand, means of functional service process matching can be exploited to search for a set of relevant subservices of a single composite service.

4.2.7 Semantic Service Discovery Architectures

Existing Semantic Web service discovery architectures and systems in the literature can be broadly categorized as centralized and decentralized by the way they handle service information storage and location in the considered service network [5, 37]. A classification of implemented Semantic Web service discovery systems is given in Figure 4.2.

Centralized service discovery systems rely on one single, possibly replicated, global directory service (repository, registry) maintained by a distinguished so called super-peer or middle agent like matchmaker, broker or mediator agent [58].

---

erty. If the property does not hold, it returns a counter-example of an execution where the property fails.

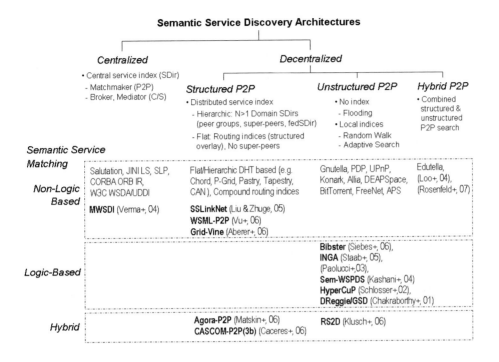

Figure 4.2: Categories of semantic Web service discovery architectures and systems.

Contrary, decentralized service discovery systems rely on distributing service storage information over several peers in a structured, unstructured or hybrid P2P network.

Semantic service discovery systems can be further classified with respect to the kind of semantic service matching means used by the intelligent agents in the network. For example, the exact keyword-based service location mechanisms of all contemporary P2P systems like JINI, SLP, Gnutella flooding, and DHT (distributed hash table) can be complemented or replaced by sophisticated logic-based semantic matching means to improve the quality of the search result.

As mentioned above, due to its generic functionality, any service matchmaker (cf. Figure 4.1) can be used in arbitrary discovery architectures and systems. In the extremes, a matchmaker can either serve as a central service directory (index) or look-up service, or can be integrated into each peer of an unstructured P2P service network to support an informed adaptive service search like in RS2D [13]. In fact, a few means of semantic service matching were originally developed for decentralized semantic P2P service retrieval in different applications.

Centralized Semantic P2P Service Discovery

In centralized semantic P2P service systems, a dedicated central service directory or matchmaker returns a list of providers of semantically relevant services to the requester. Contrary to centralized client-server middleware or brokering, the requester then directly interacts with selected providers for service provision [58]. The advantage of such centralized discovery architectures is a fast resource or service lookup time, though the central look-up server or registry like in JINI or the CORBA-ORB interface registry is a single point of failure that can be only partially mitigated by replication and caching strategies.

An application of centralized P2P service discovery is the Napster music file sharing system, and the SETI@home system that is exploiting a vast set of distributed computational resources world wide to search for extraterrestrial signals. From the Semantic Web Service discovery perspective, each of the above mentioned stand-alone Semantic Web Service matchmakers, in principle, realizes a centralized logic-based semantic service discovery system by itself. For example, the SCALLOPS e-health service coordination system uses the hybrid semantic matchmaker OWLS-MX as a central matchmaker for the selection of relevant e-health services in a medical emergency assistance application. The same matchmaker is distributed to each peer of an unstructured P2P network for decentralized OWL-S service discovery [13].

MWSDI [111] is a centralized semantic P2P service system with non-logic-based semantic service signature matching. Each peer in the system maintains one domain specific WSDL-S (SAWSDL) service registry and respective ontologies; multiple peers can form a domain oriented group. However, a distinguished central gateway or super-peer provides a global registries ontology (GRO) that maintains the complete taxonomy of all domain registries, the mappings between WSDL-S service I/O message types and concepts from shared domain ontologies in the system, associates registries to them, and serves as central look-up service for all peers. This central super-peer is replicated in form of so called auxiliary peers for reasons of scalability. For service location, any client peer (user) selects the relevant domain registries via the central GRO at the super-peer which then performs non-logic-based semantic matching (structural XMLS graph matching, NGram-based syntactic similarity, synonyms/hyponyms/hypernyms in the GRO) of service input and output concepts with those of the desired service. However, it would be hard to build the GRO, and difficult for the user to query the GRO without knowing its details in advance.

Decentralized Semantic P2P Service Discovery

Decentralized semantic service discovery systems rely on service information storage and location mechanisms that are distributed over all peers in structured, unstructured or hybrid P2P networks.

Structured Semantic P2P Service Systems. Structured P2P systems have no central directory server but a significant amount of structure of the network topology (overlay) which is tightly controlled. Resources are placed neither at random peers nor in one central directory but at specified locations for efficient querying. In other words, the service index of the system is distributed to all peers according to a given structured overlay enforcing a deterministic content distribution which can be used for routing point queries.

Prominent examples of structured P2P systems are those with flat DHT-based resource distribution and location mechanism like Chord rings, Pastry, Tapestry, CAN, P-Grid and P2PAlvis, and structured hierarchic P2P systems. Flat DHT-based systems allow to route queries with certain keys to particular peers containing the desired data. But to provide this functionality all new content in the network has to be published at the peer responsible for the respective key, if new data on a peer arrives, or a new peer joins the network.

In structured hierarchical or N-super-peer P2P systems (N>1), peers are organized in N domain oriented groups with possibly heterogeneous service location mechanisms (e.g hierarchic DHT, that is, one group with Chord ring overlay, another one with P-Grid overlay, etc.). Each group is represented by one super-peer hosting the group/domain service index. The set of super-peers, in turn, can be hierarchically structured with federated service directories in a super-peer top level overlay of the network. Peers within a group query its super-peer which interacts with other super-peers to route the query to relevant peer groups for response. The functionality of a super-peer of one peer group is not necessarily fixed, but, in case of node failure, transferable to a new peer of that group. Typically JXTA, a collection of P2P protocols, is used to realize super-peer based P2P systems, though it does not enforce such architectures.

Examples of decentralized Semantic Web service discovery in structured P2P networks are WSPDS [47], SSLinkNet [66], CASCOM-P2P$_{3b}$ [19], Grid-Vine [1], WSML-P2P [112] and Agora-P2P [60, 67]. SSLinkNet, Agora-P2P and WSML-P2P exploit keyword-based discovery in a Chord ring, respectively, P-Grid system with non-logic-based semantic profile matching of services in WSDL, respectively, WSML. The Grid-Vine system performs non-logic-based semantic P2P content retrieval by means of so-called semantic gossiping with the underlying P-Grid system. The CASCOM and Agora-P2P systems have been demonstrated for logic-based semantic OWL-S (DAML-S) service discovery in hierarchic structured P2P networks.

In the SSLinkNet [66], a Chord ring-based search is complemented by forwarding the same Web service request by the identified peers to relevant neighbors based on a given so-called semantic service link network. The semantic links between services are determined by non-logic-based semantic service matching, and are used to derive semantic relationships between service provider peers based on heuristic rules.

Similarly, the AGORA-P2P system [60, 67] uses a Chord ring as the underlying infrastructure for a distributed storage of information about OWL-S services over peers. Service input and output concept names are hashed as mere literals to unique integer keys such that peers holding the same key are offering services with equal literals in a circular key space. A service request is characterized as a syntactic multi-key query against this Chord ring. Both systems, SSLinkNet and AGORA-P2P, do not cope with the known problem of efficiently preserving the stability of Chord rings in dynamic environments.

The generic CASCOM semantic service coordination architecture has been instantiated in terms of a hierarchic structured P2P network with N interacting super-peers each hosting a domain service registry that make up a federated Web Service directory. Each peer within a group can complement a keyword-based pre-selection of OWL-S services in their super-peer domain registries with a more complex semantic matching by a selected hybrid or logic-based semantic OWL-S matchmaker (ROWL-S, PCEM or OWLS-MX) on demand. Both, the simple service discovery agent and Semantic Web Service matchmaking module are integrated into each peer (cf. Chapter 10).

The Grid-Vine system [1] performs a hybrid semantic search of semantically annotated resources by means of so-called semantic gossiping between peers about their actual semantic knowledge (also called logical layer or semantic overlay of the P2P system). The semantic overlay is defined by (a) the set of peer ontologies in RDFS or XMLS that are used to encode document annotations in RDF (each RDF triple or concept in the peer schema represents a set of documents as its instances), and (b) a set of user-specified peer schema (concept) mappings that are used by the peers to translate received queries. The numeric "semantic quality" value of these directed concept mappings, hence the non-logic-based degree of semantic similarity between query and resource annotation concept of two peers is locally assessed by the requester through a quantitative analysis of (transitive) propagation cycles of the mappings (and their previous semantic quality value) which might be wrong but not by means of logic-based reasoning about concepts. The translation links, that is the mapping and its numeric "semantic quality" are continuously exchanged and updated by the peers: Semantic gossiping among peers is the propagation of queries to peers for which no direct but transitive translation links exist. The efficient location of resources for a given and translated query by the underlying P-Grid system bases on keyword-based matching of their identifiers, that are DHT keys.

Service discovery in structured P2P networks can provide search guarantees, in the sense of total service recall in the network, while simultaneously minimizing messaging overhead. Typically, structured networks such as DHT-based P2P networks of n peers offer efficient $O(log(n))$ search complexity for locating even rare items, but they incur significantly higher organizational overheads (maintaining DHT, publishing)[14] than unstructured P2P networks. Alternatively, flooding-based or random-walks discovery in unstructured P2P networks are effective for

---

[14]For example, peer p_n publishes each of its hashed items $(term_i)$ over the DHT network, that is the item gets stored in an inverted list $(term_i, [..., p_n, ...]])$ of some peer that is found in $O(log(n))$ hops.

locating highly replicated, means popular, but not rare items. Hybrid designs of P2P networks aim to combine the best of both worlds such as using random-walks (with state-keeping to prevent walkers from revisiting same peers) for locating popular items, and structured (DHT) search techniques for locating rare items [70].

Unstructured Semantic P2P Service Systems. In unstructured P2P systems, peers initially have no index nor any precise control over the network topology (overlay) or file placement based on any knowledge of the topology. That is, they do not rely on any structured network overlay for query routing as they have no inherent restrictions on the type of service discovery they can perform.

For example, resources in unstructured P2P systems like Gnutella or Morpheus are located by means of network flooding: Each peer broadcasts a given query to all neighbour peers within a certain radius (TTL) until a service is found, or the given query TTL is zero. Such network flooding is extremely resilient to network dynamics (peers entering and leaving the system), but generates high network traffic.

This problem can be mitigated by a Random Walk search where each peer builds a local index about available services of its direct neighbour peers over time and randomly forwards a query to one of them in DFS manner until the service is found[15] as well as replication and caching strategies based on, for example, access frequencies and popularity of services [71].

Approaches to informed probabilistic adaptive P2P search like in APS [108] improve on such random walks based on estimations over dynamically observed service location information stored in the local indices of peers. In contrast to the structured P2P search, this only provides probabilistic search guarantees, that is incomplete recall.

In any case, the majority of unstructured P2P service systems only performs keyword-based service matching and does not exploit any qualitative results from logic-based or hybrid semantic service matching to improve the quality of an informed search. In fact, only a few system are available for logic-based or hybrid Semantic Web service retrieval such as DReggie/GSD [22, 23], HyperCuP [95], Sem-WSPDS [47], [82], Bibster [40], INGA [68], and RS2D [13]. These systems differ in the way of how peers perform flooding or adaptive query routing based on evolving local knowledge about the semantic overlay, that is knowledge about the semantic relationships between distributed services and ontologies in unstructured P2P networks. Besides, all existing system implementations, except INGA and Bibster, perform semantic service IO profile matching for OWL-S (DAML-S), while HyperCuP peers dynamically build a semantic overlay based on monolithic service concepts.

---

[15]This is valid in case the length of the random walk is equal to the number of peers flooded with bounded TTL or hops).

For example, [82] proposes the discovery of relevant DAML-S services in unstructured P2P networks based on both the Gnutella P2P discovery process and a complementary logic-based service matching process (OWLS-UDDI matchmaker) over the returned answer set. However, the broadcast or flooding-based search in unstructured P2P networks like Gnutella is known to suffer from traffic and load balancing problems.

Though Bibster and INGA have not been explicitly designed for Semantic Web service discovery, they could be used for this purpose. In INGA [68], peers dynamically adapt the network topology, driven by the dynamically observed history of successful or semantically similar queries, and a dynamic shortcut selection strategy, which forwards queries to a community of peers that are likely to best answer given queries. The observed results are used by each peer for maintaining a bounded local (recommender) index storing semantically labelled topic specific routing shortcuts (that connect peers sharing similar interests).

Similarly, in Bibster [40] peers have prior knowledge about a fixed semantic overlay network that is initially built by means of a special first round advertisement and local caching policy. Each peer only stores those advertisements that are semantically close to at least one of their own services, and then selects for given queries only those two neighbours with top ranked expertise according to the semantic overlay it knows in prior. Further, prior knowledge about other peers ontologies as well as their mapping to local ontologies is assumed. This is similar to the ontology-based service query routing in HyperCuP [95].

In RS2D [13], contrary to Bibster and DReggie/GSD, the peers perform an adaptive probabilistic risk-driven search for relevant OWL-S services without any fixed or prior knowledge about the semantic overlay. Each peer uses an integrated OWLS-MX matchmaker for hybrid semantic IO matching of local services with given query, and dynamically learns the average query-answer behaviour of its direct neighbours in the network. The decision to whom to forward a given semantic service request is then driven by the estimated mixed individual Bayes' conditional risk of routing failure in terms of both semantic loss and high communication costs. Peers are dynamically maintaining their local service (matchmaker) ontology-based on observations of the results which, in particular, renders RS2D independent from the use of any fixed global ontology for semantic annotation like in DReggie/GSD.

Semantic Hybrid P2P Service Systems. Hybrid P2P search infrastructures combine both structured and unstructured location mechanisms. For example, Edutella combines a super-peer network with routing indices and an efficient broadcast. In [70] a flat DHT approach is used to locate rare items, and flooding techniques are used for searching highly replicated items. A similar approach of hybrid P2P query routing that adaptively switches between different kinds of structured and unstructured search together with preliminary experimental results are reported in [94]. However, there are no hybrid P2P systems for semantic service discovery available yet.

Despite recent advances in the converging technologies of semantic Web and P2P computing [102], the scalability of semantic service discovery in structured, unstructured or hybrid P2P networks such as those for real-time mobile ad-hoc network applications is one major open problem. Research in this direction has just started. Preliminary solutions to this challenge vary in the expressivity of semantic service description, and the complexity of semantic matching means ranging from computationally heavy Semantic Web Service matchmakers like OWLS-MX in SCALLOPS and CASCOM, to those with a streamlined DL reasoner such as Krhype [52] suitable for thin clients on mobile devices in IASON [35]. An example analysis of semantic service discovery architectures for realizing a mobile e-health application is given in [21].

4.3   Semantic Service Composition Planning

Semantic Web service composition is the act of taking several semantically anno-tated component services, and bundling them together to meet the needs of a given customer. Automating this process is desirable to improve speed and efficiency of customer response, and, in the semantic Web, supported by the formal grounding of service and data annotations in logics.

4.3.1   Web Service Composition

In general, Web service composition is similar to the composition of workflows such that existing techniques for workflow pattern generation, composition, and management can be partially reused for this purpose [41]. Typically, the user has to specify an abstract workflow of the required composite Web service including both the set of nodes (desired services) and the control and data flow between these nodes of the workflow network. The concrete services instantiating these nodes are bound at runtime according to the abstract node descriptions, also called "search recipes" [20]. In particular, the mainstream approach to composition is to have a single entity responsible for manually scripting such workflows (orchestration and choreography) between WSDL services of different business partners in BPEL [83, 2]. This is largely motivated by industry to work for service composition in legally contracted business partner coalitions — in which there is, unlike in open service environment, only very limited need for automated service composition planning, if at all. Besides, neither WSDL nor BPEL or any other workflow languages like UML2 or YAWL have formal semantics which would allow for an automated logic-based composition.

In fact, the majority of existing composition planners for Semantic Web ser-vices draws its inspiration from the vast literature on logic-based AI planning [84]. In the following, we focus on these approaches to Semantic Web service com-position, and comment on the interleaving of service composition planning with discovery, and distributed plan execution. Please note that, the set of presented examples of Semantic Web Service composition planners is representative but not exhaustive.

4.3.2   AI-Planning-Based Web Service Composition

The service composition problem roughly corresponds to the state-based planning problem (I, A, G) in AI to devise a sound, complete, and executable plan which satisfies a given goal state G by executing a sequence of services as actions in A from a given initial world state I. Classical AI planning-based (planning from first principles) composition focuses on the description of services as merely deterministic state transitions (actions) with preconditions and state altering (physical) effects. Actions are applicable to actual world states based on the evaluation of preconditions and yield new (simulated) states where the effects are valid. Further, classical AI planning is performed under the assumption of a closed world with complete, fully observable initial (world) state such that no conditional or contingency planning under uncertainty is required. This is not necessarily appropriate for service composition planning in the dynamic and open-ended Semantic Web [101] where (a) the initial state can be incomplete, and actions may have several possible (conditional) outcomes and effects modeled in the domain but not known at design time. However, all existing SWS composition planners are closed-world planners of which some are able to cope with uncertainties about the domain.

A given logical goal expression and set of logic-based definitions of semantic service signature (I/O) concepts together with logic preconditions and effects from a DL-based ontology (domain or background theory) can be converted into one declarative (FOL) description of the planning domain and problem - which can serve a given logic-based AI planner as input. In particular, service outputs are encoded as special non-state altering knowledge effects, and inputs as special preconditions. The standard target language for the conversion is PDDL (Planning Domain Description Language) but alternative representation formalisms are, for example, the situation calculus, linear logic [92], high-level logic programming languages based on this calculus like GOLOG [73], Petri nets, or HTN planning task and method description format [99].

In the following, we classify existing Semantic Web service composition planners and comment on the principled interrelation between composition, discovery, and execution. Please note that the set of presented examples is representative but not exhaustive.

4.3.3   Classification of Semantic Service Composition Planners

In general, any AI planning framework for Semantic Web service composition can be characterized by

- the representation of the planning domain and problem to allow for automated reasoning on actions and states,

- the planning method applied to solve the given composition problem in the domain, and

- the parts of service semantics that are used for this purpose.

We can classify existing Semantic Web service composition planners according to the latter two criteria, which yields the following classes.

- Dynamic or static Semantic Web service composition planners depending on whether the plan generation and execution are inherently interleaved in the sense that actions (services) can be executed at planning time, or not.

- Functional-level or process-level Semantic Web service composition planners depending on whether the plan generation relies on the service profile semantics only, or the process model semantics in addition (data and control flown) [63].

Figure 4.3 shows the respective classification of existing Semantic Web service composition planners.

Static and Dynamic Composition

The majority of Semantic Web service composition planners such as GOAL [86], MetaComp (cf. Chapter 11), PLCP [89], RPCLM-SCP [63] and AGORA-SCP [92] are static classical planners. Approaches to dynamic composition planning with different degrees of interleaving plan generation and execution are rare. Unlike the static case, restricted dynamic composition planners allow the execution of information gathering but no world state altering services, hence are capable of planning under uncertainty about action outcomes at planning time. Examples of such composition planners are SHOP2 [97, 99], GOLOG-SCP [73] and OWLS-XPlan1 [56].

Advanced and reactive dynamic composition planners in stochastic domains even take non-deterministic world state changes into account during planning. While advanced dynamic planners like OWLS-XPlan2 [57] are capable of heuristic replanning subject to partially observed (but not caused) state changes that affect the current plan at planning time, their reactive counterparts like INFRAWEBS-RTC [4] fully interleave their plan generation and execution in the fashion of dynamic contingency and real-time planning.

Functional- and Process-Level Composition

As shown in Figure 4.3, most Semantic Web Service composition planners perform functional-level or service profile-based composition (FLC) planning. FLC planning considers services as atomic or composite black-box actions which functionality can solely be described in terms of their inputs, outputs, preconditions,

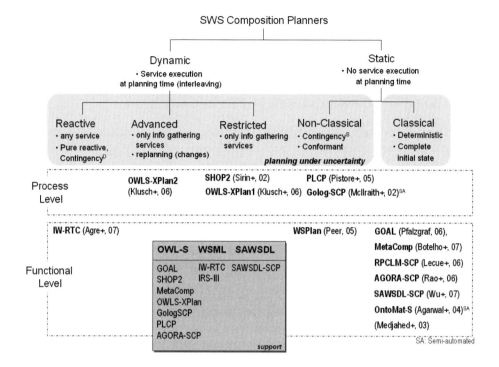

Figure 4.3: Classes of semantic Web service composition planners.

and effects, and which can be executed in a simple request-response without interaction patterns. Examples of FLC planners are GOAL [86], SAWSDL-SCP [113]
and OntoMat-S [3].

Process-level composition (PLC) planning extends FLC planning in the sense
that it also the internal complex behavior of existing services into account. Prominent examples are SHOP2 [99], PLCP [87, 89] and OWLS-XPlan [56, 57]. Both
kinds of composition planning perform, in particular, semantic service profile or
process matching which is either inherent to the underlying planning mechanism,
or achieved by a connected stand-alone Semantic Web service matchmaker. We
will discuss the interrelation between composition and semantic matching later.

Support of Semantic Web Service Description Frameworks

Remarkably, most implemented Semantic Web Service composition planners support OWL-S like GOAL, OWLS-XPlan, SHOP2, GologSCP and MetaComp, while
there is considerably less support of the standard SAWSDL and WSML available
to date. In fact, the SAWSDL-SCP planner [113] is the only one for SAWSDL,
while the IW-RTC planner [4] is, apart from the semi-automated orchestration of

WSML services in IRS-III, the only fully automated FLC planner for WSML yet.

Most composition planner feature an integrated conversion of Semantic Web Services, goals and ontologies into the internally used format of the planning domain and problem description, though a few others like the framework WSPlan [85] for static PDDL-based planning under uncertainty, and the recursive, progression-based causal-link matrix composition planner RPCLM-SCP [63] do not.

In the following, we discuss each category and selected examples of Semantic Web service composition planners in more detail.

4.3.4 Functional-Level Composition Planners

Intuitively, FLC planning generates a sequence of Semantic Web Services based on their profiles that exact or plug-in matches with the desired (goal) service. In particular, existing services S_i, S_{i+1} are chained in this plan such that the output of S_i matches with the input of S_{i+1}, while the preconditions of S_{i+1} are satisfied in the world state after execution of S_i. Depending on the considered Semantic Web Service description format (cf. Chapter 3), different approaches to logic-based, non-logic-based or hybrid semantic service profile IOPE matching are available for this purpose (cf. Figure 4.1).

In order to automatically search for a solution to the composition problem, FLC planners can exploit different AI planning techniques with inherent logic-based semantic profile IOPE- or PE-matching like WSPlan [85], respectively, MetaComp (cf. 11). The recursive forward-search planner GOAL [86] as well as the SAWSDL-SCP [113] apply non-logic-based semantic profile IO matching of OWL-S, respectively, SAWSDL services.

In AGORA-SCP [92], theorem proving with hybrid semantic profile IO matching is performed for OWL-S service composition: Both services and a request (theorem) are described in linear logic, related to classical FOL, while the SNARK theorem prover is used to prove that the request can be deduced from the set of services. The service composition plan then is extracted from the constructive proof.

The FLC planner in [75] uses proprietary composability rules for generating all possible plans of hybrid semantic profile IO matching services in a specific description format (CSSL). From these plans the requester has to select the one of best quality (QoS).

4.3.5 Process-Level Semantic Service Composition Planners

Though FLC planning methods can address conditional outputs and effects of composite services with dynamic planning under uncertainty, considering services as black-boxes does not allow them to take the internal complex service behaviour into account at planning time. Such behavior is usually described as subservice interactions by means of control constructs including conditional and iterative steps. This is the domain of process level composition (PLC) planning that extends FLC planning in the aforementioned sense.

However, only few approaches to process level composition planning for Semantic Web Services exist to date. For example, orchestration of WSML services in IRS-III [31] synthesizes abstract state machines to compose individual services in a given process flow defined in OCML[16]. Though, the functionality of the WSMX orchestration unit has not been completely defined yet.

Other automated PLC planners of OWL-S services exploit different AI planning techniques such as

- HTN (Hierarchical Task Network) planning of OWL-S process models converted to HTN methods like in SHOP2 [99],

- Neo-classical GRAPHPLAN-based planning mixed with HTN planning of OWL-S services converted to PDDL in OWLS-XPlan [56, 57],

- Value-based synthesis of OWL-S process models in a given plan template of situation calculus-based GOLOG programs [73, 74],

- Planning as model checking of OWL-S process models converted to equivalent state transition systems (STS) in the PLCP [87, 89].

In the following, we discuss each class of static and dynamic Semantic Web service composition planners together with selected examples, if available.

4.3.6 Static Semantic Service Composition Planners

The class of static AI planning-based composition covers approaches to both classical and non-classical planning under uncertainty.

Static Classical Planning

As mentioned above, classical AI planners perform (off-line) planning under the assumption of a closed, perfect world with deterministic actions and a complete initial state of a fully observable domain at design time. For example, Graphplan is a prominent classical AI planning algorithm that first performs a reachability analysis by constructing a plan graph, and then performs logic-based goal regression within this graph to find a plan that satisfies the goal. Classical AI planners are static since their plan generation and execution is strictly decoupled.

Examples of Static Classical Composition Planners

One example of a static classical Semantic Web service composition planner is GOAL [86] developed in the SmartWeb project. GOAL composes extended OWL-S services by means of a classical recursive forward-search [36]. Both, the initial

---

[16]kmi.open.ac.uk/projects/ocml/

state and the goal state are derived from the semantic representation of the user's question (goal) obtained by a multimodal dialogue system in SmartWeb. At each stage of the planning process the set of services which input parameters are applicable to the current state is determined by signature (IO) matching through polynomial subgraph isomorphism checking [76]: The instance patterns of input parameters are matched against the graph representation of the state, and a service is applied to a plan state (simulated world state) by merging the instance patterns of its output parameters with the state. As a result, GOAL does not exploit any logical concept reasoning but structural service I/O graph matching to compose services. If plan generation fails, GOAL detects non-matching paths within instance patterns and consequently produces a clarification request (ako information gathering service) conveyed to the user by the dialogue system; on response by the user the planning process is restarted in total.

Static service composition in the AGORA-SCP service composition system [92] relies on linear logic (LL) theorem proving. The profiles of available DAML-S services are translated in to a set of LL axioms, and the service request is formulated as a LL theorem to be proven over this set. In case of success, the composition plan can be extracted from the proof, transformed to a DAML-S process model and executed as a BPEL script. The AGORA planner is the only approach to decentralized composition planning in structured P2P networks [60].

An example of a static classical Semantic Web Service composition planner based on a special logic-based PDDL planner is MetaComp which we describe in detail in Chapter 11.

Static Planning under Uncertainty

Work on planning under uncertainty in AI is usually classified according to (a) the representation of uncertainty, that is whether uncertainty is modeled strictly logically, using disjunctions, or is modeled numerically (e.g. with probabilities), and (b) observability assumptions, that is whether the uncertain outcomes of actions are not observable via sensing actions (conformant planning); partially or fully observable via sensing actions (conditional or contingency planning) [26]. As mentioned above, we can have uncertainty in the initial states and in the outcome of action execution. Since the observation associated to a given state is not unique, it is also possible to model noisy sensing and lack of information. Information on action outcomes or state changes that affect the plan can be gathered either at planning time (dynamic) or thereafter (static) for replanning purposes.

Static Conditional or Contingency Planning. Static conditional or contingency planner like Cassandra and DTPOP devise a plan that accounts for each possible contingency that may arise in the planning domain. This corresponds to an optimal Markov policy in the POMDP framework for planning under uncertainty with probabilities, costs and rewards over a finite horizon. The contingency planner anticipates unexpected or uncertain outcomes of actions and events by means of planned sensing actions, and attempts to establish the goals for each different outcome of these actions through conditional branching of the plan in advance[17]. The plan execution is driven by the outcome of the integrated sensing subplans for conditional plan branches, and decoupled from its generation which classifies these planners as static.

Static Conformant planning. Conformant planners like the Conformant-FF, Buridan, and UDTPOP perform contingency planning without sensing actions. The problem of conformat planning to search for the best unconditional sequence of actions under uncertainty of intial state and action outcome can be formalized as fully non-observable MDP, as a particular case of POMDP, with a search space pruned by ignoring state observations in contingency planning. For example, conformant Graphplan planning (CGP) [100] expresses the uncertainty in the initial state as a set of completely specified possible worlds, and generates a plan graph for each of these possible worlds in parallel. For actions with uncertain outcomes the number of possible worlds is multiplied by the number of possible outcomes of the action. It then performs a regression (backward) search on them for a plan that satisfies the goal in all possible worlds which ensures that the plan can be executed without any sensory actions. Conformant planner are static in the sense that no action is executed at planning time.

Examples of Static Composition Planners under Uncertainty

The PLCP [88, 89] performs static PLC planning under uncertainty for OWL-S services. OWL-S service signatures and process models together with a given goal are converted to non-deterministic and partially observable state transition systems which are composed by a model checking-based planner (MBP)[87] to a new STS which implements the desired composed service. This STS eventually gets transformed to an executable service composition plan (in BPEL) with possible conditional and iterative behaviors. No action is executed at planning time, and uncertainty is resolved by sensing actions during plan execution.

An example of static FLC planning under uncertainty is the WSPlan framework [85] which provides the user with the option to plug in his own PDDL-based planner and to statically interleave planning (under uncertainty) with plan execution. Static interleaving refers to the cycle of plan generation, plan execution, and replanning based on the result of the executed sensing subplans (in the fashion

---

[17]Examples of decision criteria according to which contingency branches are inserted in the (conventional) plan, and what the branch conditions should be at these points, are the maximum probability of failure, and the maximum expected future reward (utility) as a function of, for example, time and resource consumption. Uncertainty is often characterized by probability distributions over the possible values of planning domain predicates.

of static conditional planning) until a sequential plan without sensing actions is generated that satifies the goal. There are no static classical PLC planner for Semantic Web Services with deterministic (sequential) process models of composite services only available.

4.3.7 Dynamic Composition Planners

The class of dynamic AI-planning-based composition covers approaches to restricted, advanced and reactive dynamic planning under uncertainty.

Restricted Dynamic Planning

Dynamic planning methods allow agents to inherently interleave plan generation and execution. In restricted dynamic planning, action execution at planning time is restricted to information gathering (book-keeping callbacks) about uncertain action outcomes. These special actions add new knowledge in form of ground facts to the partial observable initial state under the known IRP (Invocation and Reasonable Persistence) assumption [73] to ensure conflict avoidance[18]. Like in classical planning, however, world state altering services with physical effects (in opposite to knowledge effects of service outputs) are only simulated in local planning states and never get executed at planning time.

Examples of Restricted Dynamic Composition Planners

Prominent examples of restricted dynamic composition planners are SHOP2, and OWLS-XPlan1 [56] for OWL-S services of which we describe the latter in detail in Chapter 11. SHOP2 [97, 98] converts given OWL-S service process models into HTN methods and applies HTN-planning interleaved with execution of information gathering actions to compose a sequence of services that satisfies the given task. By mapping any OWL-S process model to a situation calculus-based GOLOG program, the authors prove that the plans produced are correct in the sense that they are equivalent to the action sequences found in situation calculus. HTN planning is correct and complete but undecidable due to possiblly infinite recursive decomposition of given methods to executable atomic tasks. SHOP2 detects and breaks such decomposition cycles.

Advanced Dynamic Planning

Advanced dynamic planning methods allow in addition to react on arbitrary changes in the world state that may affect the current plan already during planning

---

[18]The IRP assumption states that (a) the information gathered by invoking the service once cannot be changed by external or subsequent actions, and (b) remains the same for repeating the same call during planning. That is, the incremental execution of callbacks would have the same effect when executing them prior to planning in order to complete the initial state for closed world planning.

such as in OWLS-XPlan2. This is in contrast to static planning under uncertainty where sensing subplans of a plan are executed at run time only. However, in both restricted and advanced dynamic planning the interleaved execution of planning with world state altering services is prohibited to prevent obvious problems of planning inconsistencies and conflicts.

Examples of Advanced Dynamic Composition Planners

To the best of our knowledge, OWLS-XPlan2 [57] still is the only one implemented example of an advanced dynamic composition planner. OWLS-XPlan2 will be described in Chapter 11.

Reactive Dynamic Planning

Finally, reactive dynamic planning like in Brooks's subsumption architecture, RETE-based production rule planners, and the symbolic model checking-based planner SyPEM [15] allows the execution of arbitrary actions at planning time. Pure reactive planner produce a set of condition-action (if-then) or reaction rules for every possible situation that may be encountered, whether or not the circumstances that would lead to it can be envisaged or predicted. The inherently interleaved planning and execution is driven through the evaluation of state conditions at every single plan step to select the relevant if-then reaction rule and the immediate execution of the respective, possibly world state altering action; This cycle is repeated until the goal is hopefuly reached.

A variant of reactive dynamic planning is dynamic contingency planning like in XII and SAGE. In this case, a plan that is specified up to the information-gathering steps gets executed to that stage, and, once the information has been gathered, the rest of the plan is constructed. Interleaving planning and execution this way has the advantage that it is not necessary to plan for contingencies that do not actually arise. In contrast to pure reactive planners, reasoning is only performed at branch points predicted to be possible or likely.

In any case, reactive dynamic planning comes at the possible cost of plan optimality, and even plan existence, that is suboptimality and dead-end action planning or failure. The related ramification problem[19] is usually addressed either by restrictive assumptions on the nature of service effects on previous planning states [15] in safely explorable domains, or by integrated belief revision (TMS) in the planners knowledge base at severe computational costs.

Examples of Reactive Dynamic Composition Planners

One example of an implemented reactive dynamic composition planner is the real-time composition planner IW-RTC [4] developed in the European research project

---

[19]The problem of ensuring the consistency of the planners knowledge base and the reachability of the original goal in spite of (highly frequent) world state altering service execution during plan generation.

INFRAWEBS. It successively composes pairs of keyword-based IO matching services, executes them and proceeds with planning until the given goal is reached. Unfortunately, the authors do not provide any detailed description of the composition and matching process nor complexity analysis.

Problems of Composition Planning under Uncertainty

One problem with adopting planning under uncertainty for semantic service composition is that the execution of information gathering (book keeping) or even world state altering services at design or planning time might not be charge free, if granted by providers at all. That is, the planning agent might produce significant costs for its users even without any return value in case of plan generation or execution failure. Another problem is the known insufficient scalability of conditional or conformant planning methods to planning domains at Web scale or business application environments with potentially hundreds of thousands of services and vast instance bases. Research on exploiting conditional or conformant planning methods for Semantic Web Service composition has just started.

4.3.8 FLC Planning of Monolithic DL-Based Services

Research on AI-based FLC planning with monolithic DL-based descriptions of services has just started. Intuitively, the corresponding AI planning (plan existence) problem for the composition of such services is as follows. Given an acyclic TBox T describing the domain or background theory in a DL, ABoxes S and G which interpretations I (consistent wrt T) over infinite sets of individual (object) names are describing, respectively the initial and goal state, and a set A of operators describing deterministic, parameterized actions α which precondition and effects are specified in the same DL and transform given interpretations of concepts and roles in T ($I \rightarrow_\alpha^T I'$), is there a sequence of actions (consistent with T)[20] obtained by instantiating operators with individuals which transforms S into G?

It has been shown in [10] that the standard reasoning problems on actions, that are executability[21] and projection[22], are decidable for description logics between ALC and ALCOIQ. Furthermore, it has been shown in [77] only recently that the plan existence problem for such actions in ALCOIQ is co-NEXPTIME decidable for finite sets of individuals used to instantiate the actions, while it is known to be PSPACE-complete for propositional STRIPS-style actions. In addition, the extended plan existence problem with infinitely countable set of individuals was proven undecidable, as it is for Datalog STRIPS actions, for actions specified in ALC_U with universal role U for assertions over the whole domain by reduction

---

[20] An action is consistent with TBox T, if for every model I of T there exists I' s.t. $I \rightarrow_\alpha^T I'$.

[21] Action executability is equal to the satisfaction of action preconditions in given world states: $I \models pre_1, \forall i, 1 \leq i \leq n, I'.I \rightarrow_{\alpha_1...\alpha_i}^T I' : I' \models pre_{i+1}$.

[22] Satisfaction of assertion ϕ as a consequence or conjunctive effect of applying actions to a given state: For all models I of S and $T, I'.I \rightarrow_{\alpha_1...\alpha_n}^T I' : I' \models \phi$

to the halting problem of deterministic Turing machines. However, there is no implemented composition planner for monolithic DL-based services available to date.

4.4   Interrelations

In the following, we briefly comment on the principled relations between semantic service composition planning, discovery, and execution. Selected approaches to interleaved semantic service composition planning with negotiation are presented in the introduction to the next part of this thesis.

Semantic Web service composition planning and discovery.   From the view of semantic service discovery, the composition of complex services is of importance if no available service satisfies the given request. In this case, the matchmaker or requester agent can interact with a composition planner to successfully generate a composite service that eventually satisfies the query.

On the other hand, semantic service composition planning agents require a description of the planning domain and goal to start their planning. Both can be semi-automatically generated from the set of available semantic service descriptions together with related logic-based ontologies, the so-called background theories. In fact, from the view of composition planning, semantic service discovery is of importance for the following reasons: A semantic service matchmaker can be used to

- Prune the initial search space of the composition planner with respect to given application-specific preferences of available services, and

- Select semantically equivalent or plug-in, and execution compatible services during planning as alternative (substitute) services in case of planning failures (replanning).

There is no agreed-upon strategy for pruning the search space of Semantic Web service composition planners. Such pre-filtering of services by a matchmaker can be heuristically performed against non-functional and functional service semantics in order to speed up the corresponding planning process - but at the cost of its incompleteness. That is, composition planning over heuristically pruned search space does not, in general, solve the plan existence problem.

Another source of rhe same problem, that is correct but incomplete composition planning is the naive interleaving of planning with semantic service matching. For example, the sequential composition of stateful services from a given intial state by consecutive calls of a logic-based semantic service matchmaker by the planner only does not guarantee to find a solution if it exists: Any (not specific planning-oriented) matchmaker usually

- does not maintain any planning state information, thus ignores variable bindings that hold for service signatures (IO) and specifications (PE) according to the actual state reached by the calling (closed-world) planner, and

- performs pairwise service matching only, hence would not return services to the calling planner which combined effects (even with provided state-based instantiation) would eventually lead to a solution.

To the best of our knowledge, all available Semantic Web service matchmakers (cf. introduction to part two) are implemented as a stand-alone tool for mere semantic service matching without any composition planning support. However, functional-level composition planning is a kind of state-based semantic plug-in matching of the generated service plan with the given goal: Any FLC-planner generates a sequence of Semantic Web services based on their profiles that exact or plug-in matches with the desired (goal) service, whereas for each consecutive pair of planned services S and S' the output of S semantically matches with the input of S', and the preconditions of S' are satisfied in the planning state including the effects of S.

Examples. There are only a few implemented approaches that explicitly interleave semantic matching with composition planning.

In [64], logic-based service matching is extended with concept abduction to provide explanations of mismatches between pairs of service profiles that are iteratively used as constructive feedback during composition planning and replanning when searching for alternative services to bridge identified semantic gaps between considered IOPE profiles of services in the current plan step. A similar abduction-based matchmaking approach is presented in [29]. This scenario of explicitly interleaved discovery and composition has been implemented and tested in a non-public France Telecom research project.

In [61], the functional level composition of services specified in the DIANE service description language DSD is explicitly integrated with a DSD matchmaker module that matches service requests asking for multiple connected effects of configurable services. By using a value propagation mechanism and a cut of possible (not actual) parameter value fillings for service descriptions that cover multiple effects the authors avoid exponential complexity for determining an optimal configuration of plug-in matching service advertisements used for a composition.

In [17], the syntactic functional level service composition is based on partial matching of numerically encoded service IO data types in a service directory. Unfortunately, the justification of the proposed numeric codings for matching services appears questionable, though it was shown to efficiently work for certain applications.

The composition planner OWLS-XPlan2 [93] integrates planning-specific service IOPE matching on the grounding level: At each plan step, the planner calls the component OWLS-MXP of the matchmaker OWLS-MX 1.1 to check the compatibility of XMLS types of input and output parameters of consecutive services.

This ensures the principled executablity of the generated sequential plan at the service grounding level in WSDL.

The interactive OWL-S service composer developed at UMBC [98] uses the OWLS-UDDI matchmaker to help users filter and select relevant services while building the composition plan. At each plan step, the composer provides the user with advertised services which signatures (IO) plug-in or exact match with that of the last service in the current plan. This leads to an incremental forward chaining of services which does not guarantee completeness without respective user intervention.

The Agora-P2P service composition system [60] is the only approach to decentralized Semantic Web Service composition planning. It uses a Chord ring to publish and locate OWL-S service descriptions keyword-based while linear logic theorem proving and logic-based semantic service IO matching is applied to compose (and therefore search for relevant subservices of) the desired service.

4.4.1 Composition Planning and Execution

The semantic compatibility of subsequent services in a plan does not guarantee their correct execution in concrete terms on the grounding level. A plan is called correct, if it produces a state that satifies the given goal [63]. The principled plan executability, also called execution composability of a plan requires its data flow to be ensured during plan execution on the service grounding level [75]. This can be verified through complete (XMLS) message data type checking of semantically matching I/O parameters of every pair of subsequent services involved in the plan. For example, OWLS-XPlan2 calls a special matchmaker module that checks plan execution compatibility at each plan step during planning.

The consistent, central or decentral plan execution can be achieved by means of classical (distributed) transaction theory and systems. An advanced and implemented approach to distributed Semantic Web Service composition plan execution is presented, for example, in Chapter 12 (Semantic Web Service Execution) and [79]. However, the availability of non-local services that are not owned by the planning agent can be, in principle, refused by autonomous service providers without any prior commitment at any time. This calls for effective replanning based on alternative semantic matching services delivered by the matchmaker to the composition planner prior to, or during planning such as in OWLS-XPlan2.

4.4.2 Negotiation

Services may not be for free but pay per use. In particular, requester agents might be charged for every single invocation of services at discovery or planning time. Besides, the service pricing is often private which makes it hard, if not infeasible, for any search or composition agent to determine the total expenses of coordinated service value provision to its user.

Standard solution is to negotiate service level agreements and contracting of relevant services based on non-functional service parameters such as QoS, pricing, and reputation between service requester and provider agents involved [114]. Usually, such negotiation takes place after service discovery depending on service configurations and user preferences, followed by contracting [90]. Most existing Semantic Web service frameworks offer slots for non-functional provenance information as part of their service description.

However, the problem of how to dynamically interleave composition (re-)planning and negotiation remains open. Related work draw upon means of parallel auctioning [91], and coalition forming [80] of planning agents in different competitive settings.

4.5 Open Problems

The research field of Semantic Web service coordination is in its infancies. Hence, it comes for no surprise that there are many open problems of both semantic service discovery and composition planning that call for intensive further investigation in the domain. Some major open problems of semantic service discovery are the following.

- *Approximated matching.* How to deal with uncertain, vague or incomplete information about the functionality of available services and user preferences for service discovery? Fuzzy, probability, and possibility theory are first class candidates for the design of approximated (hybrid) semantic service matching algorithms to solve this problem. In particular, efficient reasoners for respective extensions of semantic Web (rule) languages like probabilistic pOWL, fuzzyOWL, or pDatalog can be applied to reason upon semantic service annotations under uncertainty and with preferences.

  However, there are no such semantic service matchmakers available yet. Apart from the first hybrid matchmakers for OWL-S and WSML services, OWLS-MX and WSMO-MX, the same holds for the integrated use of means of statistical analysis from data mining or information retrieval for approximative matching of semantic service descriptions.

- *Scalability.* How to reasonably trade off the leveraging of expensive logic-based service discovery means with practical requirements of resource bounded, just-in-time and light-weight service discovery in mobile ad-hoc or unstructured P2P service networks? What kind of approximated and/or adaptive semantic service discovery techniques scale best for what environment (network, user context, services distribution, etc) and application at hand? The required very large scale, comparative performance experiments under practical real-world conditions have not been conducted yet.

- *Adaptive discovery.* How to leverage semantic service discovery by means of machine learning and human-agent interaction? Though a variety of adaptive personal recommender and user interface agents have been developed in the field, none of the currently implemented semantic Web Service matchmakers is capable of flexibly adapting to its changing user, network, and application environment.

- *Privacy.* How to protect the privacy of individual user profile data that are explicit or implicit in service requests submitted to a central matchmaker, or relevant service providers? Approaches to privacy preserving Semantic Web Service discovery are still very rare, and research in this direction appears somewhat stagnant. Amongst the most powerful solutions proposed are the Rei language for annotating OWL-S services with privacy and authorization policies [28, 46], and the information flow analysis based checking of the privacy preservation of sequential OWL-S service plans [43, 44]. However, nothing is known about the scalability of these solutions in practice yet.

- *Lack of tool support and test collections.* Current easy to use tool support of Semantic Web Service discovery is still lagging behind the theoretical advancements, though there are differences to what extent this is valid for what service description framework (cf. Figure 4.1). In particular, there is no official test collection for evaluating the retrieval performance of service discovery approaches (matchmakers, search engines) for the standard SAWSDL and WSML, while there are two publicly available for OWL-S (OWLS-TC2, SWS-TC). There are no solutions for the integrated matching of different services that are specified in different languages like SAWSDL, OWL-S and WSML. Relevant work on refactoring OWL-S and WSML to the standard SAWSDL is ongoing.

Some major challenges of research and development in the domain of Semantic Web service composition planning are as follows.

- Scalable and resource efficient approaches to service composition planning under uncertainty and their use in real-world applications of the Web 3.0 and in intelligent pervasive service applications of the so called "Internet of Things" that is envisioned to interlink all kinds of computing devices without limit on the global scale.

- Efficient means of distributed composition planning of Semantic Web Services in peer-to-peer and grid computing environments.

- Easy to use tools for the common user to support discovery, negotiation, composition and execution Semantic Web Services in one framework for different Semantic Web Service formats like the standard SAWSDL, and non-standards like OWL-S, WSML, and SWSL.

- Interleaving of service composition planning with negotiation in competitive settings.

4.6 Summary

This chapter provided a brief romp through the fields of Semantic Web service discovery and composition planning. We classified existing approaches, discussed representative examples and commented on the interrelationships between both service coordination activities. Despite fast paced research and development in the past years world wide, Semantic Web service technology still is commonly considered immature with many open theoretical and practical problems as mentioned above. However, its current convergence with Web 2.0 towards a so-called service Web 3.0 in an envisioned Internet of Things helds promise to effectively revolutionize computing applications for our everday life.

References

[1] K. Aberer, P. Cudre-Mauroux, M. Hauswirth: Semantic Gossiping: fostering semantic interoperability in peer data management systems. S. Staab, H. Stuckenschmidt (eds.): Semantic Web and Peer-to-Peer, Springer, Chapter 13, 2006.

[2] G. Alonso, F. Casati, H. Kuno, V. Machiraju: Web Services. Springer, 2003

[3] S. Agarwal, S. Handschuh, S. Staab: Annotation, composition and invocation of Semantic Web Services. *Web Semantics*, 2, 2004.

[4] G. Agre, Z. Marinova: An INFRAWEBS Approach to Dynamic Composition of Semantic Web Services. *Cybernetics and Information Technologies (CIT)*, 7(1), 2007.

[5] M.S. Aktas, G. Fox, M. Pierce: Managing Dynamic Metadata as Context. Proceedings of Intl. Conference on Computational Science and Engineering (ICCSE), Istanbul, 2005

[6] S. Amer-Yahia, C. Botev, J. Shanmugasundaram: TeXQuery: A Full-Text Search Extension to XQuery. Proceedings of the World-Wide-Web Conference WWW 2004, 2004.

[7] A. Ankolekar, M. Paolucci, K. Sycara: Spinning the OWL-S Process Model - Toward the Verification of the OWL-S Process Models. Proceedingsof International Semantic Web Services Workshop (SWSW), 2004

[8] I.B. Arpinar, B. Aleman-Meza, R. Zhang, A. Maduko: Ontology-driven Web Services composition platform. Proc.of IEEE International Conference on E-Commerce Technology CEC, San Diego, USA, IEEE Press, 2004.

[9] M.A. Aslam, S. Auer, J. Shen: ¿From BPEL4WS Process Model to Full OWL-S Ontology. Proceedings of 2nd European COnference on Semantic Web Services ESWC, Buda, Montenegro, 2006.

[10] F. Baader, C. Lutz, M. Milicic, U. Sattler, F. Wolter: Integrating Description Logics and action formalisms: First results. Proc. 20th National Conference on Artificial Intelligence (AAAI), Pittsburgh, USA, AAAI Press, 2005

[11] J. Bae, L. Liu, J. Caverlee, W.B. Rouse: Process Mining, Discovery, and Integration using Distance Measures. Proceedings of International COnference on Web Services ICWS, 2006.

[12] S. Bansal, J. Vidal: Matchmaking of Web Services Based on the DAMLS Service Model. Proc. International Joint Conference on Autonomous Agents and Multiagent Systems AAMAS, 2003.

[13] U. Basters and M. Klusch: RS2D: Fast Adaptive Search for Semantic Web Services in Unstructured P2P Networks. Proceedings 5th Intl. Semantic Web Conference (ISWC), Athens, USA, Lecture Notes in Computer Science (LNCS), 4273:87-100, Springer, 2006.

[14] A. Bernstein, C. Kiefer: Imprecise RDQL: Towards Generic Retrieval in Ontologies Using Similarity Joins. Proceedings ACM Symposium on Applied Computing, Dijon, France, ACM Press, 2006.

[15] P. Bertoli, A. Cimatti, P. Traverso: Interleaving Execution and Planning for Nondeterministic, Partially Observable Domains. Proceedings of European Conference on Artificial Intelligence (ECAI), 2004.

[16] D. Bianchini, V. De Antonellis, M. Melchiori, D. Salvi: Semantic-enriched Service Discovery. Proceedings of IEEE ICDE 2nd International Workshop on Challenges in Web Information Retrieval and Integration (WIRI06), Atlanta, Georgia, USA, 2006.

[17] W. Binder, I. Constantinescu, B. Faltings, K. Haller, C. Tuerker: A Multi-Agent System for the Reliable Execution of Automatically Composed Ad-hoc Processes. Proceedings of the 2nd European Workshop on Multi-Agent Systems (EUMAS), Barcelona, Spain, 2004.

[18] L. Botelho, A. Fernandez, B. Fries, M. Klusch, L. Pereira, T. Santos, P. Pais, M. Vasirani: Service Discovery. In M. Schumacher, H. Helin (Eds.): CASCOM - Intelligent Service Coordination in the Semantic Web. Chapter 10. Birkh"auser Verlag, Springer, 2008.

[19] C. Caceres, A. Fernandez, H. Helin, O. Keller, M. Klusch: Context-aware Service Coordination for Mobile Users. Proceedings IST eHealth Conference, 2006.

[20] F. Casati, M.C. Shan: Dynamic and Adaptive Composition of E-services. *Information Systems*, 6(3), 2001.

[21] CASCOM Project Deliverable D3.2: Conceptual Architecture Design. September 2005.www.ist-cascom.org

[22] D. Chakraborty, F. Perich, S. Avancha, A. Joshi: DReggie: Semantic Service Discovery for M-Commerce Applications. Proceedings of the International Workshop on Reliable and Secure Applications in Mobile Environment, 2001.

[23] H. Chen, A. Joshi, and T. Finin: Dynamic service discovery for mobile computing: Intelligent agents meet JINI in the aether. 4(4):343-354, 2001.

[24] S. Colucci, T.C. Di Noia, E. Di Sciascio, F.M. Donini, M. Mongiello: Concept Abduction and Contraction for Semantic-based Discovery of Matches and Negotiation Spaces in an E-Marketplace. *Electronic Commerce Research and Applications*, 4(4):345361, 2005.

[25] I. Constantinescu, B. Faltings: Efficient matchmaking and directory services Proceedings of IEEE Conference on Web Intelligence WI, 2003.

[26] R. Dearden, N. Meuleauy, S. Ramakrishnany, D.E. Smith, R. Washington: Incremental Contingency Planning. Proc. of ICAPS-03 Workshop on Planning under Uncertainty, Trento, Italy, 2003.

[27] E. Della Valle, D. Cerizza, I. Celino: The Mediators Centric Approach to Automatic Web Service Discovery of Glue. Proceedings of 1st International Workshop on Mediation in Semantic Web Services (MEDIATE), CEUR Workshop proceedings, 168, 2005.

[28] G. Denker, L. Kagal, T. Finin, M. Paolucci, K. Sycara: Security For DAML Web Services: Annotation and Matchmaking. Proceedings of the Second International Semantic Web Conference (ISWC 2003), USA, 2003.

[29] T. Di Noia, E.D. Sciascio, F.M. Donini, M. Mogiello: A System for Principled Matchmaking in an Electronic Marketplace. *Electronic Commerce*, 2004.

[30] T. Di Noia, E. Di Sciascio, F.M. Donini: Semantic Matchmaking as Non-Monotonic Reasoning: A Description Logic Approach. *Artificial Intelligence Research (JAIR)*, 29:269–307, 2007.

[31] J. Domingue, S. Galizia, L. Cabral: Choreography in IRS-III: Coping with Heterogeneous Interaction Patterns in Web Services. Proc. International Semantic Web Conference, LNAI, Springer, 2005.

[32] D. Fahland, W. Reisig: ASM-based semantics for BPEL: The negative Control Flow. Proceedings of the 12th International Workshop on Abstract State Machines (ASM'05), 2005.

[33] D. Fensel, F. van Harmelen: Unifying reasoning and search to Web scale. *IEEE Internet Computing*, March/April 2007.

[34] A. Fernandez, M. Vasirani, C. Caceres, S. Ossowski: A role-based support mechanism for service description and discovery. In: huang et al. (eds.), Service-Oriented Computing: Agents, Semantics, and Engineering. LNCS 4504, Springer, 2006.

[35] U. Furbach, M. Maron, K. Read: Location based informationsystems. Künstliche Intelligenz, 3/07, BöttcherIT, 2007.

[36] M. Ghallab, D. Nau, P. Traverso: Automated planning. Elsevier, 2004.

[37] S. Grimm: Discovery - Identifying relevant services. In [104], 2007.

[38] S. Grimm, B. Motik, C. Preist: Matching semantic service descriptions with local closed-world reasoning. Proc. European Semantic Web Conference (ESWC), Springer, LNCS, 2006.

[39] L. Guo, F. Shao, C. Botev, J. Shanmugasundaram: XRANK: Ranked Keyword Search over XML Documents. Proceedings of the 2003 ACM SIGMOD International Conference on Management of Data, San Diego, USA, 2003.

[40] P. Haase, R. Siebes, F. van Harmelen: Expertise-based Peer selection in Peer-to-Peer Networks. *Knowledge and Information Systems*, Springer, 2006

[41] L. Henoque, M. Kleiner: Composition - Combining Web Service Functionality in Composite Orchestrations. Chapter 9 in [104], 2007.

[42] D. Hull, U. Sattler, E. Zolin, R. Stevens, A. Bovykin, I. Horrocks: Deciding semantic matching of stateless services. Proc. 21st National Conference on Artificial Intelligence (AAAI), AAAI Press, 2006

[43] D. Hutter, M. Klusch, M. Volkamer: Information Flow Analysis Based Security Checking of Health Service Composition Plans. Proceedings of the 1st European Conference on eHealth, Fribourg, Switzerland, 2006.

[44] D. Hutter, M. Volkamer, M. Klusch, A. Gerber: Provably Secure Execution of Composed Semantic Web Services. Proccedings of the 1st International Workshop on Privacy and Security in Agent-based Collaborative Environments (PSACE 2006), Hakodate, Japan, 2006.

[45] M.C. Jäger, G. Rojec-Goldmann, C. Liebetruth, G. Mühl, K. Geihs: Ranked Matching for Service Descriptions Using OWL-S. Proceedings of 14. GI/VDE Fachtagung Kommunikation in Verteilten Systemen KiVS, Kaiserslautern, 2005

[46] L. Kagal, T. Finin, M. Paolucci, N. Srinivasan, K. Sycara, G. Denker: Authorization and Privacy for Semantic Web Services. *IEEE Intelligent Systems*, July/August, 2004.

[47] F. B. Kashani, C.C. Shen, C. Shahabi: SWPDS: Web Service peer-to-per discovery service. Proceedings of Intl. Conference on Internet Computing, 2004.

[48] U. Keller, R. Lara, H. Lausen, A. Polleres, D. Fensel: Automatic Location of Services. Proceedings of the 2nd European Semantic Web Conference (ESWC), Heraklion, Crete, LNCS 3532, Springer, 2005.

[49] F. Kaufer and M. Klusch: Hybrid Semantic Web Service Matching with WSMO-MX. Proc. 4th IEEE European Conference on Web Services (ECOWS), Zurich, Switzerland, IEEE CS Press, 2006

[50] F. Kaufer and M. Klusch: Performance of Hybrid WSML Service Matching with WSMO-MX: Preliminary Results. Proc. First Intl. Joint ISWC Workshop SMR2 2007 on Service Matchmaking and Resource Retrieval in the Semantic Web, Busan, Korea, 2007.

[51] C. Kiefer, A. Bernstein: The Creation and Evaluation of iSPARQL Strategies for Matchmaking. Proceedings of European Semantic Web Conference, Springer, 2008.

[52] T. Kleemann, A. Sinner: Description logic based matchmaking on mobile devices. Proceedgins of 1st Workshop on Knowledge Engineering and Software Engineering (KESE 2005), 2005.

[53] M. Klein, B. König-Ries: Coupled Signature and Specification Matching for Automatic Service Binding. European Conference on Web Services (ECOWS 2004), Erfurt, 2004.

[54] M. Klusch, B. Fries: Hybrid OWL-S Service Retrieval with OWLS-MX: Benefits and Pitfalls. Proceedings 1st International Joint Workshop on Service Matchmaking and Resource Retrieval in the Semantic Web (SMR2), Busan, Korea, CEUR vol. 243, 2007.

[55] M. Klusch, P. Kapahnke, B. Fries: Hybrid Semantic Web Service Retrieval: A Case Study With OWLS-MX. Proceedings of 2nd IEEE Internataional Conference on Semantic Computing (ICSC), Santa Clara, USA, IEEE Press, 2008.

[56] M. Klusch, A. Gerber, M. Schmidt: Semantic Web Service Composition Planning with OWLS-XPlan. Proc. 1st Intl. AAAI Fall Symposium on Agents and the Semantic Web, Arlington VA, USA, AAAI Press, 2005.

[57] M. Klusch, K-U. Renner: Dynamic Re-Planning of Composite OWL-S Services. Proc. 1st IEEE Workshop on Semantic Web Service Composition, Hongkong, China, IEEE CS Press, 2006.

[58] M. Klusch, K. Sycara: Brokering and Matchmaking for Coordination of Agent Societies: A Survey. In: Coordination of Internet Agents, A. Omicini et al. (eds.), Springer

[59] M. Klusch, B. Fries, K. Sycara: Automated Semantic Web Service Discovery with OWLS-MX. Proc. 5th Intl. Conference on Autonomous Agents and Multi-Agent Systems (AAMAS), Hakodate, Japan, ACM Press, 2006

[60] P. Küngas, M. Matskin: Semantic Web Service Composition through a P2P-Based Multi-Agent Environment. Proc. of the Fourth International Workshop on Agents and Peer-to-Peer Computing (in conjunction with AAMAS 2005), Utrecht, Netherlands, LNCS 4118, 2006.

[61] U. Küster, B. König-Ries, M. Stern, M. Klein: DIANE: An Integrated Approach to Automated Service Discovery, Matchmaking and Composition. Proceedings of the World Wide Web COnference WWW, Banff, Canada, ACM Press, 2007.

[62] S. Lamparter, A. Ankolekar: Automated Selection of Configurable Web Services. 8. Internationale Tagung Wirtschaftsinformatik. Universittsverlag Karlsruhe, Karlsruhe, Germany, March 2007.

[63] F. Lecue, A. Leger: Semantic Web Service composition through a matchmaking of domain. Proc. of 4th IEEE European Conference on Web Services (ECWS), Zurich, 2006.

[64] F. Lecue, A. Delteil, A. Leger: Applying Abduction in Semantic Web Service Composition. Proceedings of IEEE International Conference on Web Services (ICWS 2007), 2007.

[65] L. Li, I. Horrocks: A software framework for matchmaking based on semantic Web technology. Proceedings of the world wide Web conference (WWW), Budapest, 2003.

[66] J. Liu, H. Zhuge: A Semantic-Link-Based Infrastructure for Web Service. Proc. of the International World Wide Web Conference, 2005.

[67] S. Liu, P. Küngas, M. Matskin: Agent-Based Web Service Composition with JADE and JXTA. Proc. of Intl Conference on Semantic Web and Web Services (SWWS), Las Vegas, USA, 2006.

[68] A. Löser, C. Tempich, B. Quilitz, W.-T. Balke, S. Staab, W. Nejdl: Searching Dynamic Communities with Personal Indexes. Proceedings of Internatioanl Semantic Web Conference, 2005.

[69] N. Lohmann: A Feature-Complete Petri Net Semantics for WS-BPEL 2.0. Proceedings of the Workshop on Formal Approaches to Business Processes and Web Services (FABPWS'07), 2007.

[70] B.T. Loo, R. Huebsch, I. Stoica, J.M. Hellerstein: The Case for a Hybrid P2P Search Infrastructure. Proceedings of rd Intl Workshop on P2P Systems (IPTPS), USA, Springer, LNCS, 2004.

[71] Q. Lu, P. Cao, E. Cohen, K. Li, S. Shenker: Search and Replication in Unstructured Peer-to-Peer Networks. Procceedings of ACM 6th ACM International Conference on Supercomputing ICS, New York, USA, 2002.

[72] A. Martens: Analyzing Web Service based Business Processes. Proceedings of Workshop on Fundamental Approaches to Software Engineering FASE, 2005.

[73] S. McIllraith, T.C. Son: Adapting Golog for composition of Semantic Web Services. Proc. International Conference on Knowledge Representation and Reasoning KRR, Toulouse, France, 2002.

[74] S. Narayanan, S. McIllraith: Simulation, verification and automated composition of Web Services. Proc. of 11th International COnference on the World Wide Web (WWW), Hawaii, 2002.

[75] B. Medjahed, A. Bouguettyaya, A.K. Elmagarmid: Composing Web Services on the semantic Web. *Very Large Data Bases (VLDB)*, 12(4), 2003.

[76] B.T. Messmer: New approaches on graph matching. PhD Thesis, University of Bern, Switzerland, 1995.

[77] M. Milicic: Planning in Action Formalisms based on DLS: First Results. Proceedings of the Intl Workshop on Description Logics, 2007.

[78] D.S. Milojicic, V. Kalogeraki, R. Lukose, K. Nagaraja, J. Pruyne, B. Richard, S. Rollins, Z. Xu: Peer-to-peer computing. Technical Report HPL-2002-57, Hewlett-Packard, 2002.

[79] T. Möller, H. Schuldt, A. Gerber, M. Klusch: Next Generation Applications in Healthcare Digital Libraries using Semantic Service Composition and Coordination. *Health Informatics*, 12 (2):107-119, SAGE publications, 2006.

[80] I. Müller, R. Kowalczyk, P. Braun: Towards Agent-Based Coalition Formation for Service Composition. Proceedings of the IEEE International Conference on Intelligent Agent Technology, Washington, USA, 2006.

[81] M. Paolucci, T. Kawamura, T.R. Payne, K. Sycara: Semantic Matching of Web Services Capabilities. Proceedings of the 1st International Semantic Web Conference (ISWC2002), 2002.

[82] M. Paolucci, K. Sycara, T. Nishimara, N. Srinivasan: Using DAML-S for P2P Discovery. Proc. of International Conference on Web Services, Erfurt, Germany, 2003.

[83] M. Papazoglou: Web Services: Principles and Technology. Pearson - Prentice Hall, September 2007.

[84] J. Peer: Web Service Composition as AI Planning: A Survey. Technical Report, University of St. Gallen, Switzerland, 2005. Available at elektra.mcm.unisg.ch/pbwsc/docs/pfwsc.pdf

[85] J. Peer: A POP-Based Replanning Agent for Automatic Web Service Composition. Proceedings of the 2nd European Semantic Web Conference (ESWC), Heraklion, Crete, LNCS 3532, Springer, 2005.

[86] A. Pfalzgraf: Ein robustes System zur automatischen Komposition semantischer Web Services in SmartWeb. Master Thesis, University of the Saarland, Saarbrücken, Germany, Juni 2006.

[87] M. Pistore, P. Traverso: Planning as model checking for extended goals in non-deterministic domains. In: Proceedings of the 7th International Joint Conference on Artificial Intelligence (IJCAI-01), 2001.

[88] M. Pistore, P. Roberti, P. Traverso: Process-Level Composition of Executable Web Services: On-the-fly Versus Once-for-all Composition Proceedings of the 2nd European Semantic Web Conference (ESWC), Heraklion, Crete, LNCS 3532, Springer, 2005.

[89] M. Pistore, P. Traverso, P. Bertoli, A. Marconi: Automated synthesis of composite BPEL4WS Web Services. Proceedings of the 2005 IEEE International Conference on Web Services, Orlando, USA, IEEE Press, 2005.

[90] C. Preist: Semantic Web Services - Goals and Vision. Chapter 6 in [104], 2007.

[91] C. Preist, C. Bartolini, A. Byde: Agent-based service composition through simultaneous negotiation in forward and reverse auctions. Proceedings of the 4th ACM Conference on Electronic Commerce, San Diego, California, USA, 2003.

[92] J. Rao, P. Kuengas, M. Matskin: Composition of Semantic Web Services using Linear Logic theorem proving. *Information Systems*, 31, 2006.

[93] K.-U. Renner, P. Kapahnke, B. Blankenburg, M. Klusch: OWLS-XPlan 2.0 - A Dynamic OWL-S Service Composition Planner. BMB+F project SCALLOPS, Internal Project Report, DFKI Saarbrücken, Germany, 2007. www.dfki.de/ klusch/owls-xplan2-report-2007.pdf

[94] A. Rosenfeld, C. Goldman, G. Kaminka, S. Kraus: An Agent Architecture for Hybrid P2P Free-Text Search. Proceedings of 11th Intl Workshop on COoperative Information Agents (CIA), Delft, Springer, LNAI 4676, 2007.

[95] M. Schlosser, M. Sintek, S. Decker, W. Nejdl: A Scalable and Ontology-based P2P Infrastructure for Semantic Web Services. Proceedings of 2nd IEEE Intl Conference on Peer-to-Peer Computing (P2P), Linkoping, Sweden, 2003

[96] B. Schnizler, D. Neumann, D. Veit, C. Weinhardt: Trading Grid Services - A Multi-attribute Combinatorial Approach. *European Journal of Operational Research*, 2006.

[97] E. Sirin, J. Hendler, B. Parsia: Semi-automatic Composition of Web Services using Semantic Descriptions. Proceedings of Intl Workshop on Web Services: Modeling, Architecture and Infrastructure workshop in conjunction with ICEIS conference, 2002.

[98] E. Sirin, B. Parsia, J. Hendler: Filtering and Selecting Semantic Web Services with Interactive Composition Techniques. *IEEE Intelligent Systems*, July/August, 2004.

[99] E. Sirin, B. Parsia, D. Wu, J. Hendler, D. Nau: HTN planning for Web Service composition using SHOP2. *Web Semantics*, 1(4), Elsevier, 2004.

[100] D.E. Smith, D.S. Weld: Conformant Graphplan. Proc. of 15th AAAI Conference on on AI, Pittsburgh, USA, 1998.

[101] B. Srivastava, J. Koehler: Web Service Composition: Current Solutions and Open Problems. Proceedings of the ICAPS 2003 Workshop on Planning for Web Services, 2003.

[102] S. Staab, H. Stuckenschmidt (eds.): Semantic Web and Peer-to-Peer. Springer, 2006.

[103] M. Stollberg, U. Keller, H. Lausen, S. Heymans: Two-phase Web Service discovery based on rich functional descriptions. Proceedings of European Semantic Web Conference, Buda, Montenegro, LNCS, Springer, 2007.

[104] R. Studer, S. Grimm, A. Abecker (eds.): Semantic Web Services. Concepts, Technologies, and Applications. Springer, 2007.

[105] K. Sycara, M. Klusch, S. Widoff, J. Lu: LARKS: Dynamic Matchmaking Among Heterogeneous Software Agents in Cyberspace. *Autonomous Agents and Multi-Agent Systems*, 5(2):173 - 204, Kluwer Academic, 2002.

[106] D. Trastour, C. Bartolini, C. Priest: Semantic Web Support for the Business-to-Business E-Commerce Lifecycle. Proceedings of the International World Wide Web Conference (WWW), 2002.

[107] P. Traverso, M. Pistore: Automated Composition of Semantic Web Services into Executable Processes. Int Semantic Web Conference, LNCS 3298, Springer, 2004.

[108] D. Tsoumakos, N. Roussopoulos: Adaptive Probabilistic Search (APS) for Peer-to-Peer Networks. Proc. Int. IEEE Conference on P2P Computing, 2003.

[109] R. Vaculin, K. Sycara: Towards automatic mediation of OWL-S process models. IEEE International Conference on Web Services (ICWS 2007), 2007.

[110] W.M.P. van der Aalst, A.J.M.M. Weijters: Process mining: a research agenda. *Computers in Industry*, 53, 2004.

[111] K. Verma, K. Sivashanmugam, A. Sheth, A. Patil, S. Oundhakar, J. Miller: METEORS WSDI: A Scalable P2P Infrastructure of Registries for Semantic Publication and Discovery of Web Services. *Information Technology and Management*, Special Issue on Universal Global Integration, Vol. 6, No. 1, 2005.

[112] L.H. Vu, M. Hauswirth, F. Porto, K. Aberer: A Search Engine for QoS-enabled Discovery of Semantic Web Services. Ecole Politechnique Federal de Lausanne, LSIR-REPORT-2006-002, Switzerland, 2006. Also available in the Special Issue of the International Journal of Business Process Integration and Management (IJBPIM) (2006).

[113] Z. Wu, K. Gomadam, A. Ranabahu, A. Sheth, J. Miller: Automatic Composition of Semantic Web Services using Process Mediation. Proceedings of the 9th Intl. Conf. on Enterprise Information Systems ICES 2007, Funchal, Portugal, 2007.

[114] J. Yan, R. Kowalczyk, J. Lin, M.B. Chhetri, S.K.Goh, J. Zhang: Autonomous service level agreement negotiation for service composition provision. *Future Generation Computing Systems*, 23(6), Elsevier, 2007.

[115] A.M. Zaremski, J.M. Wing: Specification Matching of Software Components. *ACM Transactions on Software Engineering and Methodology*, 6(4), 1997.

Chapter 5

Context-Awareness

Bruno Gonçalves, Paulo Costa and Luis Miguel Botelho

5.1 Introduction

Context-aware computing has increasingly gained the attention of the research community because, as it is the case with human interactions, context information provides the background against which it is possible to more accurately interpret communicative acts without the need to explicitly state everything that might be relevant. If, within an agent negotiation for buying some specific service, the service provider says *"the price is 20 Euros"*, the receiver would not be capable of fully interpreting the meaning of the message without using the context created by the whole conversation. Context information provides the basis for more efficient information processing mechanisms due to the possibility of discarding irrelevant information in early stages of information processing. For instance, if some patient's personal assistance agent is looking for a service that would sell him or her a specific medicine and deliver it in the patient's home, this would be achieved through the creation of a compound service consisting of an on-line pharmacy and a medicine transportation service. Using context information about the patient's location, the service composition process may discard service providers located far away from the client and create the compound service considering only a very small number of all existing services of the relevant categories. Context information also enables better adapted behavior since, being context-aware, it may be more directed towards clients requirements in the circumstances of the interaction. For instance, if a personal assistance agent is looking for an internet movie critique service for its owner, having to choose between services displaying a German, an Italian, or anEnglish user interface, the use of context information regarding the user's profile, will enable the agent to choose the service whose interface language is preferred to the client.

Context-aware computing increasing importance is manifest in the emergence of a growing number of applications that use context information captured by software and hardware sensors, such as the current time, the current temperature and humidity, the user's location, current traffic in alternative internet connections, availability and load of some service provider.

The CASCOM Project designed and implemented an architecture for context-aware agent-based service coordination for static and mobile users. Context-aware service coordination agents may adapt their behavior to their clients taking into account the context in which interactions take place. For the sake of efficiency, modularity and specialization, service coordination agents should not have to care about the problems of acquiring context information from the large diversity of sources actually existing or coping with the enormous variety of representation and encoding formats used in these sources.

This chapter provides an overview of selected topics of context-aware computing, focusing the problems of context information acquisition, modeling, and management, which are those related with context acquisition and management systems. Context information acquisition refers to the process of acquiring information that is considered to be part of the context. Often, context acquisition is implemented through software sensors (e.g., user spoken languages) or hardware sensors (e.g., room temperature). Context modeling consists of creating the model according to which context is represented. Context modeling allows to convert raw data read from the sensors into something with meaning, generally following a given ontology. For instance, the string *"English"* provided by a software sensor implemented in the user's personal assistance agent might mean *"user spoken languages = {English}"*. Context management refers to the whole activity of context processing within the context system including storing context information, taking care of context clients and their requests, and knowing when to discard particular pieces of context information. The chapter will review context definitions, theories and principles for context system design, context modeling, and context system architectures. There is of course much more about context, for instance, about the way context information may be used by context-aware systems. However, the chapter will not address such topics in detail.

Maybe the first idea of context information was the user location however, simultaneously with the effort to clarify and adequately extend its definition [2, 12, 13, 29], other kinds of information were used in context dependent applications, such as the state of network connections, the existing devices available to the user, and the social environment.

Several definitions of context can still be found, which does not contribute to creating a clear picture of context-aware applications and context acquisition and management systems. In spite of this diversity, maybe, the most accepted definition of context is the one proposed by Dey and Abowd [13], according to which *"context is any information that can be used to characterize the situation of an entity. An entity is a person, place, or object that is considered relevant to the interaction between a user and an application, including the user and application themselves"*. Although the proposal by Dey and Abowd is still the most accepted, the definition by Anagnostopoulos et al. is increasingly gaining more adepts [13]. They use the definition of Dey and Abowd but they circumscribe the notion of context to a set of situations, which describe humans, applications, and environment related to specific activities.

A context-aware system is a set of services that adapt to environmental factors, such as the location in which the system is used, nearby people and objects, as well as the changes that occur in these objects over time. With the appearance of mobile devices, context became increasingly important to improve the performance and effectiveness of applications for mobile users [17]. There are several projects [1, 5, 6, 3, 4, 16, 21, 33] that investigate how context information can be useful to improve existing services and to create new services for the next generations of mobile networks.

One of these projects is the WWI Ambient Networks [1]. This project is aimed at creating solutions beyond the third generation, promoting a scalable and low cost network that allows an easy access to the offered services. These solutions include the use of the context-aware computing paradigm to select the best connection, location services and geographical orientation among others.

Other project presented by Chalmers and Sloman [5] proposes the use of a framework that allows the management of the quality of service in mobile networks, using context information to analyze the user characteristics.

Several architectures and approaches that deal with context [2, 8, 9, 6, 10, 11, 22, 24, 27, 28] have been discussed over time, however there is still no normalized solution that satisfies all possible uses of context information.

This chapter presents some definitions of context given by several authors. Following, it presents several context models focusing context acquisition, context modeling and context processing. Next, it describes some of the developed architectures of context-aware systems. Finally, overall comments about this subject are presented.

5.2   Context Definitions

Context definitions, in computer applications, have been adapted from the way context is used in everyday language. Since there are many everyday language uses for context, an adequate and generally accepted definition of context information and context-aware applications still does not exist. The meaning of context in everyday language is related with the interpretation of written and spoken text. Text is not an encapsulated representation of a specific meaning. Rather, it is an indication that allows the anticipated construal of a meaning. That construal is based on what comes with the text, namely its context. In a sentence, each word has a meaning but the sentence global meaning can only be determined by doing inferences over its context [31]. For instance, if someone looking from a window at a car being stolen, says *"isn't that our neighbor's car?"* the pronoun *"that"* can only be understood if the listener is also looking at the same scene, that is, if the listener shares at least part of the same context with the speaker. *"Our neighbor"* can also be understood by the listener depending on the context. If the listener leaves in the same place as the speaker, then the expression gains a certain meaning. However the meaning would be different if the listener knows the speaker is talking about him and his wife.

Linguists and philosophers have made a big effort to identify the several context elements that give meaning to words. When trying to adjust everyday context definitions to computer sciences, several authors have created their own definitions of context for their applications, which lead to different views of context and different approaches to acquire context information from the environment.

Winograd [31] defines context as not only the data structures in the operating system (such as Windows and applications), but also something far beyond the application being used. Context is an operational term; something is considered context if it is used in an interaction.

For Schilit and Theimer [29], context consists of the identities of people, the objects near the application, as well as their changes. Dey [12] adds to the definition of context the emotional states, the user attention, location and orientation, date and time, and objects and persons in the user environment. The meaning of the noun phrase *"the car that has just appeared in front of you"* depends on the time in which the phrase is uttered, it depends on the direction the listener is headed to and on his or her location, and of course, on the objects (i.e., the car) on the listener's environment.

For Anagnostopoulos et al. [2], context is a set of situations that describe people, applications and environment related with a specific activity. This provides context to the context, which will enable to constrain the whole array of objects, people and events that may be considered context to only those related to a given activity. For instance, only the set of potential threats related to driving in a particular road in a given moment, not the set of all possible threats in the universe, is relevant to interpret the danger traffic sign.

The most accepted definition of context, for the scientific community, is the one by Dey and Abowd [13] which states that context is defined as any information that characterizes a situation or entity.

According to Schmidt et al. [30], context can be divided in two categories: human factors and physical environment. Human factors include user, social environment (people near the user, the relations among them, between them and the user, and between them and the application) and task (which plays a similar role to that played by the activity put forth by Anagnostopoulos and colleagues). The physical environment includes location, infrastructure (supporting the application, the user, the social context and the task) and conditions (e.g., current date and time).

Analyzing current definitions, we conclude that they are either too restrictive or too wide scoped, failing to distinguish context-aware computing from other kinds of computing.

Taken together, the points of view of Schilit and Theimer [29], and of Anagnostopoulos et al. [2] mean context includes applications, environment, and people related with a given activity, and their changes. Dey's proposal [12] also includes the emotional states, the user attention, location and orientation, date and time, and the user environment. In a strict sense, these definitions would rule out for instance current traffic conditions in a given network connection, the average waiting time per request and the current number of requests of a given application. In a broad sense, this definition would include almost everything.

For Dey and Abowd [13], context is defined as any information that characterizes a situation or entity. For Winograd [31], something is considered context if it is used in an interaction. These are obviously too broad definitions. Winograd's definition would include even the messages exchanged in the interaction. And for Dey and Abowd, almost any information would be considered context. This way, context-aware computing would be basically information processing which is not a useful definition since it does not allow us distinguishing context-aware computing from other kinds of computing.

The proposal of Schmidt et al. [30] identifies different classes of context information but it also cannot distinguish context-aware computing from other kinds of computing.

We propose that often the decision of considering or not a specific information as context should be a design task. For instance, some applications would consider the user location to be part of the context, while for others, location would not be relevant. In any case, context information should be processed differently from other classes of information or else it would not make sense to be concerned about context-aware computing. A suggestion regarding the way context information should be handled could be *"in an interaction between the initiator and the participant, it is the responsibility of the participant to acquire relevant context information even if the participant has to ask the initiator to provide (part of) it"*.

5.3 General Design Principles and Context Modeling Approaches

The design principles reviewed in this chapter are important to evaluate specific context system architectures presented in the next section. Ideally, specific architectures should comply with reviewed design principles. Whatever information is considered context in an application, it must be acquired, modeled and processed, which will transform context into something useful [2, 23]. According to Anagnostopoulos and his colleagues [2], a context system should implement a set of functionalities, such as acquisition, aggregation (creating new meaningful compound data structures integrating context information from different types of sources), discovery (discovering the relevant sources of context), and context search (discovering the relevant context information), among others.

The acquisition stage is normally associated with sensors. A great amount of context information is acquired from sensors implemented in software or hardware. Several approaches have been proposed that focus on the task of creating an interpretation of the acquired context information that makes sense for the specific application. This interpretation process is usually guided by a context ontology conceptually close to the application. An example of context acquisition might be the reading "*001A*" from a given temperature sensor placed inside a pool. The result of context interpretation, in this case, could be "*pool water temperature in Tom's place = 26 C*".

From the reviewed approaches we have identified several important aspects to be considered when developing context systems. First, we have to separate context information acquisition from context information interpretation. This separation allows context interpretation to be independent of sensor interface details. Context information acquisition can be done by software or hardware sensors. Context interpretation normally requires tools and ontologies defined in or used by the context system.

Context acquisition is not limited to only capturing context information in the moment in which it is required. Context acquisition also includes the storage of acquired context information as well as its changes over time. The variation of context information over time is usually called historic context information [19].

During acquisition, we should take into account the errors and delays introduced by processing this information. A way to avoid these errors is to use data fusion [16] (i.e., using information from several sensors to try to identify and correct possible errors). For instance, if we have time readings from several clocks, errors pertaining the reading of one of the clocks may be overcome if we use the readings of the other clocks.

Some of the acquired context information is static, while other kinds of context information may change over time. Examples of static context information are the time schedule of a given service or the nationality of a given user. Examples of dynamic context information are the user location, current time and date, and current temperature. According to Henricksen et al. [19], context information is considered static when it does not vary much over time. Static context may be directly acquired from the user or a service and stored in a central repository. Dynamic context information should be acquired by sensors and locally stored in the sensors themselves.

The proposal of Cortese et al. [8] shows the complexity of managing a large number of sensors. The proposed model assumes that the whole interaction with the user is made through sensors. This implies that the used context model has to be extensible so it can be applied to different situations with more, less, or with different sensors. These authors define two methods to get information from sensors - the methods push and pull. Using these methods, the sensors can be both proactive, always sending information to the system, or passive, sending the information only when a request is received.

Context interpretation should draw upon the definition of context ontologies. Context ontologies allow representing context information following a structure and a level of abstraction independent from context sensors and other used sources of information. Any entity that receives context information represented according to some specified context ontology can understand it, if it knows the ontology [15]. Context ontologies may be organized according to several aspects, such as used devices, application, and location, among others. The way context is acquired (from software and hardware sensors) also represents a context aspect [18].

The proposal of Anagnostopoulos [2] and his colleagues concerning context modeling states that context should be represented by classes with associations. These associations connect context elements and deal with both dynamic and static context. Additionally, the context model should allow the definition of dependencies between context elements. Christopoulou et al. [7] present a similar type of association, the synapse. These associations represent preferences and needs of the associated elements. According to this proposal, the context model should be defined by an ontology with two levels. The first level defines the model used to describe the context ontology. Following this very proposal, the first level would include the definition of "*context element*", and "*synapse*". The second level describes the context ontology using the model defined in the first level. Sticking to the same example, the second level would be the particular context elements and the particular synapses in a given application domain. The context information models presented by Anagnostopoulos and his colleagues and by Christopoulou et al. are very comprehensive models. Both synapses and dependencies are important aspects to focus when identifying the context elements.

A context acquisition and management system should be presented to applications as an abstract (i.e., hardware independent) context capturing and storage component ensuring the independence of the application with respect to the used context acquisition sensors [20]. The context system core can be built of components that implement its functionalities. Each sensor can also be built as a component that implements an abstract interface. This allows using the advantages of the component-based systems paradigm such as modularity and the unification of sensor access in a single interface [14]. As an example of a sensor implementing an abstract interface, we could think of a temperature sensor that extracts the reading "*001E*" from the environment but converts this into "*environment temperature = 30 C*" before making this information available to its clients.

The storage of context information in a system can be implemented by a centralized repository modeled following a given ontology. This repository allows the centralized access to context by context information producers and consumers [31]. The context system can also be presented as a peripheralware in a service network [26]. Generally, peripheralware consists of additional software layers placed between the middleware and services, and between the middleware and the client. Those layers perform tasks transparent to the services and to the clients. Using peripheralware allows context-awareness in services that are not prepared to deal with context. All the context information processing is done by the peripheralware in a transparent way to the services and the clients.

Prekop and Burnett [25] define a context model centered on the user activity, which is significant only when the activity takes place. This vision differs significantly from those previously mentioned because, in the previous ones, context

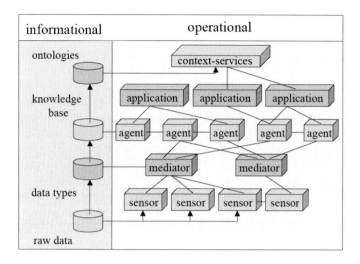

Figure 5.1: Context system architecture levels

information relates to entities, while in this one, context information relates to activities in which the entities participate. For instance, in previous mentioned models, the price of a book is context information relating to the book, and the available money to buy it is context information related to the client; in this model, both are context information of the book buying activity. This model assumes the context definition of Anagnostopoulos et al. [2], according to which, context is a set of situations that describe people, applications and environment related with a specific activity.

Several architectures were developed from the models described in this section.

5.4   Context Dependency Architectures

Context systems architectures may have two levels: operational and informative levels, as presented in Figure 5.1. The operational level comprises the system modules such as sensors, mediators that convert sensor data into higher level information, intelligent agents that gather the system knowledge, and context-aware applications (if a global perspective is adopted that views both the context system and its clients as unique system). The informative level comprises the acquired context information and knowledge. This knowledge can be represented in a simple data model, in an object-oriented model, or in an ontology model [2]. Context information is acquired by sensor networks and further subject to processes that convert it into higher level representations, usually following a context ontology, which might be more abstract or more specific of the application that requires it. Sensors can be used simply as data acquisition mechanisms but they can also be more sophisticated. Often sensors are coupled with adaptation mechanisms that create context information representations independent of the specific type of sensor. This is called sensor adaptation. Pure sensor architectures only have the operational level, since the way context information should be presented is not defined in sensor networks. However, if context adaptation performed by the sensors is done according to a given ontology, the informative level will also be present.

This section starts with sensor network architectures such as the Smart-Its Architecture. These simple architectures are totally distributed context systems consisting of a network of sensors that exchange context information packets among them. Each sensor may create new context information packets or add information to received packets. When completed, packets are sent to the context clients that have requested them.

The Merino architecture represents a sophistication of pure sensor networks because it has three kinds of sensors of different sophistication; and it includes a centralized context repository, and a user model.

All of the other reviewed architectures use similar ontology-based context modeling techniques for providing a sensor-independent abstract view of context to their clients. Besides providing sensor abstraction, all other architectures have a central repository for context information. Besides the instantaneous context, often the context repository stores historic context information. In addition to these common features, each of these reviewed architectures introduce specific differences with respect to the others.

WASP, CoBrA, Context Taylor architectures as well as the one proposed by Cortese and colleagues separate sensor information capturing from its processing. In all of them, the lower level layer extracts context information from sensors. Then, a higher level layer adapts the acquired information according to a defined ontology. This abstract representation of the context information is then subject to diverse kinds of information processing such as context fusion and inference, which result in additional pieces of context. Acquired and generated context information is stored in a repository. WASP and CoBrA have a system manager that has knowledge about all elements belonging to the architecture, manages context information requests, acquires information from the repositories and the context interpreters, and delivers it to context clients. CoBrA manager, denominated Context Broker, is a distributed agent that communicates with client agents, using an agent communication language. Besides context fusion and inference, the Context Broker also supports privacy by imposing access policies defined by each client, using a declarative language. Context Taylor has learning mechanisms that extract patterns from the context information. These patterns may be used in future context information requests.

Often, context acquisition and management architectures support both context information requests and context information subscription (push and pull). Information request mechanisms allow context clients to acquire context infor-

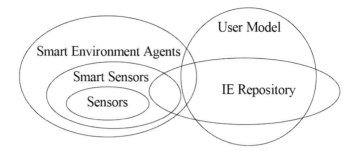

Figure 5.2: Merino architecture

mation when needed (on demand); information subscription mechanisms allow context clients to receive desired context information whenever it changes.

5.4.1 Smart-Its Architecture

The decentralized architecture proposed by Michachelles and Samulowitz [24] is ideal for mobile environments and ad hoc networks. It stores the context information acquired by sensors (*Smart-its*) in packets that are passed from sensor to sensor. These packets are denominated *sCAP* (*Smart Context-Aware Packets*). This architecture does not have a central control mechanism. Instead, sensors get to know the information acquired by their neighbors through the context packets they receive from them. A sensor only adds the context information to a packet it receives if this information has some similarity with the context contained in the packet. Each packet is organized in three parts: the acquisition plan, the probable context, and the acquisition path. The acquisition plan is a plan based on an initial model that is adapted each time the packet visits a sensor. The probable context is the information retrieved from the sensors. The acquisition path represents the list of sensors already visited. After visiting all the sensors specified in the acquisition plan, the packets are directly sent to the user or system that has requested them. The architecture proposed by Samulowitz et al. [28] also uses packets, in a similarly way as the Smart-its architecture.

5.4.2 Merino Architecture

The Merino architecture presented by Kummerfeld et al. [22] integrates three classes of sensors: normal sensors, intelligent sensors, and environment agents. The architecture also has a context information repository and a user model (see Figure 5.2). Sensors in higher layers produce higher level information, promoting a more complex vision of context. Sensors in lower level layers are confined to acquiring information from the environment. The repository stores the context information acquired from the sensors. Agents retrieve context information from

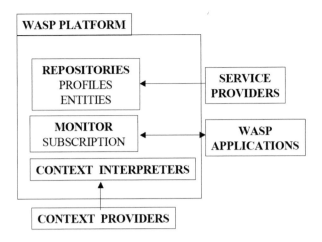

Figure 5.3: WASP architecture

the repository and produce new context information. The user model, which is controlled by an intelligent personal assistant, represents the needs of the user.

5.4.3 Architecture proposed by Cortese et al.

The architecture proposed by Cortese et al. [8] defines a logical model of architecture with two layers. This division separates sensor information capturing from its processing. In the lower layer, denominated sensors layer, the sensor information is extracted. In the upper layer, denominated semantic layer, the acquired information is adapted according to a defined ontology. The information is published in a repository where fusion agents generate additional information with a higher abstraction level.

5.4.4 WASP Architecture

The WASP architecture (*Web Architectures for Service Platforms*) [9] defines a general development environment that supports the execution of mobile services with context dependency (see Figure 5.3). The fundamental idea of this architecture is to hide the complexity introduced by context acquisition and processing from the context clients. This is done using interpretation modules that offer context to applications. These modules gather context information and make it available for the remaining platform. The platform includes repositories to support the monitoring component, which has knowledge about all elements belonging to the system. This monitoring component is responsible for the integration of WASP applications, for managing context information subscription requests, and for acquiring information from the repositories and the context interpreters. Context information is subscribed by the services registered in the platform, being further processed in the context interpreter. Ontologies are used to model context, enabling the architecture components to share knowledge among them. In order to obtain more complex context, different context supplying entities must share the same context representation. The presented architecture enables applications to obtain context information in a transparent way. Context processing problems are solved within the architecture. However, context information acquisition must be handled by the services that provide that information. The idea of hiding the context information processing complexity is an important feature of a context system.

5.4.5 CoBrA Architecture

The CoBrA architecture (*Context Broker Architecture*) [6] is an agent-based architecture that supports context awareness in intelligent systems, such as the systems that make up an intelligent house, or an intelligent vehicle (see Figure 5.4). This architecture has a central element - the context broker - that supplies a general picture of the context to the remaining agents. The context broker also supports privacy by imposing access policies defined by each client agent. The architecture incorporates the operational level in its design. The informative level is represented by the context information model. The CoBrA architecture requires the definition of a collection of ontologies to model the context. The CoBrA architecture provides a declarative language of policies that users and devices may use to limit the access to protected information. CoBrA architecture uses OWL [32] as ontology language. The context broker is an agent created to manage the shared context model. It is associated to the smart space in which the system operates, for example an intelligent house. This agent aggregates several other agents that represent smaller parts of the space.

Using this decentralized approach, communication overhead problems related with the access to a centralized mediator can be avoided. The context broker can also infer context information that cannot be easily acquired by sensors, which can be used to complete missing context elements. The context agent main function is the acquisition of context information from several sources, the fusion of this information in a coherent model and the subsequent sharing of this model with other entities in the environment. This architecture is ideal to agent networks. The use of an agent as a context broker enables CoBrA to communicate with other agent architectures, using an agent communication language. The distributed context broker results in a highly robust system, since the failure of one of the mediators does not compromise the functioning of the remaining system parts.

5.4.6 Context Taylor

This architecture proposed by Davis et al. [10, 11] is a component-based architecture that has a context service that acquires data from a set of context generation

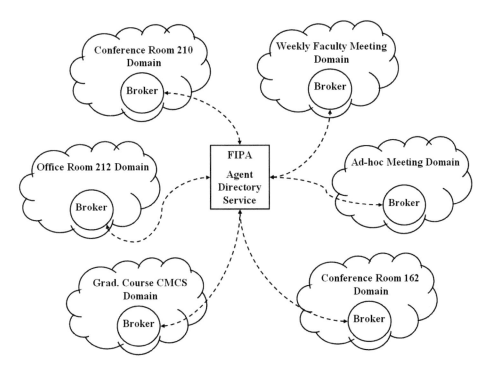

Figure 5.4: CoBrA architecture

sources. The acquired context information is stored in a repository and made available to applications via an API. Learning mechanisms extract patterns from the context information. These patterns may be used in future context information requests. The components in the architecture include generation sources, a context history repository, a learning engine, a context patterns repository, a context patterns activator, and a server that coordinates the interaction between these components. The context service works as a middleware repository that provides context about specified entities. This service manages the connection with each source of context, providing context information to applications. The structure of this architecture is presented in Figure 5.5. The server registers the context requests sent by context clients and stores all the provided context information in the context repository service. Each context entry is composed of four fields: temporal mark, user id, context type, and context state. The temporal mark allows selecting context information pertaining to a specified time interval. The user identification allows to store and access context information for different users. Each type of context corresponds to a specific representation format. The context state contains information about context of a certain type, which was observed in a certain moment. The learning mechanism applies learning algorithms to context information

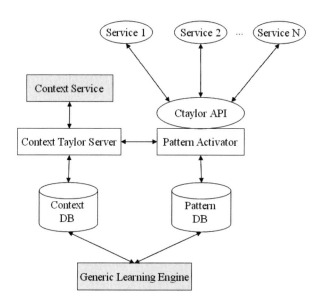

Figure 5.5: Context Taylor architecture

in the repository to abstract context patterns. These patterns are then stored in the patterns repository. Each pattern is composed of a condition, a pre-condition, a likelihood level (a value between 0 and 1 that represents the probability that the precondition predicts the condition) and a support. The conditions and pre-conditions define sets of events, and each event represents an instance of context attributes.

5.5   Summary

From the presented set of definitions, models and architectures, we conclude that a definitive solution to deal with context still does not exist. None of the described proposals addresses the whole context subject, only presenting solutions to some of the several problems related with context.

Some context definitions are too restricted ruling out important aspects of context. However most of them are too general failing to provide criteria for distinguishing context information from other kinds of information. We propose that a suitable definition of context, in the scope of context-aware computing, must allow domain and application dependent context information to be identified at design time (since particular information would righteously be considered and treated as context information in some applications but not in others); and most importantly, it should provide a clear basis for distinguishing context information from other kinds of information in terms of the way context information, but not other kinds of information, is processed. That is, definitions must have something to say about the way context information is processed in context-aware applications.

Work of more theoretical nature especially focused on context modeling and on general principles regarding context acquisition and processing proposes that context acquisition should be clearly separated from context interpretation. This work also proposes that static context information should be directly acquired from the user or other applications and may be stored in centralized repositories; while dynamic context information should be acquired by sensors and should be locally stored.

According to some authors, context representation, as specified by context ontologies, should contain several dimensions, the most important of which are entities, context elements, activities, and several kinds of associations between these (e.g., dependencies and needs). Besides individual samples of context information, it is also useful to keep historic context information.

Domain independence, improved interoperability, and the possibility to dynamically extend the context model (context ontology) are desirable properties of the context representation framework. These goals can be achieved if context ontologies have two levels: the first level describing the model that is used to represent the context ontology; and the second level representing the context ontology using the representation model defined in the first level.

Context acquisition and management systems play an important role in context-aware computation because they provide an abstraction of the context acquisition and management processes, hiding low level domain and hardware dependent details from context users and client applications. These systems should also support the two main modes of information conveying - push and pull - allowing context clients to passively receive context information whenever it changes or to receive it only upon request.

Several context acquisition and management system architectures have been proposed. These may be organized in two groups: the sensor network systems, which are more focused on the context acquisition problem; and the complete architectures, addressing both the context acquisition stage and the context processing stage, which should be totally separate processes.

Each of the proposed architectures addresses specific aspects of context acquisition and processing. For instance, sensor network architectures, such as the Smart-its, are focused on context acquisition and representation. The Merino architecture main innovation is the organization of sensors according to their level of sophistication / intelligence. It also proposes to use a context repository. Other proposals such as the WASP architecture emphasize the interaction with other applications instead of the context acquisition process.

The described complete architectures focus on important aspects that should be taken into account when designing a context system (e.g., independence of context processing from context acquisition, fusion and inference over context information, learning, and context delivery). The CoBrA architecture is more adequate for agent networks, since it provides an agent-based interface with applications, through context broker agents. The access to context information, by applications, in the other architectures is ensured by APIs. Ideally, these APIs should be flexible enough to allow adding several types of information and sensors, and to support flexible types of context searching requests. Unfortunately this is not the case.

The described architectures propose different solutions to deal with specific aspects of context-aware computing. However, none of them addresses the whole array of relevant problems. A more complete context acquisition and management system should be based on the integration of ideas put forth by the described proposals. Most of the presented architectures store all context information in central repositories which might not be a good idea, especially when there are many different sources of context acquiring a huge amount of information, and many client applications competing for system resources. A new proposal should give more attention to the integration of the sensors layer, allowing the existence and management of several types of sensors, with the context processing layer. The acquired context information should be stored in a distributed fashion. Static context information may be stored in centralized repositories; while dynamic context information should be stored locally in the sensors.

None of the architectures can be dynamically extended with new sensors of new classes of context information, in run-time. None of them supports the dynamic addition of new ontology definitions in run-time either. This is also an important feature of the context acquisition and management system developed in the CASCOM architecture.

Finally, each of the described architectures provides only one type of interface (e.g., agent-based, or API). Since context systems should be independent of their client applications, it would be a good idea to implement at least the most common types of interface.

References

[1] Ambient Networks Consortium. Ambient Networks. http://www.ambient-networks.org, 2006.

[2] C. Anagnostopoulos, A. Tsounis and S. Hadjiefthymiades: Context Awareness in Mobile Computing Environments: A Survey. Mobile e-conference, Information Society Technologies, 2004.

[3] L. Capra, W. Emmerich and C. Mascolo: Reflective Middleware Solutions for Context-Aware Applications. Proceedings of the Third international Conference on Metalevel Architectures and Separation of Crosscutting Concerns LNCS, Vol. 2192. Springer-Verlag, London, 126-133. 2001.

[4] L. Capra, W. Emmerich and C. Mascolo: CARISMA: Context-Aware Reflective mIddleware System for Mobile Applications. IEEE Transactions on Software Engineering, vol. 29, no. 10, pp. 929-945, Oct., 2003.

[5] D. Chalmers and M. Sloman: QoS and Context Awareness for Mobile Computing. Proceedings of the 1st international Symposium on Handheld and Ubiquitous Computing, LNCS Vol. 1707. Springer-Verlag, London, 380-382. 1999.

[6] H. Chen, T. Finin and A. Joshi: An Intelligent Broker for Context-Aware Systems. Adjunct Proceedings of Ubicomp 2003, Seattle, Washington, USA, October 12-15, 2003.

[7] E. Christopoulou, C. Goumopoulos, I. Zaharakis and A. Kameas: An Ontology-based Conceptual Model for Composing Context-Aware Applications. In Research Academic Computer Technology Institute, 2004.

[8] G. Cortese M. Lunghi and F. Davide: Context-Awareness for Physical Service Environments. Ambient Intelligence, IOS press, 2004.

[9] P. D. Costa, J. G. P. Filho and M. van Sinderen: Architectural Requirements for Building Context-Aware Services Platforms. IFIP workshop on Next Generation Networks, Balatonfured, Hungary, 8-10 September, 2003.

[10] J. S. Davis, D. M. Sow, M. Blount and M. R. Ebling: Context tailor: Towards a programming model for context-aware computing. Proceedings of the first International Workshop on Middleware for Pervasive and Ad Hoc Computing (MPAC)., pages 68-75, Rio De Janeiro, Brazil, 16-20 June, 2003.

[11] J. S. Davis, D. M. Sow and M. R. Ebling: Context-sensitive Invocation Using the Context Tailor Infrastructure. System Support for Ubiquitous 94 Computing Workshop at the Fifth Annual Conference on Ubiquitous Computing, October 2003.

[12] A. K. Dey: Context-Aware Computing: The CyberDesk Project. AAAI 1998 Spring Symposium on Intelligent Environments, Technical Report SS-98-02, pp 51-54, 1998.

[13] A. K. Dey and G. D. Abowd: Towards a better understanding of context and context awareness. In GVU Technical Report GIT-GVU-99-22, College of Computing, Georgia Institute of Technology, 1999.

[14] A. K. Dey, D. Salber and G. D. Abowd: A conceptual framework and a toolkit for supporting the rapid prototyping of context-aware applications. Human Computer Interaction, 2001.

[15] J. G. P. Filho and M. van Sinderen: Web Service architectures, semantics and context-awareness issues in Web Services platforms. WASP/D3.3, 16-26, 2003.

[16] H. W. Gellersen, A. Schmidt and M. Beigl: Multi-sensor context-awareness in mobile devices and smart artifacts. Mobile Networks Applications 7, 5, 341-351, October, 2002.

[17] R. Gold and C. Mascolo: Use of Context-Awareness in Mobile Peer-to-Peer Networks. Proceedings of the 8th IEEE Workshop on Future Trends of Distributed Computing Systems. IEEE Computer Society, Washington, DC, 142, 2002.

[18] K. Goslar, S. Burchholz, A. Schill and H. Vogler: A Multidimensional approach to Context-Awareness. In Proceedings of the 7th World Multiconference on Systemics, Cybernetics and Informatics (SCI2003), 2003.

[19] K. Henricksen, J. Indulska and A. Rakotonirainy: Modeling Context Information in Pervasive Computing Systems. In Pervasive '02: Proceedings of the First International Conference on Pervasive Computing, pp. 167-180, 2002.

[20] J. I. Hong and J. A. Landay: An Infrastructure Approach to Context-Aware Computing. Human-Computer Interaction, 16:287-303, 2001.

[21] P. Korpipää and J. Mäntyjärvi: An Ontology for Mobile Device Sensor-Based Context Awareness. Fourth International and Interdisciplinary Conference on Modeling and Using Context (CONTEXT 2003): 451-458. Stanford, California (USA), June 23-25, 2003.

[22] B. Kummerfeld, A. Quigley, C. Johnson and R. Hexel: Merino:Towards an intelligent environment architecture for multigranularity context description. User Modeling for Ubiquitous Computing, 2003.

[23] H. Laamanen and H. Helin: Contex-Awareness, Overview and State-of-Art. CASCOM project Technical Report, TeliaSonera, 2004.

[24] F. Michahelles and M. Samulowitz: Smart CAPs for Smart Its Context Detection for Mobile Users. Personal Ubiquitous Computing 6, 4, 269-275. January, 2002.

[25] P. Preko and M. Burnett: Activities, context and ubiquitous computing. Elsevier Science PII: S0140-3664(02)00251-7, 2002.

[26] M. Ritchie: Pre and Post Processing for Service Based Context-Awareness. Technical Report Equator-02-023, University of Glasgow / Department of Computing Science, 2002.

[27] H. K. Rubinsztejn, M. Endler, V. Sacramento, K. Gonalves and F. Nascimento: Support for Contex-Aware Collaboration. Mobility Aware Technologies and Applications, LNCS 3284, pp. 37-47, 2004.

[28] M. Samulowitz, F. Michahelles and C. Linnhoff-Popien: Adaptive interaction for enabling pervasive services. Proceedings of the 2nd ACM international Workshop on Data Engineering For Wireless and Mobile Access (Santa Barbara, California, United States). S. Banerjee, Ed. MobiDe '01. ACM Press, New York, NY, 20-26. 2001.

[29] B. Schilit and M. Theimer: Disseminating Active Map Information to Mobile Hosts. IEEE Network, 8(5):22-32, 1994.

[30] A. Schmidt, M. Beigl and H. W. Gellersen: There is more to Context than Location. Proceedings of the International Workshop on Interactive Applications of Mobile Computing (IMC98), Rostock, Germany, November 1998.

[31] T. Winograd: Arquitectures for Context. HI Journal, 2001.

[32] World Wide Web Consortium. OWL-S 1.0 Release. http://www.daml.org/services/owl-s/1.0, 2005.

[33] S. S. Yau and F. Karim: Reconfigurable Context-Sensitive Middleware for ADS Applications in Mobile Ad Hoc Network Environments. In Proceedings of the Fifth international Symposium on Autonomous Decentralized Systems. ISADS. IEEE Computer Society, Washington, DC, 319. March, 2001.

Chapter 6

Technology in Healthcare

Gert Brettlecker, César Cáceres, Alberto Fernández, Nadine Fröhlich,
Ari Kinnunen, Sascha Ossowski, Heiko Schuldt, Matteo Vasirani

6.1 Introduction

The term "e-health" was born in 1999 to represent the provision of healthcare
services through Internet [11], and was heavily promoted by the industry and
commercial sectors in order to take advantage of the power and excitement that
other "e-" terms like e-commerce and e-business had recently created in society [8,
6]. Nevertheless, the academic world would soon adopt it, leading to what some
authors call "the death of telemedicine" [14].

The term was so wide that anything to do with technology and health was
included. In this direction, the European Commission proposed the following definition for e-health [7]: "the use of modern information and communication technologies to meet needs of citizens, patients, healthcare professionals, healthcare
providers, as well as policy makers". In this definition, other disciplines like medical informatics, health informatics or telemedicine would be included.

There are numerous definitions of e-health, as the Figure 6.1 from [13] shows,
but most of them reduce to the same basic idea: e-health is the use of ICT for
health.

In order to illustrate the multiple applications that e-health embraces, a
five layer model is proposed [2, 5], as shown in Figure 6.2. At the base there
are two basic layers, the physical infrastructure and the informatic and telematic
services layers, both corresponding to the ICT. Those layers support all the basic
e-health services which will build the health applications higher up, depending on
the particular scenario. Sometimes a health application is based on only one e-
health service, which could even coincide with the use case scenario. For example,
a remote surgical operation (scenario) will be carried out from the surgery clinical
specialty (application), using the e-health service of telesurgery.

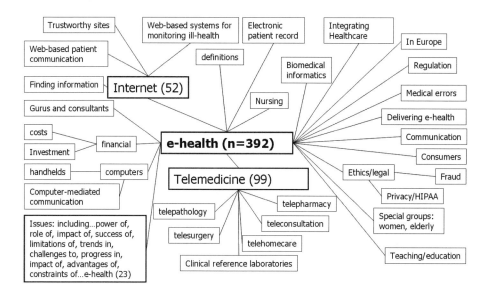

Figure 6.1: Concept map of the use of the e-health term in different papers, from [13]

6.2 Objectives

Central to all the e-health definitions is that the use of information and communication technology, such as the Internet, is required for long distance delivery of health services. The use of the Internet in e-health is likely to increase as more healthcare organizations switch to broadband Internet connections. Wireless connectivity is also another interesting characteristic that technologies are offering for this particular domain, especially for mobility that will be discussed in the next section of the chapter.

One of the main objectives of ICT in healthcare is achieving the interoperability of medical information systems and Electronic Health Records, by creating a common architecture (middleware) for delivering healthcare services and also collaborative platforms (CSCW) to improve cooperation between different disciplines in the healthcare domain.

The use of ICT is also a key stone to respond to privacy needs related with healthcare, like preserve confidentiality with a high level of security and promoting the use of e-cards in healthcare to facilitate mobility and identification.

Another objective that ICT addresses is facilitating the mobility: develop services that cover every situation we could think of (anyone, anywhere, anytime, anyhow, ...), or walking towards m-health with wireless solutions and portable devices.

Finally, ICT makes easier the management of the huge amount of information

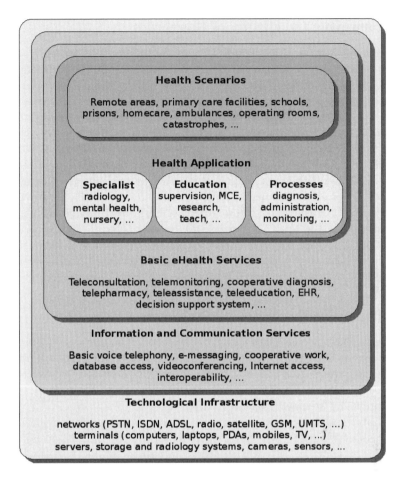

Figure 6.2: Layered model of e-health

that healthcare generates, by creating repositories of validated health information on the Internet to win the battle with bad and misleading information now existing.

In the next section we will show how the healthcare domain benefits from new technologies and what barriers exist for their implementation.

6.3 Benefits of e-Health

The benefits of using ICT for health could be grouped in three aspects [1]: improving the quality of healthcare, facilitate the access to healthcare and reducing costs.

6.3.1   Improving the Quality of Healthcare

One of the main contributions that ICT can make to improve the quality of health-care is to provide the healthcare professional with the information needed at the right time about the health of the patients. Now, thanks essentially to the computerization of the health records and the use of decision support or expert systems, some aspects can be achieved. The transfer of complex health records globally and in real time, increases the accessibility, unifies the information at every healthcare level and improves care continuity and the professional info exchange.

Collecting data and and take decision can be done in real time by workers equipped with mobile devices. Also a more efficient patient care management is possible, thanks to the optimization of healthcare resources, the improvement on the care demand management, the reduction of hospital stays and the decrease on extra medical acts and tests.

This not only leads to an improvement on productivity (e.g. time spent with bureaucratic tasks may be reduced), but also to a better care than the conventional care model, by the development of a new patient centred healthcare model.

6.3.2   Improving the Access of Healthcare

Technologies offer the possibility for anyone to access from anywhere (remote areas, for instance), anytime and in the most convenient way, to the needed healthcare or health information. In this way, ICT technologies can promote the universality and equity of healthcare access and mitigate the lack of health professionals, especially for geographically or socially isolated patients.

ICT also speeds up consultations between primary and specialized care in acute cases (enabling the possibility of a second opinion for diagnosis), and improves patient follow-up, specially in chronic illnesses.

By increasing the homecare services, it is possible to reduce the number of patient's visits and waiting lists, preventing unnecessary waste of time for both patients and professionals. In this way, treatments can be provided more rapidly and in the right place, preventing the unnecessary transfer of patients and improving their quality of life.

ICT plays also a fundamental role for the provision of information to patients. Informing patients about preventive care strategies in a faster and easier way enhances people's health knowledge and promoting self-care. The professionals can receive continuous education, preventing the professional isolation and stimulating their abilities using teleconsultations and videoconferences as learning tools

6.3.3   Reducing Costs

It is widely known that paper based systems are inefficient, with a lot of administrative procedures and possible health fraud. By improving the financial and management information administration, ICT facilitates health fraud detection.

The introduction of technologies can improve both the provision of health services and the reduction of costs in some of the processes. ICT can help to optimize administrative procedures, simplify request circuits and reduce administrative errors, for example eliminating information duplicates and redundant analysis with their associated costs.

It can also reduce both direct costs, like travel expenses (for both patients and professionals) or hospital stays, and indirect costs, speeding up the patients incorporation to their jobs. Globally, it reduces global health expenses enhancing an earlier assistance and preventing the need of further care (usually more expensive).

6.4 Barriers and Challenges of e-Health

Despite all the benefits just presented, the introduction of ICT in healthcare has had many difficulties from the technical, social, political, legal or economical point of view [12, 1, 10, 9, 3, 4, 15]. Many of these barriers are a consequence of the incredible speed of development of the technologies and the number of people and disciplines involved in the process.

The main challenges that e-health must tackle are, from a technological point of view, the lack of standards in the health industry as well as the need of the newest and leading technologies.

Also human organizations poses social barriers to the adoption of e-health. From one side, the distrust of ICT when the data are sensible and protecting electronic information's privacy, security, integrity and confidentiality is necessary. From the other side, the the users' inexperience with technologies, the limited access of patients to ICT (not only in knowledge, but also for economical or availability limitations), the adaptation of doctors to new ways of caring patients may slow down the introduction of ICT in healtcare.

Again, since e-health can (and must) be transnational, it is absolutely necessary the European Medical License for the professionals to work across borders.

Finally, the distance between the actual research and the real needs of the health system poses several problems to a wide adoption of ICT. The lack of data and methodology for the economic evaluation of e-health projects (e.g. e-health services reimbursement is not well defined) is an obstacle for the clinical routine implementation of the e-health systems as well as to obtain funds for new e-health projects.

6.5 Mobility (m-Health)

M-health means mobile healthcare. It mainly addresses mobile services which collect, transmit, filter, and processe vital patient data in real time, e.g., heart rate and blood pressure. It is especially important in applications that remotely monitor patients with chronic ailments or in home care. The overview of research in the mobile healthcare area (*m-health*) presented in this section is organized as follows: Firstly, we introduce m-health applications and describe their major requirements. Secondly, we present orthogonal technology research issues tackled by the investigated m-health projects. Thirdly, we give an overview of current and recent academic and commercial research and already available commercial products in this area.

6.5.1   m-Health Applications

Generally, m-health applications are driven by the demand of access to medical information in a mobile and ubiquitous setting. This access may either be relevant medical information retrieval by healthcare practitioners, e.g., a hospital doctor on his/her ward round, or the acquisition of relevant medical information generated by patients, e.g., telemonitoring the patient's health state outside of the hospital. In both cases, the person retrieving or generating information wants to interact with the m-health infrastructure without any obstruction or adaptation of the normal workflow or style of working. The most characteristic application requirements are:

- *Human computer interaction through mobile devices* that provide access to relevant health-related information independent of the current physical location of the user. This includes the exploitation of *networking and wireless communication*.

- *Context and location awareness*, i.e., the access to or the visualization of health-related information might depend on location and/or context.

- *Unobtrusive sensor technology* which allows for gathering physiological information from a patient without hampering his/her daily life.

- *Signal processing and pattern recognition* to derive medical relevant information out of sensor signals.

- *Fault-tolerance and reliability*. This is a unique feature in e-health applications and thus also in m-health where the usage of IT might potentially be life saving, and downtimes due to erroneous behaviour of the m-health system cannot be tolerated.

Smart Hospital / Smart Emergency Applications

At the caregiver's site, m-health applications appear in the context of smart-hospital scenarios [16, 17, 19]. These applications try to improve the daily activities of doctors and nurses. This is done by providing tools to access patient records or, more generally, clinical information systems, as well as to schedule and track patients and hospital resources in a wireless, mobile, and context-aware way.

Moreover, recent projects introduce the use of RFID technology to further improve this scenario [40].

Another application of m-health at the caregiver's site is smart emergency management [16], where information access by using mobile devices is used to support emergency services. Emergency physicians are able to access the records of their patients in advance while they are still in the ambulance car approaching the current location of a patient. If we also consider the triggering of emergency situations and access of current physiological signals, this scenario spans the bridge between the caregiver's and patient's site. Therefore, this scenario closely interacts with the m-health scenario presented in the next section.

Physiological Telemonitoring

Telemonitoring, the continuous monitoring of patients at home, is becoming a more and more important application domain in the context of m-health [22, 23, 24, 28], mainly due to the progression of chronic ailments in an aging society. First, such applications enable healthcare institutions to take care of and control therapies regarding their patients while they are out of hospital. Second, they serve as instrument for performing research and for accomplishing medical studies. Third, they allow for triggering of emergency services in case of severe health conditions. Due to the nature of the application which is continuously monitoring physiological signals, unobtrusiveness and mobility of the patient are key requirements. Finally, these applications can offer additional comfort services as by-product, like assistive services, information services and communication services, which leads us to the next m-health scenario.

Assistive Living Applications

The integration of smart-home automation is an essential aspect of assisted living for the elderly or for impaired people [16, 25, 18, 30]. The projects in this domain are the most challenging ones, because the issues of telemonitoring mentioned above are also relevant here. Elderly people tend to suffer from at least one chronic disease, which requires telemonitoring. Additional age-related impairments make independent living at home difficult and therefore assistance for daily activities is required. Moreover, the additional context information provided by a smart-home environment enhances a better interpretation of physiological sensor information, e.g., whether the patient is running or sleeping has significant influence on the blood pressure. Blood pressure readings which are normal for physical activity, may indicate a severe health condition if occurring while sleeping.

6.5.2 Technology Issues in m-Health

The different projects have different technological emphases. They either focus on infrastructure, networking and/or hardware (embedded systems and sensors).

Infrastructure

M-health projects which focus on the infrastructure have to deal with different network density and different devices (PDAs, PCs). One point of interest is the dynamic assembly of new devices. They have to solve problems in routing, naming, discovery, quality of service and security and therefore they use different kinds of architectures.

Projects which focus, among other aspects, on infrastructure issues include Akogrimo [16], projects at BMI [18], Equator [20], Pervasive Healthcare [17], and projects at VTT [25].

Networking

When projects focus on networking important research themes are smooth handovers in roaming situations, limitations in bandwidth of used respectively usable wireless networks.

Projects that address specific aspects in networking include MobiHealth [22], MyHeart [23], U-R-Safe [24], Code Blue [19].

Hardware

In m-health projects it is especially important that sensors are small, lightweight, and wearable since they are used in mobile environments and the people that wear these devices are ill and/or old. An additional constraint is low power sensing, computation, and communication as huge batteries make the devices heavy and bulky for mobile use. Thus also the memory used for data sampling and processing has to be small. It is also important that the collected data can be shown in real time.

Projects that focus on hardware include Code Blue [19], Equator [20], IM3 [21], MobiHealth [22], MyHeart [23], and U-R-Safe [24].

6.5.3   Overview of m-Health Projects

In this section, we give an overview of current research in the area of m-health. For this reason, we selected a few representative projects for a more detailed presentation.

Akogrimo

Akogrimo [16] is funded by the EC under FP6. The project integrates Next Generation Grids (NGG) and next Generation Networks. The application scenarios of Akogrimo cover smart hospitals, telemonitoring and emergency assistance. The Akogrimo NGGs are able to deal with an environment with rapidly changing context such as bandwidth, device capabilities, and location. Furthermore the architecture can be immediately deployed in Unlicensed Mobile Access (UMA) environments such as hot-spot infrastructures because it assumes a pure IP-based underlying network infrastructure.

MobiHealth

The generic BAN (body area network) software platform is the heart of the architecture of the FP5-EU project MobiHealth. It provides plug and play sensor connectivity and handles related issues such as security, QoS and hand-over. It enables monitoring, storage, and wireless transmission (e.g., by using GPRS and UMTS technologies) of vital signals data coming from the patient BAN. Possible hardware platforms for this architecture are PDAs or programmable mobile phones which can serve as Mobile Base Units (MBUs). The investigated application scenario is telemonitoring of patients at home.

MyHeart

MyHeart [23] is a research project funded by the EU under FP6. The focus of MyHeart is on preventing cardiovascular diseases by applying m-health applications. The work focuses, in particular, on the telemonitoring scenario, where sensors integrated in clothing are used to monitor heart activity and physical activity of the patient. This project emphasizes the importance of specialized sensor and device hardware to allow unobtrusive measurements. Moreover, application-specific issues and benefits for patients are evaluated.

U-R-Safe

U-R-Safe [24] is a research project funded by the EU under FP5. U-R-Safe builds a telemonitoring environment for elderly people and patients with chronic diseases. The project develops a portable device which continuously monitors physiological signals (heart activity, oxygen saturation, and fall detection) and is able to send an alarm to a medical center if an abnormality is detected. The technology issues tackled in this project cover sensor devices and wireless communication. Moreover application issues are investigated in this work.

Academic Research Projects

Some projects are hardware and sensor oriented as Code Blue. Here wireless vital signal sensors are designed to collect vital data and transmit them over a short-range wireless network to receiving devices. Furthermore a scalable software infrastructure for wireless medical devices is created. It provides routing, naming, discovery, and security for wireless medical sensors, and devices for monitoring and treating of patients. Thereby Code Blue can adapt to different network densities and different powerful wireless devices.

Equator is another sensor-based project. It aims at continuously monitoring and analyzing a patient at home by using mobile low-cost wearable devices. The devices send medical signals via wireless network connections to the grid, thereby automatically updating the patients records.

In IM3 new medical services allow wireless monitoring of vital signals independent of time and place. Patients use wearable sensors. The sensor data are collected and communicated by Medical hub devices (e.g., a cell phone or a PDA) and stored in the IM3 back-end server for remote follow-ups.

Other work in this field is more focused on the infrastructure issues and requirements demanded by m-health applications [18, 26, 25, 17]. In particular the *Center for Pervasive Healthcare* [17] is focused on aspects of infrastructure and application requirements in order to apply pervasive and nomadic computing to healthcare.

Commercial Research

Also commercial research is focusing on the area of mobile healthcare. *Healthservice 24* [27] a commercial oriented follow-up project of Mobihealth [22] is aimed at testing the feasibility of the services provided by Mobihealth in real world settings.

IBM Research [28] is working with medical device and mobile phone manufactures in order to develop *Personal Care Connect* to track vital signals.

Microsoft research [29] is developing a similar application, called *HealthGear* in order to allow for wearable and wireless monitoring of physiological signals.

The *Proactive Health Lab* of Intel research [30] is focusing on the assistive living scenario, where ubiquitous computing is improving the wellness and daily life of elderly citizens.

Continuous monitoring of physiological signals is also a research topic of HP Labs within their *BioStream* project [31]. BioStream offers a realtime operator for managing sensor streams, i.e., operators that continuously process physiological signals generated by the sensors attached to a patient.

The Philips Healthcare Systems Architecture Group [32] works on various subjects within the personal healthcare domain. One aspect of the project is to help people with chronic diseases by telemonitoring facilities. Another aspect is a smart personal coach for wellness management.

Commercial Products

There are already commercial products available that support m-health applications. These solutions are mostly device-oriented monitoring systems where sensors or in-home devices collect vital data and send them to a central system for access and analysis by physicians. Currently, these products are rather limited to specific tasks or diseases. The developed products rather focus on sensor technology or wireless communication; a product offering a reliable information management infrastructure as a backbone for m-health applications is still missing.

A group of products in this field are using telemetry functions provided by pacemakers or defibrillators in the context of cardiovascular diseases [33, 34, 35].

The sensor readings acquired by implanted devices are wireless transmitted via a mobile phone to the caregiver.

Bodymedia [36] and *MedStar* [37] allow a more general setup where mobile sensors attached to the patients body acquire the physiological signals.

Philips is offering a large set of telemonitoring solutions [38], in particular wireless measurement devices. These include, for instance, blood pressure and pulse units, pulse oximeters, ECG heart rhythm strip recorders, glucose meter devices, and even bluetooth-enabled electronic scales.

Finally, the *Lifeshirt* system of Vivometrics of is offering one of the most sophisticated sensor devices. The offered Lifeshirt senses more than 30 physiological parameters, such as pulmonary, cardiac, and other physiologic data, and producing roughly one gigabyte of data per day.

6.6 CASCOM in the Healthcare Domain

Although the CASCOM project has been designed to be general and is not restricted to a particular domain, the healthcare domain is an interesting and challenging domain for an application based on the CASCOM platform. Before analyzing the possible benefits of CASCOM in the patient care, it is useful to introduce some technical concepts related with the healthcare domain.

6.6.1 Concepts

Definitive Care

Definitive care is the set of treatments and practices to apply in order to guarantee a patient's perfect recovery from an illness or injury.

Final Outcome

The *final outcome* is nowadays not only the survival of the patient, but also his/her quality of life. In the best case, the period of incapacity is very short and afterward no permanent handicap can be seen or felt.

Total Costs

Total costs of healthcare services are rarely known with great accuracy, or at least it is very time consuming to calculate them. Total costs are considered to encompass all the expenses sustained from the beginning of the illness to the complete recovery. Generally it is believed that by making the right diagnosis and starting the definitive care on time, the total costs can be sensitively reduced.

Medical Emergency Service

A *medical emergency service* is the kind of healthcare services that must be delivered in an out-of-hospital phase.

Emergency Patient

Emergency patients are those people that run a high risk of dying or suffering from a permanent handicap, if the patient is not reached and treated on time. Emergency patients should be monitored by an alarm centre and attended by a paramedic as soon as possible, even before they can receive specialized treatment.

Alarm (or Dispatch) Centre

An *alarm centre* is an institution that handles emergency calls. In most countries common alarm numbers (e.g., 112, 911) are used to guarantee that anyone can rapidly get in contact with the appropriate authorities (police, rescue, emergency care), if needed. An alarm centre operator – on the basis of the information provided by the caller – determines the appropriate response, which in most cases means dispatching relevant units (e.g., a fire engine or an ambulance).

Criteria Based Dispatching (CBD)

In *criteria based dispatching*, an alarm centre operator follows a predefined flow-chart to interrogate the caller to estimate the medical risk, on the basis of his/her symptoms.

Computer Aided Dispatching (CAD)

In *computer aided dispatching* different technological solutions are used to estimate the patient's medical risk and to locate him/her and the nearest emergency medical service unit (e.g., ambulance), which can provide emergency care.

Emergency Care

Emergency care aims to keep the patient's airway open and secure, in order to maintain sufficient ventilation and circulation. By starting emergency care on-site and continuing it during the transfer to the healtcare centre, some additional time can be gained to start definitive care still in time.

6.7   Summary

The impact of the Information and Communication Technologies on the healthcare domain increased during the last years at an incredible pace. The evolution of the Internet provided a new empowering environment for e-health to become a reality.

In this chapter some of the benefits of the application of ICT on healthcare are described, such as improving the access to a better quality care at a lower cost. But also the drawbacks have to be taking into account, like the lack of standardization and some social and legal barriers.

One of the great advantages of e-health is the provision of services in mobility scenarios (the so called m-health). The huge investment on mobile technologies have now provided better infrastructure, networks and hardware, offering in this way an excellent opportunity for building m-health applications, like telemonitoring physiological parameters, smart emergency scenarios or assisted living for the elderly or for impaired people. In this chapter some of the main research and commercial projects on m-health are described as examples of these new services.

Although the CASCOM project has been designed to be general and is not restricted to a particular domain, the healthcare domain is quite interesting and challenging for building an application based on the CASCOM platform, as introduced in this chapter and described in the rest of the book.

References

[1] G.A. Barnes, M. Uncapher, *Getting to e-Health: The Opportunities for Using IT in the Health Care Industry.* Information Technology Association of America (ITAA), 2000.

[2] C. Caceres, *New telemedical procedures for the follow-up and caring of chronic HIV patients.* PhD Thesis. Universidad Politecnica de Madrid, 2007.

[3] *Strategy and e-Health: How to Harness the Power of the Internet for Competetive Advantage in Health Care.* A Health Care Study by Deloitte Consulting and Deloitte & Touche, 2001.

[4] *Promoting Physician Adoption of Advanced Clinical Information Systems: A Deloitte Point of View.* Deloitte Center for Health Solutions, 2006.

[5] F. Del Pozo, M. E. Hernando, and E. J. Gómez, *Telemedicine: Ubiquitous patient care.* Wiley Encyclopedia of Biomedical Engineering. John Wiley & Sons Inc., 2006.

[6] V. Della Mea, *What is e-Health (2): The death of telemedicine?*, Journal of Medical Internet Research 2001;3(2):e22.

[7] European eHealth Ministerial Declaration. Brussels, 22 May 2003. Available at: `http://ec.europa.eu/information_society/eeurope/ehealth/conference/2003/doc/min_dec_22_may_03.pdf`

[8] G. Eysenbach, *What is e-health?*, Journal of Medical Internet Research 2001;3(2):e20.

[9] A. R. Jadad, V. Goel, C. Rizo, J. Hohenadel, and A. Cortinois, *The Global e-Health Innovation Network - Building a Vehicle for the Transformation of*

the Health System in the Information Age. Business Briefing: Next Generation Healthcare, pp. 48-54, 2000.

[10] S. Laxminarayan, and B. H. Stamm, *Technology, Telemedicine and Telehealth,* Business Briefing: Global Healthcare Issue 3: pp. 93-6, 2002.

[11] K. McLendon, *E-commerce and HIM: Ready or not, here it comes,* Journal of the American Health Information Management Association, 71 (1), pp. 22-23, 2000.

[12] A. Ohinmaa, D. Hailey, and R. Roine, *The Assessment of Telemedicine: General principles and a systematic review.* INAHTA Joint Project. Finnish Office for Health Care Technology Assessment and Alberta Heritage Foundation for Medical Research, 1999.

[13] C. Pagliari, D. Sloan, P. Gregor, F. Sullivan, D. Detmer, J. P. Kahan, W. Oortwijn, S. MacGillivray, *What Is eHealth (4): A Scoping Exercise to Map the Field.* Journal of Medical Internet Research 2005;7(1):e9.

[14] E. Rosen, *The death of telemedicine?,* Telemedicine Today 2000;8(1):14-17.

[15] P. Wilson, C. Leitner, and A. Moussalli, *Mapping the Potential of eHealth: Empowering the Citizen through eHealth Tools and Services,* eHealth Conference, Cork, Ireland, 5-6 May 2004.

[16] Access to Knowledge through the Grid in a Mobile World (Akogrimo). EU IST FP6 Project: http://www.mobilegrids.org

[17] Centre for Pervasive Healthcare. University of Aarhus, Denmark: http://www.pervasivehealthcare.dk

[18] Biomedical Informatics Laboratory, Institute of Computer Science, Foundation for Research and Technology, Hellas, Greece: http://www.ics.forth.gr/eHealth/r-d-activities.html

[19] CodeBlue: Wireless Sensor Networks for Medical Care, School of Engineering and Applied Sciences, Harvard University, Cambridge, MA: http://www.eecs.harvard.edu/~mdw/proj/codeblue/

[20] Equator - Digital Care, Project funded by the Engineering and Physical Sciences Research Council, UK: http://www.equator.ac.uk/index.php/articles/summary/c63/

[21] Interactive Medical Monitoring (IM3), Interdisciplinary Institute for Broad-Band Technology, Belgium: https://projects.ibbt.be/im3/

[22] Mobihealth. EU IST FP5 Project: http://www.mobihealth.org/

[23] MyHeart. EU IST FP6 Project: http://www.hitech-projects.com/euprojects/myheart/

[24] Universal Remote Signal Acquisition For hEalth (U-R-SAFE). EU IST FP5 Project: `http://ursafe.tesa.prd.fr/ursafe/index.html`

[25] Technical Research Centre of Finland, Wellness and Healthcare: `http://www.vtt.fi/`

[26] Upkar Varshney, "Managing Wireless Health Monitoring for Patients with Disabilities," IT Professional, vol. 08, no. 6, pp. 12-16, Nov/Dec, 2006

[27] HealthService 24. EU eTen Project: `http://www.healthservice24.com`

[28] Personal Care Connect (PPC). IBM Research Zurich: `http://www.zurich.ibm.com/pcc/`

[29] HealthGear: Real-time Wearable System for Monitoring and Analyzing Physiological Signals. Microsoft Research: `http://research.microsoft.com/ nuria/healthgear/healthgear.htm`

[30] Proactive Health Lab. Intel Research: `http://www.intel.com/research/prohealth/`

[31] Bar-Or, et. Al., "BioStream: A System Architecture for Real-Time Processing of Physiological Signals", EEE Engineering in Medicine and Biology Society Conference (EMBS), San Francisco, CA, 2006: `http://www.hpl.hp.com/techreports/2004/HPL-2004-128.html`

[32] The Healthcare Systems Architecture Group (HSA). Philips Research: `http://www.extra.research.philips.com/swa/index.html`

[33] Cardionet: `http://www.cardionet.com/`

[34] Medtronic Carelink: `http://www.medtronic.com/carelink/`

[35] Biotronik Home Monitoring Service: `http://www.biotronik-healthservices.com/`

[36] Bodymedia: `http://www.bodymedia.com/main.jsp`

[37] Cybernet Medical, Medstar: `http://www.cybernetmedical.com/`

[38] Philips Telemedicine Solutions: `http://www.medical.philips.com/in/products/telemonitoring/`

[39] Vivometrics, Continuous Ambulatory Monitoring, The Lifeshirt System: `http://www.lifeshirt.com/`

[40] Siemens Business Services, Jacobi Medical Center Case Study: `http://www.it-solutions.usa.siemens.com/press/docs/ jacobimedical-casestudy.pdf`

Part II

The CASCOM Solution

Chapter 7

General Architecture

Alberto Fernández, Sascha Ossowski, Matteo Vasirani

7.1 Introduction

The CASCOM approach is a combination of agent technology, Semantic Web Service coordination, P2P, and mobile computing for intelligent peer-to-peer (IP2P) mobile service environments. IP2P environments (see Chapter 2) are extensions to conventional P2P architectures with components for mobile and ad hoc computing, wireless communications, and a broad range of pervasive devices. Basic IP2P facilities come as Web Services, while their reliable, task-oriented, resource-bounded, and adaptive co-ordination-on-the-fly characteristics call for agent-based software technology.

A major challenge in IP2P environments is to guarantee a secure spread of service requests across multiple transmission infrastructures and ensure the trustworthiness of services that may involve a variety of providers. The services of the CASCOM infrastructure are provided by peer software agents exploiting the co-ordination infrastructure to efficiently operate in dynamic environments. The IP2P infrastructure includes efficient communication means, support for context-aware adaptation techniques, as well as dynamic and secure service discovery and composition planning.

Given that the CASCOM architecture builds on an assumption that users are providing services to other users, it is essential that these services work on a broad range of devices. Therefore, the focus is on solutions that can be applied to mobile devices lacking processing capabilities of their office counterparts. Another point that is vital when adapting software to mobile devices is the limitation of wireless communication paths, in terms of data bandwith, which these devices typically employ. In the CASCOM architecture, the services are adapted not only to the constraints of mobile devices but also to the constraints of wireless communication paths (e.g., by optimizing the communication over wireless connection). In the latter case, the concept of seamless service experience is essential. Seamless service experience means an environment in which users have an easy and seamless access to electronic services, applications, and information anywhere and anytime.

The chapter is structured as follows: in Section 7.2 the technical approach of the CASCOM project is described, in Section 7.3 is envisioned a conceptual architecture that is able to provide the required functionalities, in Section 7.4 is presented an in depth description of the different elements composing the system, while in Section 7.5 are described the different possible instantiations of the CASCOM architecture.

7.2   Technical Approach

Software agents are a key technology to address the challenges of the CASCOM architecture as they offer an adequate abstraction for dealing with services from pervasive devices in IP2P environments. In turn, IP2P networks provide a suitable environment for agents to collaborate as peers sharing information, tasks, and responsibilities with each other. Agents can help manage the complexity of P2P networks, and they can be used to improve the functionality of conventional P2P systems and protocols. The inherently autonomous nature of intelligent agents helps achieving peer node autonomy, which is a requirement to operate efficiently in highly dynamic environments. The innovations of CASCOM in the agent domain concern the development of context-aware agent-based services in the Semantic Web, and flexible resource-efficient co-ordination of such services in the nomadic computing field.

Using agents in wireless environments has been an active research area in the past few years [27]. Several researchers have addressed these issues by developing agent platforms for resource-poor devices enabling them to run agent-based software (e.g., [26, 2]). However, the IP2P aspects are typically insufficiently taken into account and thus the CASCOM project aims at producing a relevant advancement in this direction. Wireless communication in agent systems has been addressed in many levels [12]. However, agent communication methods for wireless environments typically assume proxies in the fixed network. On the other hand, the CASCOM project provides solutions for agent communication in wireless environments with minimal assumption of fixed infrastructure.

Service co-ordination mechanisms of P2P systems can be applied to multiagent systems to improve their efficiency. Although this may be accepted on a conceptual level, the combination of agents and P2P environments certainly deserves more innovative research and development, especially regarding nomadic environments. However, many modern P2P overlay network algorithms (e.g., [21, 22, 24, 29]) lack support for rapid node movements and expect that the network topology remains relatively static. This assumption no longer holds in highly dynamic environments, where a node providing a service may be mobile and connected to the overlay network using a wireless connection. However, some distributed hash table algorithms taking mobility and wireless environments into account have been developed (e.g., M-CAN [20] and Warp [28]). But, the dynamic topology of IP2P networks, the fluctuating QoS of wireless network connections, and the limited capacity of mobile devices connected to such networks pose several challenges that typically have been addressed inadequately in service co-ordination architectures.

The problem of service co-ordination can be split into several subproblems: service discovery, service composition planning, execution of composite services, service execution monitoring and failure recovery by contingency re-planning. The CASCOM project advanced the state of the art in these research areas by carrying out innovative research on how these problems can be solved in open, secure IP2P environments taking into account resource-poor devices.

Most existing service discovery technologies focus on matchmaking algorithms [16]. Despite the large efforts made by the research community so far to semantically describe and reason on Web Services, efficient methods for reasoning on such descriptions still remain to be invented, and to be widely adopted by industry. That particularly holds for flexible and efficient matching algorithms to be performed in large scale and resource limited IP2P environments.

Service composition and planning can be addressed using existing artificial intelligence planning methods. However, these methods were developed for problems where the number of operators is relatively small but where plans can be quite complex. In contrast, in Web Service composition for open, large-scale IP2P service environments planning methods that can deal with huge number of possible service are required. However, plans are not necessarily very complex. This means that planning methods must follow more closely the structure of the service directories rather than be geared to generating highly complex plans. The CASCOM project developed planning mechanisms that establish plan fragments directly on top of the service directory to solve this problem.

Agent-based IP2P applications may be largely pervasive thus inherit the main characteristic of minimally intrusive pervasive applications: Context-awareness (e.g., [6]). These concepts have been intensively investigated in many contexts. However, there were neither well defined, nor commonly agreed concepts of context, situation, and context-awareness in P2P environments, not to speak about the notion of situation-aware agents and multi-agent systems in IP2P environments. The CASCOM project investigated these issues in the context of IP2P environment and developed context-aware agents providing various business application services.

7.3 Conceptual Architecture

The agent-based IP2P service co-ordination infrastructure is the basis of the CAS-COM architecture, providing functionality such as efficient, secure, and reliable communication independent of the access technology. The CASCOM architecture is an extension to conventional P2P architectures with a support for mobile computing and a broad range of mobile and pervasive devices. Users are logically

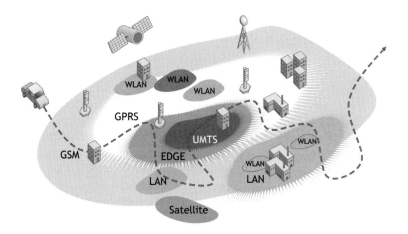

Figure 7.1: Network infrastructure

connected to the system either by using a wireless access network or by using a wireline access network. In the former case, the user most likely has a mobile device with a necessary equipment to employ the selected access technology, whereas in the latter case, a desktop computer may be used.

7.3.1   IP2P Network Infrastructure

The IP2P network infrastructure is logically situated on top of the combination of various wireless and wireline access networks providing seamless mobility between access technologies (see Figure 7.1). In general, seamless mobility means that roaming from one location to another possibly switching the underlying access technology occurs without inconvenience to the user. Such a feature will be important for the future nomadic applications and therefore an essential part of the CASCOM architecture. Figure 7.1 depicts a situation where the user drives through an urban area having available several different access technologies.

On top of seamless mobility environment, a P2P overlay network architecture is built (see Figure 7.2), which takes into account characteristics of wireless networks and resource-poor mobile devices. The fact that many P2P systems and algorithms are designed for fixed network environments implies that these solutions are not directly applicable in environments where wireless communication paths are involved. The dynamic topology of P2P networks, the fluctuating QoS of wireless connections, and the limited processing capacity of many of the devices connected to such networks, pose several challenges that have been addressed inadequately so far. Some P2P platforms consider that a client may be situated in a resource-poor device (e.g, JXTA [10]), but the communication over slow wireless connections is typically insufficiently taken into account. However, agents should be able to communicate efficiently with one another also in wireless environments.

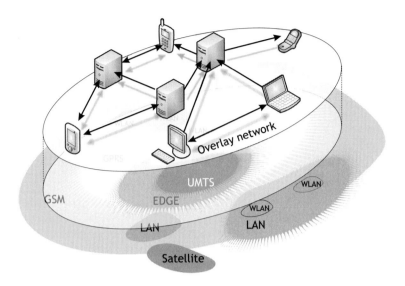

Figure 7.2: P2P overlay network

Sometimes, efficiency is not as important as, for example, reliability. The CAS-COM architecture provides necessary, efficient, and reliable agent communication means for IP2P environments.

Agent-based service discovery in IP2P environments is difficult due to the lack of a fixed infrastructure configuration and support of dynamic topologies with a changing set of members. As nodes of a P2P network move, new agents, devices, and hosts may join, or leave the network; in this way, the interconnection patterns among them change, so new routes must be dynamically discovered and maintained with minimal routing overhead and bandwidth cost.

Another challenge here is that distributed hash table (DHT) algorithms provide only keywordbased searches. However, such search method is very limited and does not fit well together with searches based on semantics. By our knowledge, for DHTs, even for multiple keyword queries, there are not known efficient approaches. Therefore, the CASCOM project considers an architecture, where the directory service plays a central role. The P2P system is used mainly for publishing and searching meta-services, which are needed for the coordination architecture to be functional for all coordination tasks. The (functional) services are then discovered through the directory service, simply because it is only possible to expose a key on a P2P infrastructure i.e., no semantic information can be taken into account.

7.3.2 Agent Architecture

The IP2P service agent and multi-agent system architecture is logically situated on top of the IP2P network infrastructure. This can be called semantic overlay

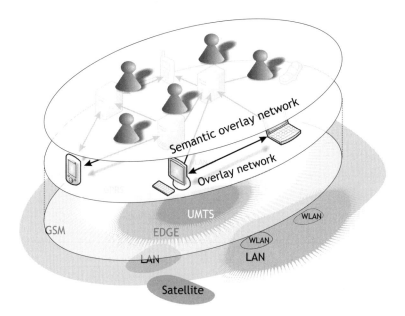

Figure 7.3: Semantic overlay network

network (see Figure 7.3). The available agents, and thus available services, depend on clients connected to the system. That is, only those agents or services are available that the (connected) clients are willing to provide. However, the CASCOM architecture has built in support for innovative service description, agent-based service discovery and mediation, service composition planning, service execution, and generic mechanism for situation-aware agents. Agent-based IP2P applications are context-sensitive and context-aware. Context-sensitivity is the ability of a device to detect its current context and changes in contextual data, such as data on the characteristics and state of used devices, the network, the agent system, and the user. Context-awareness is the ability of applications to capture and analyze the context and interrelationship between users' actions and context-sensitive devices over time.

7.4   The CASCOM Architecture in Detail

As seen in Section 7.3, the CASCOM abstract architecture aims at the innovative combination of intelligent agent technology, Semantic Web Services, peer-to-peer, and mobile computing for intelligent peer-to-peer mobile service environments. Figure 7.4 shows the different component types that make up CASCOM applications and the interactions between them. Solid arrows indicate the main direction of control flow, while dotted lines refer to the main direction of data flow. The

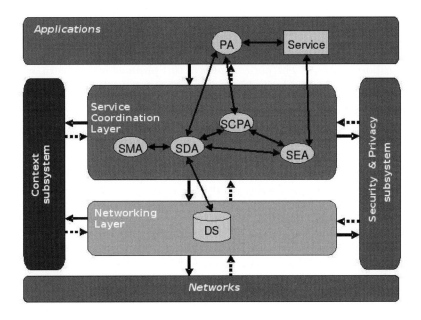

Figure 7.4: CASCOM architecture

generic architecture comprises two layers, *Networking layer* and *Service Coordination layer*, as well as two orthogonal subsystems *Context* and *Security & Privacy* subsystems.

Finally, applications that use CASCOM technology will access its functionalities through the agents at service coordination layer. A common way of doing this is through Personal Agents (PAs) representing particular users. In Figure 7.4, third party (domain) services (Web Services, agents, etc) are also located at this level.

The abstract architecture must be instantiated into a concrete one, in which several components of the same type may coexist.

7.4.1 Networking Layer

The *Networking Layer* is located just above the networks (Network Infrastructure, Figure 7.1), as a middleware to cope with the variability of the connections below, providing a generic, secure, and open intelligent P2P network infrastructure with the following functionalities:

- Efficient, secure, and reliable agent message transport communication over wireless (and wireline) communication paths independently of the access

technology. Bit-efficient ACL encoding [7] has been chosen due to the requirement for efficient communication over slow communication networks
and resource limited devices. The simplicity and ease of implementation on
small devices has been a key issue to choose FIPA-HTTP [8] as the message
transport protocol. The performance of this protocol is a concern, which the
CASCOM project addressed by using HTTP 1.1 persistent connections.

- Provide network-related context information, like QoS of a connection, network availability, etc., to the context subsystem. This context subsystem (see
  Section 7.4.3) will then acquire, store, and update context information about
  network/communication environment, including data about (available) networks and QoS of data communication that will be used within the networking layer to adapt the overlay network to changing environmental situations.

- Agent runtime environment for resource-constrained mobile devices. Among
  different agent platforms, JADE/LEAP [1] is chosen as the most appropriate
  for CASCOM: it follows the FIPA standard, allows agents to be efficiently
  executed on small devices, and is an active open source project.

- Low-level service discovery in IP2P environment. The networking layer provides some support, mainly the "low-level" IP2P service look-up, to higher
  layers where the semantic service discovery takes place.

Requesters search dynamically for services published by different providers in
a directory service (DS), which can be centralized or distributed. In the latter case,
a federation of DSs could be built, where each DS registers itself in other DSs as a
service. Thus, a DS can be found by querying entries in a DS. Such an approach was
used in the Agentcities project [5], where the directories were federated accordingly
to "application domains". Among the multiple combinations for interacting with
DSs, the CASCOM abstract architecture favours a transparent access to federated
DSs for reasons of simplicity, so that the requester interacts with a single DS that
is federated with other DSs.

Services are represented as structured objects within the directory using
OWL-S. However, directory entries are described in FIPA-SL0 language [9] because
it is independent from the descriptions of the Web Services, is general enough, has
a strong expressiveness, and keeps the architecture homogeneity. Translators were
developed to transform service descriptions into directory entries.

7.4.2 Service Coordination Layer

The *Service Coordination Layer* (Semantic overlay network in the conceptual architecture, Figure 7.3) is located between the *Networking Layer* and the *Applications*, and uses the services offered by both the *Context Subsystem* and the *Security
& Privacy Subsystem*. This layer has two main functionalities:

- Semantic service discovery (service discovery and semantic matchmaking)

- Service coordination (service composition, service execution, monitoring and contingency replanning)

In the CASCOM abstract architecture, the semantic service discovery functionality is realised by two different types of agents: *Service Discovery Agents* (SDA) and *Service Matchmaking Agents* (SMA). This was done for reasons of efficiency and flexibility, as in some application domains the matchmaking functionality may not be necessary. In much the same way, the service coordination functionality is realised by *Service Composition Planning Agents* (SCPA) and *Service Execution Agents* (SEA). Also in this case, the service composition planning might not always be required, i.e., if pre-defined (atomic and composite) services only need to be executed.

SDAs manage the discovery of required services, handling both abstract service descriptions and concrete service groundings. Usually, SDAs receive service queries from the users' *Personal Agents* (PA) and acquire relevant contextual information from the context subsystem (see Section 7.4.3). With that information, they use the service discovery functionality of the networking layer and the semantic matching functionality of SMAs, to determine services that fulfil the received service discovery request. SDAs return then a set of descriptions and their corresponding service process model and/or grounding.

SMAs provide the means to compare service specifications in a context dependent fashion. Again, they may focus on abstract service descriptions, on concrete service groundings, or both. Several semantic matchmaking approaches have been proposed [19, 25]. In CASCOM, an OWL-S service matchmaker called OWLS-MX [14] is the main component. The OWLS-MX matchmaker takes any OWL-S service as a query, and returns an ordered set of relevant services that match the query, each of which annotated with its individual degree of matching, and syntactic similarity value. The user may extend the query by specifying the desired degree, and syntactic similarity threshold.

SCPAs are capable of creating value-added composite services that match specific service specifications. Once SCPAs receive service specifications, they contact SDAs to discover existing services in a given domain (high level descriptions or concrete service groundings), constrained to the current context (that can be acquired either by receiving information from other agents or by accessing the context subsystem), and plan a composite value-added service matching the received service specification. The SCPAs make use of the OWLS-Xplan [15]. Xplan is a heuristic hybrid search planner based on the FF-planner [13]. The generated composite service will orchestrate one or more simpler services. The generated valued-added composite service may or may not contain service grounding information. In a typical interaction, when no single service is found matching a given service specification, the Service Composition functionality is used to dynamically create a value-added composite service matching the service specification, the output of which is a service description. These service descriptions may be stored or cached in some directory for later use (by agents looking for similar services' specifications).

SEAs manage the execution of composite as well as atomic service descriptions, either generated by SCPAs or pre-existing. Since the received compound service description relies on simpler services, SEAs will also coordinate the execution of these simpler services. Whenever necessary, SEAs will use SDAs to discover appropriate available service groundings for each of the simpler services invoked from the compound service description. The execution, namely the discovery of necessary service providers, will be dependent on the current context. The execution agent is based on principles of the OSIRIS process management system [23].

7.4.3   Context Subsystem

The *Context Subsystem* [17] is accessed by both the *Networking Layer* and the *Service Coordination Layer*, working as a gateway of context information between the layers. Its main functionality is to discover, acquire and store useful context information (e.g. the geographical position or the user preferences). This kind of information can be accessed by both layers either by explicitly querying the context subsystem ("pulling") or by subscribing a listener that is in charge of notifying changes and events occurring in the environment ("pushing"). The "pulling" solution permits to save resources, because the context is accessed only when needed. On the other hand, it requires more time to discover and acquire information, in the case that the needed information is not stored in a repository of historical data. The "pushing" solution offers less latency, because the context information is regularly sent to the subscriber so that it's always available, but on the other hand it uses more resources.

7.4.4   Security & Privacy Subsystem

The *Security & Privacy Subsystem* is also orthogonal to the the *Networking Layer* and the *Service Coordination Layer*. It is responsible for ensuring security and privacy of information throughout the different components of the CASCOM infrastructure. Every node of the network should keep its data confidentiality, integrity, and availability (CIA)[1]. But not only data is a security concern, also the software that deals with it, especially for network-centric systems, where the misuse, theft, and unauthorized usage of computing resources is well studied. The security and privacy requirements identified are: identification, authentication, authorisation, single sign-on, and local and network security. Also the integrity of transmitted data, non-repudiability, traceability, privacy, delegation, and nationalization need to be guaranteed.

In order to guarantee the correct treatment of data, the CASCOM project relies on two novel architectural abstractions [3]. These abstractions, namely Validation-Oriented Ontologies and Guarantors, are somehow known concepts in the

---

[1]http://www.infosecpedia.org/pedia/index.php/Main_Page

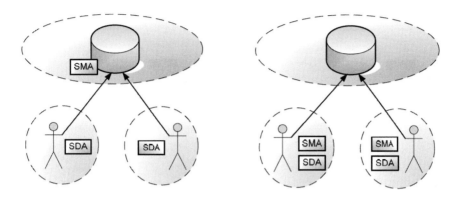

Figure 7.5: Instantiation CASCOM-1a   Figure 7.6: Instantiation CASCOM-1b

realm of security and trust management, but they have been reformulated to make them first class architectural elements.

7.5 Instantiations of the CASCOM Architecture

The CASCOM abstract architecture, in reference to service discovery, can be instantiated in different ways, on the basis of the possible network infrastructures. Four possible solutions have been considered: (1) a centralized, (2) a super-peer, (3) a structured, and (4) an unstructured pure peer-to-peer solution.

7.5.1 Centralized P2P

The first application of the CASCOM architecture is a central solution. A central directory system is used by the peers as a lookup mechanism to find services. This directory acts as a centralized peer-to-peer system: peers search for service descriptions by querying directly and only the directory.

A very simple scheme for discovering the directory service can be used by setting the access information of the directory within the SDA.

Additionally, two possibilities exist: either the matchmaker is centralized on the same host as the directory (CASCOM-1a, see Figure 7.5) or it is integrated within the peers (CASCOM-1b, see Figure 7.6).

7.5.2 Super-Peer P2P

The second instantiation of the CASCOM architecture is a super-peer P2P configuration, where multiple directories exist in a federation and they construct the look-up mechanism for the peers to find adequate services.

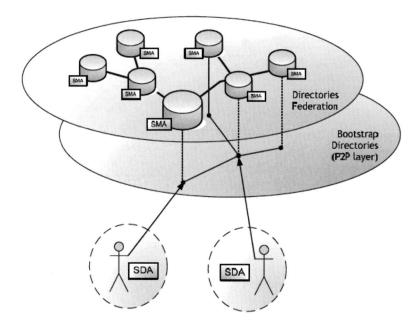

Figure 7.7: Instantiation CASCOM-2a

In addition to this super-peer structure, a pure peer-to-peer layer (typically a Distributed Hash Table) is used by the peers to find a bootstrap directory in the directory federation. This also means that some of the directories are accessible through this pure peer-to-peer system.

The basic search mechanisms invoke the federated directory services in a transparent manner, i.e. a search query may be forwarded to other federated directories. This would be totally transparent to the agents.

Concerning the matchmaker, multiple matchmakers may be hosted together with each directory (CASCOM-2a, see Figure 7.7) using an internal or an external integration. Running the SMA on the peers that query the directory is a second option (CASCOM-2b, see Figure 7.8).

7.5.3 Structured Pure P2P

The third instantiation of the CASCOM architecture is a structured pure P2P solution. Structured pure P2P systems are based on distributed indices, spread over all peers in the network. No central index is available. In contrast to hierarchical P2P systems this architecture avoids bottlenecks and asymmetries by a regular distribution of the index information over the peers. Therefore the peers of a structured P2P-system have parts of the overall index stored locally and have also parts of the routing tables.

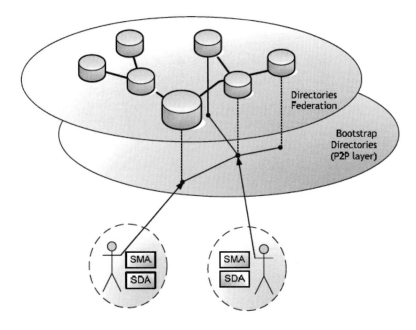

Figure 7.8: Instantiation CASCOM-2b

In relation to the underlying search strategy, a query must be forwarded from one peer to another based on the routing tables. To avoid that all peers are contacted during service discovery, additional policies must be to be included. Before starting the search, the relevant peers that hold the relevant part of the overall index must be semantically filtered. Then the search is started using only the selected peers.

The respective CASCOM architecture has no directory component, because every agent holds its own local index and it is completely decentralised. Every peer has to discover services by itself and the functionality of this agent for service discovery then depends on the chosen indexing mechanism. In CASCOM 3a (see Figure 7.9) there is no semantic matchmaker agent and the service discovery uses only the index, while in CASCOM 3b (see Figure 7.10) a matchmaker agent is used for pre-filtering the relevant peers, so that the communication load to find relevant peers in the distributed index can be reduced.

7.5.4 Unstructured Pure P2P

The fourth application of the CASCOM architecture is an unstructured pure P2P solution. In contrast to CASCOM-3, there is no information about the distributed indexing and routing tables. Examples of respective P2P service discovery solutions are Bibster [4] and GSD [11].

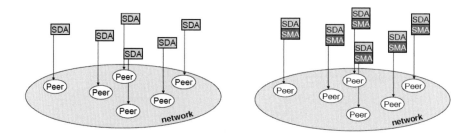

Figure 7.9: Instantiation CASCOM-3a   Figure 7.10: Instantiation CASCOM-3b

For CASCOM, our partner DFKI also developed an approach to unstructured P2P service discovery, called RS2D (risk based semantic service discovery). Each RS2D peer observes the messages it receives from the neighbourhood within a message propagation range r. These can be advertisements, queries and service replies. By caching the messages service descriptions, RS2D clusters its neighbourhood. For each direct neighbour, from whom the local peer received a message, a cluster is constructed. RS2D detects interconnections between neighbours, so clusters can be merged (see cluster $c1$ in Figure 7.11).

For each of these clusters RS2D stores a list of service descriptions. By using a semantic matchmaker, e.g. OWLS-MX, it determines the neighbouring peers to route a query to based on the risk of failure with respect to expected return of semantically relevant services. This is in contrast to Bibster and GSD. If two disjoint clusters contain a semantic similar service description the query can be routed to only one or both clusters depending on the risk-function evaluations.

Please note that RS2D is executed by each peer agent locally. That is, each peer has its own representation of its surrounding in the network. Globally viewed, the clusters may overlap each other, such that even if $p0$ does not find a matching service, its neighbour might do, as it has other clusters containing peers that are just one propagation hop out of $p0$ propagation range. In Figure 7.11 it's possible to see the overlapping clusters of peer $p0$ (dark grey - $c1$; $c2$; $c3$) and peer $p1$ (grey - $c4$; $c5$).

7.5.5   Discussion

The central setting described in Section 7.5.1 has the advantage of simplicity of maintenance. The main disadvantages are lack of robustness (i.e., single point of failure) and lack of scalability, that is the directory may form a bottleneck if many queries are sent and the query results are large. Still, the search and communication may be much more efficient, because algorithms can take advantage of the centralization of all service descriptions.

This instantiation fits well for applications in which the number of services is limited, however, for scenarios where a high number of service providers exists

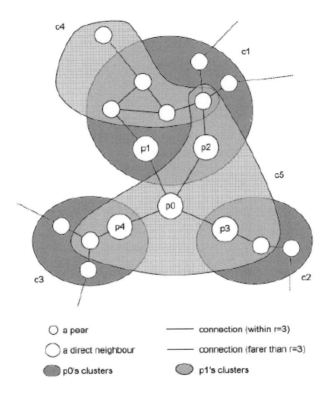

c4
c1
p1
p2
c5
p0
p4
p3
c3
c2

○ a peer   —— connection (within r=3)

◓ a direct neighbour   —— connection (farer than r=3)

⬤ p0's clusters   ⬤ p1's clusters

Figure 7.11: Instantiation CASCOM-4

this central configuration is not recommended due to its scalability problem.

The main advantage of the super-peer solution described in Section 7.5.2 is enhancing robustness and decentralization. As the network is highly structured, queries are satisfied very efficiently. The decision of how to organise services among directories (super peers) depends on the different applications, since in some domains spatial location of services is preferable to logical (categorised) distribution.

The pure P2P solution described in Section 7.5.3 has the advantage of avoiding bottlenecks and having a high degree of robustness as the directory is distributed over the peers. However, in this setting the discovery of services takes more time than with a central or hybrid directory. In addition, the computational resources needed in the peers are higher.

Finally, the main advantage of the unstructured pure P2P option (see Section 7.5.4 is the complete decentralization of the architecture with the peers having full autonomy. However, it has the drawback of resource consuming, traffic overhead and privacy concerns.

Due to the fact that the super-peer solution enhances robustness and decentralization, keeping the time a query is satisfied reasonably low, as the network is highly structured, this was the option chosen in the CASCOM project.

7.6 Summary

The driving vision of CASCOM is that ubiquitous services are provided and coordinated by an agent-based IP2P infrastructure. The architecture described in this chapter identifies the main elements necessary to attain this goal. Furthermore, it defines the interfaces between these elements and outlines their general structure, putting forward the high-level design and functionality of several software components and agents. The design is intented to impose as little restrictions as possible to concrete implementations so as to maximise flexibility and adaptability.

The architecture tends to minimise the need for user intervention through the Personal Agent. In particular, the whole process of service coordination is transparent to the user. Although in some application domains this can be seen as a disadvantage, in the emergency assistance scenarios that the CASCOM demonstrator addresses it is essential to limit the cognitive load of the user. Furthermore, this approach allows for simpler Personal Agents running on mobile devices. Finally, it is worth mentioning that if these restrictions were dropped, the CASCOM abstract architecture could easily be adapted to support more interactive architecture instantions.

References

[1] F. Bergenti, and A. Poggi. *LEAP: A FIPA Platform for Handheld and Mobile Devices*, Intelligent Agents VIII, pages 436-446, Springer, 2002.

[2] F. Bergenti, A. Poggi, B. Burg, and G. Caire. *Deploying FIPA-compliant systems on handheld devices.* IEEE Internet Computing, 5(4):20-25, 2001.

[3] R. Bianchi, A. Fontana, and F. Bergenti. *A Real-World Approach to Secure and Trusted Negotiation in MASs.* Proceedings of the fourth international joint conference on Autonomous agents and multiagent systems (AAMAS), 2005.

[4] http://bibster.semanticweb.org/

[5] I. Constantinescu, S. Willmott, and J. Dale. *Deliverable 2.3: Agentcities Network Architecture.* 2003.

[6] A. K. Dey. *Understanding and using context.* Personal and Ubiquitous Computing, 5(1):4-7, 2001.

[7] Foundation for Intelligent Physical Agents, *FIPA ACL Message Representation in Bit-Efficient Specification.* Geneva, Switzerland. Specification number SC00069G, 2002

[8] Foundation for Intelligent Physical Agents, *FIPA Agent Message Transport Protocol for HTTP Specification*. Geneva, Switzerland. Specification number SC00084F, 2002

[9] Foundation for Intelligent Physical Agents, *FIPA SL Content Language Specification*. Geneva, Switzerland. Specification number SC00008I, 2002

[10] L. Gong. *JXTA: A network programming environment*. IEEE Internet Computing, 5(3):88-95, 2001

[11] D. Chakraborty, A. Joshi, T. Finin and Y. Yesha. *GSD: A Novel Group-based Service Discovery Protocol for MANETs*. 4th IEEE Conference on Mobile and Wireless Communications Networks (MWCN), Stockholm, Sweden, 2002.

[12] H. Helin and M. Laukkanen. *Performance analysis of software agent communication in slow wireless networks*. In R. Luijten, E. Wong, K. Makki, and E. K. Park, editors, Proceedings of the Eleventh International Conference on Computer Communications and Networks (ICCCN'02), pages 354-361. IEEE, Oct. 2002.

[13] J. Hoffmann, and B. Nebel. *The FF Planning System: Fast Plan Generation Through Heuristic Search*. Journal of Artificial Intelligence Research (JAIR), (14):253?302, 2001.

[14] M. Klusch, B. Fries, M. Khalid, and K. Sycara. *OWLS-MX: Hybrid Semantic Web Service Retrieval*. Proceedings 1st International AAAI Fall Symposium on Agents and the Semantic Web, Arlington VA, USA, 2005.

[15] M. Klusch, A. Gerber, and M. Schmidt. *Semantic Web Service Composition Planning with OWLS-Xplan*. Proceedings 1st International AAAI Fall Symposium on Agents and the Semantic Web, Arlington VA, USA, 2005.

[16] M. Klusch and K. P. Sycara. *Brokering and matchmaking for coordination of agent societies: A survey*. In Coordination of Internet Agents: Models, Technologies, and Applications, pages 197-224, 2001.

[17] A. Lopes, and L. Botelho. *SEA: a Semantic Web Services Context-aware Execution Agent*. Proceedings 1st International AAAI Fall Symposium on Agents and the Semantic Web, Arlington VA, USA, 2005.

[18] D. Martin, M. Burstein, J. Hobbs, O. Lassila, D. McDermott, S. McIlraith, S. Narayanan, M. Paolucci, B. Parsia, T. Payne, E. Sirin, N. Srinivasan and K. Sycara. *OWL-S: Semantic Markup for Web Services - W3C Member Submission 22 November 2004*, http://www.w3.org/Submission/2004/SUBM-OWL-S-20041122/

[19] M. Paolucci, T. Kawamura, T. Payne, and K. Sycara. *Semantic matching of Web Services capabilities*. In Proceedings of the First International Semantic Web Conference on The Semantic Web, pages 333-347. Springer-Verlag, 2002.

[20] G. Peng, S. Li, H. Jin, and T. Ma. *M-CAN: A lookup protocol for mobile peer-to-peer environment.* In Proceedings of the 7th International Symposium on Parallel Architectures, Algorithms and Networks (ISPAN'04), pages 544-549, 2004.

[21] S. Ratnasamy, P. Francis, M. Handley, R. Karp, and S. Shenker. *A scalable contentaddressable network.* In Proceedings of the ACM SIGCOMM 01, Aug. 2001.

[22] A. Rowstron and P. Druschel. *Pastry: Scalable, decentralized object location and routing for large-scale peer-to-peer systems.* In Proceedings of the ACM/I-FIP Middleware, 2001.

[23] C. Schuler, R. Weber, H. Schuldt, and H. J. Schek. *Scalable Peer-to-Peer Process Management - The OSIRIS Approach.* In Proceedings of the 2nd International Conference on Web Services (ICWS), pages 26-34, San Diego, CA, USA, IEEE Computer Society, 2004.

[24] I. Stoica, R. Morris, D. R. Karger, M. F. Kaashoek, and H. Balakrishnan. *Chord: A scalable peer-to-peer lookup service for internet applications.* In Proceedings of the ACM SIGCOMM 01, San Diego, California, Aug. 2001.

[25] K. Sycara, M. Klusch, S. Widoff, and J. Lu. *Larks: Dynamic matchmaking among heterogeneous software agents in cyberspace.* Journal of Autonomous Agents and Multi-Agent Systems, 5(2). Kluwer Academic Press, 2002.

[26] S. Tarkoma and M. Laukkanen. *Facilitating agent messaging on PDAs.* In Fourth International Workshop on Mobile Agents for Telecommunication Applications (MATA-2002), pages 259-268, Barcelona, Spain, 2002. Springer.

[27] S. Tarkoma, M. Laukkanen, and K. Raatikainen. *Software agents for ubiquitos computing.* In R. Khosla, N. Ichalkaranje, and L. Jain, editors, *Design of Intelligent Multi-Agent Systems: Human-Centredness, Architectures, Learning and Adaptation Series: Studies in Fuzziness and Soft Computing*, volume 162, pages 31-60. 2004.

[28] B. Y. Zhao, L. Huang, A. D. Joseph, and J. D. Kubiatowicz. *Rapid mobility via type indirection.* In Proceedings of Third International Workshop on Peer-to-Peer Systems (IPTPS), San Diego, CA, USA, Feb. 2004.

[29] B. Y. Zhao, J. D. Kubiatowicz, and A. D. Joseph. *Tapestry: An infrastructure for fault-tolerant wide-area location and routing.* Technical Report CSD-01-1141, University of California at Berkeley, 2001.

Chapter 8

Agent Platform and Communication Architecture

Heikki Helin and Ahti Syreeni

8.1 Introduction

The progress in wireless network technologies and mobile devices changes the way in which people can access digital services. A user may access the same services as she would use her desktop computer, but in the nomadic environment she is able to do so anywhere, at any time and even using a variety of different kinds of devices. Such an environment places new challenges on the architecture implementing the services.

Nomadic environments differ from stationary environments in two fundamental ways. Firstly, the user is situated in an environment, where multiple data communication networks may be available. Because of the different network types and characteristics of the networks, for instance the values of Quality-of-Service (QoS) parameters (e.g., throughput, delay, or reliability) may change dramatically based on the network that the user is currently connected to. Secondly, the user may access the services using a variety of different mobile or stationary devices. The characteristics and limitations of a particular device dictate the constraints on how the user is able to access the services and what kind of content the user is provided with.

As the CASCOM architecture is based on software agent technology, we need to have an agent platform that is usable for devices with limited processing power and memory. Furthermore, the agent platform situated in a mobile device should not require any components at the fixed network. The agent communication to and from the mobile device must be designed taking into account the characteristics of wireless communication paths.

In this chapter, we present some essential enablers for agents in wireless environments. An agent platform that is usable in resource-constrained devices is an essential component of the CASCOM architecture. In contrast to previous research, the CASCOM Agent Platform, which is based on JADE/LEAP [2], is fully FIPA compliant without requiring any infrastructure components. Given that the platform contains all the components dictated by FIPA specifications, it is not that small when considering memory requirements, but it is usable in modern mobile phones. Then, we describe how agent communication over a wireless communication path is implemented in the CASCOM architecture. An appropriate communication needs a reliable message transport and efficient encoding of the messages. Agents situated in mobile devices need to communicate with other agents which may be situated in other mobile devices or in fixed network hosts. This communication may happen fully or partially over wireless communication paths. This must be taken into account when designing and implementing the communication stack (message transport and message encoding). In the CASCOM architecture, we use efficient encoding of messages by employing bit-efficient message encodings specified by FIPA [7, 9]. Further, since typically mobile devices do not have a public IP-address, which implies that mobile terminated messages cannot be sent directly, we introduce a component called CASCOM Messaging Gateway, which takes care of such situations and also improves the messaging reliability especially in cases where the mobile device changes wireless communication path (e.g., from GPRS to WLAN).

8.2   Background

In this section, we briefly summarize the FIPA architecture and give an overview of agent platforms developed for resource-limited mobile devices.

8.2.1   FIPA Agent Platform

The Foundation for Intelligent Physical Agents (FIPA) was founded in 1996 as a non-profit organization with the remit of producing standards for heterogeneous and interacting agents and agent-based systems across multiple vendors' platforms. FIPA's official mission statement expresses this more formally: "The promotion of technologies and interoperability specifications that facilitate the end-to-end interoperability of intelligent agent systems in modern commercial and industrial settings". The emphasis here is on the practical commercial and industrial uses of agent systems. The aim is to bring together the latest advances in agent research with industry best practice in software, networks and business systems.

A FIPA agent platform provides an infrastructure for deploying agents. Today's operating systems do not provide the services required for agent systems or agent societies. Therefore, there is a need for agent platforms implemented as middleware software running on top of an operating system. FIPA does not specify the internal design of an agent platform, because FIPA's main concern is achieving interoperability between agent platforms. However, FIPA requires every

FIPA-compliant agent platform to implement two mandatory services The Agent Management System (AMS), and the Agent Communication Channel (ACC). Additionally, FIPA has specified the Directory Facilitator (DF), but implementing this component is optional. The purpose of the AMS is to manage the agents' life cycles, such as starting, stopping, and quitting agents residing on the FIPA agent platform. It also maintains the mapping between an agent's identifier and its transport addresses thus acting as an agent naming service. Furthermore, the AMS is responsible for maintaining the platform profile, which describes the platform properties such as communication capabilities. The ACC is a service that implements the FIPA Message Transport Service (MTS). The ACC routes messages both between agents within one FIPA agent platform and between agents residing on different FIPA agent platforms. The DF is an optional agent maintaining information about the skills that agents have advertised with it, that is, the DF provides the FIPA agent platform with a "yellow pages" service. In the CASCOM architecture, FIPA's DF functionality is not used, but a directory system called WSDir is used (see Chapter 9 for details).

The heart of the FIPA's model for the agent systems is agent communication, where agents can pass semantically meaningful messages to one another. FIPA has specified several choices for Message Transport Protocol (MTP) and encoding of the message components. In the CASCOM architecture, HTTP is be used as a MTP and messages are encoded using FIPA's bit-efficient message encoding specifications.

8.2.2 Agent Platforms for Mobile Devices

JADE [1] is a distributed FIPA-compliant agent platform that allows agents to be executed on desktop computers in J2SE environment. When an extra component, LEAP add-on for JADE, is added to JADE, it can be also compiled for small devices, e.g., PDAs and mobile phones supporting CLDC 1.0 and MIDP 2.0 [2]. This combination is called JADE-LEAP platform (Lightweight Extensible Agent Platform). JADE-LEAP was the first FIPA compliant agent platform running on PDAs and mobile phones. In addition to the MIDP and J2SE versions, there has been a version also for PersonalJava environment, which was a predecessor of today's Java CDC configuration. However, as the PersonalJava is now obsolete, the PersonalJava version is not recommended in most recent JADE-LEAP versions.

JADE-LEAP platform supports different transport protocols and message encodings for agent messaging. Currently string encoding for Agent Communication Language (ACL) messages is supported and bit-efficient encoding is also available as an additional package. For message delivery, FIPA HTTP (restricted to XML-based message envelope encoding) and FIPA IIOP transport protocols are provided in J2SE version of JADE-LEAP. In addition, JADE-LEAP provides quite good support for FIPA compliant agent messaging as FIPA-SL content language support is available for agents. In the J2SE version of JADE-LEAP, also the subsets of FIPA-SL are provided. However, the MIDP version of JADE-LEAP

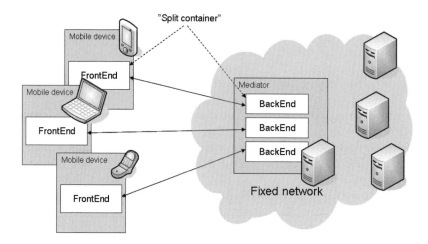

Figure 8.1: Split container model of LEAP

supports only SL0. In the J2SE version users can create their own ontologies easily as Java classes and JADE-LEAP translates the Java-objects into the content language automatically at runtime.

The JADE agent platform may consist of several hosts distributed over the network. Each host runs an agent container that connects to a main container. The main container hosts the basic FIPA services (e.g., AMS and DF), and internal messaging protocol (based on Java RMI) is being used for internal communication in platform. The main container can be replicated by a host to increase the reliability of the platform. To manage the platform easily, the J2SE version provides an optional graphical user interface for managing the agents.

The key feature of JADE-LEAP as compared to JADE is that JADE-LEAP supports the use of a split container for low-end devices, as illustrated in Figure 8.1. The container is split into two parts: the front-end and the back-end, where only the front-end part is run on the mobile device. The split container approach requires a permanent connection between these two parts of a container; agent mobility is not supported. In JADE-LEAP a new internal protocol is introduced to be used for internal communication in platform, between hosts and between the front-end and back-end. The protocol is called JICP [3] and it replaces the Java RMI based internal messaging protocol of JADE. The host in fixed network hosting the back-end of the container(s) is called the Mediator and it is mandatory; the JADE-LEAP cannot be started in a mobile device without the presence of the Mediator in a fixed network.

In addition to JADE-LEAP, there are also other agent platforms that could be used in mobile devices. MicroFIPA-OS [18] is an agent development toolkit and platform based on the FIPA-OS toolkit. This system targets at medium to high-end PDA devices that have sufficient resources to execute the PersonalJava compatible virtual machine. The MicroFIPA-OS architecture is extensible by plugging in components that either replace or extend the architecture. An example of this kind of contribution is FIPA Nomadic Application Support [15], which provides support for wireless environments, including components for efficient message transport over slow wireless communication paths [17]. The FIPA Nomadic Application Support incorporates the bit-efficient envelope and ACL messages discussed earlier. MicroFIPA-OS is no longer developed further nor supported.

Yet another example of providing an agent platform to wireless environments is A-Globe [21]. The components of the A-Globe include the agent platform, agent container, various services, and an environment simulator agent. Unlike LEAP and MicroFIPA-OS, A-Globe is not a FIPA compliant agent platform. However, this relaxation gives more freedom to design components for wireless communication and therefore more efficient solution can be made. The obvious drawback is that agents on A-Globe platform cannot directly communicate with agents residing on LEAP or MicroFIPA-OS platforms.

8.2.3 CASCOM Agent Platform

The CASCOM Agent Platform is a modified version of the JADE agent platform for devices supporting the J2ME CLDC 1.1 configuration with the MIDP 2.0 profile [4]. The version provides all the functionality of the current MIDP version of JADE-LEAP. The split-container model used in JADE-LEAP is not appropriate for the CASCOM architecture which has to support P2P architecture. In a pure P2P architecture, all devices must be able to host a complete agent platform. The issue of limited resources in mobile devices has to be solved without splitting the container.

The CASCOM Agent Platform is able to run in mobile devices and it contains limited features of JADE. This is illustrated in Figure 8.2. Agent platforms in a fixed network running on desktop computers can be original JADE, JADE-LEAP, or other FIPA-compliant platforms, and the communication between all platforms is performed using FIPA compliant protocols. In this way, there is no need to implement separate new version of JADE for J2SE environment. In addition, some features have been added from the current J2SE version or implemented as new features so that the true stand-alone execution presented in Figure 8.2 was implemented.

The CASCOM Agent Platform contains an implementation of the FIPA Agent Management System and the Agent Communication System. Agent Communication System provides a FIPA-compliant message delivery service for agents to communicate with each other. Especially the FIPA HTTP protocol is used as a message transport protocol and ACL messages are encoded using bit-efficient encoding as specified by FIPA. Details of the CASCOM agent communication architecture can be found in the next section. However, given the limitations of mobile devices and the differences between J2SE and J2ME, there are some restric-

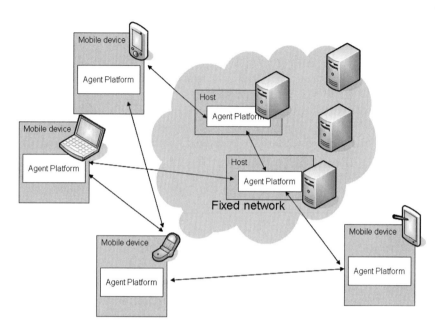

Figure 8.2: Principle of CASCOM agent platform

tions compared to full JADE. In the following, we summarize the main differences. Further details of them can be found in [5]. Firstly, the CASCOM Agent Platform cannot automatically use user-defined ontology classes written as Java classes. One has to use either abstract descriptors or add internalize and externalize methods specified by the jade.content.onto.Introspectable interface and use MicroIntrospector instead of ReflectiveIntrospector. Secondly, the distribution of the platform is not supported. Only the MainContainer is realized and all agents must run in it. Thirdly, reflection-based persistence is not implemented due to the lack of reflection APIs in MIDP, thus application-specific persistence should be implemented when needed. Lastly, agent mobility is not supported.

The architecture of the CASCOM Agent Platform follows the design of the original JADE platform. The main components are depicted in Figure 8.3. The core services of JADE are loaded at startup. The main difference to the original JADE is that internal message protocol (IMTP) does not exist, thus there cannot be more than one container because the messaging between containers would require an IMTP implementation.

Although Figure 8.3 gives a simplified overview of the CASCOM Agent Platform main components, details are more complicated as most of the JADE core

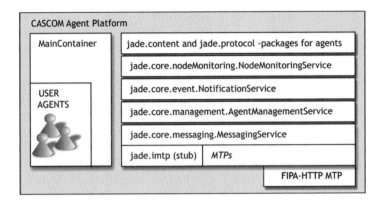

Figure 8.3: Overview of CASCOM agent platform main components

classes are still there. Many of those classes are needed to start the MainContainer and cannot be removed unless making intensive changes to the current JADE architecture.

8.2.4 CASCOM Agent Communication

In wireless environments, agents need to communicate efficiently and reliably. Therefore, the communication stack should be tailored for wireless environments. Here we took a pragmatic view to agent communication. In particular, we consider neither the reason agents are communicating, nor the semantics of messages. However, we assume that agents are communicating with one another and at least part of the communication path is implemented using wireless technologies. The latter assumption is an additional requirement in the sense that many of the solutions provided in this section are applicable also in environments where the whole communication path is implemented using wireline technologies. The agent communication in the CASCOM architecture is based on FIPA standards.

Figure 8.4 depicts a layered model of agent communication. The transport and signalling protocol layer should provide an efficient and reliable data transport service. Usually this layer should be transparent to agents, and therefore we will not discuss this layer issues in more detailed here. An overview of transport protocol issues in wireless environments can be found for example in [19].

Message Transport

A message transport protocol (MTP) defines the structure of messages sent using a transport protocol. FIPA has specified three message transport protocols: IIOP [12], HTTP [11], and WAP [13]. Out of these three protocols, HTTP is best candidate for the CASCOM architecture. In fact, assuming an off-the-shelf imple-

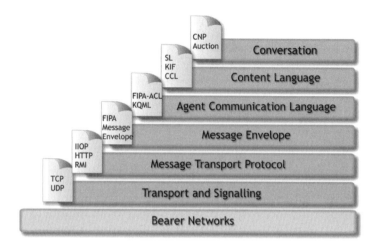

Figure 8.4: A layered model of agent communication

mentation of IIOP, it surely needs much more code than HTTP, which makes IIOP inappropriate in small devices. However, although IIOP protocol is a quite complex when employing all its features, FIPA uses only one-way request messages, and that functionality can be implemented more easily. Further, IIOP is not a good protocol in wireless environments, although its performance is acceptable given that IIOP uses binary messages. The protocol assumes a quite high bandwidth and a reliable connection because the IIOP protocol is unable to re-establish the connection after a transport connection breaks. In addition, the IIOP protocol does not allow transport connection endpoint changes. FIPA-IIOP uses a one-way request message which makes connection unreliable because the sender cannot be sure that sending the message was successful. The WAP has similar problems as IIOP, and using it in the CASCOM architecture is not recommended. Further, WAP as a FIPA message transport protocol has not standard status.

In addition to message transport protocols, at least two other options could be used in the CASCOM architecture. First, the JICP protocol, that is a message transport protocol implemented in LEAP. This protocol is designed for wireless communication and therefore it seems to be suitable for the CASCOM architecture. However, it is not clear how JICP protocol fits to a pure P2P architecture as the protocol is designed on the basis of the LEAP split-container model.

The second option is the design of a CASCOM message transport protocol that takes into account the requirements of the CASCOM architecture. However, there are several drawbacks with this option. First, designing a totally new protocol would require a significant amount of work. Second, such a protocol would be clearly proprietary and most likely would not be used widely outside of CASCOM.

The FIPA-HTTP message transport protocol [11] specifies the usage of HTTP as message transport protocol. HTTP provides somewhat better reliability than IIOP protocol because IIOP uses the one-way request method. It is fairly easy to implement at-least-once semantics with HTTP. Exactly-once semantics needed for transferring FIPA agent messages is also possible, if both peers maintain some state information.

Given all of the above, HTTP is used as a message transport protocol in the CASCOM communication architecture. It is a relatively simple protocol that can be easily implemented in small devices. The performance of HTTP is not that good, but still acceptable. Furthermore, the performance of HTTP can be improved by using persistent HTTP connections. In the CASCOM communication architecture, a persistent HTTP connection is always used between a mobile agent platform and the messaging gateway.

The design of the CASCOM Agent Platform message transport system follows the design of the JADE platform. The main principle underneath the system design was to do only small modifications to existing source codes and preserve the compatibility with JADE and FIPA standards.

Only the FIPA HTTP Transport Protocol was implemented for the J2ME environment and for the CASCOM Agent Platform. In order to meet the required security constraints of CASCOM, the platform provides an encryption service for the payload of HTTP messages. This does not mean that CASCOM implements a full-featured SSL and HTTPS. Instead, only the payload of HTTP messages is encrypted using a third party open source cryptography API available for MIDP 2.0. This solution guarantees the desired level of security, while avoiding the hard job of providing a full SSL implementation that would result in a piece of software that would hardly fit the constraints of today's mobile devices.

The overall design of the message transport system used in the CASCOM Agent Platform is illustrated in Figure 8.5. The JADE Messaging Service delivers encoded ACL Messages to the transport protocol component and the component uses available ACL Message Envelope Codecs to encode the envelope (the envelope is included in the message) to the proper FIPA encoding. The requested encoding type is specified as a parameter with the ACL Message and the message envelope. The message transport protocol component adds the encoded envelope and FIPA HTTP headers to the message and delivers it using a TCP/IP connection. If something goes wrong during the delivery, an exception is thrown to the Messaging Service.

The FIPA HTTP Transport Protocol component includes a server. When the component has been installed by the Messaging Service it has to listen to incoming messages and deliver messages to the Messaging Service once they arrive, until the component has been stopped or uninstalled by the Messaging Service. Whenever a FIPA HTTP Transport Protocol component receives a message it reads the used encoding of message envelope from the HTTP headers. If the encoding is supported, the proper ACL Message Envelope Codec is used to decode the envelope to a Java object. Then the envelope and the encoded ACL Message are passed to the JADE Messaging Service for further processing. If the envelope encoding

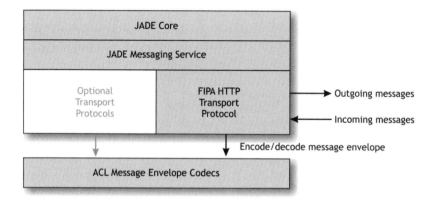

Figure 8.5: Message transport protocols in the CASCOM agent platform

is not supported (i.e., there is no available codec for it), an HTTP response error code is sent back to the sender.

The CASCOM Agent Platform design differs from that of JADE in the message envelope Codecs, in the options to use the CASCOM Message Gateway, and in the option of securing the message payload. In CASCOM, there can be different envelope Codecs available, and different message transport protocol components can use the same Codecs. The support for the CASCOM Message Gateway adds a buffer and lost a message detection mechanism for the FIPA HTTP MTP implementation. The encryption option allows securing HTTP communications even if HTTPS is not available (this is the case in most MIDP 2.0 devices).

Message Encoding

The purpose of the message encoding layer is to provide message encoding that utilizes wireless communication paths efficiently. Agent messages are encoded as follows. First the message content (expressed in some content language) and the FIPA ACL message are encoded to a payload. Then additional parameters/attributes are added to the message. In the FIPA architecture, the latter is done using message envelopes. After this, the message can be sent using a message transport protocol. Given this process, the message encoding consists of three different encodings: message envelope, ACL, and message content. Encoding of these message parts are discussed below.

Message Envelope. The purpose of the message envelope layer is to enable transport-protocol independent message handling. For example, it enables message routing so that routers (e.g., the CASCOM Messaging Gateway) do not have to understand ACL. This enables non-ACL-aware routers to forward the messages without having to concern with the message contents. On the other hand, the message envelope enables end-to-end control of messaging, when using several message transport protocols between the sender and the receiver.

FIPA has defined three concrete message envelope syntaxes. In the FIPA IIOP message transport protocol [12], the message envelope is embedded in the message transport protocol, that is, the IDL interface [20] defines the structure of the message envelope. [10] specifies an XML-based syntax for the message envelope and [8] specifies an XML-based syntax for FIPA ACL to be used in the message payload. When HTTP is used for transport protocol, HTTP MTP [12] specifies the entire agent message including the message envelope in an HTTP request. For wireless environments, there is the bit-efficient syntax for message [9]. When using it, [7] specifies a bit-efficient syntax for FIPA ACL to be used in that message payload. The bit-efficient encoding scheme encodes message envelopes efficiently by using one-octet codes for predefined message envelope parameters and other common parts of message envelope.

Bit-efficient encoding is used as the encoding scheme of message envelopes for the CASCOM communication architecture. Figure 8.6 shows the sizes (in bytes) of the message envelope transport syntaxes for the "Minimal Envelope" and the "Typical Envelope" cases, using all the different encoding options. "Minimal envelope" is an envelope which contains only the mandatory fields and the field content is the smallest possible. "Typical envelope" is more realistic one, in which there are most widely used fields with realistic field content. The bit-efficient message envelope is the most compact in both cases. This was expected. However, when the message envelope size increases, the relative difference between the encodings decreases, especially when compared to IIOP/IDL. The reason for this is that in the case of more realistic message envelope, the ratio between additional overhead and the message envelope content (i.e., the field values) increases. None of the selected encoding schemes handles the information content efficiently. As expected, the XML encoding and Java object serialization produce big message sizes. But again, the relative difference decreases when the message envelope size increases. However, for example in the case of Object serialization, the output size is still approximately four times the output size of bit-efficient encoding even in the case of realistic envelope.

Agent Communication Language (ACL). The agent communication language defines the outer language used in communication. Here we concentrate on FIPA ACL since FIPA standards are used in the CASCOM agent communication. FIPA ACL has three standard encoding schemes. The first one is based on ASCII strings, and therefore it is non-optimal and redundant. The second one is based on XML [8], which has a very verbose syntax. The third one is a bit-efficient syntax [7], which is especially suitable for wireless environments.

In the bit-efficient FIPA ACL, there are two primary ways to reduce the transfer volume over the wireless link: data reduction and intelligent caching. First, FIPA ACL messages are encoded efficiently by using one-octet codes for predefined message parameters and other common parts of the message. This is a significant improvement compared to a simple string-based coding, as it typically reduces extra overhead by 50%. Furthermore, this improvement is easy to implement and

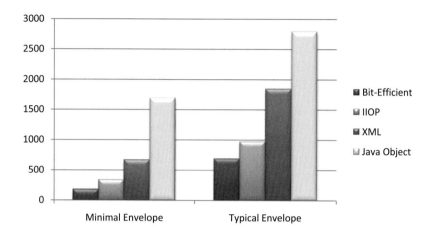

Figure 8.6: The envelope size in bytes using different encoding schemes

faster to parse than the string-based coding (comparing bytes is typically much faster than comparing strings).

Bit-efficient encoding for ACL is used in the CASCOM communication architecture. Next, we analyze the performance of different ACL encoding options. We selected four alternative methods to encode FIPA-ACL messages, which we compare against the bit-efficient encoding, totaling six different methods for ACL encoding. Firstly, the string-based FIPA-ACL encoding is measured. Especially we use the string encoding as provided by the Jade agent platform. Secondly, as the string-based messages are text information, we also analyze the data compression algorithm to compress the ACL messages. The implementation of this algorithm is the one included in Java (DeflaterOutputStream). Thirdly, a standard XML-based FIPA-ACL encoding is measured. Lastly, the standard Java serialization to output Jade's ACLMessage class is measured. Although this method is not a FIPA-compliant way to exchange ACL messages, it is, for example, used in Jade's internal communication when the agents are located on different hosts but belong to the same agent platform (that is, when Java RMI is used). Figure 8.7 shows the results of the output size measurement in bytes using a sample ACL message without the "content" field. As can be seen in Figure 8.7, the bit-efficient encoding yields the smallest output in all cases, as expected. However, the difference between the deflate encoding and the bit-efficient is insignificant. But, the deflate encoding is not a FIPA-compliant solution, and therefore cannot be used in a general case. The XML encoding output size is about twice as big as the string-based encoding. This was also expected. The serialized ACLMessage output size is notably big. This is because the Java serialization outputs the class description to each ObjectOutputStream to which the serialized objects are written. However,

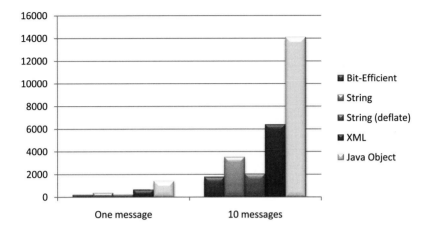

Figure 8.7: The ACL message size in bytes using different encoding schemes

the class description is output only once to each stream, that is, if two or more objects are written to the same stream, the class description is written only once. In our measurements, we use a different stream for each message, and therefore several class descriptions are needed. While this may seem unfair, it is actually the most common case. For example, when using Java RMI, a separate ObjectOutputStream has to be created for each invocation. More detailed analysis of the bit-efficient ACL can be found in [16].

Message Content. A content language is used to express the content of communication messages exchanged among agents. FIPA has specified several content languages [14]. However, each of these languages has only one concrete transport encoding syntax. Further, each content language is encoded using either S-expression or XML surface syntaxes. Both of these encoding schemes are verbose, and not very suitable for environments involving slow wireless links. XML-based languages can be encoded using some binary-XML encoding and languages based on S-expression syntax can be encoded using similar techniques as in FIPA's bit-efficient ACL encoding. Another option is to use traditional compression techniques (e.g., zip), which produce very efficient encoding, but on the other hand requires additional computing power for decompression which may not be available in a mobile device.

FIPA-SL content language is used in the CASCOM agent communication. The message content is encoded using S-expression syntax. If the message content is big, the CASCOM Agent Platform compresses the content. To analyze the effect of message content compression we used two different compression algorithms. Firstly, the message content is compressed using Java implementation of the S-rank algorithm [6] and secondly we used Zlib. Figure 8.8 shows the effect of compression

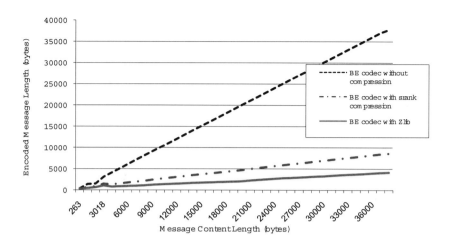

Figure 8.8: The effect compression to the message size

to the message size. Obviously, compression reduces the file size. However, the compression and decompression requires significant amount of processing power and thus it should not always be used. The CASCOM Agent Platform allows setting the threshold when the message should be compressed and when it should be sent as plain text. Figures 8.9 and 8.10 show the encoding and decoding times of a message using Nokia 6680 mobile phone. It can be seen, that although Zlib gives the best compression ratio, it also requires significantly more time to compress and decompress the content than the S-rank algorithm.

8.2.5　Messaging Gateway

Due to unreliable wireless connections, possible firewalls and NAT, the current JADE message transport system has to be improved for mobile devices. Connection to mobile devices can be lost in any time so message buffering is needed. As illustrated in Figure 8.11, devices are often in a private network (e.g., in most cases when using a GPRS connection) and also many devices in a fixed network can be behind a firewall. For these cases, there should be a gateway for agent platforms. The messaging gateway is an optional component of the CASCOM communication architecture. It is only needed in cases where mobile device has no public IP-address, but it can be used in other cases as well.

The CASCOM Messaging Gateway is a buffer for messages going to the agent platforms in mobile devices. The gateway does not address translations as the agent platforms using the gateway are expected to use the address of the gateway. That is, the agents situated in an agent platform in a private network never use their private IP-addresses as their transport addresses, but instead use

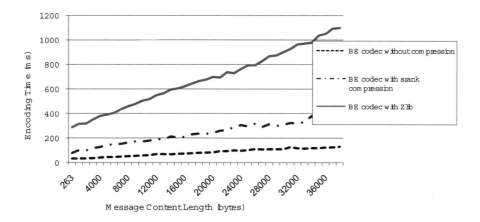

Figure 8.9: Message encoding time in Nokia 6680 mobile phone

the gateway's address. Further, the messaging gateway is totally transparent to agents. For the time being, the address of the gateway has to be given as a parameter to the CASCOM Agent Platform situated in a mobile device . This way, using the gateway is fully invisible to the agents. Besides, the gateway does not have to parse ACL messages. It forwards the messages (both directions) based on information found in the message envelope.

Once the agent platform has established connection to the CASCOM Messaging Gateway, the (HTTP) connection must be left open so that the gateway is able to send messages to the agent platform which is behind a firewall. When the connection is closed (by the platform or because of unreliable wireless connection), the gateway leaves messages in the buffer waiting for the next time the connection is established. When the connection is established again by the same agent platform, the gateway must know whether or not it should deliver all the buffered messages. In the case the agent platform has been restarted and agents have not saved their state, there is no need to send the buffered messages and they can be discarded. The information whether buffered messages should be delivered after reconnection is provided by the mobile agent platform when opening the connection.

The messaging gateway does not buffer mobile-originated messages. Platforms use their own buffers for outgoing messages, but they send them through the gateway, which routes them to the destination. However, the protocol used between the CASCOM Agent Platform and the messaging gateway ensures that no message is lost or duplicated in the case of unexpected wireless link disconnection. The protocol between the agent platform and the messaging gateway is

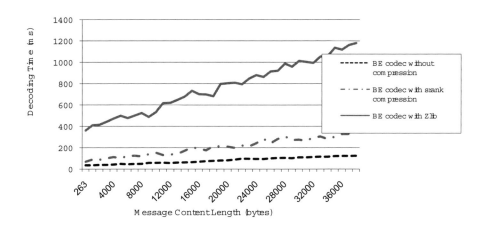

Figure 8.10: Message decoding time in Nokia 6680 mobile phone

based on HTTP. The protocol uses session identifiers in order to keep track of mobile devices. This is an important feature, since it allows roaming between different network technologies while preserving logical connections. For example, an agent situated in a mobile device can send a message to another agent in a fixed network over a GPRS connection. Before getting a reply, the mobile device roams from GPRS network to a WLAN network, and the agent at the mobile device gets a reply to its original message over a WLAN connection. The whole process is transparent to both agents.

A message transfer over a wireless connection may be in progress when an unexpected disconnection happens. In such cases, the message may be lost. The protocol of the communication between the mobile device and the messaging gateway uses message sequence numbers in order to detect if a message is lost. Should this be the case, the message is automatically retransmitted. Again, this happens transparently to the agents. Details of this protocol can be found in [5].

8.3   Summary

The agent platform and communication described above suits well for developing agent based applications for resource-poor devices. However, there are some issues that could be improved in the future.

As mentioned in Chapter 7, the end user has only one agent (the PA) in her mobile device in the CASCOM trial application. Having a full-blown FIPA-compliant agent platform for only one agent may be overkill. If only one agent in

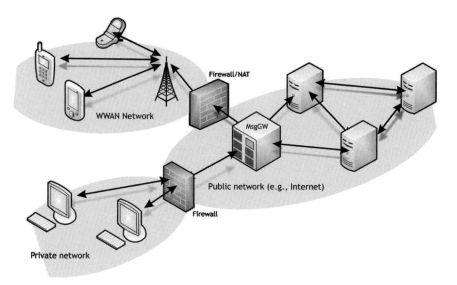

Figure 8.11: The CASCOM messaging gateway

the mobile device is needed, the agent functionality could be implemented without an agent platform and thus valuable resources in the mobile device would be saved. This, however, compromises the FIPA compliancy and thus such support was not implemented to the CASCOM architecture.

The implemented communication stack has very good support for delivering agent messages over a wireless communication path efficiently and reliably. However, more attention should be paid how agents are actually communicating. For example, if agents are sending more messages that would be absolutely necessary, scarce bandwidth will be wasted. Agents could improve their communication by choosing such communications patterns so that agent message exchanges are carried out with a minimal number of round-trips. This is especially important when using a high-latency communication path.

The CASCOM messaging gateway provides reliability to the agent communication. For example, if the wireless link is unexpectedly disconnected, no agent message is lost. However, typically applications need other kind of communication protocols as well (e.g., Web Service communication). The messaging gateway has support only for ACL communication which may not be enough for all applications. However, since the communication between a mobile device and messaging gateway is based on HTTP, it would be rather simple to add support for SOAP, as an example.

References

[1] F. Bellifemine, G. Caire, Poggi, and G. Rimassa. Jade — a white paper. *EXP — in search of Innovation (TiLab Technical Magazine)*, 3(3):20–31, September 2003.

[2] F. Bergenti, A. Poggi, B. Burg, and G. Caire. Deploying FIPA-compliant systems on handheld devices. *IEEE Internet Computing*, 5(4):20–25, 2001.

[3] G. Caire, N. Lhuillier, and G. Rimassa. A communication protocol for agents on handheld devices. In *Workshop on Ubiquitous Agents on Embedded, Wearable and Mobile Devices*, Bologna, Italy, July 2002.

[4] CASCOM Consortium. *CASCOM Project Deliverable D4.1: IP2P Network Architecture*, 2006.

[5] CASCOM Consortium. *CASCOM Project Deliverable D4.2: Technical Guide to the IP2P Service Network Environment*, 2006.

[6] P. Fenwick. A fast, constant-order, symbol ranking text compressor. Technical Report 145, Department of Computer Science, The University of Auckland, 1997.

[7] Foundation for Intelligent Physical Agents. *FIPA ACL Message Representation in Bit-Efficient Specification*. Geneva, Switzerland, October 2000. Specification number SC00069.

[8] Foundation for Intelligent Physical Agents. *FIPA ACL Message Representation in XML Specification*. Geneva, Switzerland, October 2000. Specification number SC00071.

[9] Foundation for Intelligent Physical Agents. *FIPA Agent Message Transport Envelope Representation in Bit Efficient Specification*. Geneva, Switzerland, November 2000. Specification number SC00088.

[10] Foundation for Intelligent Physical Agents. *FIPA Agent Message Transport Envelope Representation in XML Specification*. Geneva, Switzerland, November 2000. Specification number SC00085.

[11] Foundation for Intelligent Physical Agents. *FIPA Agent Message Transport Protocol for HTTP Specification*. Geneva, Switzerland, October 2000. Specification number SC00084.

[12] Foundation for Intelligent Physical Agents. *FIPA Agent Message Transport Protocol for IIOP Specification*. Geneva, Switzerland, November 2000. Specification number SC00075.

[13] Foundation for Intelligent Physical Agents. *FIPA Agent Message Transport Protocol for WAP Specification*. Geneva, Switzerland, October 2000. Specification number XC00076.

[14] Foundation for Intelligent Physical Agents. *FIPA Content Languages Specification*. Geneva, Switzerland, October 2000. Specification number SC00007.

[15] Foundation for Intelligent Physical Agents. *FIPA Nomadic Application Support Specification*. Geneva, Switzerland, November 2000. Specification number XC00014.

[16] H. Helin and M. Laukkanen. Performance analysis of software agent communication in slow wireless networks. In R. Luijten, E. Wong, K. Makki, and E. K. Park, editors, *Proceedings of the Eleventh International Conference on Computer Communications and Networks (ICCCN'02)*, pages 354–361. IEEE, October 2002.

[17] M. Laukkanen, H. Helin, and H. Laamanen. Supporting nomadic agent-based applications in the FIPA agent architecture. In C. Castelfranci and W. L. Johnson, editors, *Proceedings of the First International Joint Conference on Autonomous Agents & Multi-Agent Systems (AAMAS 2002)*, pages 1348–1355, Bologna, Italy, July 2002.

[18] M. Laukkanen, S. Tarkoma, and J. Leinonen. FIPA-OS agent platform for small-footprint devices. In J.-J. Meyer and M. Tambe, editors, *Intelligent Agents VIII, Proceedings of the Eighth International Workshop on Agent Theories, Architectures, and Languages (ATAL-2001)*, volume 2333 of *Lecture Notes in Artificial Intelligence*, pages 447–460. Springer-Verlag: Heidelberg, Germany, 2002.

[19] G. Montenegro, S. Dawkins, M. Kojo, V. Magret, and N. Vaidya. Long thin networks. Request for Comments 2757, January 2000.

[20] Object Management Group. *Common Object Request Broker Architecture: Core Specification version 3.0.3*, March 2004.

[21] D. Šišlák, M. Rollo, and M. Pěchouček. A-globe: Agent platform with inaccessibility and mobility support. In M. Klusch, S. Ossowski, V. Kashyap, and R. Unland, editors, *Cooperative Information Agents VIII*, pages 199–214, 2004.

Chapter 9

Distributed Directories of Web Services

Michael Schumacher, Alexandre de Oliveira e Sousa,
Ion Constantinescu, Tim van Pelt and Boi Faltings

9.1 Introduction

This chapter presents WSDir, the federated directory system used in CASCOM. Its main functionality is to let heterogeneous Semantic Web Service descriptions be registered and searched by certain clients. As such, it realizes a lookup function with basic retrieval schemes.

There are several main requirements for a distributed directory system. First, it should be easy to invoke by any client. This led us to define a *Web Service interface* to WSDir: it is a universally accepted standard, it provides a well-defined method to use the directory, and it allows for interacting with a heterogeneous set of clients. The sole requirement on the part of the client is that it should be able to communicate over a Web Service interface. Second, the nature of the applications to be realized requires the directory system to be distributed, for instance applying a geographical specialization of the directories. Third, the construction of the network should induce minimal overhead and should be scalable; also, the network should be robust to changes in topology and the number of interactions with the system. Fourth, the directory should allow a great number of services to be registered, and this in a very dynamic way, including lease times.

Our system is modeled as a federation: directory services form its atomic units, and the federation emerges from the registration of directory services in other directory services. Directories are virtual clusters of service entries stored in one or more directory services. To create the topology, policies are defined on all possible operations to be called on directories. For instance, they allow for routed registration and selective access to directories.

The chapter is organized as follows. In Section 9.2, we explain the service entries of Semantic Web Services that can be stored in WSDir. Sections 9.3 to 9.6 explain the architecture of WSDir by presenting *directories*, *directory services*, *directory operations*, and *policies*. In Section 9.7, we give the concrete network architecture used in CASCOM. Sections 9.8 and 9.9 discuss respectively usability and vulnerability issues of WSDir. After referring related work in Section 9.10, we conclude the chapter in Section 9.11.

9.2 Service Entries

Services are described using the Web Ontology Language for Web Services, OWL-S [4]. Internally, the directory system stores then service entries in the FIPA SL0 description language. SL0 has been chose because the whole CASCOM infrastructure is using this language for interpretability between agents. Furthermore, as we achieve with SL0 an independent way to store any kind of services and not only OWL-S descriptions.

The internal service representation contains a subset of the information provided in the original service description. This information can be used to find matching services in the directory. In addition, the original service description in OWL-S is stored in a separate slot. This field is used to retrieve the original description, e.g., to retrieve the grounding(s) of a service at service execution.

In the following, we present the information that a service entry in WSDir contains:

ServiceCategories Refers to an entry in some ontology or taxonomy of services. The value of the property is a set containing elements of the class *ServiceCategory*, which is defined in the OWL-S ontology. The information is ultimately derived from the service categories defined in the service profile.

ServiceProfileURIs This slot contains a set of profile URIs that is referred to in the service description. If the profiles are included in the service description as full-text, no URIs are stored. The URIs point to an externally stored, but (web-)retrievable service profile.

ServiceProcessURI A process URI that is defined in the service description. If none is included for the service description, the slot will be empty. If the process is included in the service description as full-text, no URI is stored. The process URI points to an externally stored, retrievable service process.

ServiceGroundings The slot that contains a set of full-text service groundings for the service. Empty set if no grounding is associated with the service (abstract service). Makes it possible to retrieve only service groundings.

OWLSServiceDescription The slot that contains the original OWL-S service description as a full-text entry. Service profile(s) and process may be referred to as URIs, though service groundings must be included as full-text.

9.3 Directories

A directory comprises a set of service entries which are managed by a collection of one or more directory services. All service entries, including directory service entries, are registered at a directory service as belonging to a specific directory. Such, directory services can form an arbitrary organisational structure (peer-to-peer, hierarchy etc.). Specifically:

- A directory can contain other directories.

- A directory supported by one or more directory services.

The above is used to characterize directories by two different types of interactions:

1. *Client-Directory* interactions: in which clients registering, deregistering, and querying the directory interact with directory services supporting the directory. They may or may not have any idea about the internals of the directory.

2. *Director-Directory* interactions: in which directory services supporting the directories interact with one another to perform the internal management of the directory (data propagation, federated queries, managing the membership of the directory service group managing the directory).

The first interaction style (*Client-Directory*) is part of the base for the creation and maintenance of a *domain directory*. The second interaction style (*Directory-Directory*) is the base for the creation and maintenance of a network directory. As directories can be used to support other directories they are seen as organizational structures. These concepts will be elaborated and exemplified in Section 9.7.1 on network topology.

9.4 Directory Services

Directory services provide a Web Service interface to a repository that holds service entries. The service entries in this store are all registered as belonging to a certain directory. The directory service forms the atomic unit of the directory federation. It allows clients to register, deregister, modify and search registrations in its repository. These registrations include service descriptions of services offered by clients as well as profiles of other directory service. By registering directory services in other directory service stores, the system becomes federated.

Figure 9.1 visually summarizes the relationship between service entries, directories and directory services. In the illustration, the directory service holds regular service entries and a directory service entry belonging to a Hospitals directory as well as entries belonging to an Insurers directory. Both directories are contained in the Body directory, which in turn is contained in the all-encompassing "." directory.

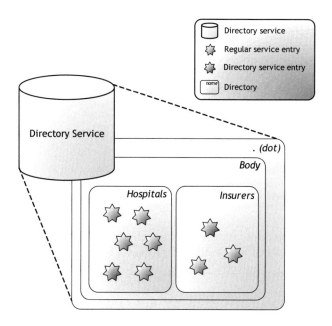

Figure 9.1: Visual recapitulation of directory system concepts

9.5   Directory Operations

The directory is able to handle five types of operations, corresponding to data manipulation primitives (*register, deregister, modify, search*) and the retrieval of meta-data information (*get-profile*). The methods are accessible remotely through a Web Service interface.

We present the operations the directory service interface offers. Before that, some of the objects that are passed as parameters are defined:

Identity-info The *identity-info* element is to be used for providing identification information regarding the invoker of a given operation in the form of an *actor-identifier*. This object can contain also a structured object providing credentials information that can be relevant to some form of authentication (e.g., a password, a X.509 certificate or a more sophisticated session key).

Directory-id The *directory-id* is a string that uniquely identifies a directory in the frame of a given directory service. It can include the names of other directories if the directory service uses a path like scheme for identifying nested directories.

Directory-token A directory-token refers to an entry registered within the directory and can be used to identify the registration entry. A directory-token contains a key (string) that uniquely identifies a particular entry in a given directory. The directory service usually generates these keys but some directories may support the registration of entries under keys specified by the client of the directory service.

Structured-object *structured-object(s)* are the data elements stored in the directory which are subsequently available for search. The only assumption about structured objects is that they have a frame-like structure similar to RDF, the SOAP XML encoding or FIPA SL0. In principle, there are no restrictions on the content of the data of the structured objects. For our experiments, the *structured-objects* are encoded in FIPA SL0.

Hereafter, we describe all operations on WSDir (except *get-profile*):

Registration

register (identity-info, directory-id, directory-token, structured-objects, lease-time)

The *register* operation enables a client to register a service description entry (as specified in the *structured-objects*) into a *directory* for a time period given by the *lease-time* parameter. If a directory-token is specified when the operation is requested then the directory should try to register the new entry using the key specified in the *directory-token*. Upon successful registration the directory service returns an *ok* message containing either a new *directory-token* or the original *directory-token* if it was specified by the user together with a new *lease-time*.

The *directory-service* can also return a *redirect* message pointing to another directory where the client could try to register its object. The detailed semantics of the *redirect* message are dependent on the policies governing the directory for which the redirect was issued. For example, this may happen for load-balancing reasons in top-level directories. To uphold the transparency of the federated nature of the system to the client, the redirection will be opaque. Note that a register policy of the directory may also forward the registration request to another directory, e.g., to balance the load of the directory.

Deregistration

deregister (identity-info, directory-id, directory-token)

The deregister operation de-registers a service that previously has been registered identified. The entry to be de-registered is included in the directory-token that has been obtained at registration.

Modification

modify (identity-info, directory-id, directory-token, structured-objects, lease-time)

The modify operation allows modifying a registered service. The structured object itself can be modified or the parameters of the entry, such as the lease-time.

Search

search (identity-info, directory-id, structured-objects, search-constraints)

The *search* operation looks in the directory for services that match a template (*structured-objects*). The request can possibly be forwarded to supporting directories, depending on the implemented search policy at the directory. As the internal service descriptions are expressed as SL0 expressions, the structured element used in the operation is also an SL0 expression. *Search-constraints* can be specified in order to restrain the search:

- The *max-time* specifies a deadline by which the constrained search should return the results.

- The *max-depth* specifies the maximum depth of propagation of the search to federated directories.

- The *max-results* element specifies the maximum number of results to be returned.

In Section 9.7.4, we show an example of how a search procedure is internally handled.

9.6   Policies

Directory services employ *directory policies* to regulate the operation of directories. Policies are defined per directory service in the *directory service profile* and determine the behaviour of a specific directory. Two types of policies can be distinguished:

Pro-active policies Policies of this type are typically used for internal management of the directories. A policy may be attached to a directory to establish the number of times per hour data is propagated within the directory, how often old entries are removed etc.

Reactive policies These policies assign a behaviour to combinations of directories and operations. The policies are executed whenever a bound operation is called. They are defined as a triple: *(directory name, operation, policy)*.

Policies can also be applied to the default directory named "***" which matches all directories that don't have a policy explicitly assigned.

From the consequent application of policies, the network topology emerges. Policies can for example define how much entries can be registered per directory, which directories can be searched by which clients, and which types of services

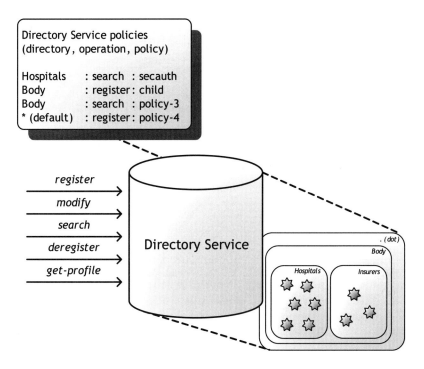

Figure 9.2: Example use of policies

will be accepted. Each directory service can define its own policies or use one of the pre-defined policies. The only requirement on the part of a policy is that it can be executed.

A straightforward example of a pre-defined policy is the *child/sibling* policy: this policy forwards all operations to both the known children (directory services registered in the service store) as well as its known siblings. The list of siblings is obtained by querying the parent directory service at which it has registered itself.

Figure 9.2 shows an example of the reactive policies that are assigned to the various directories this directory service supports. In the illustration, when a client calls the search operation on the "Hospitals" directory, a policy called "secauth" will be applied. Such a policy could for example require the client to authenticate itself before it is allowed to query the directory.

9.7 CASCOM Service Directory Architecture

WSDir allows to setup flexible distributed directory systems, especially thanks to the mechanism of policies. We present here a specific application of WSDir to build a network of directory services which are modelled as a virtual tree with multiple roots. This topology is the network architecture that has been used in the CASCOM infrastructure.

9.7.1   Network Topology

The nodes of the tree are made up by the individual directory services. This hierarchical structure with multiple entry points effectuates:

- No replication or data caching within the directory: each directory service is responsible for registrations made in its local store;

- Forwarding search only: since there is no replication, directory services will forward queries to other directory services;

- Query message duplicate checking: a given directory service will handle only the first of several identical query messages from several sources and discard the others while returning the appropriate failure message;

- No results duplicate checking: identical results may be returned by one or more directory services for a single query. This enhances the robustness of the federation at the cost of shifting the burden of filtering the results to the client.

In the network, we distinguish two types of directories: network directories and domain directories. *Network directories* are a reserved set of directories that are used for the construction of the network. In a directory federation, we can distinguish three different network directories:

- *Hidden* network directory: the directory service that forms the root of the federation by registering the top-level nodes of the network. Neither the directory service nor its registered services will be visible to the other nodes in the federation.

- *Top* network directory: visible to the network as being one of the roots of the federation multi-rooted tree. A directory service with this role could typically serve as a bootstrap service to leaf directory services. These services constitute the Top network directory.

- *Body* network directory: regular directory services that form the body of the multi-rooted tree. These directory services provide the interface to the directories that will contain most of the service registrations in the network.

Domain directories emerge from the registrations of service descriptions at the directory services that make up the directory system. By definition, domain directories are contained in the "Body Members" directory.

Hereafter, we explain the network directories in more detail. The above-mentioned roles and their place in a WSDir federation topology are depicted in Figure 9.3.

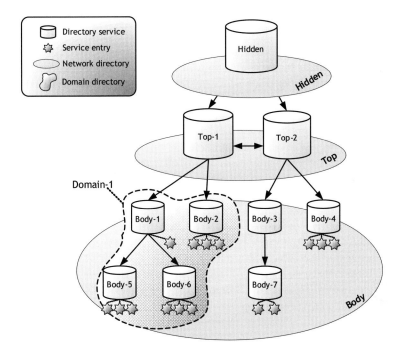

Figure 9.3: Network topology

Hidden Network Directory

The Hidden directory service node responds only to requests coming from Top directory services and exclusively regarding the "Top Members" directory. For that it holds authentication information regarding a pre-configured list of possible top-level nodes and uses this information together with information in the identity-info field of the requests. Search queries are not propagated to other directory services. The location of the hidden directory service node is pre-defined.

The existence of this domain ensures that directory services belonging to the "Top Members" directory know of their respective existence and such makes sure that every node in the network can be reached if needed. The hidden directory service is only used for bootstrapping of the top member directory services. After the system has been initialized, the hidden directory service will only be used by the top member directory services to poll to see whether new directory services have been added to the "Top" network directory. Thus, queries, registrations and other requests do not go through the hidden directory service, but will be directed at a top or body member directory service.

Top Network Directory

Upon start-up the Top directory services join the network by registering their directory-service-profiles inside the "Top Members" directory of the Hidden directory service. Also they keep track of other Top directory services currently members of the "Top Members" directory by continuously polling the "Top Members" directory of the Hidden directory service for directory-service-profiles entries. In the case that the Hidden directory service fails the Top directory services should continue to use the last retrieved membership information until the Hidden directory service will be back online. In terms of response to registration requests from clients, a Top directory service allows only for the registration of directory-service-profile entries inside the "Body Members" directory. Once the number of registrations that are hold locally goes over a given threshold the Top directory service returns redirect messages pointing requestors. Normal directory services directly registered with the current directory service. For any other kind of registration requests the Top directory services will issue redirect responses pointing at Normal directory services registered with the current directory services or other Top directory services that might be more appropriate for use. Top directory services will respond to all search requests by first trying to fulfil them locally and in the case that more results can be returned (the value of the max-results parameter in the search-constraints object has not been reached yet) it will forward the query to all other Top directory services members of the "Top Members" network directory. For determining the other Top directory services members of the "Top Members" directory the information from the last successful polling of the Hidden directory service will be used. Top directory services will respond with a failure to all other kinds of requests.

Body Network Directory

At start-up, a Body directory service will try to register its directory-service-profile in the "Body Members" directory of a Top directory service randomly picked from a pre-configured list of Top directory services. If the Top directory service cannot be reached another one is randomly picked until either the joining procedure (see next) succeeds or the list is exhausted. In the latter case the directory service will report a join failure. The directory service will follow redirect responses until the entry is successfully registered with a directory service (either Top or Body). Upon failure of the directory service used for registration the current directory service will sleep for a random time period and after than will re-initiate the initial join procedure.

For other Body directory services that try to register directory-service-profile entries inside the "Body Members" directory a Body directory service will act as a Top directory service: once the number of registrations that are hold locally goes over a given threshold the Body directory service will return redirect messages pointing requestors to child Body directory services directly registered with the current directory service.

A Body directory service will respond positively to all other requests. In particular it will forward search queries for which it could return more results than locally available to directory services locally registered in the "Body Members" directory.

9.7.2 Network Construction

At boot time, the directory makes use of a pre-defined network configuration to create a network topology. The configuration specifies management and data relations between members of the network.

Some of the network nodes might have fixed well-known addresses in order to serve as bootstrap hosts for other directory services. Depending on their role, different parts of the network are visible to bootstrapping directory services.

As mentioned before, in a typical setting, the node at the highest level will be hidden to all nodes not belonging to the "Top Members" directory.

The process of directory service registration is equivalent to the process of registering regular service entries. Directory services are registered invoking the same register method as is used for registering regular services. Instead of an OWL-S Profile, the passed structured object contains a *directory-service-profile* object.

9.7.3 Used Directory Policies

WSDir employs a set of pre-defined pro-active policies, mainly for routing purposes. Figure 9.4 gives an overview of the pre-defined policies and their hierarchy. We do note present here the details of each policy. However, we show in Figure 9.5 how these policies are applied to construct the basic network topology . Per network directory, the set of policies in place is listed.

For example, a registration request directed at a directory belonging to the "Hidden" network directory triggers the application of the *ChildRegisterPolicy*. The service registration request is forwarded to its known children, which themselves apply (by default) the *ChildSiblingRegisterPolicy*. This in turn selects the least loaded directory service among its children and among its siblings to put the service entry in its store.

The procedure for a *search* operation is similar. Requests directed at a directory service either belonging to the "Hidden" network directory or to the "Top" network directory will forward the search request to its registered children and its known siblings. The directory service instances belonging to the "Body" network directory apply the *DefaultSearchPolicy*, only searching their local store.

For the *modify*, *deregister* and *get-profile* operation, the policies that are assigned to the operations also depend on the network directory the directory service instance belongs to.

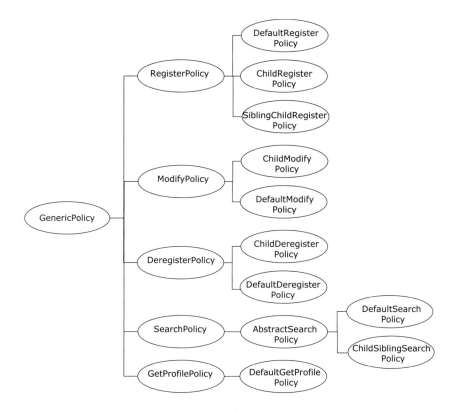

Figure 9.4: Predefined policy tree

9.7.4   Examples of Network Interactions

The following section describes two examples of the policy-governed query operation of the network of directories as presented previously. The visible network is formed from a number of "well-known" top nodes (Top-1, Top-2, Top-3) with a fixed name and transport address (but which can possibly fail) and an arbitrary number of leaf nodes which are organized in a tree topology with one of the top nodes as root.

We illustrate the process of query resolution in Figure 9.6 and 9.7: a client issues a search request for service profiles matching a template in the *Hospital* domain directory. The template is provided in the form of a *structured-object*.

1. First, the client issuing the query randomly selects one of the top level nodes (*Top-1, Top-2, Top-3*). In this example, *Top-2* is picked.

2. The *Top-2* directory service forwards the query to its siblings.

3. Directory services that have an entry for the *Hospital* domain directory in their service profile propagate the query down.

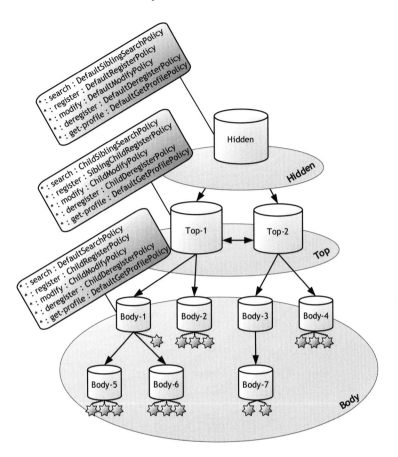

Figure 9.5: Policies in the network topology

4. To guarantee full query resolution, the query is forwarded to all directory services that are known to store entries for the *Hospital* domain directory.

5. Finally, upon finding results, the nodes holding the results will send a message back (depicted by "R=x" in the figure, where x denotes the number of matched services) to the directory service it was queried by, until it reaches the original requester. In this case, the matching service profiles in the directory services supporting the *Hospital* domain directory will be returned.

The next sections will now discuss the usability, vulnerability and performance of WSDir.

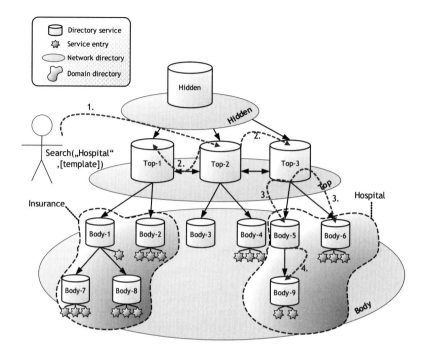

Figure 9.6: Query resolution (1)

9.8   Usability

For every instance of a WSDir's Directory Service, the user must write its own configuration file. This configuration file is accessed and read by the Directory Service during its starting procedure. The name of this file must be explicitly written in a file web.xml of the Directory Service.

The syntax of this file is based on FIPA SLO. It contains all the necessary information for the Directory Service to create its directories, associate the policies and start building a predefined network topology with other Directory Services. The user must specify the following information: i) name and address of the Directory Service; ii) name(s), address(es) and credentials of the Directory Services it should register in; iii) name of the directories it manages; iv) name of the policies that applies to directories for each operation.

Another issue regarding the WSDir's usability is monitoring its's run time activity. There are currently two ways to do this. The first one is to use a Java client which enables a human user to browse through the Directory Services and their directories. Directories and services entries are displayed in a visual tree. The user can fold/unfold directories and check which services are currently registered in a Directory Service. The second way to monitor WSDir's activity is to deploy

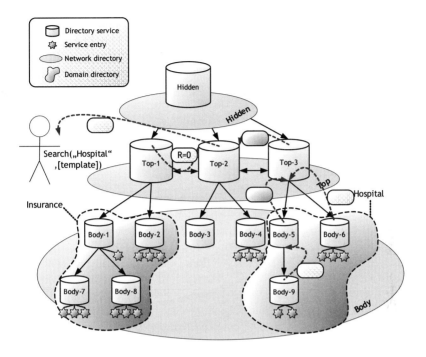

Figure 9.7: Query resolution (2)

a servlet on the same server where an instance of a Directory Service is running. Depending on this Directory Service's configuration, a user will be able to access a web page that displays a set of logs of registration requests made on it. Thus, the user can check whether his requests (registration, modification or remove) were successfully executed.

In either way, no performance information nor disfunction messages are being displayed to the user monitoring WSDir's activity. The user is then leaded to check the logs files if something wrong happened. Monitoring Directory Services performance at run time as well as errors would be a major contribution to WSDIR's usability.

On the other hand, once a topology has been decided and the configuration files have been written correctly, it is very easy to launch a federation. There exists a Java class (Startservices) that takes an ordered list of Directory Service addresses and automatically launch all of them. The user can also take advantage of another graphical tool that enables him to directly send a request to a specific Directory Service.

9.9   Vulnerability

In this section, we discuss two major issues in WSDir's vulnerability. The first one concerns server failures and breakdowns. The second one concerns more the security restrictions and users rights. In both cases, WSDir copes with those issues by using specific mechanisms. WSDir uses its loosely coupled directories and a data backup system to efficiently handle breakdowns. It implements an authentication mechanisms to identify the clients sending incoming requests.

9.9.1   Breakdowns

In the CASCOM project, we have used the network topology presented in 9.7.1, where the federation is structured in three Network layers: the Hidden layer, the Top layer and the Body layer. Although all Directory Services, regardless from which Network they belong to, can operate all requests, only those situated in the Top layer are accessed by the CASCOM's Discovery Agents. As each Network layer plays a specific role in WSDir's Federation, three breakdown scenario are discussed. Figure 9.8 illustrates the accessible Service Descriptions stored in a WSDir's Federation when all the Directory Services are running correctly. All descriptions can be accessed by a Client (the group of accessible Directory Services is defined by the quadratic border).

In a first failure scenario, a Directory Service located in the Body Network layer fails (see Figure 9.9). This failing Directory Service does not affect the rest of the Federation. However, the local set of stored Service Descriptions becomes unaccessible for any clients. The rest of the Descriptions stored in the other Directory Services are still available for the Clients, enabling them to continue working with a restricted number of Service Descriptions. The Federation still processes all five operations (search, register, deregister, modify and get Meta Data). There exists a mechanism allowing Directory Services to recover after a breakdown. This is explained in the recovery section below.

In a second failure scenario, it is a Directory Service located in the Top Network layer that fails (see Figure 9.10). The Federation is 'amputated' by the failing Directory Service's branch. In this case also, the rest of the Federation remains operational but all the Service Descriptions stored under the failing Directory Service become unavailable. Thus, several actions can be triggered while the Directory Service is down:

1. The clients (Discovery Agents) have a pre-configured list of addresses of Directory Services that are operating on the Top Layer Network. Thanks to this list, the clients can still access the Federation by picking up a new address from the list and simply contacting another Directory Service in the Top layer Network.

2. Directory Services in the Body layer Network that are operating under the failing Directory Services can also have a list of addresses of Directory Ser-

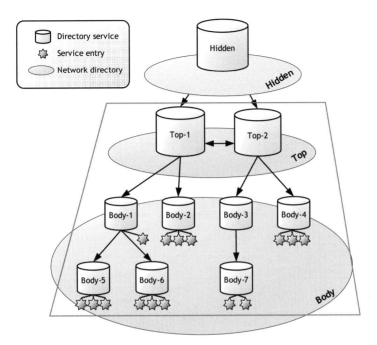

Figure 9.8: A WSDir Federation with all the Directory Services from each Network layer is working correctly. The quadratic border defines the group of currently accessible Service Descriptions stored in the Federation.

vices in the Top layer Network. Being notified that the current Directory Service in which they registered fails, they can register themselves in another Directory Service operating in the Top layer Network. Most of the Service Descriptions stored in the Federation would then be accessible again.

These two mechanisms enable the clients to continue working with the Federation as well as providing the maximum number of Service Descriptions available to those Clients. The failing Directory Service can recover using the recovering mechanism described in the following section.

In a third failure scenario, it is the Directory Service in the Hidden layer that breaks down (see Figure 9.11). In this case, the Directory Services in the Top layer cannot communicate with each other anymore. This has the effect of creating groups of available Service Descriptions. A Client requesting a Directory Service from the top layer will only receive a restricted number of Service Description. Although the Federation is still operational, it would be better for Clients to access all Service Descriptions. Thus, to cope with that, Top Network layer's Directory Services use the same mechanism as those in the Body Network layer. They can be set with a list of addresses of Directory Services operating in the Hidden Network layer and registered in them when the regular one fails. In this case, several backup

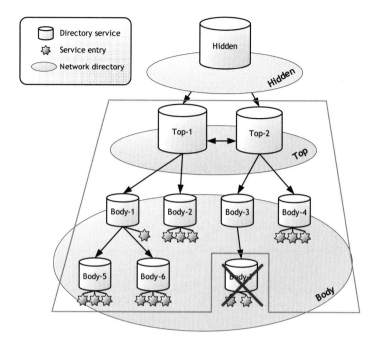

Figure 9.9: A WSDir Federation with one Directory Service from the Body Network layer is failing. The quadratic border defines the group of currently accessible Service Descriptions stored in the Federation.

Directory Services must be ready. The failing Directory Service can recover using the recovering mechanism described in the following section.

9.9.2   Recovery

WSDir has been designed to cope with breakdowns by always keeping some parts of the Federation operational. When a Directory Service is down, the Service Descriptions stored in its memory are not accessible. Once the server works fine again, the Directory Service can be restarted[1]. When it restarts, it searches for a specific internal database that has been specified in the Directory Service's configuration file. Directory Services use this database to log all insert and modification requests coming from outside clients. Delete requests erase a specific entry in the database. It contains the following columns: i) the directory token of the Service Description; ii) the lease time during which the Service Description is supposed to stay stored in the Directory Service; iii) the full registration/modification request as sent by the Client.

The directory token is the primary key of the table. It is a unique identifier

---

[1]The starting procedure is done by invoking a start method on the particular Directory Service

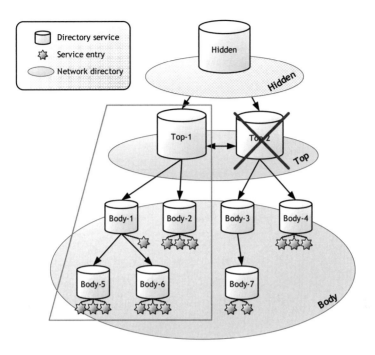

Figure 9.10: A WSDir Federation with one Directory Service from the Top Network layer is failing. The quadratic border defines the group of currently accessible Service Descriptions stored in the Federation.

for each Service Description. The lease time is also stored to ensure that when a Directory Service restarts, the elapsed time of the failure is taken into consideration. Finally, the registration/modification request is stored in the database for the following reason: rather than creating a fixed and structured schema in the database to support a specific semantic language (such as OWLS), the full request is stored as a block and then decoded by the Directory Service during recovery. By doing so, WSDir can be easily adapted to store other types of Web Service semantic languages.

9.9.3 Security

Regarding WSDir's vulnerability, there is an important issue about client authentication. For several applications, it is crucial to restrict access and interaction to trustful clients, avoiding requests from malicious entities. WSDir copes with this issue at two levels. First, clients have to provide in their requests both a sender and a receiver identification[2]. Furthermore, they may be asked to provide an encrypted password and/or a K.509 certificate. The Directory Service serving the

---

[2]This is part of the mandatory fields in the SL0 messages the Clients creates for each request

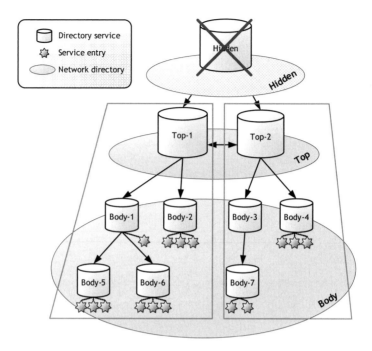

Figure 9.11: A WSDir Federation with the Directory Services from the hidden Network layer is failing. The quadratic borders define several groups of currently accessible Service Descriptions stored in the Federation.

request can then decide if the client trustful or not. On the second level, WSDir uses policies, binding operations to directories. Depending on the policies, some of the authentication information will be used to grant or deny access to a specific clients. On the other hand, as WSDir runs as a Web Service itself and uses the HTTP protocol, it may also take advantage of the HTTPS protocol. This mechanism ensures a client that it is contacting a trustful Directory Service.

9.10   Related Work

In this section, we discuss related research in Semantic Web Services discovery. We are considering only systems that have been fully implemented, as it is the case for WSDir.

The METEOR-S discovery framework [6] copes with the problem of discovering services in a scenario where service providers and requesters may use terms from different ontologies. Based on user's ontology, METEOR-S's Web Service Discovery Infrastructure organizes multiple registries[3], enabling semantic classifi-

---
[3]Web Service registries for publishing Web Services

cation of all Web Services based on domains. Their approach relies on annotating semantically service registries (for a particular domain) and exploiting such annotations during discovery. This system can be deployed in a Peer-to-Peer network, relying on the JXTA[4] project, making it scalable. Two algorithms have been implemented. One for semantic publication of Web Services and the second one for discovery of those Web Services.

This project differs from WSDir by allowing multiple ontologies to be used at the same time. This approach solves an interoperability issue that WSDir doesn't treat, although WSDir has an open architecture for any types of ontologies. In contrast to METEOR-S which implements a dedicated algorithm for discovery, WSDir can use many matchmaking modules for discovery. This thus allows WSDir to be more flexible for specific use cases.

GLUE [3] is a WSMO[5] compliant discovery engine that aims at developing an efficient system for the management of semantically described Web Services and their discovery. GLUE is built around an open source f-logic inference engine called Flora-2[6] that runs over XSB[7]. The basis of the GLUE infrastructure is a set of facilities for registering and looking up WSMO components (ontologies, goals, Web Service descriptions and mediators). With the use of these components, GLUE implements a matching mechanism that relies on wgMediators. Requester entities register a class of goals. Discovery is then performed by submitting goals. Similarly, providers register first a class of Web Service descriptions and then publish Web Service descriptions. The link between a class of Web Services and a class of goals is embedded in a dedicated wgMediator, that uses a set of f-logic rules to assert similarities. In contrast to the GLUE approach where a central storage unit is used with a single inference engine, WSDir avoids bottle neck problems by distributing its Directory Services; therefore, all requests are splitted between several Directory Services.

The WSPDS system [1] is also a peer-to-peer discovery system that is enabled with semantic matchmaking. In WSPDS, WSDL files need to be semantically annotated in order to be available for discovery. This is done by using the WSDL-S framework[8]. By doing so, the WSDL-S file doesn't have to know anything about the ontology being used by a Web Service description file such as OWL-S or WSMO. The system is built around a peer-to-peer architecture, where peers act as servants (acting both as clients and servers). Discovery queries can be sent to any servant, that will forward the query to its neighbors. All the communication is done via SOAP messages. WSDir aligns itself very closely to the WSPDS service. They use both a Web Service interface and they rely on a peer-to-peer architecture. The main difference is in the work to be done for new ontologies. In WSPDS, each

---

[4]See https://jxta.dev.java.net/

[5]WSMO - Web Service Modeling Ontology, see http://www.wsmo.org/

[6]See http://flora.sourceforge.net/

[7]XSB is an open source implementation of tabled-prolog and deductive database system. See http://xsb.sourceforge.net/

[8]see http://www.w3.org/Submission/WSDL-S/

WSDL file needs to be re-written using the WSDL-S framework. In contrast, WSDir simply needs to add the appropriate matchmaking module.

[5] describes a framework for Semantic Web Service discovery. This framework is based on context specific mappings from a user ontology to a specific domain ontology. Using these mappings, the user queries are then transformed into a specific form of query. These queries can be processed by a match making engine that takes in consideration the domain ontologies and the stored Web Services. In the prototype implementation, the match making engine is based on JESS and JENA, that uses a JESS knowledge base. When service providers store their services, the Service Registry API parses and converts the OWL ontology into a collection of JESS facts, and stores them in a knowledge base. This project unifies multiple ontologies and copes with interoperability issues, making them transparent for the user. But like the GLUE project, it has a bottle neck architecture because of its central storing unit. In contrast, WSDir uses a distributed architecture.

9.11   Summary

WSDir has been tested thoroughly in a real distributed setting spread over different countries. The system has proven to be scalable and very stable. We have integrated the system in the CASCOM use case scenario. Among others, future work could enhance the following aspects.

From the security and privacy-awareness point of view, we currently employ standard security mechanisms for accessing the directory services. In particular, if a directory service requires protecting messaging from overhearing or if it would require privacy sensible data as parameters, the access to this Web Service will be based on HTTPS. In cases where no HTTPS is available, we could couple WSDir with Guarantor agents [2] spread in the architecture in order to provide a secure tunneling between agent messages and HTTPS.

Another improvement could define security measures directly within the directory system by defining specific policies. A policy can be employed to restrict the right to perform a certain operation on a directory to only those clients that can provide the right credentials. Using this method, registration of services to a directory and search operations on directories can be restricted. For example, a directory service that does not forward any queries pertaining to a *Hospital* domain directory will simply return its entries for the domain and nothing more. This would be completely transparent to the requestor, as its view of the network topology is determined by the application of policies of the directory services underneath it.

As mentioned in the usability Section 9.8, administrating and monitoring WSDir was not a major priority during its development. Although several tools have been developed to cope with testing issues, the system lacks consistency. Some of these tools should be enhanced and packaged into a single administration package. Beyond that, a complete WSDir editor should be developed to help administrators setting up easily networks of Directory Services.

References

[1] F. Banaei-Kashani, C.-C. Chen, and C. Shahabi. Wspds: Web Services peer-to-peer discovery service. In *Proceedings of the International Symposium on Web Services and Applications(ISWS'04)*, Nevada, June 2004.

[2] R. Bianchi, A. Fontana, and F. Bergenti. A real-world approach to secure and trusted negotiation in mass. In *AAMAS '05: Proceedings of the fourth international joint conference on Autonomous agents and multiagent systems*, pages 1163–1164, New York, NY, USA, 2005. ACM Press.

[3] E. Della Valle, D. Cerizza, and I. Celino. The mediators centric approach to automatic Web Service discovery of glue. In *Proceedings of the First International Workshop on Mediation in Semantic Web Services: MEDIATE 2005*, Amsterdam, Netherlands, December 2005.

[4] D. Martin, M. Paolucci, S. McIlraith, M. Burstein, D. McDermott, D. McGuinness, B. Parsia, T. Payne, M. Sabou, M. Solanki, N. Srinivasan, and K. Sycara. Bringing semantics to Web Services: The owl-s approach. In *Proceedings of the First International Workshop on Semantic Web Services and Web Process Composition (SWSWPC 2004)*, 2004.

[5] J. Pathak, N. Koul, D. Caragea, and Honavar V. A framework for Semantic Web Services discovery. In ACM, editor, *Proceedings of the ACM 7th Intl. workshop on Web Information and Data Management (WIDM-2005)*, 2005.

[6] K. Verma, K. Sivashanmugam, A. Sheth, A. Patil, S. Oundhakar, and J. Miller. METEOR-S WSDI: A Scalable Infrastructure of Registries for Semantic Publication and Discovery of Web Services. *Journal of Information Technology and Management*, 2004.

Chapter 10

Service Discovery

Luis Botelho, Alberto Fernández, Benedikt Fries, Matthias Klusch, Lino Pereira, Tiago Santos, Pedro Pais, Matteo Vasirani

10.1 Introduction

Semantic service discovery is the process of locating Web Services based on the description of their functional and non-functional semantics. Both service oriented computing and the semantic Web envision intelligent agents to proactively pursue this task on behalf of their clients. Service discovery can be performed in different ways depending on the service description framework, on means of service selection, and on its coordination through assisted mediation or in a peer-to-peer fashion.

In the CASCOM system, semantic service discovery is realised by the interplay between a service discovery agent (SDA), a project distributed service repository (WSDir), and a semantic service matchmaker (SMA). On request, the SDA searches for relevant services in both the WSDir and in its own local service repository. Service selection is implemented through means of a rather coarse-grained keyword-based matching of services as a quick filtering operation by the SDA which is complemented by a more fine-grained logic-based analysis of service semantics by the SMA.

This chapter is structured as follows. First, we provide an overview of the discovery approach based on the interaction between SDA, WSDir, and SMA. This is followed by a more detailed description of both agents, the SDA and the SMA with focus on the integrated service matchmaking algorithms. The chapter ends with a conclusions section.

10.2 Overview

In the CASCOM system, service discovery results of the cooperation between the requester (Personal Agent), the Service Discovery Agent (SDA) that coordinates

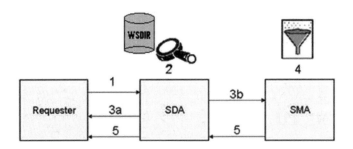

Figure 10.1: Service selection process in CASCOM

the search process, the WSDIR (a distributed service directory described in Chapter 9), and the Service Matchmaking Agent (SMA) with several integrated matchmaking algorithms. The WSDIR stores advertised OWL-S service descriptions and supports searching for them according to both functional and non-functional service semantics. The typical semantic service discovery process in CASCOM is depicted in Figure 10.1.

In step 1, the requester asks the SDA for services or service providers matching specified criteria. In step 2, the SDA extracts the specified service category from the received request and consults its own service database and the WSDIR to acquire the services that match the specified category. This coarse-grained step corresponds to a quick filtering operation that is part of the whole service selection process.

Next, the SDA matches the services that passed the quick filter with the remaining criteria specified in the request. Service selection can be entirely performed by the SDA itself based on its internal service repository or consultance of the distributed service directory (WSDir), or by calling the semantic service matchmaker SMA depending on the service selection criteria specified in the received request.

If all specified criteria involve only simple matching operations (e.g., category matching) the matching process is done by the SDA only. If the specified criteria require complex matching processes, such as preconditions and effects matchmaking, subsumption reasoning, or role-based matchmaking, the matching process is performed by the SMA. If the SDA can solely perform the matching process without the SMA, it sends the resultant set of services to the requester (step 3a). If it is necessary to involve the SMA, the SDA sends the discovered set of services together with the original request to the SMA (step 3b).

In the fourth step, the SMA selects the set of services that match according to the specified criteria. In step 5, the results are returned to the SDA and consequently to the requester. Although context processing is not explicitly represented in Figure 10.1, each agent acquires relevant context information, possibly from the context acquisition and management system (see Chapter 13), and uses it to better adapt its performance to the current situation.

In summary, the SDA can initially prune the set of available services to those that match according to a given criteria. The SDA may trigger an additional logic-based matching process on those initially selected services by the SMA. Finally, the SDA internal service database and the WSDIR store service descriptions according to different policies and ensure privacy and security.

Finally, please note that the separation between the SDA, the SMA and the WSDir, although allowing for better and easier system development and management, also has the disadvantage of requiring more intense communication of service descriptions. Besides, it has to be appropriately upgraded to also work for service discovery in totally distributed networks without service directories.

10.3   The CASCOM Service Discovery Agent

Besides service discovery, the SDA may also be used by service providers to register their services in the WSDIR or in its database. This is an important feature because the WSDIR, being a Web Service, does not provide an agent interface. Therefore, if a service registration agent interface with WSDir is desired, the SDA may be used. Currently, the SDA offers the following functionalities:

- Request a set of complete service descriptions, service profiles, service processes, or service groundings that match the specified criteria

- Register a complete service description, a service profile, a service process or service grounding.

- Associate a profile, a process, or grounding to a specified service

- Remove a complete service description, or a service profile, service process or service grounding

- Register or remove a service provider.

The separated manipulation of the several elements of the service description (service profile, service process and service grounding) is an important feature because a service can have several profiles or several groundings. Unfortunately, this separation is possible only when using the SDA internal service database; The WSDir does not support such separation. The SDA, as all other agents of the CASCOM service coordination system, uses the FIPA ACL communication language with FIPA SL contents. Figure 10.2 shows an example of a message used to request a set of complete service descriptions that match a given service profile, which is specified through an URL.

The interaction with the Service Discovery Agent is based on the FIPA Request interaction protocol, which is used for an agent to request another one to perform some specified action Figure 10.3.

The receiving agent can accept or refuse to perform the requested action. If the receiver refuses to execute the requested action, the conversation stops,

```
(REQUEST
 :sender (agent-identifier :name client@cascom)
 :receiver (set (agent-identifier :name sda@cascom))
 :content "((action
     (agent-identifier :name sda@cascom)
     (getMatchingServices
       :profileURI
         \"http://www.daml.org/services/owl-s/1.1/BravoAirProfile.owl\"
         :profileLocation \"http//localhost/BravoAirProfile.owl
         :useMatchmaker false\")))"
 :language fipa-sl
 :protocol fipa-request)
```

Figure 10.2: Example request message for relevant services

otherwise, the receiver must try to execute it. In case of success, the receiver sends the results to the sender or merely informs it that the action was successfully executed. In case of failure, the receiver must inform the sender that the execution failed, and the reasons of failure.

The SDA was completely implemented in JAVA. It uses the OWL-S API[1] to read and process OWL-S service descriptions[2]. For results of evaluating the SDA discovery agent, we refer to Chapter 16.

10.4   The CASCOM Service Matchmaker

Within the CASCOM coordination system, the semantic service selection functionality is provided by the Service Matchmaking Agent (SMA). This agent is constituted by three building blocks, each of them corresponding to a different Semantic Web Service matchmaker: the hybrid service I/O matchmaker OWLS-MX, the Precondition and Effect matchmaker PCEM, and the Role-based matchmaker ROWLS.

The OWLS-MX matchmaker (see Section 10.5) performs hybrid service signature matching through complementing logic-based semantic I/O matching with syntactic token-based similarity metrics to obtain the best of both worlds - description logics and information retrieval. The Precondition and Effect matchmaker PCEM (see Section 10.6) exploits pre-conditions and effects of service descriptions, converting them in logic predicates and using a Prolog reasoner to determine exact and inferred relations. The Role-based matchmaker ROWLS (see Section 10.7) exploits the structuring of services in terms of organisational concepts such as roles and types of social interactions.

---

[1]See http://www.mindswap.org/
[2]Further details about SDA (including a Demo) can be found at http://www.we-b-mind.org/sda

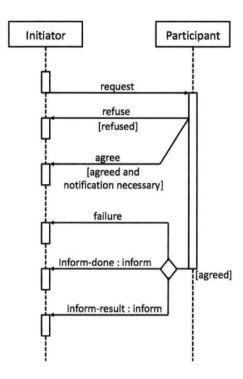

Figure 10.3: FIPA-request protocol of SDA

10.4.1 Configurations

How to properly integrate these different matchmakers into the CASCOM service matchmaker? In the project, we implemented the following configurations:

1. *Sequential.* Using the three matchmakers sequentially, where each matchmaker acts as a pre-filter of the next one in the sequence. A possible configuration can be the one depicted in Figure 10.4, where the role-based matchmaker possibly reduces the number of input services of OWLS-MX, which in turn reduces the number of input services of the PCEM matchmaker. This order has been chosen on the basis of the computational complexity of the matchmakers.

2. *Concurrent.* Running all three matchmakers with the same set of services and then combining the returned degrees of match with an aggregation function (Figure 10.5).

At the time the SMA is called by another agent, the individual configuration of utilizing the matchmaking modules can be chosen by setting a special parameter in the request message.

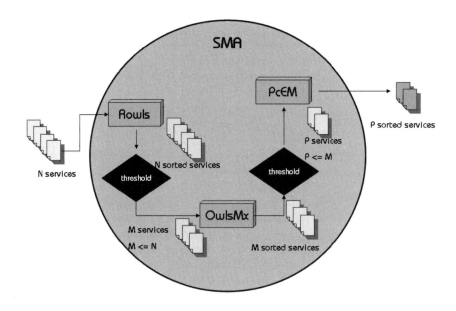

Figure 10.4: Sequential configuration

Sequential Matching by the SMA. A possible configuration is executing firstly the role-based matchmaker. The role-based matchmaker assigns to every service a real valued number between 0 and 1.

Then, a reduced set of these services are given to OWLS-MX as input. This reduced set can be composed by

- All the services which have a role-based degree of match greater than a threshold

- The first K services of the ordered set, where K is fixed

- The first M services of the ordered set, where M is a percentage of the original set size

OWLS-MX performs the matchmaking with this reduced set of services, and returns an ordered list of services, depending of the parametrization of the match-maker. There are five possible instantiations of OWLS-MX, M0 to M4, where M0 stands for a purely logic-based semantic matching, while the others instantiations additionally use a token-based syntactic similarity metric (namely, the known "Loss-of-information", "Extended Jacquard", "Cosine", and "Jensen-Shannon divergence" based similarity measure). The configurable parameters comprise the minimum degree of match, the matchmaker type and, in case of use of syntactic similarity metric, the syntactic similarity threshold. The minimum degree of match can be *EXACT, PLUG_IN, SUBSUMES, SUBSUMED_BY* or *NEAR-*

EST_NEIGHBOUR, while the syntactic similarity threshold is a real value used only for *SUBSUMED_BY* or *NEAREST_NEIGHBOUR* match.

Finally, the output of OWLS-MX is passed to the PCEM matchmaker as input. Since this matchmaker does not return a real valued degree of matching, the SMA calculates the (final) matching value as follows (cf. Section 10.6)

$$(Precondition\ Exact\ Matching \lor Precondition\ Reasoning\ Matching) \land$$
$$(Effect\ Exact\ Matching \lor Effect\ Reasoning\ Matching)$$

The return value of this formula (TRUE or FALSE) is used to create the final returned set of services. We have chosen this order of the matchmakers because the computational complexity of the role-based matchmaker ROWLS is lower than the computational complexity of OWLS-MX, which is in turn lower than the computational complexity of the PCEM matchmaker. Hence, the matchmaker that is supposed to work with the greatest set of services is the role-based one (ROWLS); OWLS-MX will work with a smaller set of services, and PCEM with an even smaller one.

The parameters that need to be set in this configuration of the SMA are

- The filter parameter of the role-based matchmaker ROWLS (threshold or K or M);

- The type of OWLS-MX matchmaker (M0, M1, M2, M3, M4), the minimum degree of match and the similarity threshold.

Aggregated Matching by the SMA. Another possible configuration of the SMA is the execution of all three matchmakers in parallel with the same set of services, and the aggregation of the results by means of special aggregation function.

For this purpose, it is necessary that every matchmaker assigns a matching value for every service. However, only the role-based matchmaker returns a real number between 0 and 1 as degree of match, while a degree of match for the PCEM matchmaker can be generated applying the above logic formula (returning a value equal to either 0 or 1). The OWLS-MX, on the other hand, returns the degree of match as a category, which can be *EXACT, PLUG_IN, SUBSUMES, SUBSUMED_BY* and *NEAREST_NEIGHBOUR*, while all the other services that are not returned can be considered having a degree of match equal to *FAIL*. So, for the OWLS-MX it is necessary to assign to every category, a real valued number between 0 and 1 (for example, *EXACT* $= 1$, *PLUG_IN* $= 0.7$, *SUBSUMES* $= 0.5$, *SUBSUMED_BY* $= 0.3$, *NEAREST_NEIGHBOUR* $= 0.1$, *FAIL* $= 0$).

Having assigned a degree of match for every service matched by every matchmaker, it is possible to combine the three results with an aggregation function, and order the original set of services on the basis of the aggregation value. Possible aggregation functions are the minimum, the product, the weighted product or more complex ones.

The parameters that need to be set in this configuration are

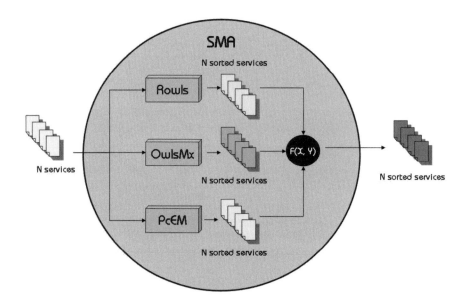

Figure 10.5: Aggregation of the three matchmakers' results by the SMA

- The type of OWLS-MX matchmaker (M0, M1, M2, M3, M4), the minimum degree of match and the similarity threshold

- The aggregation function

Predefined Configurations. In order to make easier to select the parameters of the different components of the SMA, several configurations have been programmed, which can be selected whenever the *getMatchingServices* action is requested (through the *FIPA-Request* protocol). Table 10.1 shows the predefined configurations.

SMA		ROWLS			OWLS-MX			
Param.	Mode	thres.	k filter	% filter	type	min. DOM	sim. thres.	Aggr. fun.
Default	seq.	-	-	60	M0	exact	-	-
Exact	seq.	1	-	-	M0	exact	-	-
Plugin	seq.	0.7	-	-	M1	plugin	-	-
Sub	seq.	0.5	-	-	M2	sub	-	-
Sub-by	seq.	0.3	-	-	M3	sub-by	0.5	-
NN 1	seq.	-	20	-	M4	nn	0.2	-
NN 2	seq.	0.3	-	-	M2	nn	0.5	-
Aggr. 1	aggr.	-	-	-	M1	nn	0.7	Luk.
Aggr. 2	aggr.	-	-	-	M2	nn	0.5	prod
Aggr. 3	aggr.	-	-	-	M3	nn	0.3	min
Aggr. 4	aggr.	-	-	-	M4	nn	0.5	weigh
OwlsMx	-	-	-	-	M4	nn	0.5	-
Rowsl+ OwlsMx	seq.	0.4	-	-	M4	nn	0.5	-
OwlsMx+ Pcem	seq.	-	-	-	M4	nn	0.5	-

Table 10.1: SMA predefined configurations. *Luk.* stands for Lukasiewicz t-norm ($max\{0, x + y - 1\}$), while *weigh* stands for weighted sum of the matching values returned by the 3 matchmakers ($0.5 \cdot OWLSMX + 0.3 \cdot ROWLS + 0.2 \cdot Pcem$). The minimum degree of match *nn* stands for *nearest-neighbour*, *sub* stands for *subsumes*, while *sub-by* stands for *subsumed-by*

For each possible configuration, the values for the different parameters of its internal components are reported. In case that no parameter is provided in the invocation of the matchmaking, a default configuration is selected.

10.4.2 SMA Interface

The communication protocol followed by the SMA is the FIPA-Request protocol. Only one action can be requested to the SMA, `getMatchingServices`. It accepts as parameter a URI of a OWL-S service profile as query (request), one or more service profiles (services) and, optionally, a parameter that defines the configuration of the three matchmakers (matchType). Figure 10.6 shows an example of a message sent to the SMA.

After having received the message, the SMA performs the match of the request against the list of service descriptions and, in case of successful execution of

```
(REQUEST
  :sender(agent-identifier :name sda@host1:1099/JADE
                  :addresses (sequence http://host1:7778/acc))
  :receiver(set(agent-identifier :name sma@host2:1099/JADE))
  :content "(
    (action(agent-identifier :name sda@host1:1099/JADE
                  :addresses (sequence http://host2:7778/acc))
      (getMatchingServices
        :request "http://query.owl"
        :services (sequence "http://service1.owl"
            "http://service2.owl"..."http://serviceN.owl")
        :matchType DEFAULT)))"
  :language fipa-sl
  :ontology cascom-ontology
)
```

Figure 10.6: Request message to SMA

```
(INFORM
  :sender(agent-identifier :name sma@host2:1099/JADE
                  :addresses (sequence http://host2:7778/acc))
  :receiver(set(agent-identifier :name sda@host1:1099/JADE))
  :content "(
    (result
      (action(....))
      (sequence "http://service2.owl"
          "http://serviceN.owl"..."http://service1.owl")))"
  :language fipa-sl
  :ontology cascom-ontology
)
```

Figure 10.7: Inform message from SMA

the matchmaking operation, it returns a sorted set of services (Figure 10.7).

10.5   Hybrid Semantic Service Matchmaker OWLS-MX

One option of the CASCOM matchmaker agent SMA to find relevant OWL-S services in the semantic Web is through its OWLS-MX matchmaker module. This module exploits both logic-based reasoning and content-based information retrieval (IR) techniques for OWL-S service profile I/O matching. In the following, we define the hybrid semantic filters of OWLS-MX, the generic matching algorithm, and its five variants according to the used IR similarity metrics. Familiarity with OWL-S and description logics is assumed. More details and evaluation results can be found in [4].

10.5.1 Hybrid Matching Filters

OWLS-MX computes the degree of semantic matching for a given pair of service advertisement and request by successively applying five different filters EXACT, PLUG IN, SUBSUMES, SUBSUMED-BY and NEAREST-NEIGHBOR. The first three are logic-based only whereas the last two are hybrid due to the required additional computation of syntactic similarity values.

Let T be the terminology of the OWLS-MX matchmaker ontology specified in OWL-DL (SHOIN(D)); CT_T the concept subsumption hierarchy of T; $LSC(C)$ the set of least specific concepts (direct children) C' of C, i.e. C' is immediate sub-concept of C in CT_T; $LGC(C)$ the set of least generic concepts (direct parents) C' of C, i.e., C' is immediate super-concept of C in CT_T; $Sim_{IR}(A, B) \in [0, 1]$ the numeric degree of syntactic similarity between strings A and B according to chosen IR metric IR with used term weighting scheme and document collection, and $\alpha \in [0, 1]$ given syntactic similarity threshold; $\doteq$ and $\succeq$ denote terminological concept equivalence and subsumption, respectively.

Exact Match. Service S EXACTLY matches request R $\Leftrightarrow \forall$ IN$_S$ $\exists$ IN$_R$: IN$_S \doteq$ IN$_R \wedge$ $\forall$ OUT$_R$ $\exists$ OUT$_S$: OUT$_R \doteq$ OUT$_S$. The service I/O signature perfectly matches with the request with respect to logic-based equivalence of their formal semantics.

Plug-in Match. Service S PLUGS INTO request R $\Leftrightarrow \forall$ IN$_S$ $\exists$ IN$_R$: IN$_S \succeq$ IN$_R \wedge \forall$ OUT$_R$ $\exists$ OUT$_S$: OUT$_S \in$ LSC(OUT$_R$). Relaxing the exact matching constraint, service S may require less input than it has been specified in the request R. This guarantees at a minimum that S will be executable with the provided input iff the involved OWL input concepts can be equivalently mapped to WSDL input messages and corresponding service signature data types. We assume this as a necessary constraint of each of the subsequent filters.

In addition, S is expected to return more specific output data whose logically defined semantics is exactly the same or very close to what has been requested by the user. This kind of match is borrowed from the software engineering domain, where software components are considered to plug-in match with each other as defined above but not restricting the output concepts to be direct children of those of the query.

Subsumes Match. Request R SUBSUMES service S $\Leftrightarrow \forall$ IN$_S$ $\exists$ IN$_R$: IN$_S \succeq$ IN$_R$ $\wedge \forall$ OUT$_R$ $\exists$ OUT$_S$: OUT$_R \succeq$ OUT$_S$. This filter is weaker than the plug-in filter with respect to the extent the returned output is more specific than requested by the user, since it relaxes the constraint of immediate output concept subsumption. As a consequence, the returned set of relevant services is extended in principle.

Subsumed-by Match. Request R is SUBSUMED BY service S $\Leftrightarrow \forall$ IN$_S$ $\exists$ IN$_R$: IN$_S$ $\succeq$
IN$_R$ $\wedge$ $\forall$ OUT$_R$ $\exists$ OUT$_S$: (OUT$_S$ $\doteq$ OUT$_R$ $\vee$ OUT$_S$ $\in$ LGC(OUT$_R$)) $\wedge$ SIM$_{IR}$(S,
R) $\geq \alpha$. This filter selects services whose output data is more general than
requested, hence, in this sense, subsumes the request. We focus on direct parent output concepts to avoid selecting services returning data which we think
may be too general. Of course, it depends on the individual perspective taken
by the user, the application domain, and the granularity of the underlying
ontology at hand, whether a relaxation of this constraint is appropriate, or
not.

Logic-Based Fail. Service S fails to match with request R according to the above
logic-based semantic filter criteria.

Nearest-Neighbor Match. Service S is NEAREST NEIGHBOR of request R $\Leftrightarrow \forall$ IN$_S$
$\exists$ IN$_R$: IN$_S$ $\succeq$ IN$_R$ $\wedge$ $\forall$ OUT$_R$ $\exists$ OUT$_S$: OUT$_R$ $\succeq$ OUT$_S$ $\vee$ SIM$_{IR}$(S, R) $\geq \alpha$.

Fail. Service S does not match with request R according to any of the above filters.

The OWLS-MX matching filters are sorted according to the size of results
they would return, in other words according to how relaxed the semantic matching.
In this respect, we assume that service output data that are more general than
requested relaxes a semantic match with a given query. As a consequence, we
obtain the following total order of matching filters

$$\text{EXACT} < \text{PLUG-IN} < \text{SUBSUMES} < \text{SUBSUMED-BY} <$$
$$\text{LOGIC-BASED FAIL} < \text{NEAREST-NEIGHBOR} < \text{FAIL}.$$

10.5.2   OWLS-MX Matching Algorithm

The core idea of the OWLS-MX matchmaker is to complement crisp logic-based
with approximate IR-based matching where appropriate to improve the retrieval
performance. It takes any OWL-S service as a query, and returns an ordered set of
relevant services that semantically match the query each of which annotated with
its individual degree of logical matching, and the syntactic similarity value. The
user can specify the desired degree, and individual syntactic similarity threshold.

For each given service query, OWLS-MX first classifies the respective service
I/O concepts into its local matchmaker ontology. For this purpose, it is assumed
that the type of computed terminological subsumption relation determines the
degree of semantic relation between pairs of input and concepts.

Auxiliary information on whether an individual concept is used as an input or
output concept by a registered service is attached to this concept in the ontology.
The respective lists of service identifiers are used by the matchmaker to compute
the set of relevant services that match the given query according to the five hybrid
filters.

In particular, OWLS-MX does not only pairwisely determine the degree of
logical match but syntactic similarity between the conjunctive I/O concept expressions in OWL-Lite. These expressions are built by recursively unfolding each

query and service input (output) concept in the local matchmaker ontology. As a result, the unfolded concept expressions are including primitive components of a basic shared vocabulary only.

Any failure of logical concept subsumption produced by the integrated description logic reasoner of OWLS-MX will be tolerated, if and only if the degree of syntactic similarity between the respective unfolded service and request concept expressions exceeds a given similarity threshold.

10.5.3 OWLS-MX Variants

We implemented different variants of the generic OWLS-MX algorithm, called OWLS-M1 to OWLS-M4, each of which uses the same logic-based semantic filters but different IR similarity metric $\text{SIM}_{IR}(R, S)$ for content-based service I/O matching. Based on the experimental results of measuring the performance of similarity metrics for text information retrieval provided by Cohen et.al (2003), we selected the top performing ones to build these variants. The variant OWLS-M0 performs logic-based only semantic service I/O matching.

OWLS-M0. The logic-based semantic filters EXACT, PLUG-IN, and SUBSUMES are applied as defined above, whereas the hybrid filter SUBSUMED-BY is utilized without checking the syntactic similarity constraint.

OWLS-M1 to OWLS-M4. The hybrid semantic matchmaker variants OWLS-M1, OWLS-M3, and OWLS-M4 compute the syntactic similarity value SIM_{IR} (OUT_S, OUT_R) by use of the loss-of-information measure, extended Jacquard similarity coefficient, the cosine similarity value, and the Jensen-Shannon information divergence based similarity value, respectively.

10.5.4 Implementation

We implemented the OWLS-MX matchmaker version 1.1 in Java using the OWL-S API 1.1 beta with the tableaux OWL-DL reasoner Pellet developed at the university of Maryland[3]. As the OWL-S API is tightly coupled with the Jena Semantic Web Framework, developed by the HP Labs Semantic Web research group[4], the latter is also used to modify the OWLS-MX matchmaker ontology. The OWLS-MX matchmaker is available as open source from the portal semwebcentral.org[5].

The results of the evaluation of OWLS-MX are provided in Chapter 16.

---

[3]cf. `http://www.mindswap.org`
[4]cf. `http://jena.sourceforge.net/`
[5]`http://projects.semwebcentral.org/projects/owls-mx/`

10.6   Service Precondition and Effect Matchmaker PCEM

Another option of the CASCOM matchmaker agent to determine the degree to which two service descriptions semantically match is to logically compare their pre-conditions and effects by means of its Pre-conditions and Effects Matchmaker (PCEM) module.

10.6.1   Motivation

As mentioned above, the main goal of service matchmaking algorithms is to determine the degree to which two service descriptions match. In general, matchmaking algorithms receive a description that represents the requested service, and a set of published service descriptions; and returns the degree to which each of the published service descriptions matches the request. Service matchmaking is essential for service coordination because it helps select services that better satisfy the specified requirements.

Currently, most of the matchmaking algorithms, like LARKS (Language for Advertisement and Request for Knowledge Sharing) [13], the OWL-S/UDDI [8], the RACER [6], the MaMaS (MatchMaker-Service) [7], the HotBlu [2] and the OWLS-MX (Hybrid OWL-S Web Service Matchmaker) [4] take into account the input parameters, the output parameters and the categories of the service descriptions being compared.

However, considering only their inputs, outputs and categories is often not enough for flexible service matchmaking. Sometimes, it is better to consider other service characteristics, such as service preconditions and service effects. Service matchmaking using service preconditions and effects may bring about three main advantages. First, the matching process may be much more precise than using inputs, outputs and categories alone. Matchmaking using inputs and outputs pay attention only to the classes of the service inputs and outputs and, at most, to constraints relating these parameters (see, for instance [13]). Since it is perfectly possible to have two services with input and output parameters of the same class and satisfying the same constraints, that play completely different roles, this simple matching process is not an accurate one.

The same kind of argument applies to the service categories. In most cases, service selection aims at identifying services that achieve a given effect if they are executed in some specified circumstances. This is exactly the information provided by service preconditions and effects. Second, it is not always necessary to know all the service input and output parameters. Not all services that achieve some desired effect have the same set of input and output parameters. For example, a given book selling service may require as input parameters the book name and the author name, while another one may also require the client's identification. If the request specifies only the book name and the author name, the two mentioned services would yield different matching degrees with the request. However, considering the user's actual needs, maybe each of them is as good as the other.

Third, using preconditions and effects allows the matching algorithm to reason about the compared preconditions and the compared effects. Usually, it is not necessary to find a service that achieves exactly the specified effect. Most often, like in plug-in IOPE matching (IOPE - Inputs, Outputs, Preconditions and Effects), it is enough to find a service whose effects imply the specified effects. By the same token, it is often enough to find a service whose preconditions are implied by the specified preconditions.

Only (additional) preconditions and effects matchmaking may take the mentioned facts into account. For example, if the client wants to find a service that can radiograph his finger, it is perfectly acceptable to select a service that can radiograph the client's hand or even the client's limbs. Since finger is neither a subclass of hand nor a subclass of limb, inputs, outputs and categories matchmaking algorithms would not select the service that radiographs hands or the service that radiograph limbs.

Given the described motivation, the CASCOM project decided to include preconditions and effects matchmaking in its service matchmaking agent SMA. This section describes the PCEM (Pre Conditions and Effects Matchmaking) component that implements this type of matchmaking process.

10.6.2 PCEM Architecture

This section describes the architecture of the developed preconditions and effects matchmaking component PCEM as shown in Figure 10.8.

The architecture is composed of three main modules. The first module ("Module 1 — Component Engine") controls the two other modules and determines the global matching degree of the service request with each of the available service descriptions. A detailed description of this module can be found in the section "Component Engine Module".

The second module ("Module 2 — Languages Processing") is responsible for language processing. It converts OWL ontologies into Prolog ontologies and OWL-S preconditions and effects into Prolog preconditions and effects. A detailed description of this module is presented in section "Languages Processing Module".

The third module ("Module 3 — Preconditions and Effects Matchmaking") implements the actual preconditions and effects matchmaking algorithms. It performs both exact matchmaking ("Pre-conditions and Effects Exact Match") and matchmaking using reasoning ("Pre-conditions and Effects Reasoning-based Match"). The latter uses both general purpose inference rules (e.g., deduction) and domain specific inference rules valid for certain service effects or for certain preconditions. These matchmaking algorithms are described in the section "Preconditions and Effects Matching".

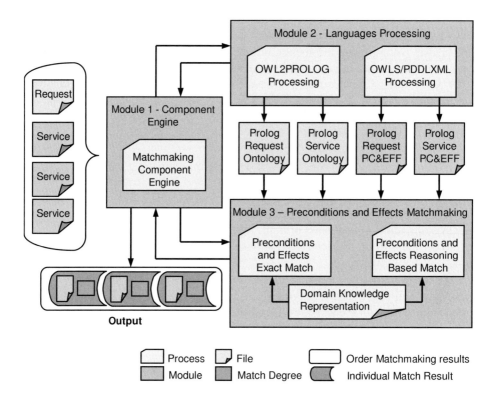

Figure 10.8: PCEM architecture

10.6.3 PCEM Engine Module

The PCEM Engine module is responsible for controlling the other two modules and for determining the final matching degree of the matched service descriptions. All matchmaking requests sent to the component are received by the Component Engine. After receiving a matchmaking request the module retrieves the OWL-S description that represents the desired service specification and the set of OWL-S descriptions of the published available services. The descriptions in the received request are sent to the Languages Processing module where the Prolog language descriptions are generated.

The next step consist of sending a request to the Preconditions and Effects Matchmaking module for determining four partial matching degrees for each of the received service descriptions: exact preconditions matching degree, exact effects matching degree, preconditions reasoning matching degree and effects reasoning matching degree. After receiving the four partial matching degrees for all service descriptions, the Component Engine computes the global matching degree for

```
1: <owl:Class rdf:ID="RightIndexFinger">
2:    <rdfs:subClassOf rdf:resource="#RightFinger">
3:    <rdfs:subClassOf>
4:      <owl:Restriction>
5:        <owl:onProperty rdf:resource="#subPartOf">
6:        <owl:allValuesFrom rdf:resource="#RightHand">
7:      </owl:Restriction>
8:    </rdfs:subClassOf>
9: </owl:Class>
```

Figure 10.9: OWL class representation

```
subClassOf(rightFinger:rightIndexFinger, finger:rightFinger).
subPartOf(rightFinger:rightIndexFinger, hand:rightHand).
```

Figure 10.10: OWL class representation in Prolog

each received service description and returns the list containing the received service descriptions and the corresponding degrees to which they match the received specification of the desired service. Unfortunately, the current implementation of the PCEM component does not sort the returned list of service descriptions by matching degree.

10.6.4 PCEM Languages Processing Module

The CASCOM service coordination layer, including the Service Matchmaker Agent SMA, uses the W3C (World Wide Web Consortium) standard OWL and de-facto standard OWL-S respectively for ontology and service descriptions. Often the representation languages used internally in the several service coordination agents differ from OWL and OWL-S therefore it is necessary to perform language conversions. Since there is no agreed upon standard for describing preconditions and effects available yet, apart from the proposal of (undecidable) SWRL, the PCEM uses Prolog as its internal representation language and reasoning tool. Therefore it is necessary to convert relevant OWL and OWL-S representations involved in any service description into the component internal Prolog representations.

OWL-S service descriptions specify, among many other things such as the already mentioned preconditions and effects, the service input and output parameters and their classes. The service parameter classes are described in domain ontologies which are represented in OWL. Therefore, it is necessary to convert the OWL representations pertaining to the classes of service parameters into the component internal Prolog format. The OWL2Prolog processing mechanism of the Languages Processing module performs those conversions.

Figure 10.10 shows the Prolog internal representations generated from the OWL representation presented in Figure 10.9.

```
service(preconditions,
       [availableBook(book:BookName),
        registeredUser(number:UserID)]).
service(effect,
       [requestedBook(book:BookName),
        not(availableBook(book:BookName))]).
```

Figure 10.11: Final preconditions and effects representation in Prolog

OWL-S service description language does not directly support the representation of service preconditions and effects [7]. Instead, the OWL-S specification suggests that conditions (including preconditions and effects) should be represented in SWRL or in PDDL among other possibilities. Since one of the most important uses of preconditions and effects is service composition planning, the project decided to choose PDDLXML, a project brewed XML surface syntax of PDDL, because PDDL is the lingua franca of the planning algorithms used in service composition. The OWL-S/PDDLXML processing mechanism of the Languages Processing module converts PDDLXML representations of preconditions and effects into the chosen internal Prolog representations. The conversion use the OWLS2PDDL converter developed at DFKI for the OWLS-XPlan composition planner (cf. Chapter 11).

(a) Preconditions	(b) Effect

`<and>`
  `<pred name="AvailableBook">`
    `<param>?Book</param>`
  `</pred>`
  `<pred name="RegisteredUser">`
    `<param>?IDUser</param>`
  `</pred>`
`</and>`
	`<and>`
	  `<and>`
	    `<pred name="RequestedBook">`
	      `<param>?Book</param>`
	    `</pred>`
	  `</and>`
	  `<not>`
	    `<pred name="AvailableBook">`
	      `<param>?Book</param>`
	    `</pred>`
	  `</not>`
	`</and>`

Table 10.2: OWL-S service preconditions and effects in PDDXML

Figure 10.11 shows the Prolog internal representations of the preconditions and effects that were generated from the OWL-S/PDDLXML representations of Table 10.2.

10.6.5 Preconditions and Effects Matching

The PCEM component performs two kinds of matching: exact matching and reasoning-based matching. Since these matching operations are done in Prolog, the module directly benefits from the Prolog built in pattern matching and reasoning capabilities. Preconditions and effects exact matching of two service descriptions (the desired service specification and the available service description) checks if the preconditions of one of the service descriptions exactly match the preconditions of the other service descriptions and if the effects of one of the service descriptions exactly match the effects of the other service description.

The exact matching of two propositions (representing either two preconditions or two effects) checks if there is a possibly empty variable substitution that, when applied to one or both propositions, results into two equal expressions. This operation is entirely performed by the matching operator of the Prolog language. As would be expected, reasoning-based matching is more complex than exact matching. Reasoning-based matching uses general inference rules (i.e., all deduction inference rules) and domain specific inference rules. All general inference rules are applicable to all kinds of effects and preconditions. Domain specific rules are applicable only to some preconditions or effects.

General purpose inference is performed by the built in Prolog reasoning mechanism using resolution and the closed world assumption. Domain specific inference rules are explicitly represented in Prolog and uniquely identified by rule identifiers. These rule identifiers are used to specify the domain specific rules that may be used with each precondition or effect. The representation of the domain specific inference rules and the specification of such rules that may be used with each precondition or effect integrate the domain specific knowledge.

The following example will help understand the developed reasoning algorithm, when domain specific inference rules are used. The example request is a service that radiographs the client right hand index finger. The only available service in the example is a service that radiographs hands. Using conventional inputs/outputs matchmaking algorithms, or using exact matching of effects, the service description does not match the request. However the two effects will be found to match, if the matching algorithm uses the domain specific inference rule according to which, if a given service causes a certain effect on a specified object then it will cause the same effect on any of the object subparts.

The following paragraphs provide a more formal account of the way service invocations, service effects and preconditions, and domain specific inference rules are represented and used by the reasoning-based preconditions and effects matching algorithm. In the following explanations, L is a first order logic language whose terms are used to represent service invocations and whose propositions are used to represent service effects and preconditions. The relationship between services and their effects and preconditions as well as domain specific inference rules are represented in the first order language ML, which is a meta language whose terms include the propositions and terms of L.

```
ServicePrecondition(α, Class(x, τ))
ServiceEffect(α, φ)
∃i Class(i,τ) ∧ SubPartOf(i, y)
```
_____
```
ServiceEffect(α|x/y, φ|x/y)
```

Figure 10.12: Domain specific inference rule 1

ML possesses several predicates, among them ServiceEffect/2, ServicePrecondition/2, Class/2, and SubPartOf/2. ServiceEffect(α,ϕ) means that ϕ is an effect of the service represented by α. α is a term of L representing a service invocation. ϕ is a proposition of L representing a service effect. ServicePrecondition(α, ϕ) means that ϕ is a precondition of the service represented by α . Class(ρ,τ) means that τ is the class of ρ. ρ is a term of L, while τ is an atom of ML representing the name of a class of a given domain. Finally, SubPartOf(ρ, σ) means that σ is a subpart of ρ. ρ and σ are both terms of L.

Using ML, the relevant aspects of the available service are represented through the following expressions:

1. ServicePrecondition(XRayService(*hand*), Class(*hand*, Hand))

2. ServiceEffect(XRayService(*hand*), Radiographed(*hand*))

In these expressions, *hand* is the input parameter of the XRayService service and "Hand" is the name of a class that represents *hands*. The requested effect is represented in the expression ServiceEffect(s, radiographed(RightIndexFinger)) in which s is an uninstantiated variable representing the desired service and RightIndexFinger is a constant representing the specific finger that has to be radiographed. The informally stated domain specific inference rule is formally represented in Figure 10.12.

In the rule represented in Figure 10.12, —x/y represents the expression that is obtained by replacing x with y. Assuming the matching algorithm learns that the rule in Figure 10.12 may be applied to the effect Radiographed/1 of the x ray service, it will apply the rule replacing its variables with their specific values in the described example as follows: α = XRayService(hand), x = hand, τ = Hand, i = RightHand, ϕ = Radiographed (hand), y = RightIndexFinger, ϕ—hand/RightIndexFinger = Radiographed (RightIndexFinger).

The rule premise $\exists i$ Class(i, Hand) $\land$ SubPartOf(i, RightIndexFinger) is satisfied since the right hand (i = RightHand) is an instance of the class Hand and the right hand index finger (RightIndexFinger) is a subpart of the right hand. Using these replacements, the instantiated conclusion of the inference rule is ServiceEffect(XRayService(RightIndexFinger), Radiographed(RightIndexFinger)), which is exactly the required effect. The rule in Figure 10.12 is translated into Prolog as shown in Figure 10.13.

```
rule(1, (serviceEffect(ReplacedService, ReplacedEffect):-
        servicePrecondition(Service, class(Object, Class)),
        serviceEffect(Service, Effect),
        class(I, Class),
        subPartOf(I, Part),
        replace(Part, Object, Effect, ReplacedEffect),
        replace(Part, Object, Service, ReplacedService))
).
```

Figure 10.13: Prolog Representation of domain specific inference rule 1

```
validation(service(xRayService(hand:Hand)),
           serviceEffect(radiographed(hand:Hand),
           validRule(1)).
```

Figure 10.14: Inference rule validation clause

The Prolog representation of domain specific inference rules uses predicate rule/2. The first argument of rule/2 is the rule identifier; and its second argument is a Prolog clause representing the rule itself. The rule conclusion is represented by the head of the clause, and the rule premises are represented by the clause body. With this design choice, the reasoning-based matching algorithm just has to assert the clauses representing domain specific rules and then rely on the Prolog built in inference mechanism to apply the rules to the desired effects and preconditions whenever necessary.

The inference rule being used in the example is not a general rule, in the sense that it cannot be applied to all preconditions and effects. For instance, it cannot be applied to a car painting service. If a car is painted blue, the car engine will not become blue, although the car engine is a subpart of the car. A given domain specific inference rule may only be applied to specified effects or preconditions. Such specifications are represented in Prolog through the predicate validation/3. The first argument of the validation/3 predicate is the service specification. The second argument is the specification of the service effect or precondition to which the rule is applicable. The third argument is the rule identifier of the applicable rule.

The validation/3 clause in Figure 10.14 states that rule number 1 may be applied to the effect radiographed(hand:Hand) of the service xRayService(hand:Hand). The hand:Hand argument means that the service input parameter Hand is of class hand.

10.6.6   Implementation

The PCEM component was developed using the OWL-S API [12], which was extended to enable processing PDDLXML conditions (in conditioned instructions), preconditions and effects for OWL-S processing; the Protege OWL-API [5] for OWL processing; and the tuProlog [9], a Java based Prolog, for the matchmaking algorithm. Prolog was chosen mainly because of its built in pattern matching and reasoning capabilities.

For results of evaluating the PCEM matchmaker, we refer to Chapter 16.

10.7   Role-Based Matchmaker ROWLS

In the following, we briefly describe the third alternative to semantic service matching used by the service matchmaker agent of the CASCOM system: the ROWLS matching component.

10.7.1   Motivation

In order to improve both the efficiency and the usability of agent-based service-oriented architectures, common organisational concepts such as social roles and types of interactions can be exploited to further characterise the context that certain semantic services can be used in.

The CASCOM abstract architecture conceives services to be delivered essentially by agents. An agent could provide an implemented Web Service by wrapping the service within an ACL interface in such a way that any agent can invoke its execution by sending the adequate (*request*) message.

However, agents are not only able to execute a service but can also engage in different types of interaction with that service. For example, in the healthcare assistance scenario, an agent providing a second opinion service should not only be able to provide a diagnostic; it may also be required to explain it, give more details, recommend a treatment, etc.

This means that the service provider is supposed to engage in several different interactions during the provision of a service. Thus, if a physician or a patient needs one or more second opinions, they should look for agents that include those additional interaction capabilities around the "basic" *second opinion* service. In a certain sense, this approach is similar to the abstraction that an object makes by providing a set of methods to manipulate the data it encapsulates. In this case, the agent provides a set of interaction capabilities based on the service.

Taking in consideration roles and interaction types can improve the *efficiency* of the matchmaking process, for example by previously filtering out those services that are incompatible in the terms of roles and interactions.

Also the *effectiveness* of the matchmaking process can be enhanced by including information regarding roles and interactions. For instance, a diagnosis service may require symptoms and medical records as inputs and produce a report as

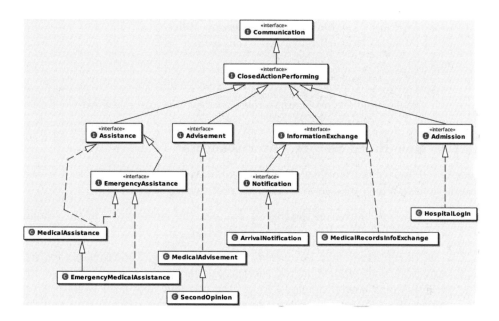

Figure 10.15: Partial interaction type ontology

output. However, the service functionality can be achieved either (i) by actually generating the report, (ii) by retrieving a previously done or (iii) by a brokering service to contact other (external) healthcare experts. In all the three cases the input and output are the same, but the role the service plays in the corresponding interactions is different.

10.7.2 Interaction Modelling

In order to develop role-based extensions to service matchmaking mechanisms, a subset of the RICA organisational model described in [11] and [10] was used.

Setting out from this basis, the first step was analysing different use case of the application domain scenario. For each use case, the types of social interaction as well as the roles (usually two) that take part in that interaction have been identified. The next step is an abstraction process in which the social (domain) roles/interactions are generalised into communicative roles/interactions.

The result of this analysis is a basic ontology of types of interactions and roles that take part in those interactions. Figure 10.15 shows an example, where the *SecondOpinion* interaction can be generalized in a *MedicalAdvisement* interaction and then in an *Advisement* interaction, in which the Advisor informs the Advisee about his beliefs with the aim of persuading the Advisee of the goodness of these beliefs. This ontology, and especially its generic (communicative) part, will be used in the service description and matchmaking extensions.

Main Role	Necessary Roles
Advisor	*Informer*
Explainer	-
Informer	-

Table 10.3: Second Opinion role-based service advertisement

10.7.3 Role-Based Service Advertisements

Role-based service descriptions comprise two kinds of information related to the interactions in which the service provider agent can engage:

1. the *main role* played in the interaction, e.g. the *advisor* role in the second opinion service;

2. a set of roles that may be *necessary* to be played by the requester for the correct accomplishment of the service. For instance, in an advisement interaction of a second opinion service, the provider may need to initiate an *information exchange* interaction in which it plays the *informee* role, and the requester plays the *informer* role. Necessary roles are given by a formula in disjunctive normal form, i.e. a disjunction of conjunctions of roles.

These two fields are repeated for each main role the service can play. A service advertisement can be graphically represented by a table with two rows, in which each column contains the main role (first row) and the necessary roles (second row). Table 10.7.3 shows a role-based service advertisement for the second opinion example.

10.7.4 Role-Based Service Requests

In the case of a service requests, a query comprises two elements:

1. *Main roles* searched. Although one role will be enough in most cases, more complex search patterns are allowed, in which the provider is able to play more than one role. As in the case of service advertisements, this expression comes as a formula in disjunctive normal form.

2. A set of roles that define the *capabilities* of the requester. These are roles the requester is able to play. This information is important if the provider requires interaction capabilities from the requesters. For example, the requester of a second opinion can inform that it is able to provide information (*informer*) if needed.

Table 10.4 shows a role-based service request for the second opinion example. The request specifies that the requester is able to play the informer and explainer roles if necessary.

Main Roles	$Advisor \wedge Explainer$
Capabilities	$Informer, Explainer$

Table 10.4: Second Opinion role-based service request

Notice that this approach is compatible with services that do not make use of the role-based extensions in their description. In case a service description does not include the role-based approach, it is assumed that it has a main role *Communicator* (the top and most general concept of the ontology) and no necessary roles are required from the requester. If the request does not include a role description, it is assumed that the requester is not interested in the role-based approach and the matchmaker will omit that phase in the service matching process.

10.7.5 Role-based Service Matching Algorithm

Within the CASCOM project, a role-based matching algorithm has been developed, which takes as input a service request (R) and a service advertisement (S), and returns the degree of match (dom) between them. Essentially, it searches the role in the advertisement S that best matches the one in the query (R).

The matching algorithm is built around the matching between two roles in the taxonomy. The semantic match of two roles R_A (*advertisement*) and R_Q (*query*) is a function that depends on two factors:

1. Level of match. This is the (subsumption) relation between the two concepts (R_A, R_Q) in the ontology. A subset of the OWLS-MX filters is considered, just the same levels of match proposed in [8]:

   (a) *exact* : if $R_A = R_Q$

   (b) *plug-in* : if R_A subsumes R_Q

   (c) *subsumes* : if R_Q subsumes R_A

   (d) *fail* : otherwise

2. The distance (number of arcs) between R_A and R_Q in the taxonomy.

All roles have the same importance and the generality (depth in the taxonomy) of the roles is not relevant. Both criteria are combined into a final degree of match which is a real number in the range [0, 1], so service providers can be selected by simply comparing these numbers. In this combination, the level of match always has higher priority: the value representing the degree of match is equal to 1 in case of an *exact* match, it varies between 1 and 0.5 in case of a *plug-in* match, rests between 0.5 and 0 in case of a *subsumes* match, and it is equal to 0 in case of a *fail*. Actually, any triple would work but 0.5 seems reasonable to keep the same scale in both levels (plug-in and subsumes).

There are infinite functions that fulfil that precondition. One equation that implements this behaviour is that in equation 10.1, where $\| R_A, R_Q \|$ is the distance between R_A and R_Q ($depth(R_A) - depth(R_Q)$) in the role ontology (if there is a subsumption relation between them). This kind of function guarantees that the value of a *plug-in* match is always greater than the value of a *subsumes* match, and it only considers the distance between the two concepts, rather than the total depth of the ontology tree[6], which may change depending on the domain. Furthermore, the smaller the distance between concepts (either in the case of *plug-in* or *subsumes* match), the more influence will have a change of distance in the degree of match (see Figure 10.16).

$$
dom(R_A, R_Q) = \begin{cases}
1 & if\ R_A = R_Q \\[2mm]
\frac{1}{2} + \frac{1}{2 \cdot e^{\| R_A, R_Q \|}} & if\ R_A\ is\ subclass\ of\ R_Q \\[2mm]
\frac{1}{2} \cdot e^{\| R_A, R_Q \|} & if\ R_Q\ is\ subclass\ of\ R_A \\[2mm]
0 & otherwise
\end{cases}
\tag{10.1}
$$

The matching algorithm compares every role in the request with the service advertisement roles, given the set of capabilities of the requester, using the aforementioned function, and returns the maximum degree of match. It uses the minimum and maximum as combination functions for the values in conjunctive and disjunctive logical expressions respectively.

10.7.6 Implementation

The role-based matchmaker was developed in Java 1.5, relying on the Mindswap OWL-S API 1.1 beta[7] for parsing OWL-S service profiles. Regarding the management of OWL ontologies, we adopted Jena Semantic Web Framework, a framework for building Semantic Web applications developed by the HP Labs Semantic Web research group[8].

For evaluation of the ROWLS matchmaker, we refer to Chapter 16.

10.8 Summary

The CASCOM project designed and implemented a service discovery process comprising a stage where desired services are sought and a stage where services found in the first stage are sorted according to the degree to which they satisfy specified

---

[6]Note that, for instance, if a linear function is used, the maximum possible distance between two concepts must be known a priori to establish the equation (e.g. $dom(x) = 1 - x/6$).

[7]http://www.mindswap.org

[8]http://jena.sourceforge.net/

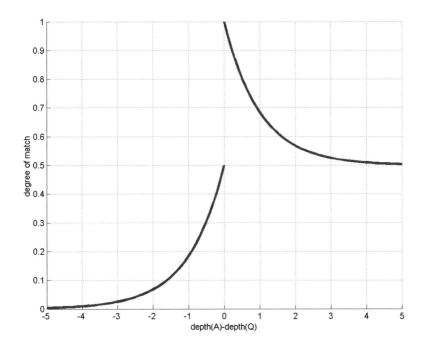

Figure 10.16: Degree of match function between two roles

criteria. In the first stage, services are sought according to simple selection criteria. The second stage uses more sophisticated matching criteria involving complex information processing such reasoning (e.g., subsumption) and role-based matchmaking.

The service discovery stage is carried out by the Service Discovery Agent (SDA), which looks for services in its own database and in the project distributed service directory (WSDir). In addition to seeking desired services, the SDA also registers, modifies and deletes service descriptions and service providers in its own database and in WSDir. The WSDir can be used directly without the SDA mediation. However, since WSDir is a Web Service, it does not offer an agent-based interface. If such an interface is required, the SDA should be used.

The fine grained service selection is performed by the Service Matchmaking Agent (SMA), using three different matching algorithms, each of which was implemented as a separated module integrated in the SMA architecture:

1. Hybrid input and output subsumption and information retrieval matchmaking algorithm (OWLS MX);

2. Preconditions and effects matchmaking algorithm, which performs exact, do-

main dependent and domain independent reasoning-based matching (PCEM); and

3. Role-based matchmaking (ROWLS).

The use of these three sophisticated matchmaking algorithms provides clear advantages in terms of both efficiency and effectiveness. For instance, role-based matchmaking may significantly reduce the number of considered services in early stages of the whole service coordination process; and reasoning-based matchmaking may identify perfectly good services, services that meet specified criteria, that would otherwise be discarded.

The three matchmaking algorithms may be combined in two distinct ways to produce the final SMA output. One of the possibilities is a sequential combination; the other is a parallel combination. In the sequential combination, each algorithm is used as a pre-filter of the next one. In the sequential combination, we have chosen to apply first the less complex algorithm (ROWLS), followed by the one with intermediate complexity (OWLS-MX), followed by the most complex of all (PCEM). This way, the more complex algorithms process fewer service descriptions. Sequential combination of the matching algorithms favors efficiency.

In the parallel combination, all algorithms are used in parallel. The results produced by each of them are aggregated in an aggregation function. Several aggregation functions (e.g., product, and minimum) may be used. Parallel combination of the algorithms favors effectiveness. Sequential or parallel combinations as well as other configuration parameters, such as the similarity threshold, are dynamically chosen during the interaction with SMA. Since these choices may be hard for SMA clients, we have predefined configurations including one that is used by default. Therefore, the SMA client has only to select one of the predefined configurations or the default one. This greatly enhances flexibility without compromising seamless interaction.

SMA and SDA interaction uses interaction protocols, agent communication language, and content language defined by FIPA; and uses ontology and service descriptions specified by the W3 Consortium. The use of standardized technologies improves interoperability and system's usability.

References

[1] A. Bernstein and C. Kiefer: Imprecise RDQL: Towards Generic Retrieval in Ontologies Using Similarity Joins. Proc. ACM Symposium on Applied Computing, Dijon, France, ACM Press, 2006.

[2] I. Constantinescu and B. Faltings: Efficient matchmaking and directory services. Proceedings of IEEE/WIC International Conference on Web Intelligence. 2003.

[3] A. Fernández, M. Vasirani, C. Cáceres and S. Ossowski: A Role-Based Support Mechanism for Service Description and Discovery. Service-Oriented Comput-

ing: Agents, Semantics, and Engineering. LNCS, 4504, pp. 132–146, Springer, 2007.

[4] M. Klusch, B. Fries and K. Sycara: Automated Semantic Web Service Discovery with OWLS-MX. Proceedings of 5th International Conference on Autonomous Agents and Multi-Agent Systems (AAMAS 2006); Hakodate; Japan; ACM Press. 2006.

[5] H. Knublauch et al.: Protege-OWL API. Available online at http://protege.stanford.edu/. September 21, 2006.

[6] L. Li and I. Horrocks: A software framework for matchmaking based on semantic web technology. Proceedings of the twelfth international conference on World Wide Web, pages 331-339. ACM Press. 2003.

[7] D. Martin, M. Burstein, J. Hobbs, O. Lassila, D. McDermott, S. McIlraith, S. Narayanan, M. Paolucci, B. Parsia, T. Payne, E. Sirin, N. Srinivasan, and K. Sycara: OWL-S 1.1 Release; http://www.daml.org/services/owl-s/1.1/overview/. 2004.

[8] M. Paolucci, T. Kawamura, T. Payne and K. Sycara: Semantic matching of Web Services capabilities. In Proceedings of the First International Semantic Web Conference on The Semantic Web, Springer-Verlag (2002) 333-347

[9] E. Denti, A. Omicini and A. Ricci: tuProlog: A Light-weight Prolog for Internet Applications and Infrastructures. Proceedings of the 3rd International Symposium on Practical Aspects of Declarative Languages (PADL 2001); Las Vegas; NV; USA; 11-12; LNCS 1990, Springer-Verlag, 2001.

[10] J. M. Serrano and S. Ossowski: A compositional framework for the specification of interaction protocols in multiagent organizations. Web Intelligence and Agent Systems: An international Journal. IOS Press. 2006.

[11] J. M. Serrano, S. Ossowski and A. Fernández: The Pragmatics of Software Agents - Analysis and Design of Agent Communication Languages. Intelligent Information Agents - The European AgentLink (Klusch et al. ed.), pp 234-274, Springer. 2002.

[12] E. Sirin and B. Parsia: The OWL-S Java API. Proceedings of the Third International Semantic Web Conference. 2004.

[13] K. Sycara, S. Widoff, M. Klusch and J. Lu: LARKS: Dynamic Matchmaking Among Heterogeneous Software Agents in Cyberspace; Journal of Autonomous Agents and Multiagent Systems. Kluwer Academic Press. 2002.

Chapter 11

Service Composition

Bastian Blankenburg, Luis Botelho, Fábio Calhau, Alberto Fernández,
Matthias Klusch, Sascha Ossowski

11.1 Introduction

One of the striking advantages of Web Service technology is the fairly simple
aggregation of complex services out of a library of other composite or atomic
services. The same is expected to hold for the domain of Semantic Web Services
such as those specified in WSMO or OWL-S. The composition of complex services
at design time is a well-understood principle which is nowadays supported by
classical workflow and AI planing based composition tools (cf. Chapter 4).

In CASCOM, we developed two composition planners for OWL-S services,
OWLS-XPlan and MetaComp, together with an approach to heuristically pre-
filtering the set of all available services which are delivered by the SMA (cf. Chapter 10) to significantly reduce the search space for both planners. Accordingly, the
CASCOM service composition planning agent, called SCPA, can be configured to
use one of the planners and either exploiting the pre-filtering module, or not.

This chapter is structured as follows. We briefly summarize the CASCOM
composition planner agent SCPA, followed by the detailed description of the pre-
filtering module, and both the OWLS-XPlan and MetaComp planning modules of
the SCPA.

11.2 CASCOM Service Composition Agent SCPA

In CASCOM, two different Service Composition Agents (SCPA) have been developed which differ in the planning engine used: one SCPA is based on XPlan [11]
while the other relies on SAPA [8]. In any case, the CASCOM SCPA takes a set of
OWL-S services, a description of the initial state and the goal state to be achieved
as input, and returns a plan that corresponds to a composite service that gets
invoked using the FIPA-Request interaction protocol.

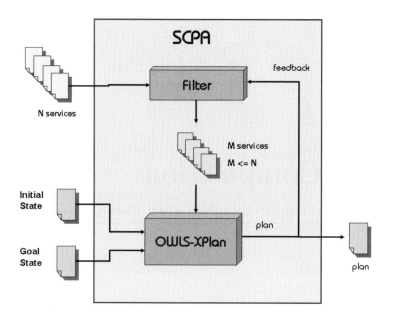

Figure 11.1: OWLS-Xplan service composition agent

The first type of SCPA, called OWLS-XPlan SCPA, relies on the service composition planner OWLS-XPlan (cf. Section 11.4). Figure 11.1 shows its internal architecture, which also contains a pre-filter component which is detailed in Section 11.3. The OWLS-XPlan SCPA may be configured to apply this prefiltering component to the set of available OWL-S services returned by the SDA which, according to the CASCOM architecture (cf. Chapter 7), is in charge of retrieving services from accessible service directories. This reduction is expected to further increase the efficiency of the overall planning process. The final service composition plan is generated by the OWLS-XPlan planner component from the given set of services, the initial and goal state ontologies, and returned for execution and to its internal prefiltering component for experience based learning.

The MetaComp SCPA (cf. Section 11.5) uses the SAPA planner instead of the XPlan planner, and does not use the prefiltering component. In fact, MetaComp asks the SDA itself for a reduced number of services so that fewer service descriptions have to be conveyed between the two agents.

The availability of two different kinds of service composition agents in CASCOM provides potential clients with added flexibility to adapt composition planning to their individual needs. More concrete, the client agent can ask the context acquisition and management system (cf. Chapter 13) for the following context information regarding the two Service Composition Agents:

- Agents availability: if the agent is available (on-line) or not

- Average waiting time per request

- Service waiting list: number of requests waiting for a service

- Average execution time

In addition, the client agent might have built its own model based on past experiences or uses third party services (such as trust and reputation) for making its decision on the selection of the composition planner agent.

11.3 Pre-Filtering for Service Composition

According to the CASCOM Architecture, the SCPA (Service Composition Planning Agent) is in charge of creating a composite service that includes several pre-existing services. In order to be able to generate such a plan that matches the original query, the SCPA needs a set of input services to set out from.

Ideally, the set of services taken into account by the SCPA to create a composite plan should comprise all services registered in the directory. However, this can be impracticable as the number of services increases, as it is expected to occur in the open IP2P environments that CASCOM targets. To overcome that problem, CASCOM suggests to reduce the set of input services that are passed on to the SCPA's composition planning component. For this purpose, filters that sort out those services registered within the directories that are less relevant to the planning process are proposed. This activity is also called *plan based service matching* of a respective service matchmaker that is cooperating with a service composition planner like in CASCOM.

Pre-selecting the set of candidate services for composition planning is not an easy task. Several ad-hoc heuristics can be thought of (e.g. services that share at least one input or output with the query, etc). In this section a more informed method for filtering services that make use of *service class information* is proposed. First, a generic framework for service-class based filtering is described, and then it is instantiated for different filters on the basis of (a) organizational information obtained from the CASCOM role ontology and (b) the service category derived from the directory structure.

11.3.1 Generic Pre-Filtering Framework

At a high level of abstraction, the service composition planning problem can be conceived as follows: let $P = \{p_1, p_2, ..., p_m\}$ be the set of all possible plans (composite services) for a given service request R, and $D = \{s_1, s_2, ..., s_n\}$ the set of input services for the proper service composition planner (i.e. the directory available). The objective of a filter F is to select a given number l of services from D, such that the search space is reduced, but the best plan of P can still be found.

Put in another way: the larger the subset of plans $P' \subseteq P$ that the planner can choose from, the higher the probability that the plan of maximum quality is among them. A good heuristic to this respect is based on *plan dimension* and on the *number of occurrences* of services in plans: a service is supposed to be the more important, the bigger the number of plans from P that it is necessary for, and the shorter the plans from P that it is required for. This information can be approximated by storing and processing the plans historically created. So, in principle, matrices might store, for every possible query, the number of plans in which each service appeared, classified by each plan dimension.

However, it soon becomes apparent that the number of services and possible queries is too big to build up all matrices of the above type. Furthermore, the continuous repetition of a very same service request R is rather unlikely. And, even more important, this approach would not be appropriate when a new service request (not planned before) is required (which, in fact, is quite usual). To overcome this drawback, it is assumed the availability of *service class information*, so as to cluster services based on certain properties. If the number of classes is not too big, the aforementioned approach becomes feasible computationally.

Figure 11.2 depicts the structure of the CASCOM approach to service composition filtering. With each outcome of a service composition request, a Historical Information Matrix H is updated. Setting out from this information, a Relevance Matrix v is revised and refined. Based on this matrix, service relevance can be determined in a straightforward manner. For each service composition request, the filtering method is based on this estimated service relevance function.

Computing Pre-filter Information

The *Historical Information Matrix* (Table 11.1) for a service class r compiles relevant characteristics of plans (composite services) that were created in the past in response to requests for services belonging to that class. In particular, for each plan dimension i and service class s it stores the number of plans of length i that made use of services of class r. Historical Information Matrices are updated as newly generated plans come in. If the service request is a logical formulae (given in disjunctive normal form), the contribution of the resulting plan is *distributed* among the affected Historical Information Matrices.

As commented above, the aim of ranking services is to try and select a set of services that cover the largest subset of the plan space, as an attempt to maximise the chance of the best plan to be contained in it. Services that formed smaller plans in the past are considered more relevant, since it is easier to cover small plans that large ones, so with less services more plans can be covered.

The Relevance Matrix specifies the relevance of a service class s to be part of a plan (composite service) that matches the query for a certain service class r. The following function is used to aggregate the information about plans contained in the *Historical Information Matrixes* (remember that all this information is about a single request class r):

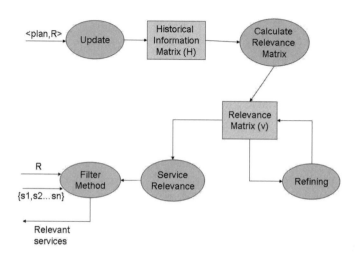

Figure 11.2: Architecture of the filter component

H^R: Historical information about plans for service class R (Request)				
Dimension	1	2	3	...
# of plans	0	50	70	...
C_1	0	7	24	...
C_2	0	10	55	...
C_3	0	30	21	...
...	...	...	...	...

Table 11.1: Example of class information about historical plans

$$Relevance(C, R) = \frac{\sum_{d=1}^{m} \frac{n_d}{d^c}}{\sum_{d=1}^{m} \frac{N_d}{d^c}} \tag{11.1}$$

where d is the dimension of the plan, m is the dimension of the longest plan stored, n_d is the number of times that C was part of a composite plan of dimension d for the request R, and N_d is the total number of plans of dimension d for that request. Note that each appearance of class C in a plan contributes to the relevance value, and that this contribution is the higher the smaller the plan dimension. c is a constant > 0 that allows adjusting the level of importance of plan dimensions. A relevance value between 0 and 1 is obtained with this calculus for every given service class C with respect to the composition of a service of class R.

The *Relevance Matrix* $v(s,r)$ can be further refined in order to take transitivity into account. Consider the following situation: A plan that achieves C_1 is searched for, and that a potential solution is to compose the services C_2 and C_3 ($C_2 \oplus C_3$ for short). However there is no service provider for C_3, but instead C_3 can be composed as $C_4 \oplus C_5 \oplus C_6$, so the final plan is $C_2 \oplus C_4 \oplus C_5 \oplus C_6$. Unfortunately, the value $v(C_4, C_1)$ is low and the service providing C_4 is discarded and not taken into account in the planning process, so the aforementioned plan cannot be found by the planner. Therefore, the relevance matrix is refined by taking *transitivity* into account, e.g. through the following update: $v(C_4, C_1) = v(C_4, C_3) \cdot v(C_3, C_1)$. The same holds for third-level dependencies (e.g.: $v(C_7, C_1) = v(C_7, C_4) \cdot v(C_4, C_3) \cdot v(C_3, C_1)$). This example motivates the definition of the $v^k(s,r)$ as a k step relevance matrix

$$
\begin{aligned}
v^1(s,r) &= v(s,r) \\
v^k(s,r) &= Max(v^{k-1}(s,r), v^{k-1}(s,s_1) \cdot v^{k-1}(s_1,r), \\
&\qquad v^{k-1}(s,s_2) \cdot v^{k-1}(s_2,r), ..., v^{k-1}(s,s_n) \cdot v^{k-1}(s_n,r))
\end{aligned}
\tag{11.2}
$$

As shown in the equation, the product is used as combination function and the maximum to aggregate the results. Note that the higher the value of k the better the estimation of the relevance of service classes. The refinement of the relevance matrix is repeated until it converges or until a timeout is received. The elevated time complexity of $O(n^3)$ for each refinement step is attenuated by the *anytime properties* of the approximation algorithm. Furthermore, recall that the number of classes n is supposed to be fixed and not overly high. Finally, note that several updates and refinements can be combined into a "batch" to be executed altogether when the system's workload is low.

There are several ways of obtaining the initial relevance matrix. If there are historical records of plans they can be used to calculate the matrix. Also, an a priori distribution can be assigned using expert (heuristic) knowledge. Still, the simplest solution is to let the service composition planning component work without filtering services until the number of plans generated is representative enough to start computing and refining the matrixes.

Service Relevance Calculus

The first step to calculate the *relevance* of a service s for a request r is the mapping of both to *classes of services*. Then, the relevance between the classes is calculated. $v(s,r)$ is used to represent the relevance of *class* s for the *class* r in the request, and $V(S,R)$ as the relevance of service S for the service request R.

Considering that, in general, the service S belongs to several classes ($s_1, s_2, ..., s_n$), if a request R only includes a class (r) in its description, then

$$
V(S,R) = \max(v(s_1,r), v(s_2,r), ..., v(s_n,r))
$$

However, if the request specifies a logical expression containing several classes of services $(r_1, r_2, ..., r_m)$, logical formulas are evaluated using the *maximum* for disjunctions and the *minimum* for conjunctions; and inside the *maximum* is used to aggregate the service classes specified by the provider. For example, if the request R includes the formula $r_1 \vee (r_2 \wedge r_3)$, and the service S belongs to the classes s_1 and s_2, the calculus is as follows:

$$V(S, R) = \max[\max(v(s_1, r_1), v(s_2, r_1)), \min(\max(v(s_1, r_2), v(s_2, r_2)),$$
$$\max(v(s_1, r_3), v(s_2, r_3)))]$$

Types of Pre-filter Composition

When a service request is analysed by the pre-filter, the set of services are first ranked by an estimation of the relevance of the service class for that request. Then, only the services belonging to the best ranked classes are passed on to the planner. In order to determine the concrete services that pass the filter three major options are considered:

a) To establish a *threshold* and filter out those services whose classes have a degree of relevance lower than that threshold.

b) To return the estimated k *best* services based on the relevance of their corresponding classes. In this case the number of services that pass the filter is pre-determined.

c) To return a *percentage* of the original set of services (based on the relevance of their corresponding classes). In this case the number of services considered in the planning process depends on the directory size.

When designing the algorithms corresponding to these filters configurations, an additional problem needs to be taken into account. Services with low (or even zero) relevance values would never be considered for planning, so they could never be part of a plan (composite service), remaining with low relevance forever. This is obviously too restrictive, as our relevance values are only estimations based on the information available at some point in time. To overcome this some services are allowed to be fed into the planner even though they are not supposed to be relevant enough according to the filter policy. Those additional services are chosen randomly. This random option is combined with the three aforementioned filter types to allow for an exploration of the service (class) space.

11.3.2 Instantiation of Pre-Filters

In the following we present two different approaches to apply the filtering framework proposed in this section. For each approach the mapping of services to classes is defined. Both methods are based on information available in the OWL-S service descriptions used by CASCOM.

Role-based Pre-filtering

In many service-oriented systems, agents are conceived as mere wrappers for Web Services. However, agents are not only able to execute a service but may also engage in different *types of interaction* related to that service, in the course of which they play several *roles*. For example, in a medical emergency assistance scenario, an agent providing a *second opinion* service should not only be able to provide a diagnostic; it may also be required to explain it, give more details, recommend a treatment, etc. Therefore, a service provider may need to engage in several different interactions, and play a variety of different *roles*, during the provision of a service.

Our role-based filtering method relies on taxonomies of roles and type of interactions (see Figure 10.15 in Chapter 10) to determine service classes. The idea is to relate roles searched in the query to roles played by agents in the composite service, that is, which are the roles typically involved in a plan when a role r is included in the query. For example, it is common that a *medical assistance* service include *travel arrangement, arrival notification, hospital log-in, medical information exchange* and *second opinion* interactions.

Following the CASCOM role-based service description approach (Section 10.7 in Chapter 10), each service provider advertises a set of possible roles from the role ontology that it can play. Similarly, in service requests it is allowed to specify the roles searched from the role ontology as a logical expression in disjunctive normal form. By establishing a mapping from the elements of the role ontology to service classes, the above filtering framework becomes applicable.

In the CASCOM role based modelling approach, the role taxonomy is supposed to be static over significant amounts of time. Still, the ontology *can* be extended to include new roles and types of interaction not considered before. In that case, the relevance matrix is updated with new rows and columns for those new roles. The relevance values for those new roles are unknown initially, but this can be overcome by randomly including some services with low relevance and, in general, by applying the bootstrapping techniques, both described in Section 11.3.1.

Category-Based Pre-Filtering

Another pertinent strategy for service classification is based on the categories (travel, medical) they belong to. Such categories are considered important information in service descriptions (in fact, the OWL-S language includes a specific field for this characteristic). There are several well known category taxonomies (NAICS, UNSPSC,...). However, CASCOM does not choose one in particular, keeping it open to the service describer.

In this filtering framework, each category is considered a class of service. Service descriptions include a set of categories. In the case of a service advertisement, this fits exactly our classes approach (set of classes). In the case of service requests, the set of categories specified are interpreted as a logical formula by connecting them with the operator or ($\vee$).

If the number of different classes (categories) is too big, the computational complexity (regarding both space and time) can become rather high. In that case, the granularity of the classes can be decreased by clustering several categories into the same class based on inheritance relations in the taxonomy tree.

The two types of classification of services presented in this section can be combined as follows:

$$Relevance(S, R) = \alpha \cdot Rel^{RB}(S, R) + (1 - \alpha) \cdot Rel^{CB}(S, R) \text{ with } \alpha \in [0..1] \quad (11.3)$$

where $Rel^{RB}(S, R)$ and $Rel^{CB}(S, R)$ are the relevance values obtained by the role and category-based filtering approaches, respectively.

11.4 Service Composition With OWLS-XPlan

Though the composition of complex Web Services attracted much interest in different fields related to service oriented computing, there are only a few implemented composition planning tools publicly available for the semantic Web such as the HTN composition planner SHOP2 for OWL-S services [15]. One problem with HTN planners is that they require task specific decomposition rules and methods developed at design time, hence are not guaranteed to solve arbitrary planning problems. That, in particular, motivated the development of our hybrid composition planner OWLS-XPlan for OWL-S 1.1 services which always finds a solution if it exists, though the corresponding planning problem remains to be NP-complete. Like SHOP2, OWLS-XPlan does perform closed world planning prepared through its integrated converter OWLS2PDDL (cf. Section 11.4.2).

While its original version enables static composition of OWL-S services in static domains, an upgraded version OWLS-XPlan 2.0 (cf. Section 11.4.4) also allows to compose OWL-S services in dynamic and stochastic environments in which changes of the world state can non-deterministically (stochastic) occur during (dynamic) planning. Such changes concern the availability of services; changes of predicates, facts, objects of the plan base. In such environments XPlan 2.0 offers an event based dynamic sequential planning of composite services. It listens for events of state changes during its planning process with heuristic partial re-planning of a new minimal and valid composition plan. This is in contrast to non-classic reactive planning with interleaved service execution, and non-classic off-line planning such as conformant, conditional, or contingency planning.

11.4.1 Architecture

The Semantic Web Service composition planner OWLS-XPlan consists of several modules for pre-processing and planning (cf. Figure 11.3). It takes a set of available

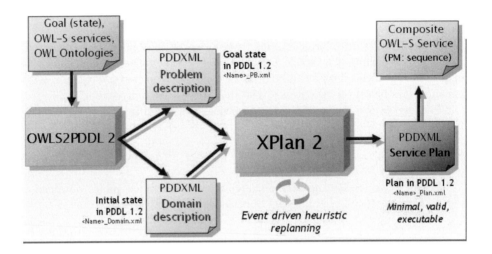

Figure 11.3: Architecture of OWLS-XPlan

OWL-S 1.1 services, related OWL ontologies, and a planning request (goal) as input, and returns a planning sequence of relevant services that satisfies the goal.

For this purpose, it first converts the domain ontology and service descriptions in OWL and OWL-S, respectively, to equivalent planning problem and domain descriptions in PDDL 2 ("Planning Domain Definition Language") using the integrated OWLS2PDDL converter (cf. Section 11.4.2). For reasons of convenience, we developed a XML dialect of PDDL, called PDDXML, that simplifies parsing, reading, and communicating PDDL descriptions using SOAP.

The planning domain description contains the definition of all types, predicates and actions, whereas the problem description includes all objects (grounded predicates, constants), the initial state, and the goal state. An operator of the planning domain corresponds to a service profile in OWL-S since both operator and profile describe patterns of how an action or service as an instance should look like. A method is a special type of operator for fixed complex services that OWLS-XPlan may use during its planning process. Both descriptions are then used by the state based action planner XPlan to create a plan in PDDL that solves the given problem in the actual domain.

Key to the translation from OWL-S to PDDXML is that any service in OWL-S corresponds to an equally named action with the same set of input parameters, logical preconditions, and effects. However, for classical (STRIPS like) action planning in AI, PDDL does not allow to describe concrete input or output values of operators such as information on specific train connections returned by a service. So we have to add special precondition and effect predicates to tell the planner that it does in general know about the output values as an effect of executing the respective action on the current world state, or the values of typed input variables allowing to match value based restrictions in preconditions of possible successor actions.

Its core AI planning module called XPlan is a heuristic hybrid FF planner based on the FF planner developed by Hoffmann and Nebel [9] (cf. Section 11.4.3). It combines guided local search with relaxed graph planning, and a simple form of hierarchical task networks (HTN) to produce a plan sequence of actions that solves a given problem. If equipped with methods, XPlan uses only those parts of methods for decomposition that are required to reach the goal state with a sequence of composed services. For stochastic domains in which the world state is changing during planning, we developed an event driven heuristic planning module XPlan 2.0 for dynamic composition of services (cf. Section 11.4.4).

11.4.2 Converter OWLS2PDDL

The purpose of the OWLS2PDDL converter is to tranlate a given OWL-DL expression in OWL-S 1.1 service descriptions and a given service composition problem into an equivalent PDDL planning problem which can be understood by AI planners such as XPlan. More concrete, the structured functional service composition problem (SWS, I, G) consists of two (user-provided) OWL-DL ontologies that represent an intial (I) and a goal (G) world state, respectively, and a set SWS of OWL-S services. In the following, we assume familiarity with OWL-DL and OWL-S. The initial state I consists of the domain knowledge base KB_0 (available services, imported OWL ontologies T with asserted instances), and the goal state G represented by a goal service functionality S_G (IOPE = input, output, precondition, effect). The problem is to find a composition sequence $P = S_1 \circ ... \circ S_n$, $S_i \in SWS$ that satisfies G (P reaches G from I).

Overview

The converter OWLS2PDDL is mapping this service composition problem to a classical action based AI planning problem in PDDL. PDDL is a modular language that allows to control its expressiveness by specifying certain *requirements*. The converter itself uses a XML dialect of PDDL 1.2, called PDDXML, with the *ADL* and *open-world* requirements for both PDDL 1.2 [2], and the Action Description Language (ADL) [13] and additional syntax for predicate cardinality restrictions [1]. An action planning problem is defined as a triple $(Init, Goal, Ops)$ consisting of

1. an initial state $Init$,

2. a goal state $Goal$,

---

[1]The PDDXML grammar in compact RelaxNG (see [5]) can be found at *http://www.dfki.de/~blankenb/owls2pddl/PDDXMLDomain.rnc* and *http://www.dfki.de/~blankenb/owls2pddl/PDDXMLProblem.rnc* for domain and problem instance definitions, respectively.

3. and a set of *Operators Ops*, where each operator describes a possible action in the considered domain. An operator is characterised by its parametrised precondition and effect, such that

   (a) an action is applicable in a given world state if and only if its precondition is fulfilled in that state.

   (b) the effect describes how a state s is transformed to its successor state if the action is applied to s.

PDDL aggregates *Init* and *Goal* states in a *PDDL problem* definition. Operators are contained in a PDDL *domain definition*. *Init* is a conjunction of predicates, whereas *Goal* is a function-free first-order logical sentence. An action precondition is, like the goal state, a function-free first-order logical sentence, whereas an effect can only be a conjunction of predicates or negated predicates, a universal quantified effect, or a conditional effect; non-deterministic disjunctions are not allowed in effect constraints (in contrast to ADL).

In summary, the OWLS2PDDL converter implements a function

$$(O \times O \times 2^S) \mapsto (D \times P)$$

where O is the set of all OWL DL ontologies, S is the set of all OWL-S 1.1 services, D is the set of all PDDL domains and P is the set of all PDDL problems. The main idea of the conversion is to map OWL-S services to planning domain operators, and to produce the PDDL problem from given OWL "Initial State" and "Goal State" ontologies. In particular, expressions in PDDL are then interpreted with standard FOL semantics corresponding to those of the decidable FOL subset OWL-DL. The interpretation of PDDL operators corresponds to that of respective ADL (Action Description Language [13]) operators which can be reduced to STRIPS operators (see [7]), which in turn are interpreted using Lifschitz' semantics (see [12]). In contrast to STRIPS, both PDDL and ADL assume the open world, but only ADL allows both disjunctions and negated literals in effect constraints (PDDL disallows disjunctive effects). The additional cardinality restrictions are interpreted under the standard description logic (DL) semantics for non-qualifying number restrictions (DL part "N").

PDDL has close to SOIN expressivity with only subsumption, equivalence and transivity of roles from OWL-DLs SHOIN expressivity missing. But these missing features can be represented by fully expanding any role specification to include also any parent and transitively holding roles. This is explained in Subsection 11.4.2. Thus, PDDL's expressiveness is sufficient to equivalently represent an OWL-S service composition problem.

The converter OWLS2PDDL generates the planning problem in PDDL for the planner XPlan, and comes in two versions: OWLS2PDDL 1.0 (2.0) of OWLS-XPlan (OWLS-XPlan 2.0) converts expressions of EXPTIME description logic SI(D) (NEXPTIME description logic SHOIN(D), corresponding to OWL-DL) to

PDDL 1.2. However, there are a few obstacles to be discussed in the following together with a simple example of a conversion.

Operators and Service Outputs

While an OWL-S service has inputs, outputs, preconditions and effects, a planning domain operator only has the latter two. The OWL-S specification states that as opposed to preconditions and effects, which refer to the world *state*, inputs and outputs represent *information* that is made available for or *produced by the service*. For an PDDL object, however, its existence cannot be bound to certain states (even with the open-world requirement).

As a solution of this problem, we model the possible creation of information by services with the help of a special `agentHasKnowledgeAbout` predicate. This predicate is set

- in the PDDL initial state: for each object representing an individual of the OWL initial state ontology;

- in the PDDL goal state: for each object representing an individual of the OWL goal state ontology;

- in the effect definition of a PDDL operator: for each PDDL operator parameter representing an output parameter of the respective OWL-S service.

We require this predicate to hold for all PDDL operator parameters representing input parameters of OWL-S services. This ensures that an action is rendered unapplicable in a state if the corresponding service's required input information is not available in that state.

Service Preconditions and Effects

OWL-S does not prescribe a specific language for defining preconditions and effects of services. Instead, one can specify the language with the OWL-S 1.1 `expressionLanguage` property. We extended the to OWL-S 1.1 `Expression` and `Condition` classes to allow for PDDXML preconditions and effects. The definition of these extended classes, `PDDXML-Expression` and `PDDXML-Condition`[2]. Currently, the converter converts only such PDDXML expressions and conditions.

Restrictions of Initial State and Action Effect

In OWL-DL, the class description of an OWL individual in any given ontology can be arbitrarily complex in the scope of OWL-DL. Since there is no notion of "initial ontologies" in OWL, restrictions resembling those of PDDL can hardly be imposed. Thus, expressions in the given OWL initial ontology which violate these restrictions are ignored by the converter when generating the initial state

---

[2]see http://www2.dfki.de/~babla/owls2pddl/pddxml.owl

and action effects. We assume that individuals which are stated to be in a given OWL class do indeed fulfill all necessary restrictions of that class.

Open vs. Closed World

Both OWL and PDDL make the open world assumption (OWA) calling for monotonic reasoning. However, XPlan does perform closed world reasoning like many action planners and service composition planners like SHOP2. Thus, the initial state is implicitly "closed" when feeding the generated PDDL planning problem description into XPlan[3]. It is not possible to include the latter (disjunctive) expression in a PDDL initial state or action effect, since disjunctions are not allowed there. Thus, when interpreting the problem as being closed-world, the conversion might not be complete.

Other Issues of Conversion

Other issues of converting OWL-DL to PDDL are as follows.

- **The PDDL type system is not general enough** to reflect the possibly complex relationships of OWL classes. Thus, the explicitly specified classes of an OWL individual are represented for the corresponding PDDXML object by unary predicates of the classes' names (this includes all superclasses).

- **No language construct for enumerations**: OWL classes which are defined via *oneOf* are converted using a disjunction of special *identity* predicates. These predicates are defined for every object in the initial state and for output parameters.

- **No domain axioms**. Our XML dialect of PDDL does not support domain axioms (which XPlan also does not support). Thus, the conversion of an OWL class definition has to be inserted at every place in the PDDXML where an object or parameter which corresponds to an OWL individual or OWL-S service parameter of that class occurs.

Conversion Rules

Figures 11.4 and 11.5 illustrate how OWL-S service descriptions, intial and goal state ontologies are translated to PDDXML. Table 11.2 summarizes how each SHOIN-expressivity OWL DL construct is converted to an equivalent PDDXML condition. In this table, the leftmost column "DL Ex." denotes the expressiveness class, Δ denotes the domain, and X^I denotes the interpretation of X. Table 11.3 summarises the conversion of transitive properties and subsumption of properties. Follwing these rules, an equivalent PDDL planning problem representation of the service composition problem can be obtained, albeit with factorial runtime and

---

[3]That is, anything which cannot be deduced (e.g. property predicate p) in the initial state is assumed to be false (i.e. $\neg p$), as opposed to being unknown (i.e. $p \vee \neg p$).

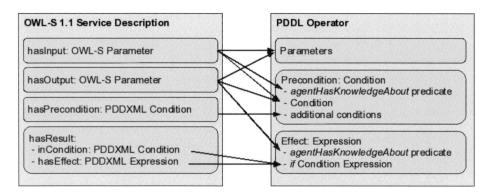

Figure 11.4: Conversion of OWL-S services to PDDXML actions

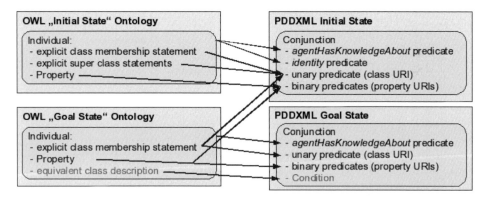

Figure 11.5: Conversion of OWL DL state ontologies to PDDXML states

space requirements in the worst case. Please note that in the current version of the converter implementation (OWLS2PDDL 2.0), the conversion of the description of equivalent classes in the goal state, transitive properties and subsumption of properties are not implemented yet; this is ongoing work.

Example of OWLS2PDDL Conversion

In the following, we provide a brief and simple example of conversion by OWLS2PDDL. Suppose that the given service, initial and goal ontologies all import a common ontology which includes some class definitions, and that there is just one service to convert as shown in Figure 11.6. The converter generates the PDDXML action shown in see Figure 11.7 for this service. The service has one input of type `Class_2`, whose definition is shown in Figure 11.8.

First, the `agentHasKnowledgeAbout` predicate is required on the input. Second, it must be ensured that only objects of the required type can be instantiated

DL			OWL	PDDXML
Ex.	Syntax	Semantics		
	A	$A^I \subseteq \Delta^I$	Class	Unary Predicate
	$\top$	$\top^I = \Delta^I$	Thing	PDDL type "object"
	R	$R^I \subseteq \Delta^I \times \Delta^I$	Property	Binary Predicate
	$R \in R_+$	$R^I = (R^I)^+$	Trans. Property	Multiple Predicates, effect
$\mathcal{S}$	$C \sqcap D$	$C^I \cap D^I$	conjunctionOf	`<and/>`
	$C \sqcup D$	$C^I \cup D^I$	disjunctionOf	`<or/>`
	$\neg C$	$\Delta^I \backslash C^I$	complementOf	`<not/>`
	$\exists R.C$	$\{x \mid \exists y.(x,y) \in R^I$ and $y \in C^I\}$	someValuesFrom	`<exists/>`
	$\forall R.C$	$\{x \mid \forall y.(x,y) \in R^I$ implies $y \in C^I\}$	allValuesFrom	`<forall/>`
$\mathcal{H}$	$R \sqsubseteq S$	$R^I \subseteq S^I$	subPropertyOf	Multiple Predicates, effect
$\mathcal{I}$	R^-	$\{(x,y) \mid (y,x) \in R^I\}$	inverseOf	Predicate
$\mathcal{N}$	$\geq nR.C$	$\{x \mid \#\{y.(x,y) \in R^I$ and $y \in C^I\} \geq n\}$	minCardinality	`<cardinality min='' ..."/>`
	$\leq nR.C$	$\{x \mid \#\{y.(x,y) \in R^I$ and $y \in C^I\} \leq n\}$	maxCardinality	`<cardinality max=" ..."/>`
$\mathcal{O}$	$\{o\}$	$\{o\}^I = \{o^I\}$	XML Type + RDF-value	Object
	$\exists T.\{o\}$	$\exists C : \{o\}^I \in T$	hasValue	`<exists/>` + special `identity` predicate

Table 11.2: Conversion and semantics of OWL DL class descriptions to PDDXML conditions

Context	OWL	PDDXML
Initial state	Transitive Property p	For all predicates $p(i,k), p(k,m)$, $i \neq k \neq m$: predicate $p(i,m)$
	p subPropertyOf p'	For all predicates $p(i,k)$: predicate $p'(i,k)$
Actions' effect	Transitive Property p	`<forall>` i,k,m `<if>` `<and>` $(i \neq k \neq m)$ $p(i,k)$ $p(k,m)$ `</and>` $p(i,m)$ `</if>` `</forall>`
	p subPropertyOf p'	`<forall>` i,k `<if>` $p(i,k)$ $p'(i,k)$ `</if>` `</forall>`

Table 11.3: Expansion of transitive and subsumed properties

```
− <service:ServiceProfile rdf:ID="ServiceProfile_1">
  − <service:presentedBy>
    − <service:Service rdf:ID="Service_1">
        <service:presents rdf:resource="#ServiceProfile_1"/>
      − <service:describedBy>
        − <j.2:AtomicProcess rdf:ID="AtomicProcess_1">
            <service:describes rdf:resource="#Service_1"/>
          − <j.2:hasOutput>
            − <j.2:Output rdf:ID="Output">
              − <j.2:parameterType rdf:datatype="http://www.w3.org/2001/XMLSchema#anyURI">
                  http://www.dfki.de/~blankenb/owls2pddxml/manual-example/manual-example.owl#Class_1
                </j.2:parameterType>
              </j.2:Output>
            </j.2:hasOutput>
          − <j.2:hasInput>
            − <j.2:Input rdf:ID="Input">
              − <j.2:parameterType rdf:datatype="http://www.w3.org/2001/XMLSchema#anyURI">
                  http://www.dfki.de/~blankenb/owls2pddxml/manual-example/manual-example.owl#Class_2
                </j.2:parameterType>
              </j.2:Input>
            </j.2:hasInput>
          </j.2:AtomicProcess>
      </service:describedBy>
    </service:Service>
  </service:presentedBy>
</service:ServiceProfile>
```

Figure 11.6: OWL-S example service

with the action. The service input class is a defined class, i.e. any individual which has a minimum cardinality of 2 on property `objectProperty_1` is a member of this class. Thus, the generated PDDXML condition contains a disjunction that states that either the parameter must explicitly be stated to be of type `Class_2`, or the cardinality restirction on the property must hold. Similarly, the conversion of the output type is also included in the action's precondition. The `agentHasKnowledgeAbout`, on the other hand, is only set in the effect, reflecting the information gain that is achieved by the service execution. The resulting initial and goal states are rather simple. The initial state consists of the following definition of `Individual_1`:

```
<Class_3 rdf:ID="Individual_1">
    <j.0:objectProperty_1>
        <Class_4 rdf:ID="Individual_2"/>
    </j.0:objectProperty_1>
</Class_3>
```

The resulting PDDXML expression which is written into the PDDXML problem definition is shown in Figure 11.9. It includes the `agentHasKnowledgeAbout` predicate, the explicit class membership statement, the `identity` predicate and the binary predicate that represents OWL property `objectProperty_1`

```
– <action name="http://www.dfk .de/~blankenb/owls2pddxml/manual-example/manual-example-service-1.cwl#Service_1'>
  – <parameters>
    <param type="object">
      ?http://www.dfki.de/~blankenb/owls2pddxml/manual-example/manual-example-service-1.owl#Input
    </param>
    – <param type="object">
      ?http://www.dfki.de/~blankenb/owls2pddxml/manual-example/manual-example-service-1.owl#Output
    </param>
  </parameters>
  – <precondition>
    – <and>
```

```
      – <pred name='agentHasKnowledgeAbout'>
        – <param>
          ?http://www.dfki.ce/~blankenb/owls2pddxml/manual-example/manual-example-service-1.owl#Input
        </param>
      </pred>
      – <or>
        <pred name="ht:p://www.dfki.de/~blankenb/owls2pddxml/manual-example/manua-example.owl#Class_2'>
          – <param>
            ?http://www.dfki.de/~blankenb/owls2pddxml/manual-example/manual-example-service-1.owl#Input
          </param>
        </pred>
        – <cardinality min="2">
          – <pred name="http://www.dfk .de/~blankenb/owls2pddxml/manual-example/manual-example.owl#objectProperty_1">
            – <param>
              ?http://www.dfki.de/~blankenb/owls2pddxml/manual-example/manual-example-service-1.owl#Input
            </param>
            <param>?individual</param>
          </pred>
        </cardinality>
      </or>
```
Converted description of Input class

```
      – <or>
        – <pred name="ht:p://www.dfki.de/~blankenb/owls2pddxml/manual-example/manua-example.owl#Class_1'>
          – <param>
            ?http://www.dfki.de/~blankenb/owls2pddxml/manual-example/manual-example-service-1.owl#Output
          </param>
        </pred>
      </or>
    </and>
  </precondition>
  – <effect>
    – <and>
      – <pred name='agentHasKnowledgeAbout'>
        – <param>
          ?http://www.dfki.ce/~blankenb/owls2pddxml/manual-example/manual-example-service-1.owl#Output
        </param>
      </pred>
    </and>
  </effect>
```
Converted description of Output class
```
</action>
```

Figure 11.7: The generated PDDXML action

11.4.3   Static Composition

As mentioned above, XPlan performs a static composition under closed world assumption. In fact, the solution of XPlan to the problem of structured functional service composition at hand corresponds to finding a sequence of services that globally plug-in matches with the given goal service functionality (cf. Figure 11.10).

XPlan Solution of the Service Composition Problem

As mentioned in previous section, the functional service composition planning problem can be mapped to a classical action planning problem by (a) identifying the given services with actions and (b) describing the domain together with the requested service in an initial, respectively, goal state ontology in the standard planning language PDDL. The solution of XPlan for this problem corresponds to a

```
- <owl:Class rdf:ID="Class_2">
  - <owl:equivalentClass>
    - <owl:Restriction>
        <owl:minCardinality rdf:datatype="http://www.w3.org/2001/XMLSchema#int">2</owl:minCardinality>
      - <owl:onProperty>
          <owl:ObjectProperty rdf:ID="objectProperty_1"/>
        </owl:onProperty>
        <owl:valuesFrom rdf:resource="http://www.w3.org/2002/07/owl#Thing"/>
      </owl:Restriction>
    </owl:equivalentClass>
  </owl:Class>
```

Figure 11.8: Common class definitions

plug-in match of the plan P considered as one composed service to the goal service S_G with goal ontology G together with an IOPE (input, output, precondition, effect) chaining of the sequecence of services within P (cf. Figure 11.10).

In addition, the executability of P on the grounding level of the reconverted actions to OWL-S services can be guaranteed by the interleaved checking of whether the I/O parameter data types in XMLS of subsequent services of P grounded in WSDL are compatible with each other which ensure the data flow within the sequence of services to be executed after planning. The reconversion is done by OWLS2PDDL 2.0 and the compatibility check is performed by the planner by means of its integrated OWLS-MXP component (partially reused from the OWLS-MX matchmaker, cf. Chapter 10).

Graphbased FF Planning with XPlan

For each sub-goal g of the determined goal agenda, at each planning step i, XPlan quickly builds a relaxed planning graph $RPG(i)$ in a fast goal reachability test heuristically ignoring negative effects of actions A, and the corresponding relaxed plan $RP(i)$ in a backward pass from g to S_i. The relaxed plan contains all paths of applicable actions that lead from g to S_i, of which only those in its first action-layer 0 are called helpful.

In the following, XPlan focuses on the helpful actions of $RP(i)$ only, hence reduces the search space. Please note that the relaxed plan is not necessarily correct due to ignorance of the Del-lists, i.e., negative effects of actions. In order to decide which helpful action to select as the next action in a valid plan sequence, XPlan applies each of them to S_i and adds the previously ignored Del-list facts yielding the complete state S_{ij}, where $j \in \{1, .., l\}$, denotes the j-th helpful action applied to state S_i.

For each of these states the relaxed plan $RPG(i, j)$ is then built to heuristically search for the relaxed plan $RP(i, j)$ with heuristically minimal length $h(RP(i, j))$. In this context, the "plan length" $h(RP(i, j))$ just denotes the sum of all actions in all action-layers of the RP.

Finally, XPlan retains the action A_{ij} with heuristically minimal goal distance, and starts the next planning step $i + 1$ with S_{ij}. If there are multiple RPs of equal length, it repeats the same decision process starting at state S_{i1} (like a breadth

```
- <and>
  - <pred name="identity">
    - <param>
        http://www.owl-ontologies.com/Ontology1183981526.owl#Individual_1
      </param>
    - <param>
        http://www.owl-ontologies.com/Ontology1183981526.owl#Individual_1
      </param>
    </pred>
  - <and>
    - <pred name="http://www.owl-ontologies.com/Ontology1183981526.owl#Class_3">
      - <param>
          http://www.owl-ontologies.com/Ontology1183981526.owl#Individual_1
        </param>
      </pred>
    </and>
  </and>
- <pred name="agentHasKnowledgeAbout">
  - <param>
      http://www.owl-ontologies.com/Ontology1183981526.owl#Individual_1
    </param>
  </pred>
- <and>
    <and/>
  - <pred name="http://www.dfki.de/~blankenb/owls2pddxml/manual-example/manual-example.owl#objectProperty_1">
    - <param>
        http://www.owl-ontologies.com/Ontology1183981526.owl#Individual_1
      </param>
    - <param>
        http://www.owl-ontologies.com/Ontology1183981526.owl#Individual_2
      </param>
    </pred>
  </and>
</and>
```

Figure 11.9: OWL initial state ontology

first search restricted on helpful actions), and then $S_{i2}, ..., S_{il}$ until a minimum is found.

Eventually, all created plans for sub-goals g of the goal agenda are respectively concatenated which yields the final plan sequence P. The plan then gets executed, and if it fails, XPlan allows re-planning from the most recent valid state produced by action execution, to avoid a total re-planning, if possible.

As mentioned above, XPlan also checks at each planning step whether the selected pairs of services to be composed are data type compatible to ensure the executability of the generated plan. For this purpose, it utilizes respective information it got from the service matchmaker (OWLS-MXP) about the available services prior to the planning process. For more details on OWLS-XPlan in general, and XPlan in particular, together with examples of service translation from OWL-S to PDDXML we refer the reader to [10, 14].

11.4.4   Dynamic Composition

For OWLS-XPlan 2.0, which has been eventually used in CASCOM, we modified the original XPlan module of OWLS-XPlan to allow for event driven heuristic re-planning of composite services during the actual planning process. The modified

(1) **Plug-in „black-box" match** of composed service P with request S_G

$\forall \text{In}(P) \exists \text{In}(S_G). \text{In}(P) \geq_T \text{In}(S_G), KB_0 \vDash \text{Pre}(P) (\text{Pre}(S_G) \rightarrow \text{Pre}(P))$

$\forall \text{Out}(P) \exists \text{Out}(S_G). \text{Out}(P) \leq_T \text{Out}(S_G), KB_n \vDash \text{Eff}(S_G) (\text{Eff}(P) \rightarrow \text{Eff}(S_G))$

(2) **Structured IOPE chaining** of services $S_i \in$ SWS within P

$\text{Out}(S_{i-1}) \leq_T \text{In}(S_i)$ and $KB_i \vDash \text{Pre}(S_i)$, with $KB_i = KB_{i-1}:\text{Eff}(S_{i-1})$

(3) Interleaved checking of **plan executability** at WSDL grounding level of services

$\rightarrow$: $\preceq_\theta$, relative query containment

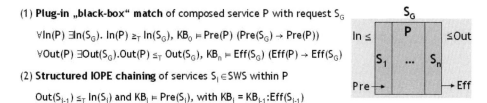

Figure 11.10: Structured functional service composition

planner XPlan 2.0 does perform, in essence, highly frequent event driven off-line re-planning under closed world asumption with heuristic computation of best reentry points for re-planning at the end of each planning step if the currently produced plan, or plan fragment is affected by the observed change.

External changes of the world state concern converted OWL ontologies, individuals and the set of available services during the internal planning process each of which potentially affecting the respective operators, actions, predicates, facts and objects in the PDDXML problem and domain descriptions as well as already generated partial plans. For event monitoring, we equipped XPlan 2.0 with an event listener for distinguished classes of events.

In particular, in each plan step i, before applying selected helpful action A to the state S_i, however, XPlan 2.0 listens for events of state changes. If no events are in its event queue, it applies A to S_i and proceeds with plan step i+1. The plan fragment from initial state S_0 to S_i is correct and, due to the selection of helpful actions in the minimal relaxed plan, approximatively optimal.

XPlan 2.0 triggers re-planning in the following cases of observed events of world state changes: (1) An operator (service) instantiation (action) becomes available. This is the case if (a) a new operator has been introduced, or (b) the world state (set of facts) changed such that an operator whose instantiation was impossible before can be instantiated now, or (c) new predicates which are part of the preconditions or effects of an operator are introduced, making it possible to instantiate this operator; (2) An operator (service) of the plan is not possible anymore, if any of the opposites of cases 1.a – 1.c holds; (3) The goal state changed due to a change of the original planning request.

Each of these cases is handled separately as described in subsequent sections. If facts or objects change, the planner searches for the first operator which precondition is satisfied by the new fact, and starts re-planning from there, while the helpful actions get instantiated with the new fact(s). The case in which a predicate p changes can be reduced (a) to the latter case of changed facts, if new facts are added; (b) to the case of change of operator o (action A), if preconditions or effects of *o* include *p*; or (c) to the case of fact changes, if the deletion of *p* implies the deletion of all instances of *p*. It is assumed that the planning state consistency is checked by means of an appropriate module as intergal part of both XPlan and XPlan 2.0.

Both versions of OWLS-XPlan have been implemented in Java and are available at the semantic Web community portal semwebcentral.org.

11.5   Service Composition With MetaComp

MetaComp is one of the service composition agents developed in the CASCOM project. Although MetaComp has been designed and implemented following basically the same approach as the OWLS-XPlan module described in the previous section, we emphasize two main differences.

First, MetaComp service discovery approach is different from that used in the filtering component of OWLS-XPlan. Second, MetaComp uses the SAPA planner [8] instead of the XPlan planner. Whereas the filtering process of OWLS-XPlan is applied to the services returned by the service discovery agent (SDA), the service discovery strategy designed for MetaComp asks the SDA for a reduced number of services so that fewer service descriptions have to be conveyed between the two agents.

Besides, MetaComp service discovery strategy is simpler than the one used in the filtering component of OWLS-XPlan. It is based on service categories (which have to be provided by the agent client), on service inputs, outputs, preconditions and effects, and it uses context information. Although simpler, we feel this strategy might yield reasonable results. However, for the purpose of the CASCOM selected problems, any of the planners (SAPA or XPlan), means either MetaComp or OWLS-XPlan would have been a good choice. The remaining of this section provides some details regarding MetaComp development and results.

11.5.1   Architecture

MetaComp receives service composition requests from its clients. Service composition requests include a partial OWL-S description specifying the service to be composed, that is, the initial state and the composition goal. The service specification (initial state and composition goal) and the descriptions of the services available to be integrated in the final compound service are sent to the planning algorithm for it to generate the compound service.

However, since both the desired service specification and the descriptions of the available services are represented in OWL-S whereas the used planning algorithm accepts only PDDL, these OWL-S descriptions, as in OWLS-XPlan, are first translated to PDDL. The planning algorithm output is merely the sequence of the elemental services that actually make up the compound service. This has to be reconverted to OWL-S so that it can be sent to the agent's client.

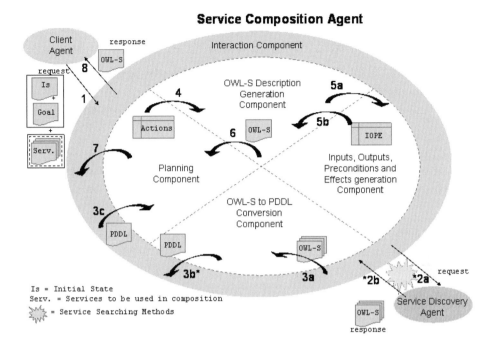

Figure 11.11: MetaComp architecture

This conversion involves two steps. First, it is necessary to generate the compound service (global) inputs, outputs, preconditions and effects from the (local) inputs, outputs, preconditions and effects of the elemental services that make up the compound service. Second, the sequence of elemental services comprising the compound service and its global inputs, outputs, preconditions and effects (generated in the first step) are converted to OWL-S. Figure 11.11 shows MetaComp component based architecture and the interactions between its components.

The agentified service composition module MetaComp consists of the following five key components:

1. the MetaComp agent interaction component AIC;

2. the converter OWLS2PDDL as described in previous section;

3. the planning component SAPA;

4. the IOPE generation component;

5. the OWL-S description generation component.

The AIC of the MetaComp agent was developed as an extension of the

JADE platform. Its main purpose is to provide an interaction framework to FIPA-compliant agents. It uses the FIPA-Request interaction protocol [6] when interacting with its clients and when interacting with the service discovery agent SDA requesting the services to be used during composition. AIC is responsible for receiving/sending messages and parsing them into a suitable format for the interaction with other components and with agents.

The purpose of the OWL-S to PDDL conversion component, the OWLS2PDDL converter taken from OWLS-XPlan, is to generate the PDDL descriptions from the received initial state description, composition goal specification, and the OWL-S descriptions of the services available for composition. For more information about the OWLS2PDDL converter we refer to Section 11.4.2.

The planning component SAPA [8] of MetaComp is responsible for generating a sequence of component services (i.e., actions) that satisfies the client request (i.e., planning goal) from the specified initial state. MetaComp uses SAPA, a domain-independent heuristic forward planner that can handle durative actions, metric resource constraints, and deadline goals. SAPA is designed to be capable of handling the multi-objective nature of metric temporal planning.

Though SAPA accepts PDDL level three (version 2.1) descriptions, following a CASCOM project decision, we have used only SAPA PDDL level one capabilities. The processing in SAPA, since it receives the two PDDL sections until it produces the plan, is made up of three steps:

1. reading and parsing the PDDL descriptions, which in case they are grammatically correct, should be transformed into a data structure to be processed by SAPA;

2. instantiation of the parameters of the available actions with object instances represented in the planning problem;

3. searching for a planning solution.

In the instantiation step, all static conditions presented in the initial state are evaluated. Static conditions are those whose truth value do not change as a result of some service execution. If a certain static condition is true in the initial state, it continues to be true in all subsequent states that result of service execution. Since their truth value never changes, once SAPA checks that they are true in the initial state, static conditions are removed from the PPDL description. This increases the planner performance.

The IOPE generation component receives the generated action sequence and the (local) parameters, preconditions and effects of each of the actions of the new composite service and generates the (global) inputs, outputs, preconditions and effects of the compound service.

The purpose of the OWL-S description generation Component is to generate the OWL-S description of the generated compound service from the sequence of component services generated by the planning component (SAPA) and the service inputs, outputs, preconditions and effects produced by the Inputs, Outputs, Preconditions and Effects generation Component.

11.5.2 Service Selection Methods

The service composition process requires a set of existing services that may be chained to form the compound service. The first step of service composition is to request the descriptions of those services to the service discovery agent. If this is not a carefully crafted process, it may result either in a huge, computationally intractable collection of services, most of which may turn out to be useless for the composition problem at hand, or in a small set of services which may be insufficient to create the desired compound service.

In this respect, we assume context information of great importance since it allows reducing the set of services requested to the service discovery agent (SDA) to only those matching the current context. This will improve efficiency in two ways. First, the SDA will only return fewer but relevant services. Second, service composition with fewer services is more efficient. Besides efficiency, context compliant services will hopefully be more adequate to the current state of affairs. Service availability and cost, and user profile are the context information considered in the service selection process.

Two service selection methods have been designed: a service category based method, where services are selected according to their category; and a method in which services are selected if at least one of their inputs, outputs, preconditions or effects matches the composition problem. However, currently, none of the designed methods has been integrated in the implemented MetaComp; this is future work.

Search Based on Service Categories

The method is focused on the service categories specified in the service composition request. In this approach, service categories are organized in a hierarchic taxonomy. After receiving the composition request, the service composition agent MetaComp asks the SDA for all available services that match the specified categories and the current context information (service availability and cost, and user profile).

The returned services (after transformation to PDDL) are used by the planning component SAPA to create the new compound service. In case the service composition is successful, the new compound service is sent to the client agent. If the services of the specified categories are not enough to perform the composition, the solution is to look for services of the category immediately above the specified category, in the given hierarchy. This process will repeat itself until the composition is successful, the maximum composition time specified by the client is reached, or no more upper levels can be found in the categories hierarchy.

Search Based on Problem Characteristics

In this method, the service composition agent MetaComp asks the SDA for all available services that match the context information and have at least one input or one precondition, one output, or one effect of the desired service. MetaComp uses the returned services in order to try to create the desired compound service. If the composition is successful, the compound service is sent to the client agent. If the service composition fails, MetaComp will ask the SDA for more services. This time, MetaComp will ask for all available services that match the context information and at least one precondition, input, output or effect that matches with the previously provided services.

MetaComp uses the newly received services plus the previously received ones and starts a new composition. The process continues until a compound service is created, the maximum composition time specified by the user is reached, or the maximum number of considered services, as specified by the client, is reached.

11.5.3   Implementation

MetaComp (with the exception of the service selection methods) was implemented in the Java programming language. Several Java based tools were used in its development: JADE (Java Agent DEvelopment Framework) [3], SAX (Simple API for XML) [4], ALL (Abstract Logic Language) [1], OWLS2PDDL (cf. Section 11.4.2) and OWL-S API [16].

JADE was used as the agent platform and for the development of Meta-Comp interaction component. SAX was used for reading PDDXML preconditions and effects. ALL provides support for the internal representation of PDDXML preconditions and effects. The OWLS2PDDL of OWLS-XPlan was used for the conversion of OWL-S service descriptions, and OWL descriptions of the initial state of the world and goal, to PDDL. The OWL-S API was used for writing the OWL-S descriptions of the compound services generated by MetaComp agent.

11.6   Summary

In this chapter, we presented that the CASCOM composition planner agent SCPA, a detailed description of the prefiltering module, and both the OWLS-XPlan and MetaComp planning modules of the SCPA. For static SWS composition planning, the SCPA can use MetaComp while OWLS-Xplan2 allows for advanced dynamic service composition (cf. Chapter 4). In any case, the search space can be tuned by prefiltering of relevant services according to the non-functional role-based matchmaker described in the previous chapter. The SCPA has been fully implemented in Java and successfully demonstrated in the CASCOM e-health application scenario.

References

[1] Adetti: Abstract Logic Language; ALL Specification. Available online at http://clts.we-b-mind.org/files/all.doc. 2002.

[2] The AIPS-98 Planning Competition Committee: PDDL the planning domain definition language. Technical Report CVC TR-98-003/DCS TR-1165, Yale Center for Computational Vision and Control, October 1998. Available at: ftp://ftp.cs.yale.edu/pub/mcdermott/software/pddl.tar.gz.

[3] F. Bellifemine, G. Caire, A. Poggi and G. Rimassa: JADE - A White Paper. EXP Magazine, In search of innovation, 3(3). 2003. Available on-line at http://exp.telecomitalialab.com

[4] D. Brownell: SAX2. O'Reilly; ISBN: 0596002378. 2002.

[5] J. Clark (Ed.): Relax NG Compact Syntax, November 2001. http://relaxng.org/compact-20021121.html.

[6] FIPA Commitee Members: Foundation for Intelligent Physical Agents: Interaction Protocol Specifications. 2002. Available on-line at http://www.fipa.org/repository/ips.php3

[7] B.C. Gazen and C.A. Knoblock: Combining the expressivity of ucpop with the efficiency of graphplan. Proceedings of the 4th European Conference ECP on Planning, London, UK, Springer-Verlag, 1997.

[8] M. B. Do and S. Kambhampati: Sapa: A Scalable Multi-objective Heuristic Metric Temporal Planner. Journal of AI Research, 20:155–194, 2003.

[9] J. Hoffmann and B. Nebel: The FF Planning System: Fast Plan Generation Through Heuristic Search. Journal of Artificial Intelligence Research (JAIR), (14):253302, 2001.

[10] M. Klusch, A. Gerber and M. Schmidt: Semantic Web Service Composition Planning with OWLS-XPlan. Proceedings of the AAAI Fall Symposium on Semantic Web and Agents, Arlington VA, USA, AAAI Press, 2005.

[11] M. Klusch and K-U. Renner: Fast Dynamic Re-Planning of Composite OWL-S Services. Proceedings of 2nd IEEE Intl Workshop on Service Composition (SerComp), IEEE CS Press, Hongkong, China, 2006.

[12] V. Lifschitz: On the semantics of STRIPS. MP. Georgeff, Amy L. Lansky (eds): Proceedings of the Intl Workshop on Reasoning about Actions and Plans, Timberline, Oregon, Morgan Kaufmann, 1986

[13] E.P. Pednault: ADL: Exploring the middle ground between STRIPS and the situation calculus. Proceedings of the Conference on Knowledge Representation and Reasoning KRR, San Francisco, CA, USA, Morgan Kaufmann, 1998.

[14] K-U. Renner, B. Blankenburg, P. Kapahnke and M. Klusch: OWLS-XPlan 2.0 - Dynamic Composition Planning of OWL-S Services (Reference Manual). SCALLOPS Project Report, 2007. Available at www.dfki.de/ klusch/owlsx-plan2.pdf

[15] E. Sirin, B. Parsia, D. Wu, J. Hendler and D. Nau: HTN planning for Web Service composition using SHOP2. Journal of Web Semantics, 1(4), 2004.

[16] E. Sirin and B. Parsia: The OWL-S Java API. Proceedings of the Third International Semantic Web Conference. 2004.

Chapter 12

Semantic Web Service Execution

Luís M. Botelho, António L. Lopes, Thorsten Möller and Heiko Schuldt

12.1   Introduction

Service execution comprises all the activities that need to be carried out at runtime to invoke one or several (Web) services in a coordinated manner. These activities include initiation, control and validation of service invocations. Since each service is supposed to create side effects as manifested by the functionality that it implements, both the service user and service provider are interested that certain properties for execution are guaranteed. The two most prominent properties are guaranteed termination and reliability, that is, sustaining a consistent state before and after execution even in the presence of failures. Those aspects become of particular interest when it comes to (i) execution in distributed environments where more than one software entity might be involved, and (ii) execution of composite services, i.e., processes.

In the conventional approach to service composition[1], the act of assembling individual atomic or composite services to a process is a manual task, done by a process designer[2]. CASCOM follows a more innovative approach in which processes are generated automatically by the service composition planning agent, using planning techniques, see Chapter 11. This chapter describes two approaches to reliable service execution, which take into account both atomic and composite services. These include augmenting the planned service composition with monitoring assertions that can be checked in order to determine if the service has been successfully executed, and in the case of failure, to allow necessary re-planning by the planning agent.

---

[1] In the literature also referred to as service orchestration.
[2] This is commonly referred to as business process modeling.

As input, service execution takes service descriptions represented by the Web Ontology Language for Services (OWL-S) and a set of actual values of the services input parameters. On successful execution a set of output values (results) will be returned to the invoker whereby the values are associated to the output parameters in the service description. Either input or output sets might be empty, or both – in this case the invoked service produces just side effects. Furthermore, execution requires grounding for each service. It consists of (i) an address to a concrete service instance and (ii) information about the protocol to be used to interact with the service instance. Consequently, leaving out the grounding in an OWL-S document results in an abstract service description independent from how it is realised. To integrate state of the art Web Services that are based on WSDL [4] and SOAP, OWL-S allows specifying so-called WSDL groundings. In this chapter we concentrate on this type as it is broadly used today. However, to underpin the applicability of OWL-S to agent-based systems, we also introduce an agent grounding. In principle, there are no limitations to develop other grounding types like for instance, grounding to methods of Java classes.

Two approaches were developed for delivering the service execution functionality in the CASCOM environment: a centralized approach (see Section 12.3), where a single specialized *Service Execution Agent* (SEA) can execute an entire composite service; and a dynamically distributed approach see Section 12.4), where different well coordinated and co operating Service Execution Agents in the environment contribute to the execution of parts of a composite service.

We have decided to adopt the agent paradigm, creating SEAs to facilitate the integration of this work in open agent societies [10], enabling these not only to execute Semantic Web Services but also to seamlessly act as service providers in a large network of agents and Web Services interoperation.

12.2   Composite Service Execution

Today's business, e.g., healthcare, and even scientific applications often involve interactions with several service providers to realize use cases that can be found in the applications. As a consequence, the services involved will be composed into processes that reproduce the use cases when executed. The composition can be done either manually by process designers probably supported by design tools, or automatically by service composition planning systems, see Chapter 11. Eventually, the planned processes and input data will be issued directly to execution systems. In a centralized approach composite services would be executed completely by one single software agent. On the opposite end, execution can also be split up at each inner service that is part of a composite service. The so produced chunks can be executed in a well coordinated manner by different while co-operating software agents, i.e., in a distributed way. Of course, all the properties that are declared in the composite service with respect to control and data flow must be maintained the same way as in a centralized approach to ensure consistent and reliable execution.

The motivation to distribute composite service execution is always to be found either in demands for scalability or by needs to optimize the execution process in inherently distributed environments such as service-oriented architectures. The reasons for optimization almost automatically emerge and can be manifold. Examples are mostly related to nonfunctional aspects like interoperability, efficiency, performance, scalability, availability, reliability, security, and so on. One concrete example that has a direct impact on efficiency, performance, and scalability is the reduction of overall data amount that has to be transferred in a distributed execution. Another one might be the automatic selection of execution agents that are currently idle, thus providing load balancing, which in turn has a positive effect on scalability. Since these advanced mechanisms always require the collection and availability of additional information at runtime this also gives motivation for the presence of a generic context information system that allows to store, handle and query them, see Chapter 13.

12.2.1 General OWL-S Execution Procedure

OWL-S [6] is an OWL-based service description language. OWL-S descriptions consist of three parts: a *Profile*, which describes *what the service does*; a *Process Model*, which describes *how the service works*; and a *Grounding*, which specifies *how to access a particular provider for the service*. The Profile and Process Model are considered to be abstract specifications in the sense that they do not specify the details of particular message formats, protocols, and network addresses by which an abstract service description is instantiated. The role of providing more concrete details belongs to the grounding part. WSDL (Web Service Description Language) provides a well-developed means of specifying these kinds of details.

For the execution of OWL-S services, the most relevant parts of an OWL-S service description are the Process Model and the Grounding. The Profile part is more relevant for discovery, matchmaking and composition processes, hence no further details will be provided in this chapter.

The Process Model describes the steps that should be performed for a successful execution of the whole service that is described. These steps represent two different views of the process: first, it produces a data transformation of the set of given inputs into the set of produced outputs; second, it produces a transition in the world from one state to another. This transition is described by the preconditions and effects of the process.

There are three types of processes: *atomic*, *simple*, and *composite*. Atomic processes are directly evocable (by passing them the appropriate messages). Atomic processes have no sub-processes, and can be executed in a single step, from the perspective of the service requester. Simple processes are not evocable and are not associated with a grounding description but, like atomic processes, they are conceived of as having single-step executions. Composite processes are decomposable into other (atomic or composite) processes. These represent several-steps executions, whereby the control flow can be described using different control constructs, such as *Sequence* (representing a sequence of steps) or *If-Then-Else* (representing conditioned steps).

The Grounding specifies the details of how to access the service. These details mainly include protocol and message formats, serialization, transport, and addresses of the service provider. The central function of an OWL-S Grounding is to show how the abstract inputs and outputs of an atomic process are to be concretely realized as messages, which carry those inputs and outputs in some specific format. The Grounding can be extended to represent specific communication capabilities, protocols or messages. WSDL and AgentGrounding are two possible extensions.

The general approach for the execution of OWL-S services consists of the following sequence of steps: (i) validate the service's pre-conditions, whereas the execution continues only if all pre-conditions are true; (ii) decompose the compound service into individual atomic services, which in turn are executed by evoking their corresponding service providers using the description of the service providers contained in the grounding section of the service description; (iii) validate the service's described effects by comparing them with the actual effects of the service execution, whereas the execution only proceeds if the service has produced the expected effects; (iv) collect the results, if there are any results, and send them to the client who requested the execution. Notice that the service may be just a *change-the-world* kind of service, i.e., it produces just side effects.

12.3   Centralized Approach for Service Execution

This section presents the research on agent technology development for context-aware execution of Semantic Web Services, more specifically, the development of a Service Execution Agent for Semantic Web Services execution. The agent uses context information to adapt the execution process to a specific situation, thus improving its effectiveness and providing a faster and better service.

Being able to engage in complex interactions and to perform difficult tasks, agents are often seen as a vehicle to provide value-added services in open large-scale environments. Using OWL-S service descriptions it was not possible up to now to have service provider agents in addition to the usual Web Services because the grounding section of OWL-S descriptions lacks the necessary expressiveness to describe the complex interactions of agents. In order to overcome this limitation, we have decided to extend the OWL-S grounding specification to enable the representation of services provided by intelligent agents. This extension is called the *AgentGrounding* [13].

We have also introduced the use of *Prolog* [5] for the formal representation of logical expressions in OWL-S control constructs. To our knowledge, the only support for control constructs that depend on formal representation of logical expressions in OWL-S is done through the use of *SWRL* [12] or *PDDL* [14].

12.3.1 Service Execution and Context-Awareness

Context-aware computing is a computing paradigm in which applications can discover and take advantage of context information to improve their behaviour in terms of effectiveness as well as performance. As described in [2] context is any information that can be used to characterize the situation of an entity. Entities may be persons, places or objects considered relevant to the interaction between a user and an application, including users and applications themselves.

We can enhance this definition by stating that the context of a certain entity is any information that can be used to characterize the situation of that entity individually or when interacting with other entities. The same concept can be transferred to application-to-application interaction environments.

Context-aware computing can be summarized as being a mechanism that collects physical or emotional state information on an entity; analyses that information, either by treating it as an isolated single variable or by combining it with other information collected in the past or present; performs some action based on the analysis; and repeats from the first step, with some adaptation based on previous iterations [1].

SEA uses a similar approach as the one described in [1] to enhance its service execution process, by adapting it to the specific situation in which the agent and its client are involved, at the time of the execution process. This is done by interacting with a general purpose (i.e., domain independent) context system [7] (see also Chapter 13) for obtaining context information, subscribing desired context events and providing relevant context information. Other agents, Web Services and sensors (both software and hardware) in the environment will interact with the context system as well, by providing relevant context information related to their own activities, which may be useful to other entities in the environment.

Throughout the execution process, SEA provides and acquires context information from and to this context system. For example, SEA provides relevant context information about itself, such as its queue of service execution requests and the average time of service execution. This will allow other entities in the environment to determine the service execution agent with the smallest workload, and hence the one that offers a faster execution service.

During the execution of a compound service, SEA invokes atomic services from specific service providers (both Web Services, and service provider agents). SEA also provides valuable information regarding these service providers' availability and average execution time. Other entities can use this information to rate service providers or to simply determine the best service provider to use in a specific situation.

Furthermore, SEA uses its own context information (as well as information from other sources and entities in the environment) to adapt the execution process to a specific situation. For instance, when selecting among several providers of some service, SEA will choose the one with better availability (with less history of being offline) and lower average execution time.

In situations such as the one where service providers are unavailable, it is faster to obtain the context information from the context system (as long as service providers can also provide context information about their own availability) than by simply trying to use the services and finding out that they are unavailable after having waited for the connection timeout to occur. If SEA learns that a given service provider is not available it will contact the service discovery agent or the service composition agent requesting that a new service provider is discovered or that the compound service is re planned. This situation-aware approach using context information on-the-fly helps SEA to provide a value-added execution service.

12.3.2   Service Execution Agent

The Service Execution Agent (SEA) is a broker agent that provides context-aware execution of services on the semantic web (whether they are provided by Web Services or agents). The agent was designed and developed considering the interactions described in Section 12.3.1 and the need to adapt to situations where the interaction with other service-oriented agents is required. Its internal architecture was clearly designed to enable the agent to receive requests from client agents, acquire and provide relevant context information, interacting with other service coordination agents when necessary and execute remote services.

This section is divided into four parts. Sections 12.3.2 and 12.3.2 describe SEA internal architecture, explaining in detail the internal components and their interactions. Section 12.3.2 describes *AgentGrounding*, an extension of the OWL-S Grounding specification that allows agents to act as service providers in the Semantic Web. Section 12.3.3 provides some details on the implementation of the agent.

Internal Architecture

The developed agent is composed of three components: the Agent Interaction Component (also referred to as Interaction Component), the Engine Component and the Service Execution Component (also referred to as Execution Component). Figure 12.1 illustrates SEA internal architecture and the interactions that occur between its components.

The Interaction Component was developed as an extension of the JADE platform and its goal is to provide an interaction framework with FIPA-compliant agents, such as its client agents (Figure 12.1, steps 1 and 10), service discovery and service composition agents (whenever SEA requests the re discovery or the re planning of specific services). This component extends the JADE platform with extra features regarding language processing, behavior execution, database information retrieval and inter components communication.

Among other things, the Interaction Component is responsible for receiving messages, parsing them into a format suitable for the Engine Component to use

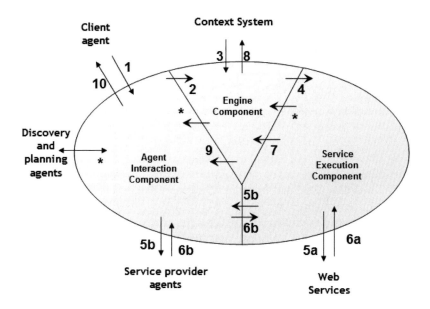

Figure 12.1: SEA's internal architecture and interactions between the several components

(Figure 12.1, step 2). The reverse process is also the responsibility of the Interaction Component — receiving data from the Engine Component and converting it into the suitable format to be sent as FIPA-ACL messages (Figure 12.1, step 9).

The Engine Component is the main component of the execution agent as it controls the agent's overall activity. It is responsible for pre processing service execution requests by acquiring/providing context information from/to the context system and deciding when to interact with other agents (such as service discovery and composition agents).

When the Engine Component receives an OWL-S service execution request (Figure 12.1, step 2), it acquires suitable context information (regarding potential service providers and other relevant information, such as client location Figure 12.1, step 3) and schedules the execution process.

The Service Execution Agent interacts with a service discovery agent (through the Interaction Component — Figure 12.1, steps *) to discover available providers for the atomic services that are used in the OWL-S compound service. If the service discovery agent cannot find adequate service providers, the Engine Component can interact with a service composition agent (again through the Interaction Component — Figure 12.1, steps *) asking it to create an OWL-S compound service that produces the same effects as the original service.

After having a service ready for execution, with suitable context information, the Engine Component sends it to the Service Execution Component (Figure 12.1, step 4), for execution. Throughout the execution process, the Engine Component is also responsible for providing context information to the context system, whether it is its own information (such as its queue of service execution requests, average execution time) or other entities' relevant context information (such as availability of providers and average execution time of services).

The Execution Component was developed as an extension of the OWL-S API and its goal is to execute OWL-S service descriptions (Figure 12.1, steps 5a and 6a) with WSDL grounding information. The extension of the OWL-S API allows performing the evaluation of logical expressions in conditioned constructs, such as the *If-then-Else* and *While* constructs, and in services' pre-conditions and effects. OWL S API was also extended in order to support the execution of services that are grounded on service provider agents (Figure 12.1, steps 5b, 6b). This extension is called *AgentGrounding* and it is explained in detail in Section 12.3.2.

When the Execution Component receives a service execution request from the Engine Component, it executes it according to the description of the service's process model. This generic execution process is described in Section 12.2.1.

After the execution of the specified service and the generation of its results, the Execution Component sends them to the Engine Component (Figure 12.1, step 7) for further analysis and post processing, which includes sending gathered context information to the context system (Figure 12.1, step 8) and sending the results to the client agent (through the Interaction Component — Figure 12.1, steps 9 and 10).

Agent Interface

When requesting the execution of a specified service, client agents interact with the Service Execution Agent through the FIPA-request interaction protocol [9]. This protocol states that when the receiver agent receives an action request, it can either agree or refuse to perform the action. The receiver (i.e., the execution agent) should notify the sender of its decision through the corresponding communicative act (FIPA-agree or FIPA-refuse).

The decision to whether or not to accept a given execution request depends on the results of a request evaluation algorithm which involves acquiring and analysing adequate context information. The Service Execution Agent (SEA) will only agree to perform a specific execution if it is possible to execute it, according to the currently available context information. For example, if necessary service providers are not available and the time required to find alternatives is longer than the given timeframe in which the client agent expects to obtain a reply to the execution request, then the execution agent refuses to perform it.

On the other hand, if the execution agent is able to perform the execution request (because service providers are immediately available), but not in the time frame requested by the client agent (again, according to available context information) it also refuses the request. The execution agent can also refuse execute requests if its workload is already too high (if its requests queue is longer than a certain defined constant).

If during the execution process the execution agent is unable to perform the entire request, it notifies the client agent by sending a FIPA-Failure message, which includes the reason for the execution failure. The FIPA-request interaction protocol also states that after successful execution of the requested action, the executer agent should return the corresponding results through a FIPA-inform message. After executing a service, SEA can send one of two different FIPA-inform messages: a message containing the results obtained from the execution of the service, or a message containing just a notification that the service was successfully executed (when no results are produced by the execution).

OWL-S Grounding Extension for Agents: AgentGrounding

WSDL is an XML format for describing network services as a set of endpoints operating on messages containing either document-oriented or procedure oriented information. The operations and messages are described abstractly, and then bound to a concrete network protocol and message format to define an endpoint. Related concrete endpoints are combined into abstract endpoints (services). WSDL is extensible to allow description of endpoints and their messages regardless of what message formats or network protocols are used to communicate [4]. In short, WSDL describes the access to a specific service provider for a described OWL-S service.

WSDL currently lacks a way of representing agent bindings, i.e., a representation for complex interactions such as the ones that take place with service provider agents. To overcome this limitation, we decided to create an extension of the OWL-S Grounding specification, named *AgentGrounding* [13]. This extension is the result of an analysis of the necessary requirements for interacting with agents when evoking the execution of atomic services. In order for an agent to act as a service provider in the Semantic Web, its complex communication schema has to be mapped into the OWL-S Grounding structure.

The AgentGrounding specification includes most of the elements that are present in Agent Communication. The AgentGrounding specification includes elements such as the name and the address of the service provider, the protocol and ontology that are used in the process, the agent communication language, and the content language. At the message content level, the AgentGrounding specification includes elements such as name and type of the service to be evoked and its input and output arguments, including the types and the mapping to OWL-S parameters.

Figure 12.2 is an example of an OWL-S service grounding using the proposed AgentGrounding extension. This description illustrates a service, provided by a FIPA compliant agent, of finding books within several different sources, with a given input title.

The AgentGrounding extension allows the specification of groundings such

```
<!-- Grounding description -->
<ag:AgentGrounding rdf:ID="HospitalFinderGrounding">
  <s:supportedBy rdf:resource="#HospitalFinderService"/>
  <g:hasAtomicProcessGrounding rdf:resource="#HospitalFinderProcessGrounding"/>
</ag:AgentGrounding>
<ag:AgentAtomicProcessGrounding rdf:ID="HospitalFinderProcessGrounding">
    <g:owlsProcess rdf:resource="#HospitalFinderProcess"/>
    <ag:agentName>hospitalinfo@cascom</ag:agentName>
    <ag:agentAddress>http://...</ag:agentAddress>
    <!-- Service Identification -->
    <ag:serviceName>find-hospital
    </ag:serviceName>
    <!-- Service Arguments -->
    <ag:hasArgumentParameter>
      <ag:ArgumentParameter rdf:ID="location">
        <ag:argumentType>java.lang.String</ag:argumentType>
        <ag:owlsParameter rdf:resource="#Location"/>
        <ag:paramIndex>1</ag:paramIndex>
      </ag:ArgumentParameter>
    </ag:hasArgumentParameter>
    <ag:serviceOutput>
      <ag:ArgumentVariable rdf:ID="hospital-info">
        <ag:argumentType>java.lang.String</ag:argumentType>
        <ag:owlsParameter rdf:resource="#HospitalInfo"/>
      </ag:ArgumentVariable>
    </ag:serviceOutput>
    <!-- Other information -->
    <ag:serviceType>action</ag:serviceType>
    <ag:protocol>fipa-request</ag:protocol>
    <ag:agentCommunicationLanguage>fipa-acl</ag:agentCommunicationLanguage>
    <ag:contentLanguage>fipa-sl</ag:contentLanguage>
    <ag:serviceOntology>hospital-finder-ontology</ag:serviceOntology>
</ag:AgentAtomicProcessGrounding>
```

Figure 12.2: Example of *AgentGrounding* description

as the one described in Figure 12.2. These groundings can be executed through a request sent to the Service Execution Agent, which in turn executes the service by invoking the specified service providers. This invocation is made by sending a message directly to the agent providing the service. All the information that is needed for sending the message is included in the *AgentGrounding* description.

The example depicted in Figure12.2 describes a service named HospitalFinderService, which is grounded to an action find-hospital that accepts, as input, a single string named location. This location argument is linked to the OWL-S service input parameter Location. The action returns, as output, also a string, named hospital-info, which is linked to the OWL-S service output parameter HospitalInfo. Other information that can be extracted from this grounding is the interaction protocol (fipa-request), the agent communication language (fipa-acl), the ontology (hospital-finder-ontology) and the content language (fipa-sl) to be used in the invocation message. The Service Execution Agent can use this information to send the FIPA message that is described in Figure 12.3.

The information extracted from the *AgentGrounding* example in Figure 12.2 plus the information regarding the concrete service input (in this example, the string '9,8324W 38,12345N'), which comes in the received service execution request, is enough for the agent to be able to create the message in Figure 12.3.

The AgentGrounding specification allows the representation of several instances of messages that can be sent to FIPA compliant agents, including the use of different performatives, agent communication languages and content languages.

12.3.3   Implementation

The Service Execution Agent was implemented using Java and component-based software as well as other tools that were extended to incorporate new functionalities into the service execution environment. These tools are the JADE agent platform [3] and the OWL-S API [19].

The JADE agent platform was integrated into the Agent Interaction Component (see Section 12.3.2) of the Service Execution Agent to enable its interaction with client agents and service provider agents. The OWL-S API is a Java implementation of the OWL-S execution engine, which supports the specification of WSDL groundings. The OWL-S API was integrated into the Execution Component of the Service Execution Agent to enable it to execute both atomic and compound services. In order to support the specification and execution of Agent-Grounding descriptions (see Section 12.3.2), we have extended the OWL-S APIs execution process engine. The extension of the execution engine allows converting AgentGrounding descriptions into agent-friendly messages, namely FIPA ACL messages, and sending these to the corresponding service provider agents. To enable the support for control constructs that depend on formal representation of logical expressions using Prolog, we extended the OWL-S API with a Prolog engine that is able to process logical expressions present in If/While clauses and pre-conditions. This extension was done through the use of TuProlog [8], an open source Java based Prolog.

12.4   Distributed Approach for Service Execution

The distributed approach for service execution differs from the centralised approach (see Section 12.3) in the sense that at runtime execution is not limited to being handled by just one execution agent but might involve several distinct agents[3]. This fundamental expansion results in the advantages described earlier

---

[3]Whether they are actually physically separated, i.e., run on different peers, is a matter of the agent platform used and the concrete deployment of agent instances. Consequently, the distributed approach imposes no constraints on the organisation of agents beyond what is implicated by the agent platform used. On the other hand, not physically separated would mean that they run on one peer within different threads or processes.

```
(REQUEST
 :sender (agent−identifier :name sea@cascom)
 :receiver (set (agent−identifier :name hospitalinfo@cascom
   :addresses (sequence http://...)))
 :content "((action
     (agent−identifier :name hospitalinfo@cascom)
     (find−hospital :location \"9,8324W 38,12345N\")))"
   :language fipa−sl
   :ontology hospital−finder−ontology
   :protocol fipa−request)
```

Figure 12.3: Message generated from the example in Figure 12.2

in this chapter but brings in new characteristics that need to be tackled in order to retain reliable execution.

The following sections present presents research results in the area of distributed execution of composite Semantic Web Services. Section 12.4.1 starts by pointing to the general assumptions. The main part of this chapter describes the basic concept and structure of the distributed approach and the protocol that represents the interaction model between client agents and execution agents. The chapter concludes by briefly presenting the implementation of the service execution system that was developed at the University of Basel.

To start out, distributed service execution invariably requires a certain strategy to organise and co-ordinate distribution. Basically, such a strategy includes a method to control the flow of execution among the participating agents and the invocation of the service itself. In general, various kinds of such strategies can be designed. The properties of the approach that has been developed in the CASCOM project will be described in Section 12.4.2.

12.4.1   General Assumptions

For distributed service execution, we first assume that a composite service contains an arbitrary number of service invocations whereby the composition structure is equal to a directed acyclic graph, i.e., combined sequential and parallel flows together forming processes as denoted in [16]. Second, as a basis for correct process execution, each service invocation is assumed to be atomic and compensatable. This means that the effects of a service can be undone, if necessary, after the invocation has returned. Otherwise, unwanted side effects of aborted or reset executions may remain and exactly-once execution semantic could not be guaranteed. For services which do not comply with the atomicity requirement, we assume that a wrapper can be built which adds this functionality. Third, we assume that services are stateless, i.e., that they never have to remember anything beyond interaction. In our approach, execution state (i.e., intermediate results) is solely stored by the execution system, as part of the process (composite service) instance. Finally, our approach considers the crash failure model, which means that components such as services and machines may fail by prematurely halting their execution.

12.4.2   Execution Strategy

Carrying out execution of composite services in a distributed environment consisting of more than one execution agent requires the definition of a certain strategy. The strategy is built on three core properties: First, it defines how to divide the composite service into sections which can be executed in a distributed way afterwards. Second, it defines where and when to distribute those sections to different execution agents. Finally, it defines a mechanism for control between the participating agents to guarantee consistent execution. Altogether they imply the way execution will be actually done at runtime.

The selection or design of an execution strategy needs always to be accompanied by an analysis of the service environment. The two main aspects that such an analysis would cover are (i) the technologies used, like SOAP based Web Service interactions, and (ii) the deployment structure of service providers and their (physical) relation to service clients (agents in the CASCOM architecture).

In the following, three different dimensions for categorisation of execution strategies are described. Sections 12.4.2 and 12.4.2 describe two general purpose approaches, which have their own characteristics regarding the three dimensions. The former one was chosen for implementation of the distributed service execution agent and we will outline some advantages and disadvantages.

In general, a strategy for distributed execution of composite services must initially define whether execution control takes place in a centralised or decentralised way. The centralised approach requires a dedicated manager agent that takes the responsibility of supervising and co-ordinating execution after receipt of the composite service. In doing so, the manager agent invokes the actual execution agents according to the control structure of the composite service. The execution agents in turn invoke the actual services and await the results of the service invocations. In contrast to the centralised approach the decentralised approach does not require a dedicated agent, that is, the co-ordination role is no longer limited to stay at a single manager agent. In theory, the co-ordination role either can be forwarded among the participating agents or the agents coalesce to share the co-ordination role. Whereas the manager agent in the centralised approach turns out to become a bottleneck and a single point of failure both problems are eliminated in the decentralised approach. On the other hand, a decentralised approach comes with the trade-off that more advanced control mechanisms are required, accompanied by higher (communication) efforts in case of failure handling and initial preparation before execution (see Section 12.4.2). In addition, the decentralized approach allows for balancing the load among different agents and for taking into account the dynamics of practical settings where agents might frequently leave or others join.

Starting from the process model of OWL-S services, execution can be further classified depending on whether the services are atomic or composite (see Section 12.2.1). While execution of an atomic OWL-S service implicates just one service invocation, the number of service invocations for composite OWL-S services intuitively relates to the number of atomic services out of which they are *composed*. In general, we always refer to composite services since execution of atomic services in fact does not require an advanced distributed execution strategy. The reason is that invocation of a Web Service is defined as a request reply pattern between a service client and the provider that cannot be further split up. As a conclusion, it is now obvious what the smallest granularity for sections of a composite service is: the atomic services. At the same time it is also the preferred granularity as it directly maps to the OWL-S process model[4]. Hence, it is not remarkable

---

[4]The process model basically relates to a directed graph, whereby the nodes are (atomic)

that most execution strategies would size the sections for distribution equal to the atomic services. Finally, the general assumption is that agents execute those sections of the composite service. For instance, the most straightforward approach would associate each atomic service within a composite service to one execution agent which invokes it, i.e., a composite service consisting of n atomic services would require n execution agents ($n \geq 1$).

Yet another aspect for categorisation of execution strategies relates to whether execution agents and (Web) service providers are tightly integrated/coupled or not. By tightly integrated we mean that an execution agent basically wraps one or more services, that is, both run on the same machine, probably even in the same process. In addition, the implementation of the invocation of the Web Service by the wrapper agent itself might bypass the whole Web Services communication stack and might be done without this overhead by direct programmatic calls. Furthermore, this type mostly comes along with the intention that an execution agent wraps a fixed set of services, i.e., the set of services is expected to never change. As opposed to tight integration, remote coupling means that the execution agent and the (Web) service provider are distant from each other, that is, the execution agent invokes the service in the standard way using its communication layer and protocol. For instance, the today's broadly adopted Web Service stack: HTTP based SOAP or REST. Finally, this type mostly comes along with a generic design of the execution agent which is able to invoke any remote service.

Dynamically Distributed Execution Strategy with Remote Coupling of Execution Agent and Web Services

The approach described hereafter was designed to address recent developments in service-oriented architectures in which the spreading and application of Web Service standards like WSDL and SOAP have reached a level where Web Service providers almost always apply those technologies to publish and provide access to their Web Services. As a matter of fact, the question had to be raised whether a tight coupling of execution agents and Web Services is appropriate, assumable, even feasible in practice or whether a strategy can be found which fits well to the current exploitation of Web Services: A strategy which considers remote invocation of services using the common Web Services communication stack and which is still robust against failures. As a result, this strategy supports the requirement that service providers want to remain Web Services conform with respect to the service interfaces.

Figure 12.4 illustrates the course of the dynamically-distributed and decentralized excution strategy based on a very simple scenario where a composite service containing a sequence of three Web Service invocations $WS1$ to $WS3$ should be executed. It is also assumed that a composite service is split up into sections equal to the atomic services inside. The strategy works as follows.

---

services and vertices represent the control flow.

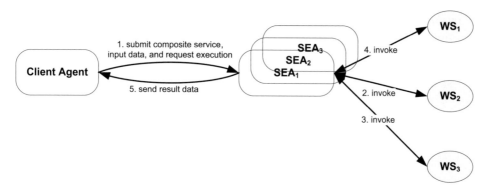

Figure 12.4: Dynamically-distributed execution strategy with remote coupling of execution agent and Web Services

1. The client agent submits a valid OWL-S composite service description together with the input data to one available execution agent, SEA_1 in this case.

2. SEA_1 parses the service description and immediately starts invoking the first Web Service $WS1$. After return of the result from $WS1$ the first section is finished.

3. A decision step follows to determine whether execution of the next section should be made by the same agent or whether the execution state should be transferred to another execution agent and continue there. In this decision step arbitrary heuristics can be used to figure out how to continue, i.e., on which agent to continue. For instance, it would be possible to design context based heuristics making it possible to adapt dynamically to overloaded, slow, expensive, or failure-prone context situations and transfer execution state to other execution agents with superior context situations. Additionally, it is also possible to face the effort for transferring execution state to another execution agent with the benefit available there. As a result, the system can be adapted to the circumstances that exist in practical settings by designing distribution heuristics that incorporate the characteristics[5].

4. Execution of the next section might continue on SEA_1 until $WS3$ returned its result. The same decision step is done after each section.

5. In step 5 the composite service output (result) is returned to the client agent.

The heuristics based approach for distribution is able to cope with external

---

[5]Two simple heuristics have been implemented for the prototype. First, a CPU load based heuristic. A transfer of the execution state takes place only if the average CPU load on the current execution agent exceeded a certain threshold in a preceding timeframe. For validation purposes, a round-robin heuristic has been implemented that transfers to another execution agent in either case but always selects that execution agent that has been used least recently.

failure situations but not with crash situations of the current execution agent itself. To overcome this problem, two possibilities exist. It is either possible to persist the current execution state at the current agent, or to replicate the execution state online to another execution agent. Whereas the first solution is only appropriate for short interruptions whereby the agent gets rebooted immediately afterwards and restarts the interrupted execution, the second solution is more robust since execution can be immediately overtaken by the agent which has the replicated execution state. Therefore we intend to extend the implementation of the execution agent with the latter solution.

Provided that the heuristics based decision always returns with the result to continue at the same execution agent, execution is in fact not distributed and the communication effort is minimal. According to the actual heuristic used, this situation represents the optimal execution environment then. On the opposite end, transfer to another agent on each decision computation represents the most suboptimal execution environment according to the heuristic and also involves the highest communication overhead. Therefore it turns out that the more precarious the context environment is the more efforts must be undertaken.

Another characteristic of this strategy is that its properties do not deteriorate assuming that (Web) service providers would be tightly integrated with agents. Assuming this change the execution agent which currently does invocations should then communicate to other agents using ACL messages instead of using the Web Services stack. Consequently, only the message layer for service invocations needs to be replaced/extended by a communication layer for ACL messages.

Fully Distributed Execution Strategy with Tight Integration of Execution Agent and Web Services

The determinative characteristic of this strategy is the assumption that execution agents and (Web) service providers are tightly or locally integrated, as described above. Consequently, execution agents need to be deployed and made available for every pre-existing service provider in the infrastructure. This property distinguishs it from the dynamically-distributed strategy described in the preceding section. This approach for distributed while decentralized composite service execution is related to techniques described in [18] and [15].

Figure 12.5 illustrates the course of the fully-distributed and decentralized execution strategy. Likewise Figure 12.4 it also assumes a very simple scenario where a composite service containing a sequence of three Web Service invocations $WS1$ to $WS3$ should be executed. The client agent — according to the setting in the CASCOM architecture this would actually be the SCPA — submits the valid OWL-S composite service description together with the input data to any available execution agent, for instance SEA_0. This execution agent parses the given service description for the first atomic service provider, which is $WS1$. With this information the agent resolves the execution agent SEA_1 as it is the wrapper of $WS1$ — notice that we assume the availability of some kind of directory containing

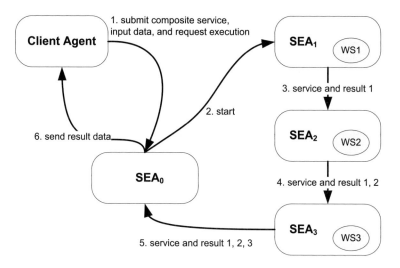

Figure 12.5: Course of fully-distributed execution strategy with tight integration of SEA and service provider

a mapping from service providers to execution agents. In the next step SEA_0 forwards the complete service description and input data to SEA_1 co-requesting execution start. By forwarding the complete service description each agent is able to resolve the next agent to forward control and results to because this information can be read from the process model of the service description. Remember that the process model specifies the control and data flow, i.e., the order and type of service invocations. In the scenario, after completion of execution of $WS1$, SEA_1 would resolve the agent for $WS2$ which is SEA_2 and again forward the complete service description together with the input data and result 1 produced by $WS1$. This procedure continues until SEA_3 has finished invocation of $WS3$ with result 3. In step 5 SEA_3 sends results 1 to 3 back to SEA_0 which just maps them to the composite service's output (result). Provided that all service invocations returned without failures the result is sent back to the client agent in step 6.

In case of failures on one execution agent, failed service invocations, or in case of violated pre- or post-conditions execution either has to be rolled back or a re-planning could be initiated trying to find alternative services and continue execution if an alternative was found. Assuming transactional properties of the services (as stated in Section 12.4.1) a roll back can be done based on the fact that each execution agent knows its adjacent predecessor(s) from the process model of the composite service. A rollback then requires moving back along the control path step by step and rolling back each service invocation done.

The downside of the simple variant of this approach is that intermediate results produced by service invocations and input data will be forwarded in any case no matter if they are actually required on every execution agent, i.e., the data flow is not optimal and that SEA and atomic service need to be tightly coupled. For instance, in the scenario illustrated in Figure 12.5, if $WS1$ produces large volumes of data as result 1 they will be forwarded to SEA_2 and SEA_3 in any case. In a first optimised version data (input and output data, intermediate results) would only be forwarded between the agents where it is required, thus reducing the overall data communication amount. Furthermore, it is not necessary to forward the composite OWL-S service description from agent to agent. In a second optimisation step this can be optimised to split the composite service into its atomic services sections and extend the execution strategy with an initial distribution of the sections to each agent, i.e., each execution agent receives just its own task within the composite service. In the scenario above this initial step could be done by SEA_0. To complete this optimisation each agent also needs knowledge about its adjacent predecessor(s) and successor(s) for control flow navigation. The successor(s) is/are required for normal forward navigation whereas the predecessor(s) is/are required for backwards navigation in case of roll back.

12.4.3   Interaction Model

The execution agent shows a non-proactive behaviour. It must be actively contacted by a client agent that wants to request execution of a composite OWL-S service[6]. In general, there is no limitation about what kind of agent can act as the client agent. However, the overall CASCOM architecture was designed for dynamic planning of composite services by a dedicated planner agent. This planner agent issues a service (together with the actual inputs) to the execution agent after it has finished the planning, triggers execution start, and asynchronously awaits the results. As problems might occur during execution — for instance, a Web Service invocation might fail because it might be temporarily not available — the interaction model also includes a re-planning sub-interaction. In case of a problem the execution agent would temporarily suspend execution and ask the planner agent for planning of a contingency service. As a result, the types of interactions that have to be supported are extended asynchronous request/reply interactions.

Each execution agent publishes a main interaction interface by which all communication with a client agent takes place. This main interface is formalized by an agent ontology that defines the concepts, predicates, and actions to create meaningful ACL message content. Furthermore, an internal interaction interface exists by which execution agents communicate among themselves during execution; the latter one is not described here.

Not just because of the asynchronous invocation model but especially because of the required usage patterns which are beyond the simple request/reply pattern, all interactions between calling agent and execution agent are stateful, thus forming an interaction protocol. Each new invocation of one of the execution

---

[6]In fact, both atomic and composite OWL-S services can be issued the same way to an execution agent.

agent's methods implicitly creates a new session which lasts until the final result was sent back to the invoking agent — no matter if the result is positive or negative. The state on both sides is encapsulated by finite state automata as provided by the JADE framework. As a recommended starting point for simple request/reply agent conversations FIPA has specified the standard *Achieve Rational Effect* protocol [9]. However, we have specified and implemented an extended version of the protocol, named *Achieve Rational Effect ** protocol, since the original protocol is not sufficient with respect to the requirements of service execution interaction. For example, if some client agent requests the execution of some composite OWL-S service from an execution agent, it is useful even necessary for monitoring and re-planning purposes that the requestor gets notified about execution progress. This notification informs about the position of control flow within the composite service, respectively the effects achieved so far. In short, the *Achieve Rational Effect ** protocol extends the standard FIPA Achieve Rational Effect protocol with two optional features:

1. The possibility to send any kind of intermediate or feedback ACL messages (information) to the initiator before the final result (inform or failure) is sent to the initiator. Consecutive messages of this kind can be sent, but may alternate with 2.).

2. The possibility to send return requests (ACL messages) back to the initiator to *ask* for additional information which might be required to achieve the original rational effect. A return request must be answered by the initiator until a new return request can be done or a new feedback message can be sent.

Figure 12.6 shows the defined order and cardinalities of the ACL message flow for the *Achieve Rational Effect ** protocol. For the interfacing with the execution agent the extension part is used to provide the initiating agent with up to date information about the current state of the execution. The second part is used to trigger re-planning of composite OWL-S services in case of problems during execution, for instance, if an atomic service part of the composite service became suddenly unavailable.

12.4.4 Implementation

The distributed service execution is implemented in Java as autonomous agents that can be deployed within the CASCOM agent platform [11] as well as the JADE platform [3]. The implementation derives from and incorporates concepts of the OSIRIS process management system [17]. This system essentially represents a peer-to-peer message oriented middleware with an integrated component framework. The component framework allows to implement and run custom components each delivering a pre-defined service and able to communicate with other (remote) components. The messaging layer basically realizes the publish/subscribe

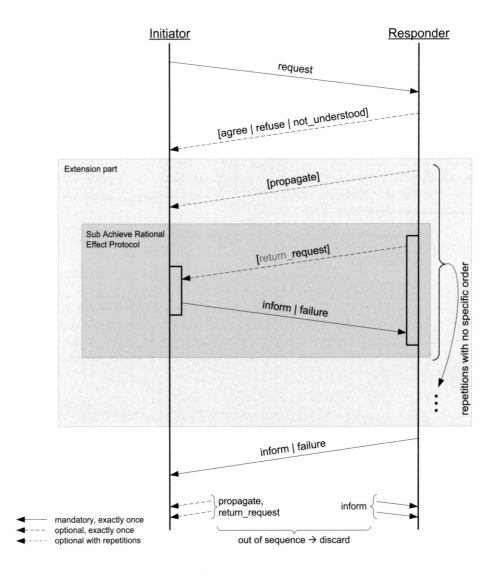

Figure 12.6: Message flow for interactions of a client agent (initiator) with the service execution agent (responder)

messaging paradigm as well as addressing of specific receivers. Furthermore, it incorporates advanced concepts such as eager and lazy replication, and freshness properties. On top of the middleware, a distributed while decentralized process execution engine (implemented as components) was developed. This means that several peers may be involved in the execution of a composite service whereby no central co-ordinator is required. Its execution strategy can be compared to the one presented in Section 12.4.2. Finally, the internal design of the OSIRIS system is strictly multithreaded, comparable to the SEDA approach [20].

The OSIRIS system was extended to support execution of Semantic Web Services. All its functionality is represented to the outside by agents, whereby for a minimum deployment just one agent is sufficient — of course, such a deployment in fact would be not distributed. Furthermore, all execution agents in a distributed deployment are equal in their functionality accessible by client agents, which means that all of them are available to be used in the same way, thus presenting a true P2P structure. In fact, all the functionality implemented is encapsulated by one so called agent *Behaviour*. Conceptually, a behaviour represents a task that an agent can carry out. Each agent can be added any number of different behaviours at any time, thus adding it any number of tasks that it can do. Consequently, a great flexibility is achieved with respect to who can implement OWL-S service execution functionality: The behaviour can be added to any agent, thus extending the agent to which it is added with OWL-S service execution functionality.

Another aspect that has been incorporated in the implementation is the distinction between call-by-value and call-by-reference semantics. Execution requests by a client agent can be made in either of those types with respect to both the OWL-S service description itself and the actual input data. Using the call-by-value style means to embed the data value itself in a request[7]. On the other hand, call-by-reference style means to embed only a reference[8] to the data value in a request that must be resolved by the execution agent afterwards.

12.5 Summary

In this chapter an agent based framework has been presented that enables the execution of composite (as well as atomic) Semantic Web Services that are described based on OWL-S and WSDL. From a systems point of view, two comprehensive approaches are provided: (i) a centralized solution where a single Execution Agent solely takes over the responsibility for executing a given service and (ii) a distributed approach where a set of P2P-organized Execution Agents co-operate to share the execution task among them. The centralized solution employs context information to determine the appropriate service providers for each situation to distribute and balance the execution work. The distributed approach goes even

---

[7]The data format for both the OWL-S service description and input data is serialised XML.

[8]The implementation allows using URLs to reference (external) data that is available somewhere in the Web.

one step further by providing built-in scalability support not only with respect to the number of service providers but also in terms of an increasing number of client agents. Here, scalability is supported at two levels: First, at a micro level by a multithreaded implementation that allows an Execution Agent to handle multiple execution requests concurrently. Second, at a macro or infrastructure level by the possibility to dynamically migrate execution from one agent to another. This is beneficial when for instance the overall execution time and/or throughput can be optimized, or when the load among the different execution agents can be balanced. This optimization is based on a generic cost model that is open to incorporate different measures like, for instance, service costs, data and communication costs, reliability of computing resources, and resource consumption of services. This means that the assessment whether an ongoing execution would profit from a transfer to another agent is open to allow (i) incorporating domain-specific requirements and (ii) context information. This gives a great flexibility to apply this approach to various environments having different preconditions, requirements, and properties. Furthermore, the migration procedure does not require any centralized supervision and was developed to happen completely self-dependent and decentralized.

The following two subsections discuss alternative approaches to service execution that can be taken into account when starting from different assumptions.

12.5.1   Late Binding of Service Provider Instance during Execution

The overall CASCOM architecture approch considers that Execution Agents take *instantiated* service descriptions as their input, that is, service descriptions that are already grounded to a particular service provider (instance). This means that in the CASCOM setting the Service Composition Planner Agent already decides about which concrete service provider it will use when creating a new composite service. This approach is highly beneficial for services which are created ad-hoc, and are only very infrequently executed, immediately after the service is composed.

However, when services are executed frequently or when the execution of the service is time-consuming, then it can no longer be guaranteed that the groundings are still valid, while the service type may still be appropriate. In this case, it is beneficial when planning and service execution is further decoupled. A first approach considers only service types as output of the planner, while the groundings for the complete service is done at instantiation time. This approach is particularly useful for short running services such that the groundings remain valid during service execution. Second, the grounding might be done prior to the invocation of an atomic service during the execution of a composite service. Deferring the decision on the service grounding to instantiation or execution time frees the composition planner agent from this additional task and will reduce the composition time. This shift of service provider selection to happen *closer* to the service invocation has the potential to improve the overall system behaviour in very dynamic service environments. The higher the probability that an optimal service provider selection that was done at time t_1 becomes suboptimal at a later point in time t_2, the more important this becomes. An example that illustrates this would be either a long delay between service composition and execution, or a (very) long running composite service consisting of, say, three subsequent atomic service invocations. If service providers are already selected before execution it might happen that the one associated to the third atomic service is not available anymore when the actual service invocation is due, thus, would raise a failure. The task of binding the abstract service type to an instance will be under the responsibility of the execution agent. To accomplish this binding, additional queries to discover service providers must be done by the execution agent.

However, this aspect is of rather minor importance to the CASCOM system: First, service execution immediately follows service composition, i.e., there is almost no delay in between. Second, the envisioned application scenarios are rather characterized by short running composite services compared to the extent that is considered usual in other application domains like scientific workflows. Finally, the dynamic failure handling by composition re-planning provides a method to cope with services that become unavailable during execution.

Nevertheless, the implementations of both the centralized and the distributed approach are prepared for late binding of service instances during execution but need to be extended to closely integrate with the Service Discovery Agent.

12.5.2 Tight Integration of Service Providers and Execution Agents

The discussion of tight integration versus remote coupling of service providers and execution agents has already been raised and discussed in detail in Section 12.4.2. The CASCOM systems assumes a remote coupling of service providers and execution agents because of the status quo in the way Web Services are deployed today and how they can be accessed – not only from a technical point of view but also from a organizational point of view: Service providers are unwilling to deploy additional software layers that would integrate their services with inter-organizational service infrastructures for several reasons. The most important one is that they are afraid of loosing control over their services.

Still, in intra-organizational deployments it would be more easily possible to use the approach for distributed execution of composite services that has been described in Section 12.4.2. Even then one aspect remains to be further considered, which is the adequacy for ad hoc automated service composition where the resulting composite services are usually executed only once.

References

[1] D. Abowd, A. K. Dey, R. Orr and J. Brotherton: Context-awareness in wearable and ubiquitous computing. *Virtual Reality*, 3:200–211, 1998.

[2] G. D. Abowd, A. K. Dey, P. J. Brown, N. Davies, M. Smith and P. Steggles: Towards a better understanding of context and context-awareness. In *HUC '99: Proceedings of the 1st international symposium on Handheld and Ubiquitous Computing*, pages 304–307, London, UK, 1999. Springer-Verlag.

[3] F. Bellifemine and G. Rimassa: Developing multi-agent systems with a FIPA-compliant agent framework. *Software-Practice and Experience*, 31(2):103–128, 2001.

[4] E. Christensen, F. Curbera, G. Meredith and S. Weerawarana: Web Services Description Language (WSDL) 1.1. `http://www.w3.org/TR/wsdl`, 2001.

[5] W F. Clocksin and C. S. Mellish: *Programming in Prolog*. Springer-Verlag New York, Inc., New York, NY, USA, 1981.

[6] OWL Services Coalition. OWL-S: Semantic Markup for Web Services, 2003.

[7] P. Costa and L. Botelho: Generic context acquisition and management framework. In *Proceedings of the First European Young Researchers Workshop on Service Oriented Computing*, 2005.

[8] E. Denti, A. Omicini and A. Ricci: Multi-paradigm java-prolog integration in tuProlog. *Sci. Comput. Program.*, 57(2):217–250, 2005.

[9] Foundation for Intelligent Physical Agents. FIPA Communicative Act Library Specification. `http://www.fipa.org/specs/fipa00037`, 2000. Specification number SC00037.

[10] H. Helin, M. Klusch, A. Lopes, A. Fernandez, M. Schumacher, H. Schuldt, F. Bergenti, and A. Kinnunen: Context-aware Business Application Service Co-ordination in Mobile Computing Environments. In *Proceedings of the 2005 Workshop on Ambient Intelligence - Agents for Ubiquitous Environments*, Ultrecht, The Netherlands, July 2005.

[11] H. Helin, T. van Pelt, M. Schumacher and A. Syreeni. Efficient Networking for Pervasive eHealth Applications. In GI-Edition, editor, *Proceedings of the European Conference on EHealth (ECEH06)*, volume P-91 of *Lecture Notes in Informatics*, October 2006.

[12] I. Horrocks, P.F. Patel-Schneider, H. Boley, S. Tabet, B. Grosof and M. Dean: SWRL: A Semantic Web Rule Language combining OWL and RuleML. `http://www.w3.org/Submission/SWRL`, 2004.

[13] A. Lopes and L.M. Botelho: SEA: a Semantic Web Services Context-aware Execution Agent. In *AAAI Fall Symposium on Agents and the Semantic Web*, Arlington, VA, USA, 2005.

[14] D. McDermott: PDDL – the planning domain definition language, 1998.

[15] M. G. Nanda, S. Chandra and V. Sarkar: Decentralizing execution of composite Web Services. In *OOPSLA '04: Proceedings of the 19th annual ACM*

SIGPLAN conference on Object-oriented programming, systems, languages, and applications, pages 170–187, New York, NY, USA, 2004. ACM Press.

[16] H. Schuldt, G. Alonso, C. Beeri and H.-J. Schek: Atomicity and Isolation for Transactional Processes. *ACM Transactions on Database Systems (TODS)*, 27(1):63–116, March 2002.

[17] C. Schuler, H. Schuldt, C. Türker, R. Weber and H.-J. Schek: Peer-to-peer execution of (transactional) processes. *International Journal of Cooperative Information Systems (IJCIS)*, 4(14):377–405, 2005.

[18] C. Schuler, R. Weber, H. Schuldt and H.-J. Schek: Scalable Peer-to-Peer Process Management - The OSIRIS Approach. In *Proceedings of the 2nd International Conference on Web Services (ICWS)*, pages 26–34, San Diego, CA, USA, July 2004. IEEE Computer Society.

[19] E Sirin: OWL-S API project website. http://www.mindswap.org/2004/owl-s/api, 2004.

[20] M. Welsh, D. E. Culler and E. A. Brewer: SEDA: An architecture for well-conditioned, scalable internet services. In *Symposium on Operating Systems Principles (SOSP-18)*, pages 230–243, Banff, Canada, 2001.

Chapter 13

Context-Awareness System

Paulo Costa, Bruno Gonçalves and Luis Miguel Botelho

13.1 Introduction

Computer application basic inputs, such as keyboard strokes or pointing devices, supply only limited information about the surrounding environment. The necessity of context information grows as applications need to adapt to the environment in which they are used. This adaptation increases the application's performance and makes sure that the results are well adapted to the specific circumstances. The main objective of context-aware computing is the development of applications that, without being limited by usual input devices, acquire and use context information to better adapt to the circumstances in which interactions take place.

Since context can be acquired by a wide range of input devices (i.e., domain dependent sensors), context systems were created to provide a simple and unique source of information for applications. Context systems can then be understood as extensions of the basic input that an application can receive [4].

This chapter describes the CASCOM approach to context acquisition and management — GCMAS (General Context Management and Acquisition System). The proposal was developed under the assumption that specific information is considered context if it complies with the following definition:

> "Context is all the information related to persons, objects, locations and applications, participating or being referred in a specific interaction, which is not strictly necessary for the interaction to be accomplished, although the use of this information allows improving the quality of the interaction and often the system's performance."

The presented definition integrates aspects from the definitions put forth by Anagnostopoulos et al. [1], and by Dey and Abowd [4], which are probably the most accepted ones in the scientific community. It emphasizes the central role of interactions, and sets a clear distinction between information that is essential to the interaction and context information which, although not being essential, may be used to improve it. This distinction is humbly suggested by the authors of this chapter with the goal of providing some guidance about the difference between context-aware computing and computing in general. According to this view of context information, while non-context information (i.e., information that is strictly necessary for the task at hand) should be explicitly provided to the system when requesting it to perform some task, context information (i.e., information not strictly necessary) should be acquired by the system that receives the request, even if it has to ask it back to the requester.

The following example may shed some light on this issue. Imagine someone, say Tom, that wants to use the CASCOM Agent System to locate a Healthcare Centre. Tom might send a request to the CASCOM Agent System saying "Find me a Healthcare Centre". This is the information explicitly sent in the message initiating the interaction. However, being a context-aware system, the CASCOM Agent System knows that Tom's location is important for discovering a Healthcare Centre more appropriate to Tom's situation. Therefore, it asks Tom's location to GCMAS, the CASCOM Context System. Having Tom's location, the CASCOM Agent System will be capable of discovering the Healthcare Centre closest to Tom. In this example, Tom's location is context information hence acquiring it is the responsibility of the CASCOM Agent System.

Other context definitions may be found in the context-awareness state of the art chapter (Chapter 5), in particular in Section 5.2.

GCMAS is responsible for acquiring, monitoring, representing and storing context information. The system is organized in two layers - an infrastructure layer and an application layer. The infrastructure layer incorporates mechanisms that allow applications to provide context information, request context information and subscribe information about selected context events. Application dependent context processing mechanisms are included in the application layer, which provides mechanisms for context modeling, aggregation, and reasoning adapted to the type of application that accesses the system.

The chapter begins with the system requirements. Following, it presents context representation decisions, namely the content and structure of the ontologies used to model context in GCMAS. Next, it presents the description of GCMAS architecture explaining each of its components and functionalities. Finally, in the last section, it presents a discussion of the context system, briefly describing an example in which GCMAS is used in one of the CASCOM medical emergency scenarios, and presenting results and conclusions.

13.2   System Requirements

This section presents a set of requirements assuming, without loosing generality, that context information is acquired by sensors, which is in fact the most accepted choice. The described requirements are classified in two types: functional and non-functional. The discussed requirements were identified through a review of the literature on context acquisition and management (see Chapter 5), in particular those aspects proposing design principles for context systems and context modeling (Section 5.3).

The following functional requirements, which apply in general to all context systems, are analyzed:

- Separating context capturing from context interpretation;

- Sensor information acquisition should not depend on the specific sensor but on its interface, which must comply with the specified ontology;

- Capability of acquiring information from sensors according to the specified ontology regarding the sensor;

- Easy communication between remote or local sensors and applications;

- Supporting client applications implemented using diverse paradigms and technologies;

- Provide historical context information;

- Provide static context information volunteered by applications;

- Transparent mechanism for locating the best source of context information for each context request, using sensor properties (e.g., sensor owner and hosting device);

- Run-time addition of new sensors; and

- Context information subscription mechanism.

Context capturing should be isolated from context interpretation. In this requirement, context capturing refers, for example, to reading "0300000050" from a specific location sensor; and context interpretation would be generating the following information "Ann's location is (x =30.0 m, y= 0.5 m) relative to the central point in the north doorway of the Interdisciplinary Complex building". This separation allows the interpretation mechanisms to be developed without the concern of how context information is obtained. In GCMAS this requirement is fulfilled because context interpreters, aggregators and reasoners (application layer) allow an additional abstraction of the data provided by the sensor widgets, generating application dependent information.

The context extraction mechanisms should not depend on sensors, but on the interfaces that sensors present to the system. This requirement is satisfied in GCMAS through sensor widgets, which provide an abstraction of the data acquired by each sensor.

Context systems should be capable of acquiring information from sensors according to the specified ontology regarding the sensor. This ensures compatibility between sensors and applications. GCMAS is capable of acquiring context information from any registered sensor, in accordance with the specified ontology.

Both remote and local sensors and applications should be allowed to easily communicate. The fact of sensors and applications being distributed (remote) should not have a negative impact on the easiness with which they communicate. GCMAS includes interfaces that allow sensors and applications, both remote and local, to connect to each other without difficulties. The same interface is used irrespective of whether or not the client application and the sensor widget are running on the same or on different devices.

Context systems should be prepared to receive requests from applications implemented with diverse paradigms and technologies (e.g., object oriented technologies, component-based technologies, or agent-based technologies), which communicate using different protocols. This was achieved through the inclusion of several types of system interfaces. Currently, we have implemented interfaces suitable for component-based applications and for agent-based applications. The application designer just has to select the kind of interface more adequate to the application technology.

Context systems should provide historical context information. When requested by the application, the system should provide historical information about specified aspects of the context. GCMAS includes a history storing mechanism that allows accessing to historic context information. The interface for requesting context information allows specifying the desired number of context information samples.

Context systems should also store static context information provided by their client applications. Static context is context information that does not change much over time. Rapidly changing context information is dynamic or volatile context. GCMAS has a context repository and a specific interface through which it may receive and store context information requested or volunteered by its client applications. For example, some Personal Assistance Agent may want to provide its owner gender, nationality and birth date to the context system. This information may then be requested by the physician agent where the user is being treated.

Context systems must be capable of transparently locating the best source of context information for each context information request. GCMAS has a yellow pages service where sensors register themselves as they are added to the system. This service allows GCMAS to locate required sources of context information. For instance, if a given client application requests the patient's location in a medical emergency scenario, and GCMAS has different classes of context information sources (e.g., location, gender, spoken language, birth date and nationality among others), and several specific sensors within the same class (e.g., location sensors for several users), GCMAS yellow pages service will identify the location sensor of the specific patient. Sensor descriptions in the GCMAS yellow pages service allow the inclusion of sensor properties which may be used to guide their location.

It should be possible to add new sensors to the system anytime while the system is running, without requiring the system to be reinitialized. GCMAS supports the dynamic addition of new sensors in run-time. Besides, it should also be possible to add new sensors even if the information they provide is not specified in the system ontology at the moment of their addition. GCMAS supports this requirement by allowing the sensor registration mechanism to add the definitions of the new sensor information to the context ontology. Imagine, as an example, that a software sensor providing the room temperature is to be added to GCMAS. Suppose also that the used context ontology does not include the "room temperature" concept. The sensor addition mechanism will start adding the "room temperature" concept to the ontology, and then it will register the new sensor in the system's yellow pages.

Finally, context systems should implement an alert mechanism that notifies their client applications when changes occur in specified aspects of the context. GCMAS design includes a context subscription mechanism through which client applications may subscribe specified classes of context information. When context information of the specified classes changes, the subscription mechanism sends the subscribed context information to the subscriber. In an fictitious scenario, the hospital Intensive Care Unit Agent needs to be informed of the updated heart rate and blood pressure values of a patient being carried by an ambulance to the hospital. Instead of repeatedly issuing requests for the patient's heart rate and blood pressure to GCMAS,it just needs to subscribe these two classes of context information. GCMAS will autonomously send updated information to the agent.

This section considers also a set of non-functional requirements, which apply to context systems in general and even to the generality of information management systems: performance/response time, usability, generality and reliability/robustness.

Context systems should have short response times. To fulfill this requirement GCMAS was developed with the concern of optimizing its performance, by avoiding unnecessary processing, component communication and memory usage. Since GCMAS allows the existence of redundant components, adequate load balance policies could be defined which would improve the systems response time.

To ensure their usability, context systems should provide intuitive and complete interfaces to their functionalities. GCMAS implements a set of interfaces that enable adding new sensors easily, and a simple access of applications to the system functionalities.

Context systems should be as general as possible so that they can be used by several types of applications. Any application of any domain can use GCMAS, providing that it knows its communication protocols and the applicable context ontology.

To ensure their reliability context systems should possess sensor failure control system so that they continue to function even if several sensors fail. GCMAS fulfills this requirement. GCMAS allows redundant components, for instance redundant sensors. This way, even if one instance of a given component fails, the redundant one will replace it.

13.3   Context Representation

To enable GCMAS and their client applications to interpret context, GCMAS represents context according to specified publicly available ontologies, as suggested by most authors, such as Dey and Abowd [4], Anagnostopoulos [1], and Chen and Kotz [2], whose work is described in the section on design principles and context modeling (Section 5.3) of Chapter 5. The definition of the context ontology, also known as context modeling, is a very important step for the development of a context system.

The simplest way to define the context ontology is proposed by Dey and his colleagues [5]. According to these authors, two of the main components of the context ontology are context elements (sources of context information), such as sensors; and context entities representing persons, places, applications and objects which the sensors refer to.

GCMAS ontology uses a similar approach. It defines the class "context element", representing a context information supplier such as a sensor or a record in the context repository. It also defines the class "context entity", representing the person, object, application or place referred by each context supplier (i.e., a location sensor is represented by a context element; the person that is located by that sensor is represented by a context entity). Each individual sensor can then be located in the context ontology as a "context entity"/"context element" pair. The context ontology used in GCMAS is organized in three layers: the base ontology, the distribution ontology and the context data ontology (see Figure 13.1). The base ontology describes the basic concepts of the GCMAS ontology such as context element, context entity, context value, context property and the relations between these concepts. The base ontology may also be seen as a meta-ontology defining the primitive concepts used to actually represent the context ontology of a specific domain.

The distribution ontology represents the distribution of context elements and entities on a specific scenario. The distribution ontology uses the base classes defined in the base ontology. Context information of a specific domain is described in terms of context elements, context entities, context values, and the relations between them.

The context data ontology represents a view of the context information that is closer to object oriented implementation languages. It defines the classes of context information, from the point of view of the implementation.

Both the base ontology and the distribution ontology are described in OWL ontology definition language [9]. Since the context data ontology needs to be close to the description of an object oriented programming language, it is defined in XML Schema [8].

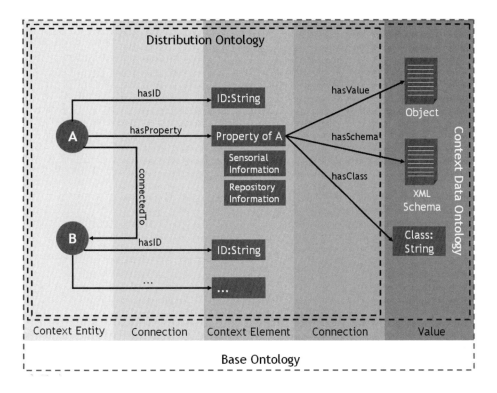

Figure 13.1: GCMAS ontology description

13.3.1 Base Ontology

The base ontology defines all the basic concepts that may be used to define a concrete domain context ontology. These include context elements, which represent context sources; context entities, which represent relevant persons and objects; and relations, which represent associations between context elements and entities. All elements defined in the domain context ontology must extend the classes defined in the base ontology. Besides the fundamental concepts (context elements, context entities and relations), the base ontology also defines relation links to the context data ontology, which represent the path of the classes of a specific context information, the XML Schema of the context data ontology defining those context information classes, and the actual value of the context information. These are represented by the *hasClass*, *hasSchema* and *hasValue* relations, as can be seen in Figure 13.1.

The classes defined in this ontology represent general context entities, general context elements and the basic relations between them. All context entities must be uniquely identified through the *hasID* relation. Entities are associated with their context objects by the *hasProperty* relation. Entities may also be associated with

Class	Description
ContextObject	Represents the context element and associated context information. Contains the context element ontology class, the object oriented class path, the XML Schema representation of context, and the context information itself.
ContextEntity	Represents a context entity. Contains the entity unique identifier, and the entity ontology class and description.
Link	Represents a relation that connects two ontology classes.
SensorProperty	Represents sensor properties. This class does not have direct connection to the ontology but uses its information. It is used for sensor registration and discovery.

Table 13.1: Base ontology classes description

other entities using the *connectedTo* relation (see Figure 13.1). This relation allows the association between entities and elements that are related on the application scenario (i.e., the entity *userA* connects to entity *deviceA* through a *connectedTo* relation meaning that this user has an associated device).

Each context element has three properties: *value*, representing the context information itself, linked through the *hasValue* relation; *schema*, representing its XML Schema [8], linked through the *hasSchema* relation; and its class path information, representing the class of context information (as represented in the object oriented implementation language), linked through the *hasClass* relation (i.e., the *LocationSensor* context element is represented by the object oriented class *gcmas.ontology.element.LocationSensor*). Context elements are also associated to their related context entities by the *hasOwner* relation.

The base ontology concepts defined above are represented by the classes *ContextObject, ContextEntity, Link* and *SensorProperty*. Table 13.1 represents a brief description of these classes. All context information supplied by the system is represented as instances of the *ContextObject* class. The system is responsible for translating sensorial information into *ContextObjects*. These objects represent both the context element and the context information itself. Context information is structured according to the corresponding XML Schema and stored, in XML serialized form, in the value attribute, representing the *hasValue* ontology relation.

Storing context in serialized form allows the system to store all relevant types of context information (i.e., a *ContextObject* object for a room temperature sensor could be like this one: context element — *temperatureSensorForRoomA*, the ontology instance of the class *TemperatureSensor*, representing the sensor that measures that room temperature; *hasClass - gcmas.ontology.element.Temperature*, the class path to the context class (as represented in the object oriented implementation language); *hasSchema*, XML Schema representation context class or a path to the file where it is represented; *hasValue*, an XML representation of context information).

As described in the base ontology, the *ContextObject* is related to a context entity represented by a *ContextEntity* object. This object represents context entities used in the context system and possesses information about them.

Link objects represent relations between ontology classes. Although most of the relations between *ContextObjects* and *ContextEntities* are made directly through the defined class attributes, it may be necessary to represent other relations such as those between entities.

SensorProperty objects were created to normalize sensor registration in the system. These objects specify the context element the sensor belongs to, and the context entity associated to it (i.e., a *SensorProperty* object for a room temperature sensor could be like this one: context entity *roomA*, the instance of the class *Room* (which extends the base ontology class *ContextEntity*) representing the room where the temperature is measured which is associated with context element *temperatureSensorForRoomA*, the instance of the class *TemperatureSensor*, representing the sensor that measures that room's temperature).

13.3.2 Distribution Ontology

The distribution ontology represents the specific context information in a given domain. This ontology extends the classes defined in the base ontology to represent the context entities and context elements identified in the given scenario.

In a simple example of a distribution ontology, in a scenario where there is a need to locate people, each person is identified as a context entity and belongs to the ontology class *Person*, extending the *ContextEntity* base class. All persons are instances of this class. The location sensor is identified as a context element and belongs to the *LocationSensor* ontology class, extending the *ContextElement* base class. All location sensors will be instances of this class (i.e., *BobSensor* is an instance of *LocationSensor*). Each instance of a *LocationSensor* is linked to the corresponding instance of *Person* by the *hasSensor* relation. This relation extends the *hasProperty* base ontology relation (see Figure 13.1).

The context distribution ontology represents all defined context elements, context entities and all their instances for a given application scenario.

13.3.3 Context Data Ontology

The context data ontology defines the structure of context information in a way that is closer to object oriented implementation languages.

Although Jena [6] framework is used to process OWL descriptions, there is not a direct link between OWL classes and those in object oriented programming languages.

XML Schema language is used to define context in the context data ontology layer because XML Schema definitions are very close to object oriented programming language descriptions. The context data ontology creates a bridge between the OWL ontology description and an object oriented implementation language. The XML Schema declarations define classes of context information (as represented in its object oriented implementation language) and are directly connected to the sources of context information, the context elements, through the hasSchema relation. The other properties, *hasValue* and *hasClass*, point to the value and class path of the context element.

The *LocationSensor* context element is a simple example of a context data ontology definition. This element connects to the *gcmas.ontology.element.LocationSensor* program class, defined by the *hasClass* relation. The XML Schema description of this class is defined by the *hasSchema* relation. The description specifies that location is represented by three floating point values — latitude, longitude and altitude.

When the system acquires information from a given sensor, the information is transformed according to the defined XML Schema and stored into the *hasValue* attribute of the returned *ContextObject* object (see Section 13.3.1).

13.4   Context System Architecture

GCMAS architecture is a mixed of a component-based system and a development framework. System components represent sensors, repositories and system functionalities as identified in the system requirements section. To enable applications to easily access the system, GCMAS provides a set of alternative kinds of interfaces to all its functionalities. The system also provides the necessary tools to convert information provided by low level context sources such as sensors into higher abstraction level representations. The provided tools also support the simple inclusion of new sensor types into the system in run-time.

Different architectures were presented in the section on context system architectures (Section 5.4) of the context state of the art review chapter (Chapter 5). GCMAS includes many of the desirable features, which are scattered by several of these architectures.

13.4.1   System Overview

GCMAS operates in two perspectives, as a sensor development framework and as an application interface.

In the sensor developing perspective, the system is responsible for sensor adaptation which provides hardware independent access to sensor information. Sensor adaptation consists of acquiring and transforming the context information provided by sensors into a higher level representation compliant with the context ontology. This adaptation is made by specific components, the sensor widgets. Since there is a large range of sensor types, in order for the system to be easily adapted to all of them, general sensor adaptation tools were developed and are distributed with the system. These tools provide the means to interact with the system core components in a general way. New sensors and corresponding ontology definitions may be dynamically added to the system using these tools.

From an application perspective, the system has to implement ways of communicating with different types of applications, by providing basic interfaces to the system functionalities. The system allows the search for context and context historic information, the subscription of context events, and it also allows applications to provide context to the system. System functionalities are directly associated to specific components.

Each of the system functionalities is accessible through several types of interfaces (component-based interfaces and agent-based interfaces). This variety allows different types of applications to communicate with the system using more convenient communication protocols.

The system architecture consists of two main layers (see Figure 13.2) — the system infrastructure layer, which contains most of the system core functionalities; and the application specific layer, which contains functionalities more specific to each type of application. The application layer can be seen as an extension to GCMAS.

The system infrastructure layer possesses the basic components for context acquisition, storage and delivery. These components provide methods to process context information as defined by the context ontology, allowing context to be treated in a transparent way. By abstracting away from sensor extracted data, the system becomes open to all classes of context information, as long as they can be defined in the context ontology. The context ontology may be modified in run-time (e.g., new elements may be added when a new sensor is added to the system in run-time), allowing the system to handle new types of context information without being previously specifically prepared for that.

The functionalities provided by the system infrastructure layer allow applications to request context and context historic information, using the context query component; to register themselves on the system for receiving notifications each time context changes, using the event subscription component; and to provide context information to the system, so that it can be available to other applications, using the context storage component. Core components such as ontology manipulators, yellow pages server, and the sensor development tools also belong to the system infrastructure layer.

The application specific layer allows converting existing context information into a format more close to the application, aggregating information from several sources into single objects that make more sense to the application, and inferring new context information from existing context information acquired by the context system. Given its domain dependent nature, the components in the application layer must be developed on the side of the application.

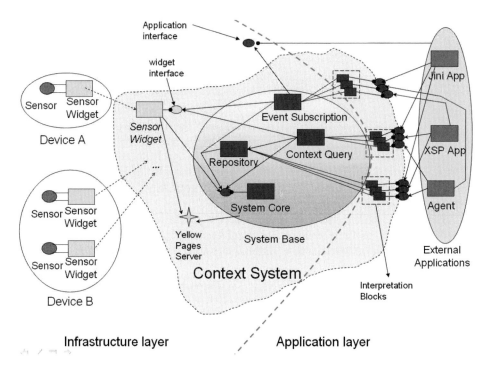

Figure 13.2: GCMAS architecture

13.4.2   Detailed Component Description

GCMAS is presented to applications as a black-box system. Its architecture is depicted in Figure 13.2. The figure shows only the existing application interfaces but the system can be extended with new ones. The system infrastructure layer is composed of sensors and sensor widgets, repository components, context query components, event subscription components, yellow pages server and the system core. Currently, the application layer consists only of the context interpreter which converts context information as provided by the system into a different application oriented format. The context interpreter has been designed but it has not been implemented yet.

In order to maintain the desired system redundancy, which is responsible for its robustness and efficiency, each of the system infrastructure layer components can have multiple instances running simultaneously possibly on different devices, allowing the distribution of the received requests. This is mandatory for sensor widgets since they run on the sensor side.

As shown in Figure 13.2, GCMAS provides interfaces to communicate with Jini-based applications [7], XSP-based[1] applications (both of which are component-

---

[1]XSP (eXtended Service Platform) is a tool for component-based systems development and

based interafces), and agent-based applications. GCAMS allows the inclusion of more types of application interfaces.

Sensor Widgets

Sensor widgets allow sensors to communicate with GCMAS. They provide mechanisms to register sensors on the system's yellow pages server. They convert sensorial information into objects of the defined context ontology. Sensor widgets implement interfaces that handle system requests, such as context queries, and context event subscriptions.

Sensor registration allows GCMAS to be aware of their existence. Sensor registration is done by registering the widget associated to that sensor in the system's yellow pages server (see Section 13.4.2). Since widgets are seen by the system as any other component, their registration in the system's yellow pages is similar to the registration of other components. The widget must supply information about the instance of context element that represents the sensor, and the instance of context entity that represents the entity associated to the sensor (see Section 13.3). This information is encapsulated in a *SensorProperty* object and stored on the yellow pages to be used as an identifier.

When the context query component (see Section 13.4.2) processes the received context request, it locates the appropriate sensor widget and sends it the request. In response, the sensor widget, after extracting and transforming the sensorial information, supplies the requested context information, encapsulated in a *ContextObject* object, to the query component (see Section 13.3.1).

Context extracted from the sensor is transformed according to the defined context ontology. This results in creating an object defined by the corresponding XML Schema included in the context data ontology. This object is then serialized and encapsulated inside a *ContextObject* object, so that the system can manipulate it in a transparent way.

A set of tools named *Schema Class Builder* are used to support the XML Schema manipulation and serialization. These tools allow the creation of Java classes from XML Schema, and the serialization and de-serialization of instances of these classes. The *Schema Class Builder* was developed by the "We, the Body, and the Mind" research lab of ADETTI in partnership with *Accedo*.

System requests for event notification (i.e., event subscription) work in a different way. The system component responsible for this functionality, the event subscription component (see Section 13.4.2), requests the sensor widget to start supplying it the new context information each time it detects a change in the subscribed context. The event subscription component supplies the sensor widget an internal event notification interface in order for the widget to send the information to applications through it. Each time a change is detected, the widget sends the

---

deployment developed by the *We, the Body, and the Mind* research group of Adetti[2] and by Accedo Consulting[3].

new context information encapsulated in a *ContextObject* through the supplied interface.

Context historic information is also managed by the sensor widget. Context history is locally stored, in the sensor widget, as a limited list of context samples, and can be requested by applications. Each time a new sample of context is acquired from the sensor it is stored on the historic list. Older samples are deleted when the list's retention time or list size is reached. Context historic information is made available by the sensor widgets as an array of *ContextObjects*, each one containing an encapsulated sample of context.

Since the sensor widget component is the only one in the system infrastructure layer that needs to be developed according to each specific type of sensor, the system provides basic sensor development tools named the general sensor adaptation tool. These tools allow the development of new sensor widgets, including all necessary system interfaces, yellow pages registration and ontology updating.

New classes of context information can be added to the system's ontology by the sensor widget. The general sensor adaptation tools provide the necessary means for sensor widget developers to incorporate new ontology information into GCMAS during sensor registration. New ontology definitions can include new classes of context elements and entities, along with their instances, and new XML Schema definitions of context information, or only new instances of already defined context elements and entities. Ontology update requests are then processed by the system core (see Section 13.4.2).

Repository Component

The repository component, which relies on a relational database, is responsible for storing and supplying context information provided by applications. Since the process of information storage in the repository is slower than context storage in sensors, the repository should only be used for context information that does not change frequently, that is, for static context.

The information sent by applications must be transformed accordingly to the XML Schema defined by the context ontology and incorporated into a ContextObject object (see Section 13.3.1). This way, any type of information can be received and stored as long as it is defined in the ontology. This same type of object is returned by the repository component when a context query is made.

The information in the repository is stored in serialized format, which is retrieved from the *hasValue* attribute of the received ContextObject. This ensures that GCMAS remains independent of the type and contents of context information.

The external interfaces implemented by this component only define context storage methods and ontology update methods. Context queries are made through the context query interface (see Section 13.4.2).

Although the context repository should in principle be used for static context information, it is also possible to obtain context historic information from the repository. Context historic information samples are stored in the database in the same way as context information. Historic information is retrieved from the repository as an array of *ContextObjects*, each containing a context sample.

Context Query Component

The context query component is responsible for processing and responding to context queries. Context queries may be encapsulated in one of two possible objects: the *QueryObject* and the *HistoryQueryObject*. Both objects provide information about the entity which the context refers to and the context element that provides it. History queries also require information about the timestamp or number of samples to be retrieved from the history. This information allows the query component to precisely identify the necessary source of context information, and the associated sensor widget (see Section 13.4.2) or repository database records (see Section 13.4.2).

Event Subscription Component

Event subscription implies that external applications must register themselves on the system in order to receive the new context information each time the desired context changes. Each new sample of context information is encapsulated in a ContextObject object. In order to do so the system must know the interface to invoke on the application side so that applications can receive the new context. The system offers several application side interfaces, developed to simplify the task of sending context to applications. All applications that want to receive context events must implement these interfaces. For each type of application, a specific interface of this kind can be developed as long as it extends the basic application side interface.

Context subscriptions are encapsulated in *SubscribeObject* objects. This object contains the same information as *QueryObject*. Additionally, applications must also supply a link to the application side interface that will receive the new information. After locating the responsible sensor widget on the yellow pages, the event subscription component requests it (see Section 13.4.2) to start sending context information to the specified event subscription interface. Each time new context information is received from a sensor, the event subscription component consults the relation of applications that have subscribed it, and subsequently sends them the new information.

Yellow Pages Server

The system's yellow pages server is the point where all system components are registered, allowing system components to locate each other. In the proposed architecture, it is possible to have multiple instances of the system components running simultaneously. The yellow pages server is responsible for differentiating each instance of the components and for locating the requested instances. Each component instance may be distinguished from the others through an attribute representing its sequential number.

System Core

The system core is responsible for system startup and for ontology related functionalities. System startup may be configured in configuration files. These files define which interfaces are made available by the system, the number of instances for each component to be launched, and the specification of the file containing the ontology. Ontology manipulation tools enable system components to search for ontology descriptions and for relations between sensors, context elements and context entities. It also supplies the system with methods for translating ontology instances into ontology representative objects (see Section 13.3.1). The system uses the Jena framework [6] to store and manipulate its ontology. The ontology is stored in a system database for faster access, and made available for applications through an ontology definition file.

Context Interpreter

In the application layer, the context interpreter (i.e., context interpretation module) converts the gathered context information into an application suitable representation, in accordance to the specified context ontology. The context interpreter uses the aggregation mechanism to integrate information from several sensors into a single data structure, and the context reasoning mechanism to infer new context information from already existing information. The aggregation mechanism is used when it is necessary to create new compound pieces of context information from existing correlated context information. The reasoning mechanism is used when it is necessary to infer new context. It defines reasoning mechanisms that produce new context from collected context information, enriching it with new information.

13.4.3   System Deployment

Until this moment, the current section has presented GCMAS as a general purpose tool for the creation of particular context acquisition and management systems for specific applications. This subsection presents some brief guidelines pertaining the development and deployment of a context system for a specific application. Since the application to be developed is a context information acquisition and management system, the analysis process includes the identification of the context entities and the context elements in the chosen application domain. Following the context definition presented in the introductory text of this chapter, the identification of relevant context elements and entities may be achieved, starting with identifying the relevant interactions of the context client application. After identifying all entities, we identify the context information associated with them, their properties

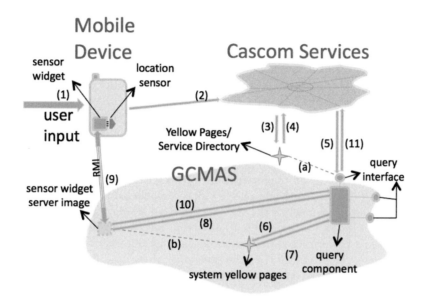

Figure 13.3: Example of interaction

and relationships.

13.5   Summary

GCMAS was developed to be used with the CASCOM system. The following example shows the way GCMAS and the CASCOM Agent System cooperate to provide valuable and context-aware assistance in a specific imagined scenario. As described in Section 1.3 (emergency assistance application), when the CASCOM Agent System needs to find the medical care centre nearest to the patient, it first needs to know where the patient is. The CASCOM Agent System simply needs to request the patient's location to the developed context system. This interaction is depicted in Figure 13.3. The interaction starts when the user logs in the CASCOM system, through his or her Personal Agent, and issues a help request, requiring medical assistance (1). The request is passed to the CASCOM Agent System (2). Since user location information is necessary to select the closest medical centre, the CASCOM Agent System queries the CASCOM service discovery for a GCMAS instance (3) and requests the user location from GCMAS query interface (4). The query component of GCMAS locates the sensor widget representing the user location's sensor, using the GCMAS internal yellow pages (5). For this, the query component uses the user and sensor classes described in the ontology supplied by the CASCOM Agent System. After locating the adequate sensor widget (a) (the widget of the user location sensor, which has a remote interface coupled with the sensor on the user's mobile phone), the query component requests it to provide its current context information (6). The sensor widget gets the information from its sensor (7), transforms it into an ontology defined object and sends it to the query component (8), which in turn passes it to the CASCOM Agent System (9), which requested it. The CASCOM Agent System then uses the user's location to locate the medical centre closest to the user.

Since GCMAS is an innovative application we cannot establish a direct comparison with other approaches. Analyzing the proposals described in context awareness state of the art chapter (see Chapter 5), it is possible to state that these applications were designed to solve specific problems of context-aware computing.

GCMAS, the proposed context system, represents a domain independent and adaptable solution to most of the problems related with context acquisition and management. GCMAS is adaptable to any situation as long as its context can be described using the proposed framework for context ontology representation. The system domain independence (i.e., the possibility to be used in different domains) arises from the ontology design and from the total independence from particular context information contents.

Tests made to GCMAS after its development provide evidence regarding the relative advantages of its architecture over related approaches. In terms of domain independence and adaptation, GCMAS goes beyond other analyzed systems. These results can be seen on Table 13.2.

The system evaluation was based on some of the interactions extracted from the CASCOM main scenario. Comparison with other approaches was based on a mere qualitative analysis of the architectures. The possibility of having multiple instances of the system components improves its robustness. If an instance of the component fails other instances can replace it. The system continues to work even if some of its components are not available.

The existence of several external interfaces allows client applications to interact with the context system using the application preferred type of interface.

The system may be extended to the application level through the context interpretation module. This allows the system to become more adapted to specific domains requiring more information than explicitly available from the system's context sources. Context interpretation also changes the way context information is represented so that applications can better understand it.

GCMAS supports the introduction of ubiquitous computing paradigm into applications. By removing the burden of obtaining information from sensors, registering and locating sensorial devices, and managing stored contextual information, application developers can focus only on application specific problems and on using the information provided by GCMAS. Applications and application designers may use the context ontology to know what kind of context information is available in the system.

By combining this system with other platforms, for instance the CASCOM agent-based service coordination platform, it is possible to take advantage of

Test	Result
Context Information Retrieval	Applications were able to retrieve context information (regarding context entities and elements in the context ontology) from the system. These results apply to both sensorial context information and repository context information.
Context Information Diversity	Applications were able to retrieve different types of context information from the system, all of them defined by the system ontology.
Application Connectivity Diversity	Different types of applications interacted with GCMAS using different interfaces, and obtaining the same context information for the same type of request. Tests were made with three different application interfaces — XSP, Jini and agent-based interfaces.
Context Information Storage	The system was able to store a predetermined number of context samples in its sensors. Queries where made to each one of these in order to obtain this information and to show its availability. Location sensors and battery sensors where used in these tests.
Sensor Property Search	The system was capable of distinguishing two instances of sensor widgets of the same class. Queries to both instances were made in order to test their availability. These tests involved two location sensors belonging to different users.
Ontology Updates	The system was able to update a new definition in the context ontology. This new definition was necessary to the addition of a new sensor in run-time. After the new sensor has been added to the system, the client application was able to retrieve context information from it. Ontology update was made during sensor registration.

Table 13.2: Functional test results

context-awareness without the burden of acquiring the relevant context information. CASCOM service coordination system uses context information to find, compose and execute services required by the user so that they become better adapted to the situation. Future versions of this system may include the definition and implementation of new types of external interfaces and the implementation of context interpretation modules.

References

[1] C. Anagnostopoulos, A. Tsounis and S. Hadjiefthymiades: Context Awareness in Mobile Computing Environments: A Survey. Mobile e-conference, Information Society Technologies, 2004.

[2] G. Chen and D. Kotz: A Survey of Context-Aware Mobile Computing Research. Dartmouth College, Hanover, NH, USA, 2000.

[3] E. Christopoulou, C. Goumopoulos, I. Zaharakis and A. Kameas: An Ontology-based Conceptual Model for Composing Context-Aware Applications. Research Academic Computer Technology Institute, 2004.

[4] A. K. Dey and G. D. Abowd: Towards a better understanding of context and context awareness. GVU Technical Report GIT-GVU-99-22, College of Computing, Georgia Institute of Technology, 1999.

[5] A. K. Dey, G. D. Abowd, Gregory, D. and Salber, D: A Conceptual Framework and a Toolkit for Supporting the Rapid Prototyping of Context-Aware Applications. Human-Computer Interaction - Special Issue: Context-aware Computing, 16, 2-4, pp. 97-166, 2001.

[6] B. McBride: Jena: A Semantic Web Toolkit. IEEE Internet Computing, 6-6, 1089-7801, pp.55-59, IEEE Educational Activities Department, Piscataway, NJ, USA, 2002.

[7] Sun Microsystems. JINI Network Technology. http://www.sun.com/software/jini, 1999

[8] World Wide Web Consortium. XML Schema 1.1 Release. http://www.w3.org/XML/Schema, 2004.

[9] World Wide Web Consortium. OWL-S 1.0 Release. http://www.daml.org/services/owl-s/1.0, 2005.

Chapter 14

Security, Privacy and Trust

Federico Bergenti

14.1 Introduction

The literature about trust in multiagent systems collects a huge number of works that analyse almost any facets of this concept from nearly every point of view. Nevertheless, an accepted and stable formal model of trust in agent societies is still missing. In this chapter, we address this remarkable flaw of the current research by reporting the main contributions of the CASCOM project on this topic: *(i)* a stochastic model of trust that measurably captures trust in two-party interactions, and *(ii)* a general-purpose framework that the CASCOM platform provides to enable the realization of secure, privacy-aware and trust-aware multiagent systems.

Interaction is a key feature of agenthood ("the" key feature, we may say) and secure, trusted and privacy-aware interactions are what we truly want from real-world multiagent systems. While it is easy to identify a minimum set of requirements capable of providing guarantees for security in multi-party interactions, e.g., authorization and authentication, we are not yet ready to identify similar requirements for trusted and privacy-aware interactions.

The work done in the CASCOM project on these problems is along the lines of the research that is trying to identify a set of abstractions and mechanisms to guarantee trust- and privacy-awareness in multi-agent interactions. In particular, the final objective of our work is about providing the CASCOM platforms with a set of facilities to allow developers to easily and intuitively create not only secure but also privacy- and trust-aware multiagent systems. In order to achieve our goal, we developed a stochastic model of trust capable of formally showing that interactions mediated by a trusted third party, that we call *guarantor*, are rationally convenient over direct interactions. This result ensures that privacy- and trust-awareness can be obtained by mediated interactions and it provides a solid base for the design of the framework for privacy and trust awareness that we integrated in the CASCOM platform.

This chapter is organized as follows: next section frames the problem that we address in order to focus on the ideas and the abstractions behind our stochastic model. Section 14.3 provides the foundations of our model and it quantifies the increment of the utility that agents perceive because of the mediation of a guarantor. Then, Section 14.4 deals with the decision-making strategies of rational agents and it shows a worst-case specialization of our model that justifies why agents are more likely to choose guarantor-mediated over direct interactions. Section 14.5 reports on how our stochastic model is concretized into the CASCOM platform by means of a framework that facilitates the realization of trust- and privacy-aware multiagent systems. This framework relies on secure messaging within the CAS-COM platform and Section 14.5 also gives some technical details on this. Finally, Section 14.6 summarizes the lessons learned from this work.

14.2   Two-Party Interactions

Most of the work reported in this chapter is about the study of the interaction between two agents only, X and Y. This study is very generic and its results can be applied in many situations. In any case, we needed to focus our work on a special case of general interest in order to devise a formal framework for our study. This is the reason why we take the assumption that, from the point of view of security, trust and privacy, we can always reduce any two-party interaction to the special case of two agents mutually signing a contract. With no loss of generality, from now on we will always refer to the joint act of signing a contract as a means to study any other form of two-party interaction.

Having said this, we can state our working scenario as follows: X is interested in signing a contract with Y and it is in the process of deciding whether to do it directly or through the mediation of a trusted third party, the guarantor G, that can act as a middleman for transactions. We take a rational standpoint and we assume that X discriminates between direct and mediated interaction on the basis of its utility function. Moreover, we assume incomplete information and we say that X cannot take a fully-informed decision; rather, it has to face some risks.

This scenario models some interesting properties of real-world interactions and it provides a sufficiently simple case to allow for a formal analysis. Moreover, we believe that many interactions that are possibly occurring in nowadays multiagent systems can be approximated with acceptable accurancy to a network of two-party interactions. The comprehensive study of scenarios involving many jointly interacting agents is still in progress and it is subject of a future work.

The two-party scenario that we use to define our stochastic model of trust relies on an underlying assumption that is worth some discussion. In particular, we always assume that agents exchange the terms of the contract under negotiation using individuals of a known and shared ontology, which is described in some known and shared logic formalism, e.g., OWL [14]. This assumption allows agents to manage the information contained in the contract in a friendly way and to reason about the contract with a reasonable accurancy.

All in all, the assumption of modelling contracts between negotiating agents in terms of individuals of known and shared ontologies is absolutely general and has some remarkable advantages. First, complex contracts can be described using a combination of simple ontologies, with a potential reduction of the complexity of published ontologies. We can freely compose simple ontologies into complex descriptions of contracts, thus avoiding duplication of definitions and possible ambiguities. The second advantage that we see in using ontologies for modelling contracts is that it greatly simplifies the creation and validation of proposals and agreements. The creation of a proposal is reduced to the creation of one or more individuals of known ontologies. The control of the suitability of a proposal reduces to checking whether a candidate proposal actually belongs to the family of admissible proposals described in the referenced ontology. The problems of creation and validation of individuals of ontologies are both well studied and they are largely supported by a number of available tools like reasoners (see, e.g., [15]) and query engines (see e.g., [10]). We need no special-purpose instrument to manage contracts: any available tool capable of processing ontologies is suitable for the purpose. Finally, ontologies expressed in common formats are easily mapped into human-readable documents for a subsequent inspection of the agreements that agents may have autonomously signed.

Nevertheless, the obvious assumption of using ontologies to describe the terms of a contract has some important drawbacks that we need to consider carefully. In fact, any attempt to use them in real-world scenarios immediately encounters a problem: How an agent could trust the constraint of a new ontology? Suppose that a seller requires possible customers to sign contracts using an ontology that it made available in some public repository. This ontology may model some property as being "required by local laws." How could customers trust this requirement if they have no trust relationship with the seller that created the ontology? Could a customer (in some sense) validate the ontology to decide whether to trust it or not? Obviously, there is no way to validate the adherence of an ontology to real-world laws without involving highly specialized jurists. No potential customer would be in the position of performing this sort of validation.

Another facet of this problem occurs in the case of an ontology that is partially non-disclosed to final users. Let us suppose that the aforementioned seller splitted its ontology into two parts: a public part describing valid proposals and agreements, and a private part used to model the policies that it employees to fix prices and accept orders, i.e., the policies that it uses to reason on proposals. This last part contains background knowledge on the marketing strategies of the seller and it is vital not to disclose it to potential competitors. In this case, a full fledged reasoning on the ontology is possible only by accessing the whole ontology, and only partial reasoning is available to customers.

All in all, these exemplified facets of the problem all root in the requirement that ontologies used to model contracts must be provided by trusted and liable signers. Unfortunately, this is not sufficient to provide a solid base for modelling the trust relationships in real-world contracts. In fact, we need to take into account legal validity in a larger scope and therefore the problem of checking the identities of involved agents is obviously crucial. A simple static control of identities by means of certificates [6, 7] is inadequate because, e.g., certificates can be revoked and keys can be stolen. We definitely need a dynamic approach to the validation of identities, i.e., the identification of agents in a secure, privacy- and trust-aware multiagent system can be performed only through a set of runtime services capable of validating certificates and thus performing a trusted source of identification.

The problem of checking identities is closely related to the concrete representation of identities. For example, in some European countries persons are uniquely identified by an alphanumeric code that groups the full name of the person, his/her birth date, his/her birthplace and a checksum. Similarly, corporations are designated with their VAT identification number. The identification code is the only means that we have to validate the identity of a legal person, whether physical or not. Therefore, one of the very basic issues that we have to tackle is how to represent identities in an agent-processable way. In our model, we decided to design an ontology describing legal persons and their attributes and to associate this ontology with a set of general-purpose services for addressing the majority of problems related to identification. The connection between this ontology and its services is reinforced by means of a common trusted signer.

It is worth noting that, in order to fully exploit the possibility of having runtime services capable of providing warranties regarding sensitive tasks on an ontology, both the ontology and its associated services must have the same levels of trust and security. In fact, we have — at least — two interesting cases. In the first, two negotiating agents both trust the publisher of the ontology. They exchange proposals until an agreement is reached and they mutually check their identities using an untrusted service. Since they do not trust the identity-verification service, they can both suppose that they are signing an agreement with an unknown party. The second case is about an identity-verification service that receives both an ontology and an identity as input, and that it verifies the identity in a secured database. What happens if someone gives formally valid — compliant with the ontology — but legally void identity? Since the given identity matches the record in the database of identities, the service would return an affirmative answer, but this identity is legally void and therefore unusable in signing real-world contracts. These two simple examples show that both ontology and associated services must be trusted and secured. If any of the two does not have a suitable level of trust and security, their combined use will result in an insecure interaction.

14.3   A Model of Mediated Interactions

This section presents a set of abstractions and accounts for their relationships in order to setup a stochastic model of interactions between agent X, agent Y and (possibly) guarantor G.

14.3.1 Abstractions

The problem of providing a quantitative definition of trust in societies of rational agents has been addressed in many different ways, e.g., see [13]. While we recognize the critical importance of cognitive models of trust, e.g., see [5], we date back to the abstract and coarse-grained definition of trust given in [8] to come to a stochastic interpretation of this notion. In particular, if we recall that:

> "Trust is the subjective probability by which an individual, A, expects that another individual, B, performs a given action on which its welfare depends,"

it is quite reasonable to model trust as an estimation of the probability by which B will perform the target action. Many factors contribute to this estimation [11, 12]; nonetheless we prefer to adopt a blackbox approach that discards all these factors and we model trust as a random variable $\mathbf{t}$ that ranges in the interval $[t_{min}, t_{max}]$. Clearly t_{min} and t_{max} are both between zero and one and we assume $t_{max} \geq t_{min}$ with no loss of generality.

Then, we assume the rationality of agent A and we require that the estimation of the probability by which B will perform the target action is done using some reasonable amount of information regarding B and its actual intention of performing the action. This guarantees that the real probability of B performing the action lays in $[t_{min}, t_{max}]$, with t_{min} and t_{max} reasonably close around it.

Having said this, our model of two-party interactions is based on the following quantities, where X and Y are agents and c is a contract:

- $p_{c,X}$: the probability that X would carry out successfully all the obligations stated in c.

- $t_{c,X,Y}$: the measure of trust that X has in Y with respect to c, i.e., an estimation of $p_{c,Y}$ from the point of view of X.

The study of all possible different forms of contracts is subject of a large literature and even restricting it to the types of contracts that we normally consider in multiagent systems [4], the diversity of possibilities is remarkable. We acknowledge this literature but, for the sake of simplicity and for the need of quantitative tractability, we stick on a very simple model of contract. This model involves only two signers, X and Y, and it is totally described by two triples — each signer knows only one of the two triples. In detail, from the point of view of agent X — the notation is symmetrical for Y — a contract c is described by a triple, that we call *subjective evaluation* of c, which contains:

- A *reward* $R_{c,X}$ that agent X receives upon success of contract c;

- An *investment* $I_{c,X}$ that agent X makes in contract c, i.e., a certain assured value that it releases when signing contract c; and

- A *penalty* $P_{c,X}$ that agent X receives if the contract fails because of Y.

Such values are not restricted to be monetary, rather they quantify the level of satisfaction of X. All in all, such quantities are subjective and therefore we cannot assess any mathematical relations between the values of the triples of two different agents, even though they refer to the same contract.

More in detail, a contract c has the following properties from the point of view of X:

- If the contract is honoured, then agent X will receive $R_{c,X}$ with probability one; and

- If the contract fails because of agent Y, agent X will receive $P_{c,X}$ with probability one.

Another assumption that we take concerns the relative ordering of reward, investment and penalty in a single subjective evaluation. We are interested in contracts whose parameters are ordered as follows:

$$P_{c,X} \leq I_{c,X} \leq R_{c,X} \qquad (14.1)$$

This inequality captures the essence of risky contracts. Moreover, it implies that we are interested in agents that sign contracts with the intent of honouring them. Any failure in honouring a contract turns into a loss of utility (see later on) $I_{c,X} - P_{c,X}$. Furthermore, agents in our model do not reason about their possible failure in honouring a contract, they just assume that they can honour all contracts they sign; nevertheless the uncertainty about the other signer remains.

The abstraction of *guarantor* was introduced and discussed in detail in [3, 2]. For the sake of completeness, we recall here that guarantors are sources of highly trusted information and they are sort of trust catalysts, i.e., they are trusted by other agents and they form connecting nodes in the network of trust. If agent X requests a piece of information from guarantor G, it assigns a correctness probability of one to the received response. Nevertheless, we introduce some failure probability in order to account for the idea that the use of additional information, i.e., the information that guarantor G provides, always introduces some risk, even though the information source is highly trusted and reliable.

14.3.2   Expectation of the Utility of Agents

We analyse here the utility that agents estimate in the process of signing a contract. This utility is considered in two forms: with and without the mediation of a guarantor. We refer to the first case as *mediated* interaction, and we say that the second case is a *direct* interaction. We start with the formalization of direct interactions because their treatment is obviously simpler.

Direct Interaction

Taking into account the abstractions that we previously defined, we can explicitly write the expected value of the utility that agent X receives from signing a contract with agent Y as:

$$\overline{U}^r_{X,c} = R_{c,X} \cdot p_{c,Y} + P_{c,X} \cdot (1 - p_{c,Y}) \tag{14.2}$$

where the superscript "r" indicates that the real probability is used in this equation, and not an estimation of its value.

Unfortunately, this utility is not available to any agent since $p_{c,Y}$ is not observable. Instead, agent X estimates the expected utility using its trust in the other party (agent Y):

$$\overline{U}^e_{X,c} = R_{c,X} \cdot t_{c,X,Y} + P_{c,X} \cdot (1 - t_{c,X,Y}) \tag{14.3}$$

Taking into account that agent X invests a certain value when it signs the contract, and that any contract has some probability $p^s_{c,X}$ of being finally signed, the total average utility perceived by agent X is:

$$\begin{aligned}
\overline{U}^r_X &= \overline{U}^r_{X,c} \cdot p^s_{c,X} + I_{c,X} \cdot (1 - p^s_{c,X}) \\
&= [R_{c,X} \cdot p_{c,Y} + P_{c,X} \cdot (1 - p_{c,Y})] \cdot p^s_{c,X} + I_{c,X} \cdot (1 - p^s_{c,X})
\end{aligned} \tag{14.4}$$

As before, the agent can only estimate the total utility, thus obtaining:

$$\begin{aligned}
\overline{U}^e_X &= \overline{U}^e_{X,c} \cdot p^s_{c,X} + I_{c,X} \cdot (1 - p^s_{c,X}) \\
&= [R_{c,X} \cdot t_{c,X,Y} + P_{c,X} \cdot (1 - t_{c,X,Y})] \cdot p^s_{c,X} + I_{c,X} \cdot (1 - p^s_{c,X})
\end{aligned} \tag{14.5}$$

Mediated Interaction

We can adapt the previous equations to the case in which the contract is evaluated using additional information obtained from a guarantor. In this case, the failure probability that we associate with a guarantor has to be considered. This failure probability accounts for the possible uncertainty of the information that the guarantor provides. In particular, we assume that an error of a guarantor may cause a failure of the contract. In this case agent X receives $P_{c,X}$. This risk is acceptable if we assume that in the case of an error, the guarantor itself, and not contractors, pays the penalty.

Under this assumption, the new expected value of the utility of signing contract c is:

$$\overline{U}^{G,r}_{X,c} = R_{c,X} \cdot P\{c \text{ honoured}\} + P_{c,X} \cdot P\{c \text{ not honoured}\} \tag{14.6}$$

where the superscript "G" indicates that some information from the guarantor is considered when signing the contract.

Under the assumption that p^G_k is the probability of the guarantor to provide erroneous information and that any error of the guarantor immediately causes the contract to fail, it is possible to express the total contract success and failure probabilities:

$$\begin{aligned}
P\{c \text{ honoured}\} &= p_{c,Y} \cdot p^G_k \tag{14.7} \\
P\{c \text{ not honoured}\} &= (1 - p_{c,Y}) \cdot p^G_k + 1 - p^G_k \\
&= 1 - p_{c,Y} \cdot p^G_k \tag{14.8}
\end{aligned}$$

where the latter is obtained by means of:

$$P\{c \text{ not honoured}\} = P\{c \text{ not honoured}|\text{Guarantor succeeds}\} +$$
$$P\{c \text{ not honoured}|\text{Guarantor fails}\} \qquad (14.9)$$

Using (14.7), we can rewrite (14.4) as:

$$\overline{U}_{X,c}^{G,r} = R_{c,X} \cdot p_{c,Y} \cdot p_k^G + P_{c,X} \cdot (1 - p_{c,Y} \cdot p_k^G) \qquad (14.10)$$

Then, using this equality in (14.4), we obtain the total average utility of signing the contract using information from a guarantor as:

$$\overline{U}_X^{G,r} = \overline{U}_{X,c}^{G,r} \cdot p_{c,X}^s + I_{c,X} \cdot (1 - p_{c,X}^s)$$
$$= [R_{c,X} \cdot p_{c,Y} \cdot p_k^G + P_{c,X} \cdot (1 - p_{c,Y} \cdot p_k^G)] \cdot p_{c,X}^s +$$
$$+ I_{c,X} \cdot (1 - p_{c,X}^s) \qquad (14.11)$$

Since agents assign a trust of 1 to guarantors, most of the estimations of agent X are not changed by the mediation. In particular, the estimation of the contract success probability remains unchanged; therefore the estimation of the average utility of the contract does not change. Also, the estimation of the expected utility as a function of the probability of signing (14.5) is not influenced. As explained in the following section, the mediation of the guarantor influences only the decision making strategy.

14.4   Decision Making Strategy

Using the previous results, we can introduce a rationality principle in our model by means of a decision making strategy that use a utility function to discriminate on the inclusion of the mediation of a guarantor into a generic interaction.

14.4.1   Trust PDF and the Risk Factor

As we said in the introductory part of Section 14.3, we model trust from the point of view of an agent as the estimation of the probability of having a contract honoured by its counterpart. An underlying assumption of this definition is that this estimation, and the real probability of the contract being honoured, both lie in the interval $[t_{min}, t_{max}]$. In essence, trust is a random variable $\mathbf{t}$ whose *Probability Density Function (PDF)* depends on the decision making strategies of the agents involved in the contract.

Taking $\mathbf{t}$ and a rationality principle into account, it is easy to evaluate the probability of agent X signing a given contract c. In particular, we can state our rationality principle as follows: X decides to sign a contract c with Y if the estimated expected utility that it perceives is greater than the investment required to sign the contract. Which leads immediately to the following:

$$
\begin{aligned}
p^s_{c,X} &= P\{\overline{U}^e_{X,c} > I_{c,X}\} \\
&= P\{R_{c,X} \cdot t_{c,X,Y} + P_{c,X} \cdot (1 - t_{c,X,Y}) > I_{c,X}\}
\end{aligned}
\tag{14.12}
$$

A further elaboration of this equation yields to:

$$
\begin{aligned}
p^s_{c,X} &= P\{t_{c,X,Y} \cdot (R_{c,X} - P_{c,X}) > I_{c,X} - P_{c,X}\} \\
&= P\left\{t_{c,X,Y} > \frac{I_{c,X} - P_{c,X}}{R_{c,X} - P_{c,X}}\right\}
\end{aligned}
\tag{14.13}
$$

Where we supposed that $R_{c,X} - P_{c,X}$ is not zero. Now, if we define:

$$
\kappa_{c,X} \doteq \frac{I_{c,X} - P_{c,X}}{R_{c,X} - P_{c,X}}
\tag{14.14}
$$

it is possible to express $p^s_{c,X}$ as:

$$
p^s_{c,X} = P\{t_{c,X,Y} > \kappa_{c,X}\}
\tag{14.15}
$$

This last equation indicates that agent X signs contract c if its trust in the counterpart with respect to c exceeds $\kappa_{c,X}$, which we call *risk factor*. This factor depends only on X's subjective evaluation of contract c and it describes the risk that X perceives in signing contract c. This, allows to rephrase the decision making strategy as:

> *Agent X signs a contract c with a counterpart Y if and only if its trust in Y for contract c is greater then the risk factor of c.*

It is worth noting that the risk factor $\kappa_{c,X}$ is a number between zero and one. Furthermore, it is the quotient of two quantities that have a precise meaning on their own:

- The numerator $N_{c,X} = I_{c,X} - P_{c,X}$ expresses the gain that agent X obtains when rejecting contract c, compared to the case in which the contract is accepted but actually not honoured.

- The denominator $H_{c,X} = R_{c,X} - P_{c,X}$ represents the gain that the contract yields in case of success with respect to failure.

Then, e.g., if we consider the boundary cases:

- $\kappa_{c,X} = 1$ means that the contract will never be signed, because the investment equals the utility, but the first is guaranteed while the second is not.

- $\kappa_{c,X} = 0$ means that the contract has no risk, since the investment equals the penalty, which is assured with probability 1. Therefore the contract will always be accepted.

More generally, if $\kappa_{c,X} \leq t_{min}$ the contract is always rejected, while if $t_{max} \leq \kappa_{c,X}$ the contract is always accepted. This consideration accounts also for the boundary cases analysis explained above.

Having introduced the risk factor $\kappa_{c,X}$, it is possible to rewrite (14.4) with some emphasis on it. In particular:

$$
\begin{aligned}
\overline{U}^r_X &= [R_{c,X} \cdot p_{c,Y} + P_{c,X} \cdot (1 - p_{c,Y})] \cdot p^s_{c,X} + I_{c,X} \cdot (1 - p^s_{c,X}) \\
&= [(R_{c,X} - P_{c,X})p_{c,Y} + P_{c,X}] \cdot p^s_{c,X} + I_{c,X}(1 - p^s_{c,X}). \quad (14.16)
\end{aligned}
$$

Now, explicitly showing $p^s_{c,X}$ and subsequently $(R_{c,X} - P_{c,X})$:

$$
\begin{aligned}
\overline{U}^r_X &= [(R_{c,X} - P_{c,X})p_{c,Y} + P_{c,X} - I_{c,X}] \cdot p^s_{c,X} + I_{c,X} \\
&= (R_{c,X} - P_{c,X}) \cdot (p_{c,Y} - \kappa_{c,X}) \cdot p^s_{c,X} + I_{c,X}. \quad (14.17)
\end{aligned}
$$

This last equation gives the possibility to draw some interesting considerations. First, $\overline{U}^r_X$ is bounded between $P_{c,X}$ and $R_{c,X}$. Furthermore, $\overline{U}^r_X$ is a linear function of $p^s_{c,X}$ and its slope is $(R_{c,X} - P_{c,X}) \cdot (p_{c,Y} - \kappa_{c,X})$. Since $(R_{c,X} - P_{c,X})$ is non negative because of (14.1), the sign of the slope is influenced by $(p_{c,Y} - \kappa_{c,X})$ only. This ultimately means that the risk factor is an indicator of convenience in terms of the average utility:

- If the success probability of the contract is greater than $\kappa_{c,X}$, then the average utility (of X) increases with the probability of signing the contract, i.e., the contract is advantageous.

- If the risk factor is lower than $\kappa_{c,X}$, the contract is disadvantageous and the average utility decreases with $p^s_{c,X}$.

- If $\kappa_{c,X} = p_{c,Y}$, the average utility is constant.

14.4.2   The Role of the PDF of Trust

The only working assumption on **t** that we accepted up to now is that **t** is a random variable bounded by t_{min} and t_{max}. Here, we further elaborate on trust as a random variable and, without breaking our blackbox approach, we go for the worst case and we assume that **t** is uniformly distributed in the interval $[t_{min}, t_{max}]$. This new assumption allows us to study the influence of the mediation of a guarantor on the average utility perceived by agents.

In accordance with (14.15), we can express the signing probability as the probability that $t_{c,X,Y} \geq \kappa_{c,X}$. Therefore:

$$
p^s_{c,X} = P\{t_{c,X,Y} > \kappa_{c,X}\} = \int_{\kappa_{c,X}}^{+\infty} f(t_{c,X,Y}) \, dt_{c,X,Y} \quad (14.18)
$$

Then,

$$p_{c,X}^s = \begin{cases} 1 & \kappa_{c,X} \leq t_{min} \\ \frac{t_{max} - \kappa_{c,X}}{t_{max} - t_{min}} & t_{min} < \kappa_{c,X} < t_{max} \\ 0 & t_{max} \leq \kappa_{c,X} \end{cases} \qquad (14.19)$$

Now, we focus our analysis of the utility on the most interesting case in which $t_{min} \leq \kappa_{c,X} \leq t_{max}$, i.e., we exclude the edge cases. Moreover, we assume that $\mathbf{t}$ has a symmetric PDF. Introducing (14.19) in (14.17) we obtain the average utility as a function of t_{min} and t_{max}:

$$\overline{U}_X^r = (R_{c,X} - P_{c,X}) \cdot (p_{c,Y} - \kappa_{c,X}) \cdot \frac{t_{max} - \kappa_{c,X}}{t_{max} - t_{min}} + I_{c,X}. \qquad (14.20)$$

Then, using the symmetry of the PDF of $\mathbf{t}$ with width δ it is possible to rewrite (14.19) as:

$$p_{c,X}^s = \begin{cases} 1 & \kappa_{c,X} \leq t_{min} \\ \frac{t_{max} - \kappa_{c,X}}{t_{max} - t_{min}} & t_{min} < \kappa_{c,X} < t_{max} \\ 0 & t_{max} \leq k \end{cases} \qquad (14.21)$$

And then:

$$p_{c,X}^s = \begin{cases} 1 & \kappa_{c,X} \leq t_{min} \\ \frac{p_{c,Y} + \delta - \kappa_{c,X}}{2\delta} & t_{min} < \kappa_{c,X} < t_{max} \\ 0 & t_{max} \leq k \end{cases} \qquad (14.22)$$

which expresses $p_{c,X}^s$ as a function of δ. Substituting this equation in (14.20) and excluding the edge cases, we obtain:

$$\overline{U}_X^r = (R_{c,X} - P_{c,X}) \cdot (p_{c,Y} - \kappa_{c,X}) \cdot \frac{p_{c,Y} + \delta - \kappa_{c,X}}{2\delta} + I_{c,X}. \qquad (14.23)$$

This equation expresses the average utility as a function of the width of the PDF of $\mathbf{t}$. Moreover, since the utility $\overline{U}_X^r$ is a hyperbolic function of δ, any small decrease of δ implies a much higher increase of the average utility and vice versa.

(14.23) has the following interesting consequence on the behaviour of the utility. If agent X takes its decision of signing a contract c using a symmetric PDF centred around $p_{c,Y}$ and if the contract does not fail because of X, then for all $\delta \in \Re^+$ such that $t_{min} - \delta \geq 0$ and $t_{max} + \delta \leq 1$, we have that $\overline{U}_X^r(\delta)$ is non-increasing. In fact, $\overline{U}_X^r$ is piecewise differentiable and the differentiation of (14.23) for $t_{min} < \kappa_{c,X} < t_{max}$ yields:

$$\begin{aligned} \frac{\partial \overline{U}_X^r}{\partial \delta} &= (R_{c,X} - P_{c,X}) \cdot (p_{c,Y} - \kappa_{c,X}) \cdot \frac{2\delta - 2(p_{c,Y} - \kappa_{c,X} + \delta)}{4\delta^2} \\ &= -\frac{(R_{c,X} - P_{c,X}) \cdot (p_{c,Y} - \kappa_{c,X})^2}{2\delta^2} \end{aligned} \qquad (14.24)$$

Taking into account that a subjective evaluation is well formed if $R_{c,X} \geq P_{c,X}$, the partial derivative is always non-positive, i.e., an increment of the estimation (which introduces uncertainty), always worsens the performance of the agent's decision strategy and its relative utility.

The explicit choice of a PDF for **t** allows elaborating on the inclusion of mediation into an interaction. The two parameters $\kappa_{c,X}$ and $p_{c,Y}$ are kept fixed, since the mediation of a guarantor does not change or influence them. On the contrary, the total error probability is modified to account for the additional probability of error that the guarantor brings. Using (14.7), it is possible to directly substitute $p_{c,Y}$ with $p_{c,Y} \cdot p_k^G$ in (14.23) to express the total success and failure probabilities, thus obtaining a version of (14.23) for the case of mediated interactions. To stress the fact that the width of the estimation is different when introducing a guarantor in the interaction, we use the notation δ^G instead of δ:

$$
\overline{U}_X^{G,r} = \begin{cases} H_{c,X} \cdot M^G + I_{c,X} & \kappa_{c,X} \leq t_{min} \\ H_{c,X} \cdot M^G \cdot \frac{p_{c,Y} + \delta^G - \kappa_{c,X}}{2\delta^G} + I_{c,X} & t_{min} < \kappa_{c,X} < t_{max} \\ I_{c,X} & t_{max} \leq \kappa_{c,X} \end{cases} \quad (14.25)
$$

Where we defined (see later on) $M^G = (p_{c,Y} \cdot p_k^G - \kappa_{c,X})$.

14.4.3 Worst-Case Analysis

In order to study the effect of mediation in our model, we recall that our main working assumption is that guarantors provide additional information to agents, thus allowing for a more precise, i.e., narrower, estimation of $p_{c,Y}$. Anyway, guarantors, although highly reliable, introduce additional error probability that must be compensated by improvements in the estimation of trust.

In order to quantify the performance of a guarantor as a middleman in an interaction between agent X and Y, we calculate the amount of additional information that a guarantor needs to provide in order to keep the average utility of agent X fixed.

The comparison of the two utilities expressed in (14.23) and (14.25) allows calculating the width of the guarantor-mediated estimation of trust for which the utility equals the case without mediation. If we introduce $\hat{\delta}^G$ in $\left[0, \frac{1}{2}\right]$ as a function of δ and p_k^G such that:

$$
\overline{U}_X^r(\delta, p_{c,Y}) = \overline{U}_X^{G,r}(\hat{\delta}^G, p_{c,Y} \cdot p_k^G) \quad (14.26)
$$

we can compare (14.23) and (14.25) to obtain:

$$
(p_{c,Y} - \kappa_{c,X}) \cdot \frac{p_{c,Y} + \delta - \kappa_{c,X}}{\delta} = (p_{c,Y} \, p_k^G - \kappa_{c,X}) \cdot \frac{p_{c,Y} + \hat{\delta}^G - \kappa_{c,X}}{\hat{\delta}^G} \quad (14.27)
$$

where we subtracted $I_{c,X}$ on both sides and multiplied by $\frac{2}{R_{c,X} - P_{c,X}}$. Then, introducing $M = (p_{c,Y} - \kappa_{c,X})$ and $M^G = (p_{c,Y} \, p_k^G - \kappa_{c,X})$:

$$
M \cdot \frac{\delta + M}{\delta} = M^G \cdot \frac{\hat{\delta}^G + M}{\hat{\delta}^G} \quad (14.28)
$$

and dividing by M^G yields:

$$\frac{M}{M^G} \cdot \frac{\delta + M}{\delta} = \frac{\hat{\delta}^G + M}{\hat{\delta}^G} \tag{14.29}$$

which allows making $\hat{\delta}^G$ explicit:

$$\hat{\delta}^G = \frac{M}{\frac{M}{M^G} \cdot \frac{\delta + M}{\delta} - 1} = \frac{M M^G \delta}{M(\delta + M) - M^G \delta} \tag{14.30}$$

that holds if $M^G \neq 0$.

It should be quite clear that $2\,\hat{\delta}^G$ is the breakeven point that makes agent X choose to go for a mediated interaction rather than for a direct interaction:

- If the guarantor provides enough information to restrict the estimation of trust to a width less than $2\,\hat{\delta}^G$, the use of mediation is advantageous.

- If the estimation remains larger than $2\,\hat{\delta}^G$, the error probability introduced by the guarantor decreases the average utility.

Finally, it is worth noting that this decision strategy is purely ideal because agent X does not know p_k^G.

In order to ground our model in everyday experience, we recall that we are interested in guarantors that introduce a very low error probability, and therefore we study the behaviour of $\hat{\delta}^G$ as p_k^G tends to 1. What we obtain from this study is that if agent X makes its decisions assuming that $\mathbf{t}$ has a symmetric PDF and that the contract will not fail because of X itself, for all $\delta \in \left[0, \frac{1}{2}\right]$, $\delta - \hat{\delta}^G$ tends to 0 in a hyperbolic way as p_k^G tends to 1.

Because of editorial reasons, we cannot provide details on the demonstration of this result. Anyway, this result shows that if a guarantor introduces a (sufficiently) low probability of error, the use of its mediation is advantageous and the rewards that it brings rapidly increase as the probability of error decreases.

14.5   Integration in the CASCOM Platform

Security, privacy- and trust-awareness are crosscutting features of the CASCOM platform that are spread across all its layers to provide application developers with different services at different layers. For the sake of readability, we somehow oversimplify the description and we allocate such features to the IP2P Network Layer and to the Service Coordination Layer only. See other chapters in this book for an in-depth description of these layers and of the overall architecture of the CASCOM platform.

14.5.1   IP2P Network Layer

The IP2P Network layer provides application developers with most of the standard security features that we need to guarantee an adequate level of security for real-world communications between software entities. In detail, this layer transparently accommodates cryptography and non-repudiability of pairwise communications. Application developers are not involved in securing communications and, once activated, the secured transport mechanism is in charge of the whole process of encryption and decryption of all inbound and outbound messages.

Basically, messages are filtered using a standard asymmetric cryptography method; security and non-repudiability are guaranteed because agents are requested mandatory to complete the registration of their services with Directory Facilitators with an X.509 certificate to be used in communications. Client agents accessing the services of service-provider agents provide their X.509 certificate in the act of requesting services.

The adopted cryptography scheme may be very demanding in terms of communication bandwidth and this is not always acceptable in a mobile environment. In order to provide application developers with a fine-grained control over the cryptography overhead, we allow the level of security to be customized on a message basis. For each and every single outbound message, an agent can choose to encrypt the message or not, and for encrypted messages it can choose between encrypting the whole ACL message or only its SL content.

The security module of the IP2P Network Layer is embedded deep in the core of the CASCOM platform as a pluggable service and it is ubiquitously deployable because it is both MIDP and J2SE compliant. It uses a downsized version of the Bouncy Castle Crypto API [1] and its memory footprint and runtime requirements are compatible with nowadays mobile devices. New `ACLCodec` and `SLCodec` [9] implementations are provided to guarantee the possibility of fine tuning the overhead of encryption on message basis.

14.5.2   Service Coordination Layer

The Service Coordination layer sits on top of the IP2P Network layer and it exploits its services to provide novel, agent-level services with a high level of abstraction. This is the reason why we use to say that the Service Coordination layer raises the level of abstraction of the secure messaging services of the IP2P Network layer towards the realization of full privacy- and trust-awareness services. In detail, such services provide:

- Guarantor-mediated ACL messaging that ensures trustworthy and possibly anonymized communications.

- Privacy-awareness storage mechanisms.

Unfortunately, we cannot provide application developers with a transparent tool like we did for secure messaging at the IP2P Network layer. Policies for ensuring privacy-awareness have to take into account the intended usage and the inherent nature of transmitted data for being correctly applied. At the service coordination layer, transmitted data is no longer an opaque stream of bytes, rather it is a source of possibly classified information that agents may need to protect against malevolent usage. ACL messages containing classified data are easily interleaved with messages that do not contain them and we need application developers to classify which message is potentially privacy-critical. Therefore, the CASCOM privacy- and trust-awareness services are agent-level services that developers must explicitly address. This is the reason why we developed a framework for CASCOM-based applications capable of providing a direct support to developers in the classification of data for communication and storage.

We designed our framework to match a set of fundamental requirements, that resulted in strict development guidelines, as follows.

- Security. All communications must be secured and directed to trusted parties.

- Traceability. Messages must be signed by senders, while responses must be signed, directly or indirectly, by a guarantor. The framework transparently enforces this property and it provides a transparent tracing service that logs all communications.

- Locality. The number of trusted parties involved in a communication must be kept minimal.

- Transparency. The use of guarantors in trustworthy communications must be transparent to application developers, i.e., she/he is not directly involved in the use guarantors' services.

- Ease of use. The framework must provide high level procedures to perform common tasks, as well as low level, more specific procedures devoted to fine-grained and less common tasks.

- Standardization. Information exchange, including messages and certificates, must be performed using well-known and accepted formats.

Following such requirements, the design of the CASCOM framework for privacy- and trust-awareness is split into two views: *(i)* the *Client view* that groups the classes that agents exploit to access the services of the privacy- and trust-awareness framework, and *(ii)* the *Guarantor view* that contains the components that guarantors use to implement their functionality. These views are connected through a Java interface, named `Guarantor`, that plays the logical role of a remote interface that guarantors implement and that agents exploit to communicate with guarantors. Such a design uses the well-known *half object plus protocol* design pattern and application developers are only interested in the use of the stubs of the `Guarantor` interface.

It is worth noting that the client view represents a mandatory interface while the guarantor view is only one of the possible internal implementation of guarantors. Obviously, the client view plays a substantially more relevant role in this design.

The use of the services that the client view of the framework provides always starts with an authentication phase that clients perform to achieve a mutual recognition with a guarantor. Once a client is authenticated with a guarantor, it can exploit the mediation of the guarantor to request for services in a trustworthy and possibly anonymized way. In detail, a client can perform three kinds of requests for services:

- Direct requests: requests for services whose outcome is used by the client itself;

- Indirect requests: requests that are performed on behalf of some other client.

Direct requests are ordinary requests for services, except for the following two constraints:

- Parameters and results are transported on a secured channel;

- The guarantor acts as a middleman and it is responsible for tracing the request to guarantee non-repudiability;

- The client is responsible for providing a distributed timestamp to allow for traceability of complex interactions.

Indirect requests are a delegation mechanism that allow a client (B, delegated) to have a service performed on behalf of another client (A, delegator). Indirect requests are implemented with the following steps:

- Client A requests its guarantor to grant indirect requests to client B;

- If the guarantor can honor the request of A, it accepts requests from B and serve them as if they were requested by A;

- The guarantor stops serving indirect requests from B when the delegation expires, e.g., because the maximum number of requests from B is reached or because of time limitations.

An indirect request starts when A creates a delegation token for B using the `Guarantor` interface. If the guarantor can grant the delegation, a globally unique token that identifies the delegation is created and it is provided to B. The delegated client B uses this token to finally access the services through the guarantor with no further authentication, i.e., there is no mutual recognition between B and the guarantor.

Indirect requests allows chaining trust and constructing a network of trust on the fly, thus avoiding static structures that mutual recognition of guarantors imply. Moreover, they are a good way to allow a third party having a service done without explicitly requesting mutual recognition, i.e., it is a good way to carry out anonymized communications.

The guarantor view of the framework describes how guarantors implement their services with the requested level of security and privacy awareness. Every guarantor decides its own optimized approach to provide services as long as the `Guarantor` interface is honoured and therefore the guarantor view of the framework is only one of the possible ways to implement guarantors. Anyway, high-quality guarantors are not easy to implement because they need to deal with somehow tricky issues, e.g., the global uniqueness of the generated tokens and the correct tracing of invocations, and therefore the guarantor view of the framework plays an important role for real-world applications.

One of the principal components of the guarantor view of the framework is the so called *sensitive data storage*. This is a general-purpose means for data storage that is meant to allow for a seamless treatment of sensitive data. It is worth noting that every Nation in the European Community adopted laws to provide guarantees to citizens regarding the treatment of their sensitive data. Such laws are all rooted in a note of the European Commission and they all contain strict technical requirements that databases of sensitive data must follow. The sensitive data store ensures that the basic principles of the correct treatment of sensitive data are respected and it ensures the possibility of fine tuning its policies to comply with national laws.

The second part of the guarantor view of the framework is the so called *message tracer*. This component provides all needed mechanisms for tracing direct and indirect requests served or rejected by the guarantor. Such requests are stored in a sensitive data store that saves all information regarding requests. It is worth noting that the use of a distributed time stamp in indirect requests allows to correlate traces of different guarantors, and therefore it supports backward tracing of communications across a complex network of clients and guarantors.

14.6 Summary

The work reported in this chapter has two main objectives: *(i)* it studies trust from a quantitative point of view and it demonstrates that mediated interactions are mandatory to achieve privacy- and trust-awareness in real-world multiagent systems; and *(ii)* it shows an overview of the infrastructure that CASCOM platform provides to provide application developers with a real-world support for these abstractions. Such an infrastructure provides notable features that are not discussed here and that play a fundamental role from the point of view of scalability and reliability of CASCOM-based applications (see other chapters in this book regarding these issues).

This work is not meant to be conclusive and many points remain open. One of the major planned developments regards the study of concrete trust estimators, and the introduction of the resulting PDFs in our model.

Another very important open point regards the study of the effects of delegation of tasks and goals through a chain of delegated guarantors.

Finally, the study of one of the main features of guarantors, i.e., the possibility of anonymising interactions, is still in search of a formalization — and of a stochastic model — even though its characteristics and possible uses are clearly understood [2] because this kind of interaction allows to prevent unwanted spread of sensitive information.

Acknowledgment

The author would like to thank Roberto Bianchi, Andrea Fontana and Danilo Bonardi for their inspired contribution to the ideas and the results reported in this chapter.

References

[1] Bouncy Castle Crypto API Web site. http://www.bouncycastle.org

[2] F. Bergenti, R. Bianchi and A. Fontana: Secure and Trusted Interactions in Societies of Electronic Agents. In Proceedings of *The 4th Workshop on the Law and Electronic Agents (LEA 2005)*, 1–12. Bologna, Italy. 2005. Wolf Legal Publishers.

[3] R. Bianchi, A. Fontana and F. Bergenti: A Real–World Approach to Secure and Trusted Negotiation in MASs. In Proceedings of *The 4th International Joint Conference on Agents and Multi-Agents Systems (AAMAS)*, 1163–1164. Utrecht. The Netherlands. 2005. ACM Press.

[4] R.W.H. Bons: *Designing Trustworthy Trade Procedures for Open Electronic Commerce*. Ph.D.diss., EURIDIS and Faculty of Business Administration, Erasmus University, Rotterdam, The Netherlands. 1999.

[5] C. Castelfranchi and R. Falcone: Principles of Trust for MAS: Cognitive Anatomy, Social Importance, and Quantification. In Proceedings of *The International Conference of Multi-agent Systems (ICMAS)*, 72–79. Paris, France. 2005. ACM Press.

[6] C. Ellison: *SPKI Requirements*. IETF RFC 2692. 1999.

[7] C. Ellison, B. Frantz, B. Lampson, R. Rivest, B. Thomas T. Ylonen: *SPKI Certificate Theory*. IETF RFC 2693. 1999

[8] D. Gambetta (Ed.). *Trust: Making and Breaking Co-operative Relations*. Basil Blackwell, Inc. 1988.

[9] JADE Team. *JADE Programmers Guide*. Available at http://jade.tilab.it

[10] JENA Web site. http://jena.sourceforge.net

[11] N.R. Jennings, S. Parsons, C. Sierra and R. Faratin: Automated Negotiation. In Proceedings of *The 5th International Conference on the Practical Application of Intelligent Agents and Multi-Agents Systems (PAAM-2000)*, 23–30. Manchester, UK. 2000.

[12] S. Marsh: *Formalising Trust as a Computational Concept.* Ph.D. dissertation, Department of Mathematics and Computer Science, University of Stirling, Stirling, UK. 1994.

[13] MINDSWAP Team. *A Definition of Trust for Computing with Social Networks* Technical report, University of Maryland, College Park, February 2005.

[14] OWL Web site. `http://www.w3.org/2004/OWL`

[15] Racer Web site. `http://www.sts.tu-harburg.de/~r.f.moeller/racer`

Part III

Trials and Results

Chapter 15

Qualitative Analysis

Mihael Cankar, Nadine Fröhlich, Heimo Laamanen, Thorsten Möller, and Heiko Schuldt

15.1 Introduction

Software development aims at providing support for users in order to better cope with specific problems they face in their professional and/or daily life. Thus, developers have to carefully analyze requirements and needs of prospective users. But this process is very difficult and often characterized by misunderstandings between developers and users. In a trial, users evaluate a software application and give valuable feedback whether or not it meets their expectations and how it can be improved.

The CASCOM project involves laboratory trials and field trials to obtain qualitative feedback from end users. The main objectives of the trial activities in the CASCOM project are the following:

- Proving the CASCOM architecture and its implementation.

- Evaluating the acceptance of the system and the suitability of the selected technology in the chosen application domain.

- Verify whether the CASCOM service coordination framework meets the business needs of multiple service providers and network operators.

To make the trials realistic, they are conducted under controlled conditions using real network services, resources, devices, and terminals.

As the CASCOM architecture is very generic and universally applicable, the trials are based on a concrete application scenario in a concrete application domain. The partners of the CASCOM project decided to use *emergency medical assistance* as application domain (see Chapter 1). The concrete trial scenario of the trials in Innsbruck and Basel is shown in Figure 15.1. The scenario used in the Helsinki trials slightly differs in details. This scenario is based on the fact that

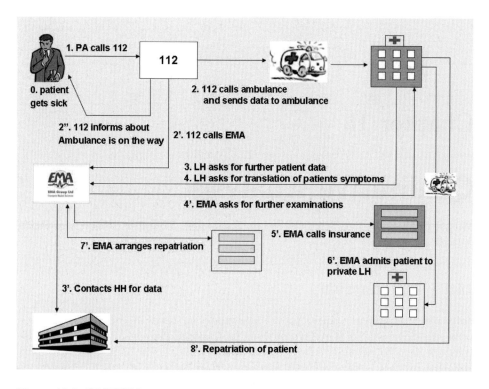

Figure 15.1: CASCOM emergency assistance application scenario used for the field trials

people on the move can get into situations where they need immediate medical assistance. It consists of two phases, a pre-hospital and a hospital phase.

Pre-hospital phase: In the scenario it is assumed that a Finnish tourist, is on vacation in Austria when he feels a pain in his chest. Before leaving for Austria, he has installed the necessary CASCOM software on his smart phone and activates it to initiate an emergency call. After initiation he has to answer a few questions about his symptoms. The questions appear on the GUI of the smart phone. Subsequently an emergency call is set up by the patient's personal agent, and the 112 agent (emergency dispatch center) is contacted. This agent contacts the nearest ambulance and informs about the medical case of the patient. This information basically contains data collected on the initial questionnaire, old patient data (e.g., ECGs, X-rays), some personal data but also the patient's position determined by a location-based service. The location-based service allows directing the emergency car to the patient. Through all this information physicians in the ambulance are able to prepare the patient's treatment. Furthermore EMA — a Finnish emergency assistance organization — is contacted by the 112 agent. Meanwhile the patient receives a message that the ambulance is on its way.

After primary care, the ambulance physicians decide about the local hospital (LH) for the patient and bring him there. The emergency physicians at the hospital also receive patient information to prepare the patient's treatment.

Then the *hospital phase* follows: The LH needs further patient data and requests it from EMA. EMA makes this data immediately available which significantly saves time in this critical situation. Subsequently, the LH requests EMA to provide a translation of the patient records. Moreover, EMA monitors the quality of the patient's treatment. If the quality is not adequate, it requests the LH to do further examinations. When the patient's situation demands repatriation to the home hospital (HH), EMA takes care of calling the insurance and asking about cost coverage. It organizes the transport to an private LH or the transfer back home and informs the hospital about the arrival of the patient. Furthermore the home hospital can get patient data via CASCOM services and use them to prepare the continuation of the patient's treatment. The scenario demands flexible planning and re-planning activities that are transparent to the user.

For the trials, only the first part of this scenario (the pre-hospital phase) was implemented and tested.

In what follows, the different trial activities will be described in more detail. The CASCOM consortium has successfully carried out the following trials: a usability lab trial in Helsinki (Finland) and field trials in Basel (Switzerland) and Innsbruck (Austria). The latter has been strongly supported by both emergency physicians and IT staff at the University Hospital in Innsbruck. The description of the CASCOM trials is structured as follows:

- Test set-up (testers and test environment.)

- Execution (test sequences and assessment.)

- Results (including proposed and implemented improvements on the different agents.)

This chapter concludes with a summary on all the activities related to the quantitative analysis of the CASCOM system.

15.2   Usability Trials in Helsinki

The test of the personal agent that is the patient's system view took place in a usability laboratory at TeliaSonera's premises in Helsinki and the test of the physician's system view was executed in a non-moving ambulance.

The purpose of these activities was to study the usability and handling of the user interface and to eliminate worst usability failures before the field trials in order to get better usability at the Innsbruck trials. The user feedback captured in this trial provided valuable information to improve the user interface of the system. It has been proven that such laboratory tests executed with expert testers and rigorous analysis give accurate results even for mobile services [3]. But they

Figure 15.2: Usability tests in Helsinki

do not necessarily reveal whether the product will be usable in its eventual usage context. For example, disruptions in a mobile environment may cause problems if the patient's tasks are cognitively heavy. Emulating the mental state of a user in a medical emergency is impossible in a test situation. This has implications that may bias the results in this report. The field tests that were conducted in a real environment and thus under more realistic conditions answered some of these issues.

15.2.1   Test Set-Up

Testers

As described before, for the work in the project it is important to capture feedback from the users to prove the concept of CASCOM and improve the CASCOM software. But the primary goal of the tests was not statistical validity and therefore a small number of users was sufficient. In Helsinki there were four testers for testing the patient's emergency application and two paramedics were interviewed in the ambulance to study the needs of the ambulance unit. Furthermore two doctors and a nurse were interviewed for background information on the recovery of patients from abroad.

Test Environment

The equipment used for the trials in Helsinki was the following: Nokia N93 Series 60 phones for testing the patient's view of the system and an IBM ThinkPad tablet PC with pen control for testing the physician's view. A backend system consisting of Dell Precisions equipped with Windows XP Pro SP 2, Java JDK 1.5.0_10, JADE 3.4 and Linux Fedora Core 3 OS, Java JDK 1.5.0_05, and the

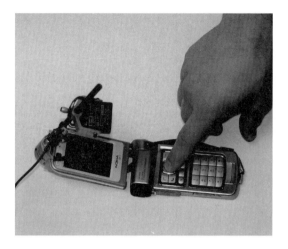

Figure 15.3: Test setup of smart phone for usability tests

CASCOM trial version. Thereby the server Dell Precision 690 has the following configuration: Intel Xeon 5160 with 3.00 GHz, 1333 MHz, 4 MB Cache, and 4 GB RAM. The other server, a Dell PowerEdge 1800, has a 2 kpl Intel Xeon 3 Ghz Processor and 4 GB RAM. For the network connections WLAN (TeliaSonera HomeRun) and UMTS as wireless networks (TeliaSonera 3G service) were used. Furthermore, as fixed network TeliaSonera ethernet was used.

15.2.2 Execution

The actual usability trials started with a warm-up phase for getting familiar with devices and their usage. Here testers had to solve simple tasks such as sending a text message to a friend, playing a game and finding the CASCOM application. After that, testers tested the application. They were asked to imagine themselves in the following situation: "You suddenly feel a pressing, continuous, and strong pain in your chest. There is no-one nearby and you do not know the local language. Thus you decide to use the application to get help." The testers were encouraged to think aloud during the test as these comments are valuable clues for improvement. Thereby testers were recorded with a video camera, which made it possible to check details and user feedback later. During the trials, a special camera directly installed on the smartphone was used (see Figure 15.3). The duration of each test was about 40 minutes except the test in the ambulance, which needed more time.

15.2.3 Results

The usability trials gave important suggestions for improving the software for better matching the user's requirements. Some of the suggested changes were implemented before the field trials.

As these usability tests were the very first tests with potential users, the evaluation of the test results concentrated on flaws in the usability in order to avoid failures in the actual field trial. Thus, good and well working functionalities were not the main topic. However, in general, all the test users expressed as their opinion that they would use in the future emergency services based on the CASCOM technology even though they had some psychological hindrance related to trustworthiness of this kind of systems. This kind of service conflicts with their learned behaviour in case of emergency situation.

In addition, they were willing to pay for the service either directly as an annual or monthly fee or embedded in other services, such as travel insurance.

The overall flow (input from the users and output to the users) of requesting emergency help worked in an acceptable way, and users did not request any major changes. Intelligent phones, such as Nokia N93, seem to be proper user equipment for the CASCOM service. The computing and communication power and quality of display are adequate for the CASCOM services.

In the following sections, the main suggestions and possible solutions are described.

Personal Agent

Reporting emergencies: Participants said they would rather call 112 to report an emergency, as it is a learned way of behaving. They like the personal contact and find comfort in talking to someone. The CASCOM system cannot offer this, but the traditional way fails in unknown environments (e.g., foreign countries). But the CASCOM application could be improved by giving additional feedback such as information about the arrival of the ambulance, self-help recommendations and contact information of the hospital.

Starting the application: Participants not familiar with the series 60 devices had trouble finding the application. This is mostly caused by the user interface of the phone, but it needs to be addressed. One idea is to make the application visible in the idle state of the phone and thus easier to find. Another idea is to have an additional hardware button, but this idea is discarded as it is too expensive.

Confirmation of emergency reports: Participants expressed varying levels of need for privacy control. Of course, local legislation in countries may make additional requirements. If a confirmation or authorization proves to be necessary, there are many possible methods, all of which have their pros and cons. The PIN code of the phone is usually well remembered, but perhaps less so in an emergency? Voice and fingerprint recognition are interesting, but people's behavior in an emergency may make recognition more difficult than in ideal conditions. Until

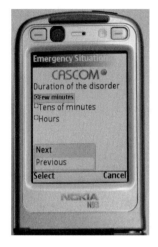

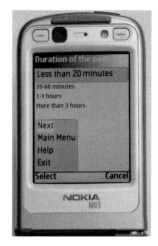

Figure 15.4: Radio buttons   Figure 15.5: Radio buttons improved

now, no viable solution has been identified.

Terminology: The test setting of the usability test did not allow to properly verify the understandability of the questions used to report a medical situation. The users were in a very artificial situation and seemed to answer something just to get on with the test. As it is not possible to create a less artificial environment the texts have to be checked again with medical experts.

Radio buttons not clear: It is possible to move focus without moving selection. Users had to verify that they have chosen the correct option. Moving the cursor should also move the selection, then middle-clicking should accept it and move to the next screen, i.e., the same way as on the main page of the application. Also, fonts on the screen changed depending on where the focus was. This should be corrected so that font size remains fixed. These suggestions are implemented now. Figure 15.4 shows the situation before and Figure 15.5 shows the situation after the improvement.

Next and Back do not work as expected: The left softkey of the old version leads to a new menu with 'next' or 'previous'. The user should always be able to get back to the previous screen while making selections. Returning to the main menu should be possible from 'Options' (left softkey). The softkeys should follow a familiar logic. On a series 60 Nokia handset, for example, the following should be used: Pressing the left softkey label should open the 'Options' menu with the choices: 'Next', 'Main menu', Help', 'Exit' (see Figure 15.5). Pressing the right softkey label should effect a 'Back', that is, it should take the user one step back.

Permission to use network: Before opening a new wireless link the mobile phone's policy is to ask for a permission. The application should not make a request to use the network while the user is doing something. In the worst case, the user has spent time answering the questions, then finds the network does not work for

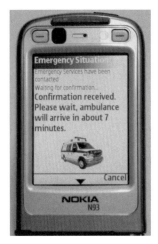   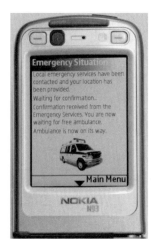

Figure 15.6: Message for the patient   Figure 15.7: Message slightly improved

some reason. The application should open a network session when it is launched. At this time users are not surprised about it, and any problems with the network are obvious before answering any questions. Ideally the application should know which network to use and just open it.

This problem can be solved by configuration and it is Java Microedition specific. Thus for the prototype it is not really relevant but it should be fixed in the end version.

Not enough feedback: After placing an emergency call the message "Ambulance is on its way" is not comforting enough. Users wanted to be sure the ambulance knows where they are and would have liked to have the estimated arrival time. The message should be adapted adequately. Furthermore, it was not clear to the testers what the 'Cancel' button means - cancel the emergency or cancel the application? In response to this feedback, the message has been improved but it should still be made more concrete. The cancel button has been replaced by a 'Main Menu' button. The screen used in the Helsinki trials is shown in Figure 15.6 and the improved screen is shown in Figure 15.7.

Ambulance Unit

Given that only two paramedics tested the ambulance units, the results are less detailed than those for the personal agent. However, given the very early state of the prototype user interface, the following recommendations can be made even with the small number of participants.

When driving to the scene: The address and navigation guidance are the most important information. These should be made prominent on the first view. As most ambulances already have a separate navigation system, the CASCOM application should concentrate on giving the crucial patient details in a clear way. The paramedics have little time to get familiar with the patient's medical background. Only the most critical patient information is useful. If a summary of the medical history is available, it should be highlighted. Images (ECG etc.) are not always needed.

Device form factor: The device must suit a variety of needs. Paramedics need to view the information in the driver's cabin, as well as enter data on location and in the back of the ambulance. The device must be easily portable and rugged. Writing (entering data) must be easy and not prone to errors. Handwriting recognition is not currently very good at this. Either it should be possible to enter data by choosing options from a list, or a keyboard should be used. The screen should be sufficiently sized for legibility and viewing patient history images. The device has to be relatively small as there is already a lot of stuff to carry on the car. Thus it should be no larger than the A4 format.

Device placement: The paramedics' focus is on the patient. Entering information must be easy without having to concentrate on the device trying to keep it from falling. The device should have a docking station to keep it in place and provide power. Writing should be possible in the docking station while helping the patient. One further idea is to consider a different or an additional display in the driver's cabin for viewing the navigation map and the patient info.

Patient recovery from abroad: As it was not possible to study a recovery scenario on location, the following is a very general list of suggestions. Talking to the patient can be very helpful to assess the gravity of the situation. Once EMA is contacted by the local hospital, the patient's agent could be updated with EMA contact information and advice to get in touch. Several interviewees mentioned that seeing the patient would be very helpful. Perhaps the patient could use the personal agent to upload images of himself. Once the system is running and electronic data from many patients are in, they can be analyzed to notice patterns. Currently EMA nurses depend on talking to other personnel to notice such patterns.

15.3 Field Trials in Innsbruck and Basel

The field trials consisted of two parts. The first part has evaluated the personal agent and was executed at the University of Basel (Switzerland) with students from the university as testers. The second part of the field trials did analyze the physician's view of the system was conducted in Innsbruck (Austria). It took place at the trauma station and in a driving emergency car at TILAK (Tiroler Krankenanstalten GmbH, the umbrella organization of the state hospitals of the Austrian state Tyrol). Here two internationally renowned physicians thoroughly and carefully tested the CASCOM application and provided highly positive and valuable feedback.

The aim of the *usability trials* in Helsinki described in Section 15.2 was to improve usability by finding worst failures before the actual trial and correct them. It was conducted under controlled conditions as this is a good way for first usability testings. In contrast, the *field trials* were conducted under more realistic conditions partly in a real hospital environment. Furthermore we got the possibility to use real healthcare Web Services in the trials, the health@net Web Services. These services provide access to patient health records. They were developed in the health@net project where TILAK and the University for Health Science, Medical Informatics and Technology (UMIT) cooperate to implement a local health network that allows Tyrolean hospitals and general practitioners to share health-related information of patients [5, 6].

TILAK and UMIT offered professional support for the trials as they are interested in working with new and innovative technologies. Therefore, the experts evaluation of the CASCOM application is of high relevance. All physicians at TILAK have been very much in favour of the overall CASCOM idea and its technical implementation. In particular, they very positively evaluated the CASCOM system as a whole, both from a functional (early access to important patient data) and from a non-functional point of view (response time, etc.).

Hence, the field trials focus more on the interaction with the overall system and problems that cannot be recognized under laboratory conditions, e.g., the handling of the application and the devices in special places. Nevertheless, it has turned out that the usability tests gave valuable feedback to improve the CASCOM user interfaces -- these improvements have been applied before the start of the Innsbruck field trials.

15.3.1   Test Set-Up

Testers

In the field trials in Innsbruck two physicians tested the physician's application view in their daily working environment (the emergency department and the emergency car). In the part of the field trials executed in Basel, there were six students who took over the role of patients equipped with mobile devices where the CASCOM application suite has been installed.

Test Environment

In these trials not exactly the same hardware and software configuration as in the usability trials in Helsinki was used, in order to have a broader test field. Thus the equipment used for the trials in Innsbruck and Basel was the following: Smartphones of type HTC TyTN using UMTS for testing the patient application, and Ultra Mobile PCs of type Asus R2H for testing the physician's view. In addition, ANYCOM GP-700 Bluetooth GPS Receivers were used for the HTC TyTNs, as these smartphones do not support GPS but GPS location tracking was needed for the execution of the trials. For each platform a Java Virtual Machine implementation needed to be available. In the case of mobile devices this is defined to be

Figure 15.8: Crew of the emergency car

at least a Java Micro Edition compatible runtime (J2ME MIDP 2.0). For fixed devices this is defined to be at least a Java 2 Standard Edition 1.4.2. As server a computer located at the TILAK with the following parameters was used: HP ML530 G2, Dual Xeon 2,4 GHz, 6 GB RAM, Vmware machines using 1*1 Gbit LAN connection, Vmware ESX 2.5.3. Up to 8 machines can be hosted in parallel on this device.

For security reasons, this server was placed inside the local demilitarized network zone (DMZ). The network setup mostly relied on wireless and fixed network communication technologies. In the TILAK buildings, wireless network (WLAN) has been available. It was used for the trial in the stationary emergency department. For trial activities carried out in the emergency car we used UMTS and GSM (GPRS) based communication. The test environment used during this trial is depicted in Figure 15.9. The patient data which has been accessed during the trial activities was provided by the health@net project via dedicated Semantic Web Services. It has turned out that CASCOM is an even more challenging use case for health@net. Due to the good liaison to health@net, CASCOM has received excellent support and has been able to make use of the health@net services (for privacy reasons not on productive data from the TILAK clinical information system but on anonymous patient data).

15.3.2 Execution

Before starting the trials, all testers received a short introduction to the system and its functions as well as an explanation of the handling of the devices to present an overview of the overall system. The real trials started with a warm-up phase for getting familiar with the devices and their usage. Here testers had to solve a

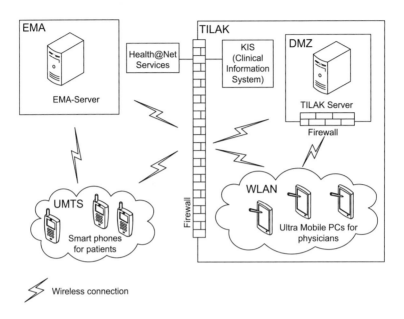

Figure 15.9: Test environment

simple task such as opening a website. After that, testers tried out the application
by using it as if they were involved in a real medical emergency. They were asked
to perform tasks and were encouraged to think aloud during the test as these
comments are valuable clues for improvement. All activities during the actual
trials were recorded with a video camera. When studying usability details, portable
cameras allow a moderator to follow a user and record his/her interaction with a
mobile device [4]. Thus, it was possible to check details and user feedback later. The
trial was completed by interviews based on questionnaires to capture main points
of feedback. The interviews were done immediately after the tests to be as reliable
as possible. The Innsbruck trials with the physicians lasted approximately two
hours each. The duration of the Basel trials with the students was approximately
30 minutes per person.

15.3.3   Results

The results of the trials were very valuable as they proved the architecture and the
implementation of the CASCOM software. Moreover they gave important suggestions for further improvements of the software so that it even better fits the user's
requirements.

Personal Agent (Basel)

The Basel students who tested the patient's view had a good overall opinion about the software. They said the application's functionality would meet their needs and they thought the masks and the structure of the application are good and it is easy to learn and easy to use. Furthermore the application is stable and has a good performance. All these points are especially important in emergency situations.

Testers had different opinions about what is the most relevant functionality of the system. Some stated it is that the application tries to find the best hospital, others liked most that the application submits medical patient data to the hospital before the patient arrives there, and it was also seen as an important feature that she/he might be able to have such a service in a country where the patient does not speak the local language.

Three persons said they would feel safer with the application, one said he would not and two did not know. All six students like the application and four would recommend it to others. Although the testers liked the application, they gave very good suggestions for improving it. Subsequently these suggestions are listed:

Reporting emergencies: Similar to the testers in Finland, participants said it is not easy for them to think of using an application in an emergency situation instead of making a call, as there is nobody who calms them, no explanations, no feedback. Some testers wanted to have the additional possibility to make a call to the hospital or to receive a call from the hospital to get direct feedback from a physician. Other testers proposed to extend the application for non-emergency cases. When a patient does not need a emergency car, the application could provide a map with the way to the hospital.

Starting the application: Testers doubted that the number of questions that have to be answered before the emergency call is appropriate. Some noticed there are not enough questions; others thought there are too many questions for an emergency case. As in the Helsinki trials, testers proposed to have a software emergency button or maybe a key combination for starting the application very quickly and avoiding trouble in finding the application.

Terminology: Another point of criticism was that the questions are often very specific and sometimes participants do not know what to answer. E.g., for some of them it was not clear what to answer in the mask 'Severity of pain' (see Figure 15.10). A proposal was to have in all the dialogs the possibility to answer 'I don't know'. This suggestion is quite similar to that given in the Helsinki trials but we have to discuss with medical emergency professionals whether this is the right way to improve the user interface.

Not enough feedback: As in the usability trial the users stated that the message 'Ambulance is on its way' is not comforting enough in an emergency situation. Users wanted to be sure the emergency car knows where they are and would have liked to have the estimated arrival time. The message should be adapted adequately. The improvements that have been made until now are not enough (see

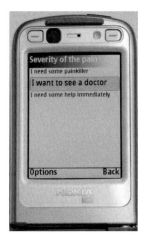

Figure 15.10: Do you want to see a doctor?

Figure 15.7).

Readability problems: Users thought that the font size of the application and buttons is too small. Further, they reported that the title of some dialogs could not be seen in full length (see Figure 15.10).

No save prompt: There is no saving prompt after the user has filled in the fields for personal data. Thus if the wrong button is pressed, all inputs are lost. Furthermore, it is possible to make nonsensical entries, e.g., impossible dates, which is not relevant in an emergency case, but improving it might increase the confidence in the system.

Inconsistent handling: The handling of the application is not always consistent. Sometimes switching between keyboard and stylus is necessary to complete a task. This is not intuitive and can be confusing in emergency situations.

Ambulance Unit (Innsbruck)

The trials in Innsbruck in which the physicians view of the system was tested were also very successful as all parts of the system worked very well and there were only minor problems with the network. Thus, the participants were highly pleased with the application. Their feedback indicated that the user interface is comfortable and easy to use, design and handling are consistent, the structure is clear and data is well readable.

In particular, they liked the early availability of patients' medical records because it makes the preparation of upcoming medical cases easier (see Figure 15.11). They also think the CASCOM application might help to lower wrong diagnoses and to save the lives of old people and people with chronic diseases.

Although the testers were very satisfied with our prototype they had valuable

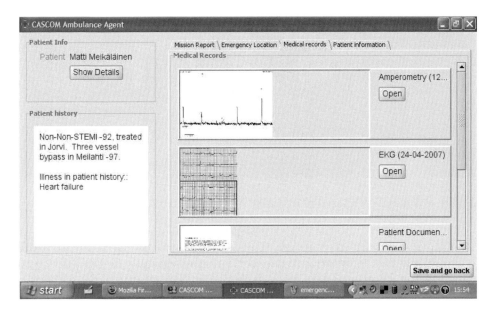

Figure 15.11: Early information

ideas for improving the application. Suggestions from the test physicians were:

When driving to the scene: In contrast to the testers in Helsinki the participants thought the navigation dialog is not needed as they have a separate navigation system in their car. For them, only the address is relevant. The physician of the emergency car thought just like the participants in Helsinki a whole discharge letter is too much. He only needs the most relevant data. But the physician at the station needs all information (but not older than 5 years). Maybe it would make sense to split up the application for using in the hospital and in the emergency car.

Device form factor: We used a different device than in the Helsinki trials. It is smaller and better portable, but the display is still large enough for showing patient data. But it does not fulfil the requirement of break resistance and protection the physicians in the emergency car need, and maybe it is too heavy. By contrast, the physicians at the trauma station do not need such a device. They would prefer to use the already available laptops or PCs. In Figure 15.12 the devices used in the usability trials in Helsinki and in the field trials in Innsbruck are shown.

Device placement: The smaller device makes the device placement much easier.

Furthermore we received following suggestion for improving the software:

Contact information of relatives: The physicians said it would be useful to store contact information especially telephone numbers of relatives, to inform them in an emergency case.

Figure 15.12: TabletPC used in Helsinki   Figure 15.13: Ultra mobile PC

Integration with other devices: The participant of the emergency car team expressed the wish to integrate online monitoring systems, e.g. an ECG device, to reduce efforts for manual data input during an emergency situation especially in the emergency car.

Integration with clinical information system: The participants at the trauma station said they would need integration with the clinical information system to avoid handling too many applications. In emergency cases, this is particularly important. More precisely, this means that they should be able to enter information on the patient using the ambulance agent in case it is made sure that this information is automatically transferred to the patients health record in the hospitals clinical information system.

15.4   Summary

In summary, all trials activities have proven the functionality and the expected properties of the overall system. However, in addition to that positive feedback, all groups of testers had some ideas for further improvements. Some problems found in the Helsinki trials were improved before the trials in Innsbruck and Basel.

Especially the trials with emergency physicians in real-world environments in Innsbruck were very successful. The application and in particular the P2P communication infrastructure was very stable and reliable even under demanding conditions. The physicians participating in these trials had no problems with the structure and the user interface of the application. They were very satisfied with the main idea behind application and stated in the interviews that they are convinced of the usefulness of the application. They finally confirmed that they would use the system, when finally available, both in their professional life (as emergency physician on the way to or waiting for patients) and in their private life when travelling abroad. It is also important to note that the physicians at the trauma station and in the emergency car have partly different requirements, e.g., regarding the devices on which the application runs. This needs to be taken into account when devices for particular usage are selected.

References

[1] J. Nielsen. Why You Only Need to Test With 5 Users. http://www.useit.com/alertbox/20000319.html, 2000.

[2] K. A. Ericsson and H. A. Simon. Verbal reports as data. Psychological Review 87, American Psychological Association, Washington, DC, USA, 1980.

[3] A. Kaikkonen, Kallio T., A. Keklinen, A. Kankainen, and M Cankar. Usability Testing of Mobile Applications: A Comparison between Laboratory and Field Testing. *Journal of Usability Studies*, 1:4–16, November 2005.

[4] V. Roto, A. Oulasvirta, T. Haikarainen, H. Lehmuskallio, and T. Nyyssnen. Examining mobile phone use in the wild with quasi-experimentation. Technical Report 2004-1, HIIT, August 2004.

[5] T. Schabetsberger, E. Ammenwerth, R. Breu, G. Goebel, A. Hoerbst, R. Penz, K. Schindelwig, H. Toth, R. Vogl, and F. Wozak. E-Health Approach to Link-up the Actors in the Health Care System of Austria. In *Ubiquity: Technologies for Better Health in Aging Societies. Proceedings of MIE2006*, volume 124 of *Studies in Health Technology and Informatics*, Amsterdam, 2006. IOS Press, A. Hasman and R. Haux and J. van der Lei and E. De Clercq and F. France.

[6] F. Wozak, M. Breu, R. Breu, R. Penz, T. Schabetsberger, R. Vogl, and E. Ammenwerth. Medical Datagrids as Infrastructure for a Shared Electronic Health Record (SEHR) as an Open Source Reference Implementation for Austria. In *Gesundheitsversorgung im Netz*, pages 121–124, Germany Berlin, 2006. Akademische Verlagsgesellschaft AKA GmbH, G. Steyrer and T. Tolxdorf.

Chapter 16

Quantitative Analysis

Danilo Bonardi, Luís Botelho, Matthias Klusch, António L. Lopes,
Thorsten Möller, Alexandre de Oliveira e Sousa, and Matteo Vasirani

16.1   Introduction

The different software agents and technologies that were introduced in earlier chapters of this book were also subject to a quantitative evaluation. The main objective of these tests was to verify that they can be effectively used in real world settings. Consequently, the measurements taken are mainly targeted to assess performance and scalability of CASCOM's meta services. Qualitative measures on the application level are not covered in this chapter and can be found in Chapter 15.

All tests that are subsequently described must be considered in the context of their network characteristics. Where possible, controlled environments and local services have been used, but in some cases it is opportune to use and rely on the standard Internet infrastructure respectively public services.

16.2   Service Matchmaker Agent

16.2.1   Test Environment

We have done four kinds of tests with the SMA. All the service descriptors were located on a local server at URJC. This was done so that the performance evaluation could not be affected by external factors like network delays or bandwidth.

Along all the tests, two different SMA configurations were evaluated. In the first configuration (in what follows, we will refer to it as cfg. 1), all the three matchmakers were invoked sequentially (first the role-based matchmaker, then OwlsMX and finally the precondiftion-effect matchmaker). This is the most fine-grained configuration of the SMA, but also the most time consuming, due to the presence of the logic reasoning matchmaker. In the second configuration (cfg. 2), only the role-based matchmaker and OwlsMX were invoked sequentially.

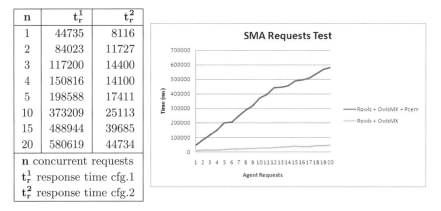

n	t_r^1	t_r^2
1	44735	8116
2	84023	11727
3	117200	14400
4	150816	14100
5	198588	17411
10	373209	25113
15	488944	39685
20	580619	44734

n concurrent requests
t_r^1 response time cfg.1
t_r^2 response time cfg.2

Figure 16.1: SMA response time as a function of concurrent requests

16.2.2   Test 1

The objective of the first test was to understand how the SMA reacts to an increasing number of requests, sent by several agents, with the same services and query combination. The services to match were nine services from the medical domain, with a query that matches with all the descriptors.

The results are depicted in Figure 16.1. The plot shows that the response time grows linearly with the number of requests in both of the two configurations, although in the second case the response time of SMA is considerably lower.

16.2.3   Test 2

The second test aimed at evaluating how the SMA manages an increasing number of services that match with the given query. The services and the query were the same as in the previous test. In this test we used only one agent request.

The results are depicted in Figure 16.2. Also in this case the response time of SMA, with a growing number of matching services, increases almost linearly.

16.2.4   Test 3

The objective of the third test was to understand how the presence of matching and non-matching services affects the computation of the SMA. The request was composed of fifty non-matching services from the medical transportation domain, and an increasing number of matching services.

The result of the last test depicted in Figure 16.3 is aligned with the previous tests. It is worth noting that for the first configuration (cfg. 1), even if the total number of services in the request is greater with respect to the second test, the response time is similar. For example, in the second test, the response time of a request with 20 matching services was 71399 ms, while in the third test, the

n	t_r^1	t_r^2
1	21514	4475
2	30438	7261
3	26773	5941
4	28662	7674
5	35828	6192
10	50039	8859
15	56260	12837
20	71399	12224
n matching services		
t_r^1 response time cfg.1		
t_r^2 response time cfg.2		

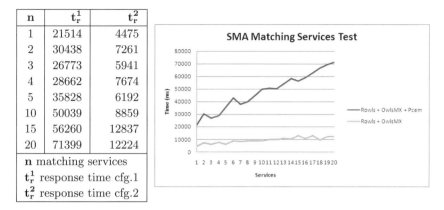

Figure 16.2: SMA response time as a function of matching services

n	t_r^1	t_r^2
1	34401	23889
2	38468	21961
3	45175	20380
4	48004	20099
5	46704	25124
10	73168	28135
15	77410	26077
20	88509	26221
n matching services		
t_r^1 response time cfg.1		
t_r^2 response time cfg.2		

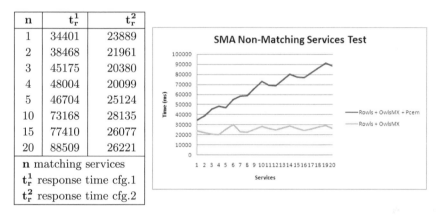

Figure 16.3: SMA response time with non-matching services

response time of a request with 20 matching services and 50 non-matching services was 88509 ms. This shows that the SMA response time is more sensitive to the number of matching services than to the total number of services. This is because if one of the three matchmakers detects a non-matching service, this service is filtered out and not passed to the other matchmakers in the sequence.

16.2.5   Test 4

The objective of the last test is to check the retrieval performance of the match-maker as a whole, that is, to determine the quality of the answer set of the five variants of the hybrid OWLS-MX matchmaker in terms of recall and precision (R/P). For details about the hybrid matching filters and text similarity measure from information retrieval (IR) used by each of the OWLS-MX variants and the

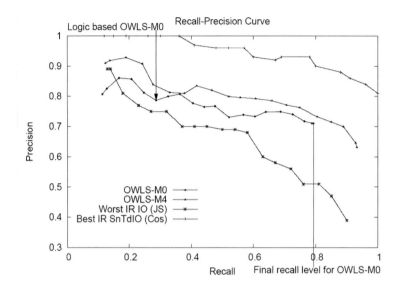

Figure 16.4: Retrieval performance of the matchmaker as a whole

R/P experiments conducted we refer to [2]. The R/P performance measurements were done against the OWL-S service retrieval test collection OWLS-TC2[1] that also includes the CASCOM services and adopted the evaluation strategy of micro-averaging the individual recall/precision (R/P) curves. The micro-averaged R/P curves of the top and worse performing IR similarity metric together with those for the OWLS-MX variants are shown in Figure 16.4.

This preliminary result provides strong evidence in favor of the proposition that building Semantic Web Service matchmakers purely on crisp logic based reasoning may be insufficient. A preliminary quantitative analysis of these results showed that even the best IR similarity metric (Cosine/TF-IDF) alone performed close to the pure logic based OWLS-M0 which can be significantly outperformed by hybrid semantic matching with OWLS-M1 to OWLS-M4 in terms of both recall and precision. Second, the hybrid matchmakers OWLS-MX, in turn, can be outperformed by each of the selected syntactic IR similarity metrics to the extent additional parameters with natural language text content are considered.

[1]The OWLS-TC2 is available at http://projects.semwebcentral.org/projects/owls-tc

n	t_r^f	t_r^{nf}
1	44250	46125
5	33141	30078
10	44593	37203
15	76984	39844
20	81281	42864
25	89203	43453
30	84360	45123
35	85157	46983
40	94672	48223
45	111453	50241
50	126047	52123

n concurrent requests
t_r^f service found [ms]
t_r^{nf} service not found [ms]

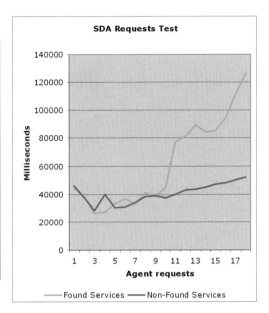

Figure 16.5: SDA response time as a function of non-matching services

16.3 Service Discovery Agent

16.3.1 Test Environment

The SDA possesses a large variety of functionality. In the evaluation, we decided to concentrate on the find service feature because this is related to OWL-S and exhibits some algorithmic complexity. We performed two kinds of test, that both comprise a growing number of requests to the SDA agent. In the first test, all the requests were executed successfully; in the second, all the agents requested a service which could not be found.

16.3.2 Test Results and Discussion

The results of the test depicted in Figure 16.5 evidence a consistent difference between the two kinds of requests. The results also show that the find service feature of the SDA is quick, especially since the SDA cache has been bypassed in these tests.

If we analyze the detail each request sent to the SDA, we can determine what the most time-consuming tasks are in the overall process. Figure 16.6 shows a pie chart which illustrates the sub-tasks that have to be performed by each search request sent to the SDA.

The results depicted in Figure 16.6 were obtained by the average result of 200

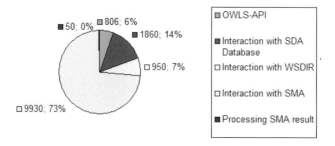

Figure 16.6: SDA search time [ms] percentages

search requests sent to the SDA, which had, at the time, 200 services registered in the service directories. As can be seen from the picture, the most time-consuming tasks (around 73%) is in fact the matching process that is carried out together with the SMA. The remaining time (around 27%) is consumed by the operations related to the acquisition of services from the service directories and processing the acquired service descriptions using the OWL-S API.

16.4   Service Composition Planner Agent

As mentioned in Chapter 11, two different Service Composition Agents (SCPA) have been developed in CASCOM that differ in the planner engine used: one is based on XPlan [4] while the other relies on SAPA [1]. In any case, the chosen CASCOM SCPA takes a set of OWL-S services, a description of the initial state and the goal state to be achieved as input, and returns a plan that corresponds to a composite service that gets invoked using the FIPA-Request interaction protocol.

16.4.1   OWLS-XPlan

We evaluated the performance of XPlan, using the publicly available benchmark of the international planning competition IPC3, and compared the results with that of the four top performing IPC3 participants, i.e., FF planner, Sim-Planner, and the HTN planners TLPlan, and Shop2. XPlan was tested without task specific methods. Planning performance was measured in terms of (a) the planning completeness, i.e., the total percentage of solved problems, (b) the average plan length, and (c) the average plan quality, i.e., the average distance of individual plans from the optimal plan length in relation to the complexity of the given problems2. In summary, the experimental performance results of both versions of OWLSXPlan show that service composition planning can be done reasonably

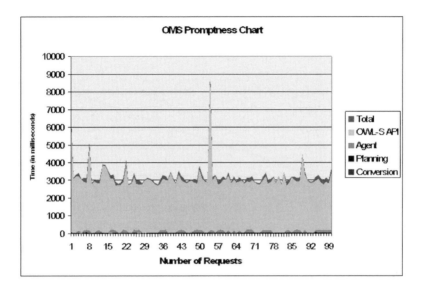

Figure 16.7: Service composition in the OMS domain for 100 requests.

efficient and effective for low to medium complex planning domains (up to 15k objects), in particular the limited e-health planning domain considered in the project CASCOM during the field trial.

For more information and preliminary evaluation of XPlan 2.0, we refer to [4]. Evaluation results for the static version OWLS-XPlan 1.0 are provided in [3].

16.4.2 MetaComp

The alternative composition planner that can be used by the CASCOM SCPA, that is SAPA as part of the module MetaComp (cf. Chapter 11), was evaluated with respect to domain independence, performance and scalability. The evaluation tests were carried out using an Intel(R) Pentium(R) M processor 1.60 GHz, equipped with 512 MB of RAM memory. Since the designed service selection methods have not been integrated in MetaComp, the evaluation tests address only the agent remaining features.

The domain independence hypothesis was evaluated through testing the agent in different application domains namely the medical records translation domain (Medical Records), the online medicine selling domain, the box depots transport (Depots) domain, the package delivery domain (DriverLog), and the aero travel domain (ZenoTravel). The agent successfully generated compound services in all of these domains. Although this does not prove that MetaComp is completely domain independent, it constitutes significant evidence supporting the domain independence hypothesis.

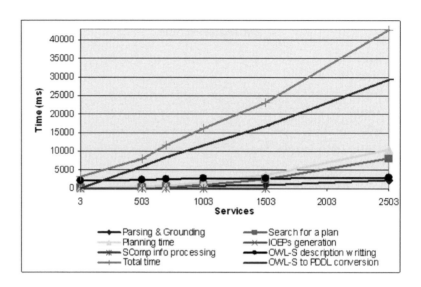

Figure 16.8: Average service composition times vs. number of available services

MetaComp performance and scalability were assessed in the Online Medicine Selling Domain (OMS). Of all the domains we have used in our tests, the OMS domain was chosen because it is the only one for which OWL-S descriptions of its services exist, allowing us to estimate the complete execution time, including the OWL-S to PDDL conversion. Figure 16.7 shows the performance results in the OMS domain, with 100 requests and no additional services besides those required to achieve the composition goal.

The total execution time per request was about 3.4 seconds. The average planning was 26.95 ms per request, which is practically imperceptible for the end user. Another component that is also hardly noticeable by the user (in this test) is the OWLS2PDDL converter, due to the reduced number of services to convert. OWL-S API is responsible for about 95% of the total execution time.

We have increased the number of services considered for composition to assess the agent scalability. Fifty compositions for 503, 703, 1503 and 2503 services were carried out in the OMS domain. The average times are presented in Figure 16.8. For 503 services, the average time spent in composition was 8 seconds. For 703 services, this time was 12 seconds. For 1503, the average total time was 24 seconds. Finally, for 2503 services, the average time spent in composition increased to 43 seconds.

These results show that MetaComp performs within a reasonable time frame while the number of services considered for composition is less than 500 services. Unfortunately, when this number increases, performance rapidly worsens to impractical values. The times spent writing the OWL-S description of the compound

n	t_r^w	t_r^f
1	14688	12703
5	54594	38828
10	92390	64031
15	129422	92484
20	170875	127172
25	224891	179266
30	263907	190141
35	369875	206688
40	399031	254610
45	422203	302968
50	451468	312734

n concurrent requests
t_r^w service working [ms]
t_r^f service failure [ms]

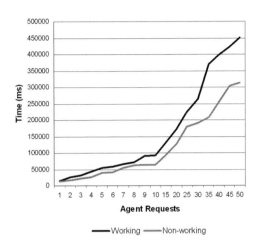

Figure 16.9: SEA response time as a function of concurrent requests and service failures

service, and generating its inputs, outputs, preconditions and effects do not change because the solution plan is always the same. As the number of available services for composition increases, the planning time also increases, becoming larger than the time for writing the OWL-S description. Given the enormous growth of the number of considered services, the largest increase happens in the OWL-S to PDDL conversion time.

In summary, the results show the excellent performance of SAPA as one alternative planning component of the CASCOM SCPA. For compound services involving a small number of elemental services (which we assume to be the case for most service composition environments), the generation of the OWL-S description of the compound service from the output of the planning component consumes about 95% of the total time spent to handle each composition request. This quite unexpected result is due to using the OWLS-API, which is still under considerable development. It is assumed that this may be improved in the near future.

16.5 Service Execution Agent

16.5.1 Test Environment

Probably the most interesting measure to explore the performance of the Service Execution Agent (SEA) is the time it takes to execute a given service as a function of concurrent requests (using alternating input data). Consequently, this test has been conducted in two different cases: one where the service is correctly executed and the other where the service execution has some (random) run time error in input. In these two tests, the real existing Healt@Net Web Service *Find Patient* has been used, annotated by a locally stored OWL-S descriptor. This means that the test environment can not be taken as entirely controlled since it uses — and relies on — the standard Internet infrastructure and its properties. However, this decision was made on purpose to include the dynamics of the Internet and to get insights on how this might effect the test in terms of time variations.

16.5.2   Test Results and Discussion

As it can be seen from Figure 16.9, the SEA is initially fast in both cases. Nevertheless, the plot evidences a continuous raise of the execution time with increasing number of concurrent requests higher than what was expected. As detailed analysis revealed, there is one main reason for this, which goes back to implementation details: the current implementation of the FIPA interaction protocol part of the JADE platform – used as a basis by the SEA – works as a barrier that serializes incoming parallel requests, that is, incoming requests are put into a queue and each request is handled one after the other. This means that the SEA currently conducts just one execution at a time although its internal structure behind this barrier was particularly designed and implemented to support concurrent (composite) service executions. Only by an extension of this behavior in the near future the SEA can demonstrate its full potential in terms of responsiveness to increasing load.

The observation that the execution in case of input failure is faster than the normal one is no surprise and a result of the fact that in this case the invoked Web Service produces a fault, that is, it does not run the functionality that it represents.

Because of the fact that the standard Internet infrastructure was part of the test, the results must be considered in the context of its network and utilization characteristics. The plot in Figure 16.9 does not show strong outliers. This indicates that both the Internet infrastructure as well as the invoked service offered nearly constant runtime characteristics at the time when the test was conducted.

16.6   WSDir

16.6.1   Test Environment

The objective of the test environment was to compare the response time of the directory federation towards multiple simultaneous search requests (only abstract search) coming from an increasing number of clients and registered services descriptions. For that, we have decomposed the evaluation of WSDir into three scenarios. Based on the topology used in CASCOM, the number of directory services were different for each scenario. Actually, each time a set of service descriptions is stored in the federation (evenly balanced) and the set of clients accesses as much

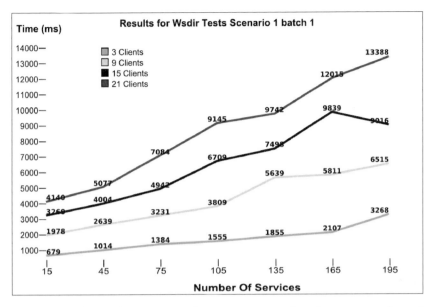

Figure 16.10: WSDIR Average search request processing time per number of services for scenario 1

as possible different directory services in the Top Network layer. All the directory services were partially distributed (some were running on the same servers) in a secured network. The clients were all running at the same time in threads on the same computer. Each client performed three random searches to produce different results.

16.6.2 Topology and Scenario

In CASCOM, WSDIR is distributed across three network layers: a Hidden Layer, a Top Layer and a Body Layer. Agents only access the directory services located on the Top Layer. Each scenario has a specific number of directory services in the Top Layer and the Body Layer (the Hidden Layer always contains one directory service). The three used scenarios were the following:

1. Scenario 1: three directory services on the Top Layer and six on the Body Layer.

2. Scenario 2: six directory services on the Top Layer and six on the body layer.

3. Scenario 3: ten directory services on the Top Layer and twenty on the Body Layer.

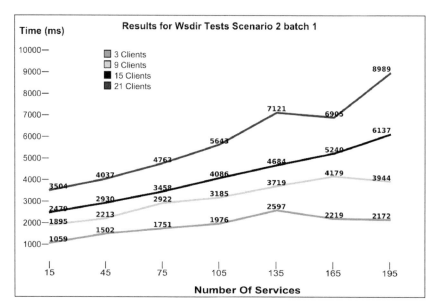

Figure 16.11: WSDIR Average search request processing time per number of services for scenario 2

16.6.3 Test Results and Discussion

The following figures show the average response time in milliseconds per number of stored services. Each line corresponds to a given number of simultaneous clients requesting the federation.

Note that scenario 2 (see Figure 16.11) shows the best results. This implies that Top Layer's directory services play an essential role in the scalability of the system. This observation can be explained as follows: not enough directory services on the Top Layer (scenario 1) cannot serve too many clients and too many directory services on the Top Layer (scenario 3) produce too many messages within the federation, thus loosing more time on internal communication. For a given number of clients, we see that the time increases linearly. The abstract search algorithm is in $O(n)$ complexity. The variations on the lines are due to run time performance clean up of the directory services and random queries (a query that matches a lot of services takes more time to be processed).

16.7 Summary

To complement the qualitative analysis presented in Chapter 15 which has proven the applicability of the overall CASCOM system to the healthcare domain, also CASCOM's performance and scalability characteristics underwent a series of quantitative evaluations.

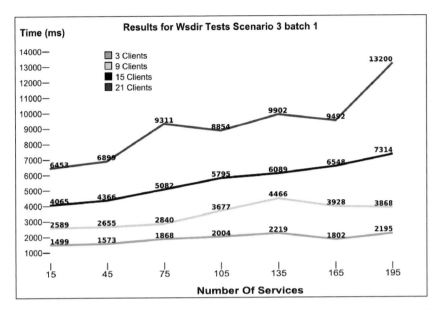

Figure 16.12: WSDIR Average search request processing time per number of services for scenario 3

For the quantitative analysis, each component of the CASCOM system was evaluated independently, i.e., without interactions and dependencies with the other components. This approach has the advantage that it allows to individually focus on the most crucial aspects and the most important characteristics of each agent. The results showed that no agent is a potential performance bottleneck or limits the scalability of the overall system.

References

[1] M. B. Do and S. Kambhampati. Sapa: A Scalable Multi-objective Heuristic Metric Temporal Planner. *Journal of AI Research*, 20:155–194, 2003.

[2] M. Klusch, B. Fries, and K. Sycara. Automated Semantic Web Service Discovery with OWLS-MX. In *Proceedings of the 5th Int'l Conf. on Autonomous Agents and Multi-Agent Systems (AAMAS)*, Hakodate, Japan, 2006. ACM Press.

[3] M. Klusch, A. Gerber, and M. Schmidt. Semantic Web Service Composition Planning with OWLS-XPlan. In *Proceedings of the AAAI Fall Symposium on Semantic Web and Agents*, Arlington VA, USA, 2005. AAAI Press.

[4] M. Klusch and K-U. Renner. Fast Dynamic Re-Planning of Composite OWL-S Services. In *Proceedings of 2nd IEEE Intl Workshop on Service Composition (SerComp)*, Hongkong, China, 2006. IEEE CS Press.

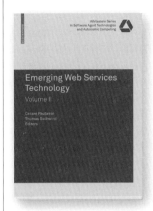

WHITESTEIN SERIES IN SOFTWARE
AGENT TECHNOLOGIES AND
AUTONOMIC COMPUTING

Emerging Web Services Technology, Vol. II

WEWST 2007, Halle (Saale), Germany, November 2007.
Selected Revised Papers.

Gschwind, T., IBM Research GmbH, Zürich, Switzerland / **Pautasso, C.**, University of Lugano, Switzerland (eds)

BIRKHÄUSER

WSSAT — Whitestein Series in Software Agent Technologies and Autonomic Computing
Emerging Web Services Technology, Vol. II
2008. 203 p. Softcover
ISBN 978-3-7643-8863-8

Web-service-oriented frameworks are ubiquitous today. This book contains contributions to the state-of-the-art of the most recent topics, such as grid-based computing, mobility issues for web services, dynamic web services, and model driven engineering.

Selected revised papers from the peer-reviewed 2007 European Conference on Web Services (ECOWS) and the peer-reviewed 2007 Workshop on Emerging Web Services Technology (WEWST). Keynote by Prof. Schahram Dustdar.

From the content:
0. Emerging Web Services Technologies - Some Research Challenges Ahead.- 1. Service selection by choreography-driven matching.- 2. Enabling Business Experts to Discover Web Services for Business Process.- 3. Evaluation of Semantic Service Discovery - A Survey and Directions for Future Research.- 4. A Framework for Dynamic Web Services Composition.- 5. Composite Web Services.- 6. Management Requirements of Web Service Compositions.- 7. BPEL-DT - Data-aware Extension of BPEL to Support Data-Intensive Service Applications.- 8. Towards Resource-Oriented BPEL.- 9. SSL-over-SOAP: Towards a Token-based Key Establishment Framework for Web Services.- 10. A Framework for QoS-based Resource Brokering in Grid Computing.- 11. Model-Driven Performance Evaluation for Service Engineering.

www.birkhauser.ch

Whitestein Series in Software Agent Technologies and Autonomic Computing

Edited by
Monique Calisti (Editor-in-Chief), Marius Walliser, Stefan Brantschen, and Marc Herbstritt

This series reports new developments in agent-based software technologies and agent-oriented software engineering methodologies, with particular emphasis on applications in the area of autonomic computing and communications.
The spectrum of the series includes research monographs, high quality notes resulting from research and industrial projects, outstanding Ph.D. theses, and the proceedings of carefully selected conferences. The series is targeted at promoting advanced research and facilitating know-how transfer to industrial use.

■ **Ma, H.**, CWI, Amsterdam, The Netherlands, / **Leung, H.F.**, Chinese University of Hong Kong, Hong Kong, China

Bidding Strategies in Agent-Based Continous Double Auctions

Online auctions are a platform to trade goods on the Internet. In this context, negotiation capabilities for software agents in continuous double auctions (CDAs) are a central concern. Agents need to be able to prepare bids for and evaluate offers on behalf of the users they represent with the aim of obtaining the maximum benefit for their users. For the agents, their bids are decided according to some bidding strategy. In CDAs, this is a complex decision problem because of the inherent uncertainty and dynamics of the auction market. This book presents a new bidding strategy for agents to adopt in CDAs and proposes tools to enhance the performance of existing bidding strategies in CDAs.

2008. 150 pages. Softcover.
ISBN 978-3-7643-8729-7

■ **Pěchouček, M.**, Czech Technical University, Prague, Czech Republic / **Thompson, S.G.**, BT. Labs, Suffolk, U.K. / **Voos, H.**, University of Applied Sciences, Ravensburg-Weingarten, Germany (eds.)

Defense Industry Applications of Autonomous Agents and Multi-Agent Systems

Defense and security related applications are increasingly being tackled using technologies developed in the field of Intelligent Agent research. The contributions in this book describe work in the development of command and control systems, military communications systems, information systems, surveillance systems, autonomous vehicles, simulators and Human Computer Interactions. The broad nature of the application domain is matched by the diversity of techniques presented in this book. The book provides a single reference point for the state-of-the-art in the field.

2007. 180 pages. Softcover.
ISBN 978-3-7643-8570-5

■ **Calisti, M.**, Whitestein Technologies AG, Zürich, Switzerland / **van der Meer, S.**, Waterford Institute of Technology, Ireland / **Strassner, J.**, Motorola, Inc., Schaumburg, IL, USA (eds.)

Advanced Autonomic Networking and Communication

This book presents a comprehensive reference of state-of-the-art efforts and early results in the area of autonomic networking and communication.
The book consists of three three parts consisting of papers from industrial and academic perspectives. The first part focuses on architectures and modeling strategies. Part two is dedicated to

middleware and service infrastructure as facilitators of autonomic communications. The last part addresses autonomic networks, specifically how networks can be equipped with autonomic functionality and thus migrate to autonomic networks.

2007. 200 pages. Softcover.
ISBN 978-3-7643-8568-2

■ **Annicchiarico, R.**, Fondazione Santa Lucia IRCCS, Rome, Italy / **Cortés, U.**, Universidad Malaga, Spain / **Urdiales, C.**, Universidad Polytècnica de Catalunya, Barcelona, Spain (eds.)

Agent Technology and e-Health

2007. 156 pages. Softcover.
ISBN 978-3-7643-8546-0

■ **Moreno, A.** University of Tarragona, Spain / **Pavón, J.**, University of Madrid, Spain (eds.)

Issues in Multi-Agent Systems The AgentCities.ES Experience

2007. 240 pages. Softcover.
ISBN 978-3-7643-8542-2

■ **Pautasso, C.**, IBM Zürich, Switzerland / **Bussler, C.**, Cisco Systems Inc., San Jose, USA (eds.)

Emerging Web Services Technology

2007. 182 pages. Softcover.
ISBN 978-3-7643-8447-0

BIRKHÄUSER